BOULDER
BRITAIN

Ape Index

www.apeindex.com

Katie Mundy on Cave Right Hand, 6B+, Bowden Doors (page 222). Photo: Mark Savage.

BOULDER
BRITAIN

The essential guide to British bouldering

Niall Grimes

Ape Index

Contents

The South West   page 38

Wales   page 94

The North West   page 144

The Lakes   page 186

Pete Robins on The Yorkshireman, 7B+, Kyloe in the Woods (page 221, problem 18). Photo: Adam Long.

Northumberland page 212

Yorkshire page 246

The Peak page 308

The Midlands............ page 368

Southern Sandstone page 390

Scotland page 404

Copyright © 2011 Niall Grimes / Ape Index
Published by Ape Index
www.apeindex.com
All rights reserved.
ISBN: 978-0-9570578-0-7
First published 2011
Distributed by Cordee www.cordee.co.uk

Contents

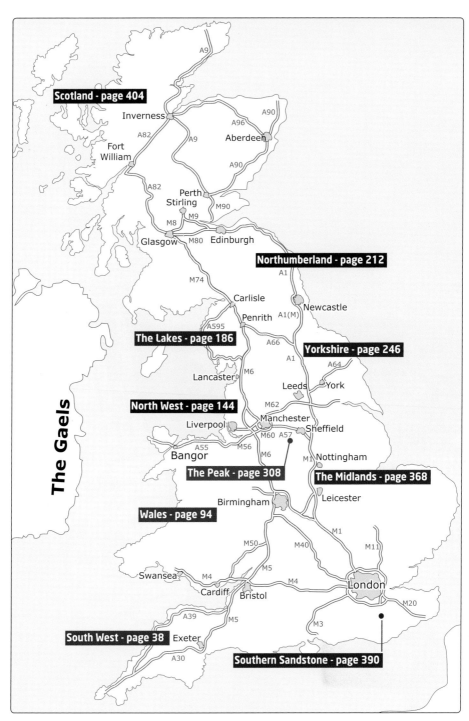

Scotland - page 404

Inverness

A9

A82

Fort
William

Aberdeen

A96

A90

A90

A82

Perth
Stirling

M90

M8 M9

Glasgow M80 Edinburgh

Northumberland - page 212

A1

M74

Carlisle

Penrith A1(M) Newcastle

The Lakes - page 186

A595

A66

Yorkshire - page 246

A1

A64

Lancaster

M6

Leeds York

North West - page 144

M62

Liverpool

Manchester

M60 A57 Sheffield

A55

M56

Bangor

M6

The Peak - page 308

M1 Nottingham

The Midlands - page 368

Birmingham

Leicester

Wales - page 94

M1

M50

M40

M11

Swansea

M4

M5

M4

Cardiff

Bristol

London

M20

South West - page 38

A39

M5

M3

Exeter

Southern Sandstone - page 390

A30

The Gaels

Crags alphabetically

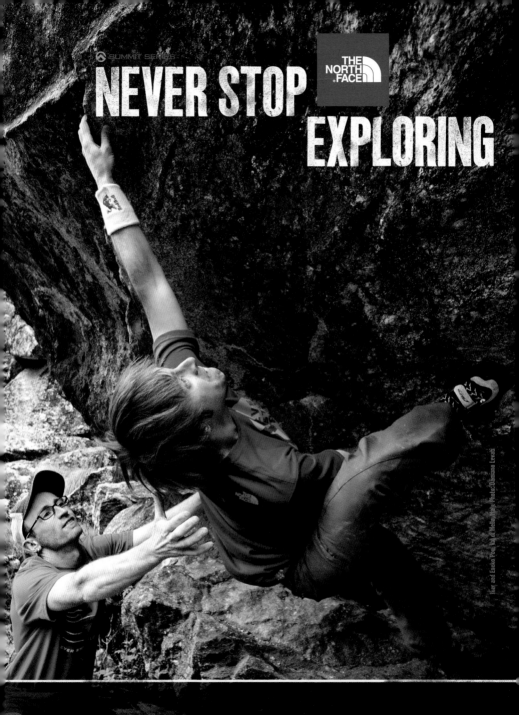

NEVER STOP EXPLORING

THE NORTH FACE

Foreword

Well somebody had to do it, a guide to the UK, and for bouldering of all things.

How times have changed since Beetham was mucking about climbing boulders upside down with his pals at the turn of the 20th century. There's a lot of rocks, pebbles and craglets in these isles now which people have thought worth documenting. Promises of a lifetime of moods, textures and vistas. From the frictionless shale of Cornwall, with its bizarre wave sculpted features and sea views, all the way up until things start getting really bumpy once you hit Scotland.

This guide does what guides have to do, which is get you there and hint at what you're in for. Simply knowing where the majority of the bouldering crags are in the UK is no mean feat in itself. And all too often these days I find myself longing for a path on my remote adventures. The County is my bouldering home in the UK but I feel comfy without a map for most of Northern England and Scotland nowadays. Over the years I've climbed from the far south of the UK at St Ives and Godrevy, all the way up to Torridon in the North West of Scotland. The difference between areas in the UK is startling. The bleakness of places like Queens Crag is a stark contrast to the whooping valleys of the Churnet with teenage screams from Alton Towers floating through the air, yet both are sandstone. On the coastal crags with the sea as the main topic for your optics, its roaring flow reveals and then snatches back many a classic problem. In Sheffield, the furthest city from any sea, you're more likely to encounter a sea of pads and many a friend, where an estranged look would often greet you elsewhere in the country here you will often blend in almost too easily.

The UK never has quantity in abundance, only Scotland has potential for 300+ problem venues and much of these haven't been developed yet and are guarded by the Scotch Midge for all the pleasant months. Font, Swiss, Hueco this is not. It is its own thing, like the twee towns and villages you encounter on the way, cobbled streets, lichenous drystone walls. Lone oak trees and a singular crows caw on a quiet dewy autumn morning. All the aspects hold their own secrets. Sometimes the venues are just a good excuse to experience an area. And what better excuse is there than climbing to visit these humble microcosms? Just remember we are always a guest when we visit somewhere so we should treat places like we're lucky to have been invited in to assuage their tranquility. Which we are. Thank you to all the developers who have shared their secrets.

Dan Varian

John Fletcher on Blacking out the Friction, 7C, at Godrevy (page 48, problem 15). Photo: Barnaby Carver.

Introduction

If you're reading this, then it exists. Even if it's only my old uncle Algernon Carruthers, and he has bought the only copy, then that doesn't matter. The fact is that it is out there and it is a thing and I am finished. And that was never something I was sure would happen.

I began this project many years ago. As in MANY years ago. I had an idea. It grew, it developed and it changed. I had it, then some time later the idea had me. For many years now I have travelled the UK, lugging a camera, a tripod, a print out and a packet of biscuits up a bracken covered hillside. Caked in sweat, tired and cursing. Checking out remote bluffs, photographing, doing some problems. Once the idea had gotten a hold of me it shook me and pushed me and made me go to many far corners of the land.

I had shelved the idea several times. The task was too big and doing it felt too lonely. I frequently wondered why I was doing it and seldom came up with any good reason. Why a bouldering book? Why me? But time and again, when I had relaxed into an enjoyable lifestyle like normal people, the idea would scream in my ear again to do it.

The last time was about two years ago talking to Tom and Rachel in the Showroom in Sheffield. They remembered that I had once been doing it and asked me about it. I told them I was out of it, gladly, but described it to them. As I did I couldn't help but think, 'That's a great idea'. So there again I started it.

Well, now it's done. And despite my constant cursings I have loved every minute of it. Doing this book has been an adventure and has taken me on a great personal journey. I'll never forget the feeling I got from first happening upon many of the remote, beautiful and unique bouldering venues. Thorn Crag, Dinas Rock, Hartland Quay, Carn Brea, Moelfre, Elephantitus, Armathwaite, Queens Crag, Bridestones, Fisherground, Grinshill, Ogmore, Forest Rock, Callerhues, Hutton Roof and Combeshead Tor. All great spots, some big, some little, and all with something to offer.

I hope that I have done the crags a service here. I hope that I have described them in a fair and good light. Sometimes local guides can be too enthusiastic leading ultimately to a disappointing visit. I have tried here to be honest about places while at the same time remaining positive about them. Every venue in here is fab, but sometimes you need to have realistic expectations.

Many things have happened in my life during it but now I'm glad it is finished so I can focus on other things. I really want to thank my wife Helen for all her help in this project, and to say how much it has meant. Even at these late stages, as deadlines have come and gone, she has been nothing but supportive. Despite the fact that my constant beavering at this book must be a drag, I have always felt both a tolerance and expectation of quality. I really appreciated it. I also want to thank our lovely daughter Erin for making what would otherwise be a laborious, work-heavy time feel fantastic. She can't speak yet but if she could I know what she'd say:

"Daddy, you're not still writing that stupid book about rocks are you?"

And of course there's Sophie too. She's good for keeping my feet on the ground.

I hope you like this book and that it will take you to some of the areas I have discovered for myself. It has allowed me to see so many beautiful places and do so much great climbing. Perhaps most of all, as this book has relied on the help and generosity of so many people, both friends and strangers, I have been left with a great impression of the climbers and boulderers of the land. The spirit and generosity of almost everyone I have dealt with has been a privilege to see.

Now it's late at night and I am behind a computer. But I can't help remembering walking up to Mynydd Dinas on a late June afternoon. I had spent most of the day visiting a couple of underwhelming venues in blustery drizzle. Expecting the same I had to force myself to drive another hour based on a few sentences in a download. I drove inland from Fishguard, into wild uplands, just as the sun came out. Cardigan Bay revealed itself wide and blue. The instuctions were accurate and from the parking I spotted the outcrops. As I started the walk in I got a call from home with some truly great news. Elated, I sprung through tufted grass, the fresh wind blowing off the sea. The western sun warmed me. I got to the little outcrops, dark boulders that seemed little travelled and very, very special. I put my boots on. I couldn't imagine a nicer place in the world.

Niall Grimes

Chris Plant on Cyclops, 6A+, Hutton Roof (page 165, problem 14). Photo: Mark Edwards.

Sources and info

It goes without saying that this book is heavily reliant on the sources of bouldering information countrywide. We are lucky to have such a great range of guidebooks to our bouldering areas and the quality and depth of knowledge are an inspiration. The Lakes, Northumberland, Yorkshire, the Peak, Wales, Shropshire, Scotland and Southern Sandstone are all blessed with great publications. The spirit and motivation behind their creation is a great thing.

We also have a superb tradition of web-based information. These sites, such as Lakesbloc, Yorkshiregrit, Peakbouldering, Javu and Esotericrock, have been an invaluable resource. The fact that the information is available for free belies the fact that their standards are sometimes every bit as high as that of printed works. It speaks highly of the creators of these sites.

I also owe a huge thank you to individuals who have provided information on their local areas. I was blown away by these people's enthusiasm and generosity. I have hopefully namechecked these people individually in the appropriate sections or in acknowledgements. A big thumbs up to you all, especially those in the South West, South Wales, Scotland and Guernsey.

I acknowledge the debt to the hard work of all the individuals who have compiled this information. Without them this guide would not have been possible.

Also listed here is where to get more info, as per the Info section in the guides. I have not traced these sources back through their history as each guide does this, but have concentrated on those which I have used and are currently available. Some books are not available at the time of writing but are due out in the near future.

Below is a list of the major sources. Where there is a source for an individual venue it is listed in that section. Most books are available from their associated websites, local climbing shops and their websites or via Cordee (www.cordee.co.uk).

Bouldering in Scotland (Stone Country, 2008)
Burbage, Millstone and Beyond (BMC, 2005)
Eastern Grit (Rockfax, 2006)
Froggatt to Black Rocks (BMC, 2010)
Lakes Bouldering (Rockfax, 2006)
Leicestershire Rock Climbs
  (BMC, not available at time of writing)
Lancashire Rock (BMC, 2006)
Nesscliffe (Nick Dixon, 2007)
North East England (CMC / Smartboys, 2003)
North Wales Bouldering
  (Northern Soul, 2004)
Northern England (Rockfax, 2008)
Northumberland Bouldering Guide
  (NMC, 2004)
Parisella's (Ground Up, 2009)
Peak Bouldering (Rockfax, 2000)
Peak District Bouldering (Vertebrate, 2011)
Portland (CC, 2008)
Sandstone (BMC, not available at time of writing)
Shropshire Bouldering
  (www.highsports.co.uk, 2006)
Southern Sandstone (CC, 2008)
Southern Sandstone Bouldering
  (SSB Guides, 2011)
Stanage (BMC, 2007)
The Roaches (BMC, 2009)
Western Grit (Rockfax, 2009)
Yorkshire Gritstone
  (YMC, not available at time of writing)
Yorkshire Gritstone Bouldering
  (Total Climbing, 2008)

Yorkshire Gritstone Bouldering Volume 2
  (Total Climbing, 2011)
Yorkshire Gritstone Bouldering (Rockfax, 2000)
www.betaguides.com
  - North York Moors and nationwide info
www.clevelandmc.com
  - Cleveland Mountaineering Club
www.climbers-club.co.uk
www.climbonline.co.uk
www.dumby.info - Dumbarton bouldering
www.esotericbouldering.co.uk
  - Bouldering around Bristol
www.javu.co.uk
  - Dartmoor and general south west info
www.lakesbloc.co.uk
www.northwalesbouldering.com
www.thebmc.co.uk
www.peakbouldering.info
www.stonecountry.co.uk
www.ssbouldering.co.uk - Southern Sandstone
www.swbg.co.uk
  - South Wales Bouldering Guide
www.thenmc.org.uk
  - Northumberian Mountaineering Club
www.total-climbing.com
www.rockfax.com
www.ukbouldering.com
  - Good bouldering forum
UKClimbing.com - general climbing info
www.v-publishing.co.uk
  - Vertebrate Publishing
www.yorkshiregrit.com

16

Acknowledgements

This book is the result of input from so many people. A huge thanks to all those who wrote sections, checked scripts, provided information, accommodation, support and inspiration. And a huge thank you to the proof reader. Thanks Lynn.

Adi Gill, Adrian Hatherall, Al Williams, Andrew Hinde, Andrew Shilling, Anne Bush, Barnaby Carver, Ben Read, Ben Tyrrell, Bill Walton, Bob Moulton, Brian Bush, Chris Plant, Chris Smith, Dan Varian, Dave Biggs, Dave Henderson, Dave MacLeod, Dave Westlake, Duncan Martin, Ellis Ash, Flo Scheimpflug, George Smith, Grant Edwards, Greg Chapman, Iain McKenzie, James Arran, James Squire, Jamie Maddison, Jenny Hack, John Earl, John Watson, Jon Pearson, Jon Ratcliffe, Jon Rettie, Jonathan Bean, Kev Hughes, Lee Robinson, Lynn Robinson, Matt West, Mike Adams, Neil Arch, Neil Kershaw, Nik Jennings, Owen McShane, Pete O'Donovan, Pete Robins, Rae Cowie, Rich Hession, Richie Betts, Rob Dyer, Rob Sanderson, Robin Nicholson, Simon Young, Steve Crowe, Steve Quinton, Stuart Cathcart, Ted Kingsnorth, Tim Wilkinson, Tom Newberry, Tom Randall.

What about the photos! A titanic thank you to all those lovely people whose beautiful pictures grace these pages. Needless to say without them this book would be one step up from a telephone directory.

Adam Lincoln, Adam Long, Alex Messenger, Alice Brockington, Amanda Lyons, Amanda McKenzie, Andrew Poland, Barnaby Carver, Carrie Hill, Claire MacLeod, Dan Arkle, Dave Biggs, Dave Ripley, David Simmonite, Ellis Ash, Fraser Harle, Ian Taylor, James O'Neil, James Squire, Jamie Maddison, Jamie Moss, Jen Randall, Jo Gilbert, John Coefield, John Watson, Jon Bassindale, Jon Pearson, Jonathan Bean, Kevin Avery, Lee Robinson, Mark Savage, Matt West, Mike Adams, Mike Hutton, Nic Mullin, Pete Robins, Ray Wood, Richie Betts, Sean Bell, Steve Le Feuvre, Stuart Brooks, Tom Peckitt.

Apologies to anyone I've missed.

A note from the BMC

All land in Britain belongs to someone and it is important to remember that access for climbing is often reliant on users acting as stewards of the countryside and behaving in a responsible manner. Climbers are generally very good at this, with a strong code of ethics held by the community as a whole, but it is every climber's responsibility to ensure that access to the crags we all hold dear remains open.

There are several types of access in England and Wales:

Open Access land: this is land designated under the Countryside Rights of Way Act 2000 as an area where the public has a right to roam across the entire area, not just along the right of way network.

Public Rights of Way: these are marked as footpaths, bridleways, restricted byways or open byways and provide a network of access routes across the country for use by any member of the public.

Private land: the BMC liaises with landowners of land which is not open access in England and Wales to agree permissive access to climbing sites where necessary.

In Scotland there is a freedom of access across virtually all land in Scotland providing it is conducted responsibly.

Most dog owners are well aware that dogs should be kept away from livestock, but what can be less understood is the impact of dogs upon wildlife and in particular ground nesting birds. These birds choose nest sites on moorland away from paths meaning that human disturbance is unlikely, however dogs tend to run across open moorland off the path network and can disturb these nests. During the spring whilst on moorland areas, keeping your dog under close control on a lead is the responsible way to do your bit and help ground nesting birds successfully fledge their chicks.

The one stop shop for all access information in England and Wales is the BMC's Regional Access Database (RAD) which can be found at: www.thebmc.co.uk/rad. This database is an up-to-date resource with any access information relating to crags that climbers may need to know about and is well worth checking before a day's climbing to prevent a wasted journey.

Any access issues or queries can be fielded through the BMC access team in England and Wales and MCofS in Scotland. Contact details for these are below:

England: Rob Dyer (robd@thebmc.co.uk)
Wales: Elfyn Jones (elfyn@thebmc.co.uk)
Scotland: Hebe Carus (hebe@mcofs.org.uk)

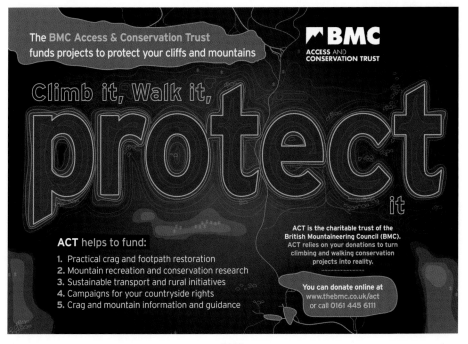

Now Hear This

For God's sake read these easy notes and try to take them in.

// The Rock

Please treat the rock with care and respect. It can wear out and it will never come back.

Never hammer, chip or vigorously brush the rock. Just use a soft nylon brush.

Dirty soles wear away the rock. Clean your feet.

Tread lightly. Messy footwork destroys the rock's surface.

Never climb on damp or wet sandstone. Moisture greatly weakens it.

Eroded problems are especially vulnerable. Let them rest.

Don't use Font-style 'pof' resin. It spoils problems.

// The Environment

Respect any agreed access restrictions. See thebmc.co.uk/rad for information.

Dogs can frighten and kill wildlife. Keep them under control.

Landings are vulnerable. Protect the ground with a bouldering mat.

Try to avoid crossing fences and walls in the countryside. Use a gate.

Use chalk sparingly. Huge white patches and tick marks are an eyesore.

Take litter home with you. Not just yours but any you find.

Go to the toilet considerately. If you can't go at home them bear others in mind.

Don't piss under overhangs or in dry spots. The rain won't wash it away.

// Other People

Always bear other people in mind and be polite to those sharing your space, climbers and non-climbers. They have as much right to be there too, sometimes more.

Farmers rely on the countryside for their livelihood. Make sure your behaviour doesn't cause them any trouble.

Always park considerately. Never block any gates or driveways.

Try to make your impact a good one. It's a great life and our likes will not be there again.

Some words in foreign

Here are some translations of key words used in the book for Johnny Foreigner.

// English	// français	// Espanol	// Deutsch
approach	une approche	Aproximación	Zustieg
arete	une arête	Arista	Kantenkletterei
boulder	un bloc, un rocher	bloc	Boulder
bouldering	faire du bloc, le bloc	bulder	bouldern
bouldering mat	un crash-pad	colchoneta	Crashpad
climbing	l'escalade (f)	escalada	klettern
conditions	les conditions (f)	condiciones	Bedingungen, Conditions
corner	un dièdre	diedro	Verschneidung
crack	une fissure	fisura	Riß
crag	une falaise	sector/zona	Gebiet, Sektor
crimp	une réglette	regleta	Leiste
damp	humide	humido/humida	feucht, nass
descent	la descente	descenso	Abstieg
dyno	un jeté	lanzamiento	Dynamo
exposed	exposé/e	expuesto	ausgesetzt
family-friendly	familial	apto para niños	familienfreundlich
fingery	très à doigts	de dedos	kleingriffig
flake	une écaille	laja	Schuppe
granite	le granit	granito	Granit
grit	le grès	grit	Gritstone
groove	une fente; un dièdre	diedro	Rille
highball	haut	Tsunami	Highball
landing	l'aterissage	caida	Absprunggelände
limestone	le calcaire	calcario	Kalk
midge	un moucheron	mosquito	Mücke
mountain	une montagne	montaña	Berg
overhang	un dévers / un surplomb	desnivel	Überhang
pad	un crash-pad	colchonetta	Crashpad, Matte
parking	un parking	parking	Parkplatz
path	un sentier; un chemin	camino	Weg, Pfad
pebble	un caillou	piedra	Kiesel
pocket	un trou	agujero	Loch
powerful	très physique; péchonneux	escalada de fuerza	athletisch
quarry	une carrier	cantera	Steinbruch
quick drying	qui sèche vite	secado rápido	schnell trocknend
rhyloite	le rhyolite	riolita	Rhyloit
roof	un toit	techo	Dach
sandstone	le grès	arenisca	Sandstein
sea	la mer	mar	Meer
shade	l'ombre	sombra	Schatten
sit start, sitter	un départ assis	sit start	Sitzstart
slab	une dalle	placa tumbada	Platte
sloper	un aplat	romo	Aufleger
steep	qui déverse, déversant	vertical	steil
sun	le soleil	sol	Sonne
tidal	à mare	marea	Gezeiten
train (as in railway)	un train	tren	Zug
training	entraînement	entrenamiento	Training
traverse	une traverse	travesia	Traverse, Quergang
undercut	une inverse	invertido	Untergriff
vertical	vertical	vertical	senkrecht
walk	un promenade	caminar	Spaziergang
wall	un mur	pared	Wand
wet	mouillé/e	mojado/mojada	nass

Chris Doyle on Cave Life, 8A, Parisella's Cave (page 130, problem 5). Photo: Alex Messenger.

Tom Peckitt on Big Kicks, 7C, Lord's Seat (page 273, problem 30). Photo: Jon Pearson.

// Problem inclusion

The book seeks to give a good visit to each venue listed. It in no way seeks to be definitive, nor even to give all the best problems. It seeks to give you a great flavour for the place. For most venues there is a vast amount of further problems, often just as good as those listed in this book. Go for an explore. If you like it, get the local guide.

// Sit starts

Problems are taken as being non-eliminate standing starts unless otherwise stated. Any problem that starts from sitting will have the words 'sitter' or 'sit start' in italics immediately after the grade unless this is blindingly obvious. If a description says 'Start sitting, from small pockets,' this doesn't mean you have to sit in the pockets. It's where your hands go. On topos I have tried to start the arrowed problem lines on the first handholds used in the problem then roughly trace the line of the hands. Hence on a sit start problem the arrowed line comes quite close to the ground. On stand ups it is much higher.

If the problem has an optional sit start these are sometimes mentioned in italics. In the example below:

8 Wave Arete 6A *Sitter.*

This means that the problem goes from a sitter at the grade of 6A. Whereas:

10 Index Bulge 5 *Sitter 7A.*

means that the problem is a 5 from standing or 7A from a sit start.

// Traverses

Traverses are marked in yellow to avoid confusion with intersecting up-problems. It doesn't mean that people who traverse are cowards.

// Highballs

If problems are particulary highball this is often mentioned in the text. However if this is obvious it may not be. Use your sense. And remember, short problems can be as risky as tall ones.

// Disclaimer

Climbing is dangerous. The author accepts no responsiblity for any harm that comes your way while using this book. Every effort has been made to ensure the information is correct but you must still use your own judgement.

// Grades

I have used Fontainebleau, or Font, grades in this book. While Fred Nicole and Daniel Woods might be working hard to extend the system in the upper levels, I have spent many hours in the lab growing the system backwards. Hence I bring you the grade of Font 1! The system's flexibility in the lower grades is the reason I opted for Font grades. If you don't understand bouldering grades or are more familiar with a different system then see the chart below. Fundamentally, the bigger the number the harder it is. It's that simple.

Font grades	V grade	British technical grade
8C	V15	
8B+	V14	7b
8B	V13	
8A+	V12	
8A	V11	7a
7C+	V10	
7C	V9	
7B+	V8½	
7B	V8	6c
7A+	V7	
7A	V6	
6C+	V5	
6C		6b
6B+	V4	
6B	V3	6a
6A+	V2	
6A		
5+	V1	5c
5	V0+	5b
4+	V0	5a
4	V0-	4c
3+		4b
3		4a
2+		3c
2		3b
1+		3a
1		

Notes

// UKBouldering.com

UKBouldering.com has a great forum where among some random topics you will find lots of up-to-date information on crucial topics such as conditions to many of the more fickle venues included in this book. Many of the users are very committed and knowledgable local activists who will gladly give you all the beta you will need to a visit to their local area. There are mines of information on every section covered on these pages. Join in.

// UKClimbing.com

The country's biggest climbing website with a huge photo gallery and very active forum, although not always talking about climbing. A very well developed logbook system gives info on all the venues and most of the problems covered in this book. Again, the forum can be handy for information on climbs, accommodation etc.

Ken Palmer on Hanging Flake, 6C, Combeshead Tor (page 65, problem 22). Photo: David Simmonite.

~~ ●	crags and boulders
BH	bunkhouse
YH	youth hostel
C	cafe
PH	pub
S	shop
▲	campsite
●	train station
◯	town or city
◯	lake
	trees
P	car park
O j2	motorway junction
=	motorway
|||	roads
O	roundabout
·····	track
⁚⁚⁚⁚	path

// Topo symbols

 // Approach time: The time it takes me to walk from the car park to the main bouldering area.

 // Problem range: The upper figure is the number of problems, based on the most comprehensive guide for any area. The lower figure is the range at which the venue is best.

 // Climbing style: An indication of the styles of climbing available. Can you work out what they mean?

 // Sunshine: Imagine the sun is a kind of clock. The red in the middle shows which hours the venue is in the sun. Example, top left the venue comes into the sun about midday until sunset. Top right from mid-afternoon to sunset. Bottom left, sun all day. Bottom right, dawn till mid afternoon.

 // Shelter: A sheltered venue, one that's good for keeping out of the wind. Good for cold gusty days.

 // Exposed: A venue that catches the wind and weather. Good for hot and midgy days, bad for cold ones or softies.

 // Seepage: A venue that is prone to dampness. This can be a dank, north facing venue, or a venue that seeps in winter or after rain, or a tidal one that retains moisture.

 // Rainproof: A venue that provides shelter and remains climbable when it rains. It can still suffer from seepage.

// Tidal: A venue where the climbing or approach is limited by the tide to some degree.

// Maps

Hopefully the maps are self-explanatory. Use the key above to help. Almost all maps are orientated north so there is no north marker. Where a map is not orientated to the north there will be a red north marker.

// GPS coordinates

At the top of each section, in the coloured title bar, are the latitude and longitude coordinates for the main parking spot for that venue for use in satellite navigation systems.

// Family friendly

This is a venue where there has somewhere nice, grass or the seaside, for the family to hang out and relax while the alpha parent or child has a boulder. It doesn't mean that it's easy to get to with a buggy: approach times are always given and awkward approaches are usually noted. In essence it means somewhere that is nice to have a picnic.

// Info

This is where to go to get more info on the venue. If other publications cover the venue yet have less information than is included here they are generally not mentioned.

ORGANIC

www.organicclimbing.com

d. woods. rocklands: laura griffiths photo

Premium bouldering gear, proudly made in the USA. Now with soy foam.

Waddage

There's always been boulders but for bouldering we need people. Here's a list off the top of my head of the people to whom we owe the sport. The people who have pushed it all forward, the innovators, the hardcore, the scenesters, the spotters, the documenters, the comedians and the rogues. Without them there would be nothing to write about.

As I say this is pretty much off the top of my head and not in any particular order. There will be people on it who deserve to be on it, and that is good. There will be people who think they should be on it but who shouldn't, so aren't. That's good too. There are people who should be on it and who aren't. That's probably bad, but you'll live with it. Console yourself with the thought of people who are on it but shouldn't. Remember, love *all* the people.

Tony Barley	Naomi Buys	Paul Houghoughi	Rob Gawthorpe
Shauna Coxsey	Grant Edwards	Ken Wood	Greg Chapman
Malcolm Smith	Lee Robinson	John Gaskins	Chez George
Tim Rankin	Mark Stokes	Jonathan Lagoe	Chris Hamper
George Smith	Phil Davidson	Paul Ingham	Will Atkinson
Nigel Poustie	Tim Carruthers	Pete Whillance	Hank Pasquill
Ali Coull	Quentin Fisher	Ray Wood	Jon Pearson
Gav Symonds	Dave Cuthbertson	Mark Leach	Graham Desroy
Niall McNair	Alan Cameron-Duff	Zaff Ali	Andi Turner
Steve Bancroft	Dave Wheeler	Jonathan Bean	Claude Dean Frankland
Tom Newberry	Rupert Davies	Jerry Moffatt	Dave Westlake
Steve Blake	Al Rouse	John Watson	Claude E Benson
Jordan Buys	Dan Varian	Mark Sharratt	Ryan Plews
Tim Wilkinson	John Coefield	Mina Leslie-Wujastyk	Richard Duffy
Bob Smith	Pete Hurley	Jon Barton	Nic Ward
Johnny Dawes	James Ibbertson	Stuart Littlefair	James Putrell
John Redhead	Owen Samuels	Justin Critchlow	Don Whillans
Pete Kirton	Pierre Allain	Stuart Cathcart	Michael Duffy
Chris Davies	Katherine Schirrmacher	Martin Boysen	Ron Fawcett
Tommy Smith	Will Perrin	Mick Adams	Alan James
Murray Hamilton	Andy Swann	Joe Brown	Fred Nicole
Ben Stokes	Matt Birch	Dave Birkett	Dave Buchanan
Tyler Landman	John Wainwright	Adam Wainwright	John Dunne
Dave Ripley	Simon Young	Kev Hughes	Pete Chadwick
Chris Graham	Adam Long	Tom Proctor	John Syrett
Ian Stronghill	Tom Walkington	John Earl	Suzan Dudink
Nick Dixon	Ray McHaffie	Pete Robins	William Cecil Slingsby
Gaz Parry	Simon Panton	Leah Crane	Ruth Smitton
Paul Smitton	Katy Whittaker	Mike Hammill	Ben Farley
Peter Wycislik	Jonny Woodward	Dougie Hall	Allan Manson
Gavin Foster	Danny Cattell	Al Williams	Ian Cummings
Ken Palmer	Dalvinder Sodhi	Richard Hessian	Diane Merrick
Ben Read	Nibile	James McHaffie	Barnaby Carver
Richie Betts	Sam Cattell	Liam Fyfe	Jim Arnold
Pete Kitson	John Gill	Fred Botterill	Jamie Cassidy
Steve Dunning	Paul Savage	Bob Hutchinson	Neil Kershaw
Ian Vickers	Tim Clifford	Will Sim	Andy Popp
Ryan Pasquil	Jerry Peel	Tom Peckitt	Al Harris
Martin Crook	Dave MacLeod	Andy Whall	Dave Noden
Neil Dyer	Will Perrin	Micky Page	Robin Mueller
Paul Pritchard	Big Annie	John Allen	Paul Higginson
Rae Cowie	Adam Hocking	Steve Rhodes	Martin Veale
Mark Katz	Ned Feehally	Steve Crowe	Arthur Dolphin
Joe Healey	Allan Austin	Ryan Pasquill	Liam Desroy
Rob Sanderson	Dave Henderson	Andy Brown	Umpleby
Robin Barley	Richie Patterson	Chris Doyle	Andy Earl
Jason Myers	Lucinda Whittaker	Ben Moon	Pete Zeigenfuss
Bernard Newman	Gill Peet	James O'Neil	Jim Kimber

Graded List

It's wrong to six decimal places!

Don't take this too seriously. In fact, if you find yourself in a third world country suddenly under attack from a violent intestinal bug then these should be the first pages to go. To be honest, they are just randomly distributed through their grades with a few of the cooler ones at the top of each set. If any are right then don't hestitate in letting me know. But still, it fills a few pages, and you can't argue with that.

// 8C
Shadowplay, Little Font
Walk Away Sit Start, Fairy Steps
Il Pirata, Trowbarrow

// 8B+
Voyager Sit Start,
 Burbage North
Pilgrimage, Parisella's Cave
Kaizen, Woodwell
Monk Life, Kyloe in the Woods
7 of 9, Glen Nevis
Bulbhaul, Almscliff
Leviathan, Kyloe in the Woods

// 8B
High Fidelity, Caley
Cypher, Slipstones
The Ace, Plantation
Voyager, Burbage North
Pool of Bethesda Sit Start,
 Cromlech Boulders
Isla de Encanta, Trowbarrow
Keen Roof, Raven Tor
Pressure, Dumbarton
Walk Away, Fairy Steps
Gaskins Problem, Pillbox
Fat Lip, Raven Tor
Super Furry Animal, Slipstones
Anasthesia, Woodwell

// 8A+
Pool of Bethesda, Cromlech
Blood Sport, Shaftoe
Ivan Dobsky, Ravensheugh
Cherry Falls, Almscliff
The Bitch, Back Bowden
Work Hard, Curbar
One Infinity, Bathford
Mr Fantastic, Cromlech
Carpenter's Apprentice,
 Dinas Rock
Wife of Fyfe, Dinas Rock
Downset, Elephantitus
8 Ball, Gardom's
Don't Pierdol, High Rocks
Catapult, Kyloe in the Woods

Little Women, Little Font
Super Submarine, Longridge
Bonnie, Parisella's Cave
Drink Driving, Pillbox
Ark Royal, Queens Crag
A Bigger Belly, Rubicon
Compact Culture, Sheep Pen
Toe-Fu, Simon's Seat
Inertia Reel Trav, The Roaches
Shallow Groove, Trowbarrow
The Full Traverse, Warton

// 8A
Careless Torque, Plantation
Diesel Power, Cromlech Boulders
Queen Kong, Queens Crag
The Art of Self Destruction,
 Woodwell
XXXX, Bowderstone
Preparation H, Hepburn
The Joker, Plantation
All Elements, Bathford
The Fonz, Brimham
Westworld, Burbage West
Ranieri's Reach, Caley
Caseg Groove Sit Start, Caseg
Sabotage, Dumbarton
Sway On, Gallt yr Ogof
Supercede, Hartland
Mako, Hound Tor
Under Pressure, Pantymwyn
Guy Fawkes, Portland
The Crack in the Shadows,
 Queens Crag
Red Dragon, Queens Crag
Abba Gold, Saddle Tor
Menace, Sheep Pen
Dead Baron, Shipley Glen
Endangered Species,
 Thorn Crag
Stokes Croft, Torridon
Humble Pie Disorder,
 Wavelength
Not Bad Nige, Woodwell

// 7C+
Eyes of Silence, Callerhues
Jason's Roof, Crookrise

Lou Ferrino, Parisella's Cave
Main Vein, Caseg
Groove is in the Heart, Clodgy
Monoblock, Pex Hill
Tusk, Elephantitus
Providence, Godrevy
Wish, High Rocks
Psycho Cowboy, Pentire
Ben's Roof, Raven Tor
I Am Curious Yellow, Ilkley
Sparks, Pantymwyn
Check oot me Pipes,
 Ravensheugh
Trigger Cut, Parisella's Cave
Rational Bandit, Pentire
Thug Mental, Pantymwyn
Porn Makes Me Horny,
 Porth Ysgo
Pump up the Power, Raven Tor
The Magician, Ravensheugh
Saddle Tor Traverse, Saddle Tor
Jerry's Problem, Sheep Pen
The Power of RAAA, St Bees
Haston Dyno, The Breck
Colorado Dreaming, Tintagel
The Keel, Almscliff
Silverback, Dumbarton
Cruel Intentions, Wainstones

// 7C
The Big Smile, Wavelength
Big Kicks, Lord's Seat
Tetris, The Roaches
Be Ruthless, Pantymwyn
Cowboy Junkie, Pentire
Little Northumberland,
 Nesscliffe
Blockbuster, Caley
Fat Cat Roof, Dinas Rock
Ben's Wall, Curbar
Beetle Back, Glen Nevis
Blacking out the Friction,
 Godrevy
Gloss Over the Mat, Hartland
Bus Stop, Cromlech Boulders
Resurrection, High Rocks
Lock, Stock and Barrel,
 Loch Katrine
Ivory Mountain, Bonehill

You'll be wishing for rain...

// 7C (continued)
Red Quinne, Northcott
Love Pie, Wavelength
The Wave Traverse, Bonehill
Brad Pit, Plantation
Powerband, Raven Tor
Vitruvian Man, Trowbarrow
Not Bad Dave, Woodwell
In Bloom, Dumbarton
Tim's Crack, St Bees
Improper Opera, Bowderstone
Ache Ball, Hartland
Niche Dyno, Brimham
Terry, Caley
Rock Attrocity, Parisella's Cave
Learning to Fly, Kyloe Crag
Jerry's Roof, Cromlech Boulders
Crouching Start,
    Hidden Foothold, Cromlech
Lipo Suction, Wetherby
Smackhead, Gallt yr Ogof

// 7B+
The Essence, Torridon
The Arete, Gillercombe
West Side Story, Burbage West
Bad Moon Rising, Thorn Crag
Inaudible Vaudeville,
    Bowderstone
The Yorkshireman,
    Kyloe in the Woods
Under The Bridge, Pantymwyn
Ram Air, Ramshaw
Thug Mentality, Pantymwyn
Dialogue, Ramshaw
Prime Time, Kyloe Crag
The Groove, Clodgy
The Shield, Dumbarton
ur hot, Godrevy
Beth's Traverse, Goldsborough
Ringpiece, Ilkley
Hitchhiker's Direct,
    Kyloe in the Woods
Dick Williams, Secret Garden
Full AD Traverse,
    Bourton Combe
Cubby's Lip, Kyloe in the Woods
J-Lo, Northcott
Gasoline Straight Up,
    Pantymwyn
Pet Sounds, Porth Ysgo
Reiver, Ravensheugh
The Press, Rubicon
Lay-By Arete, Slipstones
Barrel Traverse, The Barrel
Blind Date, Burbage North
Kids, Tintagel
The Rib, Burbage South
Texas Hold 'Em, Trowbarrow
Wavelength, Wavelength

// 7B
Chocolate Wall, Pillbox
Braichmelyn Traverse,
    Braichmelyn
The Mission, Torridon
Ben's Groove, Caley
The Universal, Applecross
Wright's Traverse, Churnet
Hooby's Special, Ogmore-by-Sea
Big Marine, Longridge
T Crack, Cratcliffe
Millstone Grit, Shipley Glen
For Liechtenstein, Wainstones
The Dark Side, Bonehill
Ears of Perception, Bowderstone
Bustach Prow, Bustach
Deliverance, Plantation
Breakaway, Pex Hill
Big Al Qaeda, Robin Hood's
The Gimp, Caseg
The Iron Bar, Clemmitt's
Salad Fingers, Clodgy
Undercuts Traverse,
    Combeshead
Jerry's Traverse, Cratcliffe
Ultimate Retro Party, Cromlech
Weedkiller Traverse, Raven Tor
Ground Force, Carrock Fell
Soft on the G, Gardom's
Carnage, Hartland
Slopy Traverse, Lynmouth
Left Wall Traverse, Parisella's
Simple Simon, Churnet
Liquid Sunshine, Portland
McNab, Lord's Seat
Worldline, Queens Crag
The Main Issue, Reiff
Super Trouper, Saddle Tor
Mile High Guy, Carrock Fell
Bow Wow Prow, St Bees
Voodoo People, Warton

// 7A+
Malcolm's Arete, Torridon
Yellow Desert Scream, St Bees
Demon Wall Roof, Almscliff
Armathwaite Traverse,
    Armathwaite
The Famous Grouse, Bell Tor
Beaver Cleaver, Parisella's Cave
Picnic Sarcastic, Bowderstone
Ousal Low, Churnet
A Northern Soul, Hepburn
Hank's Wall, Brownstones
The Sphinx, Burbage North
Crouching the Mahogany,
    Callerhues
Don't Mess with the Shek,
    Applecross
Snoopy, Carn Brea
Punk's Life, Carrock Fell
Boomerang, Clodgy

Pantys Down, Pantymwyn
Cromlech Roof Crack, Cromlech
Toll Boothe Arete, Portland
Rob's Wall, Fisherground
Perfect Evening Light, Godrevy
Hitchhiker's Guide to the Galaxy,
    Kyloe in the Woods
Seventh Wave Traverse,
    Lynmouth
Slim, Parisella's Cave
Lung La, Grinshill
The Duergar, Ravensheugh
The Pinch, Sheep Pen
Foal's Chopper, Saddle Tor
Cowboy Arete, Pentire
Whaleback, Simon's Seat
Yew Tree Traverse, Pleasley Vale
The Queen is Dead,
    Queens Crag
Dulcinea, Simonside
Stomping With Bez, Portland
Ames Low, Huntsham
Split Lip, Portland
The Crack, Reiff
A Bigger Tail, Rubicon
Dancing Queen, Saddle Tor
Lightning Strike, Portland
Red Baron, Shipley Glen
Sulky Little Boys, Slipstones
Clash of the Titans, St Bees
The Minimum, The Barrel
Hard Arete, The Roaches
Shallow Grave, Trowbarrow
The Witch, Wavelength

// 7A
TP and QC, Reiff
Hanging Slab, The Roaches
Elephantitus, Elephantitus
And For My Next Trick,
    Thorn Crag
Tierdrop, Ramshaw
Northumberland Wonderland,
    Nesscliffe
Popcorn Party, Porth Ysgo
The Nose, Burbage North
Mugsy, Dumbarton
Joker's Traverse, Brimham
Small Brown, Crookrise
Nicotine Alley, Bowles
Mark's Roof Original, Gardom's
Bloodstone Arete, Carn Brea
Slapstick, Bowderstone
Mr Pepperpot, Bridestones
Superman, High Rocks
Prowed, Hound Tor
Hamper's Hang, Apparent North
Prow, Armathwaite
Barbastelle, Back Bowden
The Crack, Braichmelyn
Double Dyno, Bonehill
Nürburgring, Bridestones

// 7A (Continued)
The Alliance, Burbage South
Sick Happy, Bustach
Gnasher, Sheep Pen
Yorkshire 8A, Rothley
Green Traverse, Plantation
Plumline Traverse, Warton
Sing a Rainbow, Carrock Fell
The Porthole, Huntsham
Red Handed, Reiff
Kingdom of Rain, Sheep Pen
Screaming Slave, Woodwell
High Speed Imp Act, Churnet
Little Extra, Raven Tor
Johnny's Wall, Cromlech
Bend in the Rainbow, Longridge
Gorilla Warfare, Curbar
Launch Pad, Dinas Rock
Firestarter, Pantymwyn
Trigonometry, Godrevy
Rheumatology, Hepburn
Darth Vadar, High Rocks
The Traverse, Langdale
Riding Hannah, Dinas Rock
Cyclone, Lynmouth
Beach Ball, Secret Garden
Red Quinne Traverse, Northcott
Hooby's Roof, Ogmore-by-Sea
G Spotting, Pac Man
Fingers Start, Churnet
Pillbox Original, Pillbox
Help the Aged, Plantation
The Greek, Pillbox
Paradise, Clemmitt's
Really Cool Toys, Porth Ysgo
Petty Thief, Portland
Stinging Nettle, Stone Farm
Cave Problem, Robin Hood's
Crystalline Entity, Carn Brea
C3PO, The Roaches
Red Wall Traverse, Trowbarrow
The Prow, Wainstones
Monster Tide, Lynmouth
Utopia Traverse, Wavelength
Mega Traverse, Wetherby

// 6C+
Hueco Crack, St Bees
Ogwen Jazz, Caseg Fraith
Klem's Bulge, Sheep Pen
The Pocket, Langdale
Jocks and Geordies, Kyloe in
Caseg Groove, Caseg
The Golden Bicep, Huntsham
Pommel, Brimham
Rouse's Wall, Carrock Fell
Gentle Jess, Dinas Rock
Sloper Patrol, Almscliff
Stazi, Nesscliffe
Central Wall, Braichmelyn
Sky Pilot, Glen Nevis
Sorcerer Direct, Forest Rock

Pebble Wall, Almscliff
Pac Man Arete, Pac Man
The Sheep, Burbage South
Boulevard, Callerhues
Monty Python's Direct, Kyloe in
I Can, I Can't, Carrock Fell
Dyno from Undercut,
    Combeshead
Fast Cars, Porth Ysgo
Razor Roof, Cratcliffe
The Edge Problem, Cromlech
Fight Club, Loch Katrine
The Overhang, Langdale
Cube Traverse, Bonehill
Oh Yeah, Caseg Fraith
The Ramp, Gallt yr Ogof
Midnight in a Perfect World,
    Glen Nevis
Loose Cannon, Cromlech
Northern Track, Clodgy
Little Prow Traverse, Hound Tor
Toe Dragon, Sheep Pen
Slugtaste, Huntsham
Pongo, Dumbarton
Tourist Trap, Loch Katrine
The Joker and the Thief,
    Lynmouth
Tom's Reverse, Woodwell
Sugarfix, Warton
Marsh Dyno, RAC
Weight Watcher, Sheep Pen
Bluebell Traverse, The Breck
King of Drunks, Wavelength
Fish Arete, Wimberry

// 6C
Naked Edge, Simon's Seat
Hart's Arete, Pex Hill
Eliminator, Grinshill
Stretch and Mantel,
    The Roaches
Ron's Crack 1, Crookrise
The Traverse, Harmer's
Manson's Wall, Shipley Glen
Hanging Flakes, Combeshead
Not to be Taken Away,
    Plantation
Viking Invasion, RAC
And She Was, Simon's Seat
Gorilla, Dumbarton
Banana Finger Direct,
    Burbage North
The Crack, Bowderstone
Boot Boys Start, Raven Tor
Wish, Hound Tor
Nameless Arete, Northcott
Font Traverse, Shaftoe
Oyster, Ogmore-by-Sea
Jawa, Loch Katrine
Mantel Masterclass,
    Back Bowden
The Scoop, Bonehill

Pervert's Traverse, Combeshead
Strong Struggle, Harrison's
Hoodoo People, Warton
Limbo Dancer, Hound Tor
Purple Haze, Tintagel
Rippled Wall, Bonehill
The Neb Roof, Shaftoe
Labyrinth, Warton
Pudding Basin, Huntsham
The Knob, Loch Katrine
Swamp Monster, Torridon
Readheads Roof, Wainstones
Back Wall Traverse,
    Hobson Moor
Berlin's Fallen, Nesscliffe
Roadside Arete, Cromlech
Black Wall Traverse, Salisbury
Karma Sutra, Pac Man
Utopia Left-Hand, Wavelength

// 6B+
Conan the Librarian,
    Mother Cap
Magician's Newphew,
    Queens Crag
Beach Boys Arete, Porth Ysgo
Dog Shooter, Sheep Pen
Virgin Traverse, Almscliff
Fandango, Bowles
Tobacco Road, Bowles
Boardman's Arete, Carrock Fell
Heel Hook Traverse, Cromlech
Sadcocs Wall, Crookrise
Strawberries, Curbar
Pocket Dyno, Godrevy
Layaway, Harmer's
Happy Days, Brimham
Bloody Helman Start, Helman
Gone for a Bourton,
    Bourton Combe
Cube Arete, Bonehill
Old Kent Road, High Rocks
Pink Gin, Kyloe in the Woods
Robbed Arete, Ogmore-by-Sea
Higginson Scar, Porth Ysgo
Sanctified, Woodwell
Johnny's Slab, Porth Ysgo
Wave Arete, Bonehill
Marsh Arete, RAC
The Lurch, Ramshaw
The Coppinger, Tintagel
Wamdue Project, Trowbarrow
Boysen's Groove, Wavelength
Local Hero, Wimberry
Griff's Traverse, Bridestones
Utopia Central, Wavelength

// 6B
The Gypsy, Almscliff
Burnt Heather, Thorn Crag
Nicotine Stain, Burbage North
Caseg Fraith Arete, Caseg Fraith

// 6B (Continued)

Toto, Dumbarton
Boysen's Route, Frodsham
Rippled Arete, Bonehill
Rippled Wall Traverse, Bonehill
Pond Traverse, Brownstones
Remergence, Burbage North
Cae Du Crack, Cae Du
Back Stabber, Caley
Footpath, Callerhues
Vicicle Graffiti, Carrock Fell
Charlie's Overhang, Newstones
Boysen's Arete, Harrison's
Little Groove, Carrock Fell
Crystal Wall, Combeshead
Freddie's Nightmare,
   Mynydd Dinas
Arch, Badger Rock
Pocket Traverse, Cromlech
Monkey Boy, Dinas Rock
World's Hardest V3, Gillercombe
Maizie Gunn's, Glen Nevis
No Grieving, Helman
Little Prow, Hound Tor
Ouzel Thorn, Thorn Crag
Kebab Legs, Wavelength
The Ramp, Porth Ysgo
Noel's Arete, Rothley
A Miller's Tale, Rubicon
Foul Bite, Saddle Tor
Immaculato, Nesscliffe
Aerobic Wall, Hound Tor
Hanging Arete, Rothley
Red Rum, Kyloe in the Woods
Art School, Loch Katrine
Technical Master, Millstone
Ousal High, Churnet
Wavelength Central, Wavelength
Lip Traverse, Mynydd Dinas
Ass Creek Traverse, Grinshill
Ripple, Newstones
J Dog, Northcott
Pump Traverse, Parisella's
Unmarked Grave, Porth Ysgo
Southern Soul, Portland
The Pinches, Ramshaw
Teewhuppo, Reiff
Hidden Traverse, Saddle Tor
Staffs Flyer, The Roaches
The Shelf, Wavelength

// 6A+

Jumping Jack Flash,
   Goldsborough
Rabbitstone Crack, Queens Crag
Flying Arete, Almscliff
Mr Smooth, Caley
Go West, Burbage West
The Seam, Gromlech
Cracked Boulder Traverse,
   Combeshead
5c Wall, Hound Tor

JRA, Clodgy
Battle of the Bulge, Helman
Digitation, Brownstones
Watercolour Challenge,
   Loch Katrine
Frontside Traverse, RAC
Gorilla, Gorilla, Hutton Roof
Lean-To, Carrock Fell
Pocket Wall, Cromlech
Crucifixion, Fairy Steps
Strong Arete, Fisherground
Left Flake Direct, RAC
West Face Route, Harrison's
Silent Running, Holmfirth
Bjorn Again, Saddle Tor
Cyclops, Hutton Roof
Tall Wall, Caseg Fraith
Bogmen, Torridon
Pete's Slab, Mynydd Dinas
Pebble Arete, Plantation
Klem's Arete, Sheep Pen
Black Crack, Tintagel

// 6A

Morrell's Wall, Almscliff
The Sorcerer, Back Bowden
The Ramp, Braichmelyn
The Wave, Carn Brea
Poodle Traverse, Dinas Rock
Pock, Burbage South
Otley Wall, Caley
Carnage Arete, Hartland
The Scoops, Huntsham
Hubris, Goldsborough
Soft Centre, Shaftoe
Trauma Arete, Hepburn
Cut Steps, High Rocks
High Traverse, Honister
Twister, Lynmouth
Main Overhang, Moelfre
Limbo, Ravensheugh
Lay-By, Slipstones
Chickenheads, Caley
Bob's Bastard, Caley
Crease Direct, Crookrise
Home Rule, Dumbarton
Right Groove, The Roaches
Jalapeno Arete, Thorn Crag
Perrin's Crack, Porth Ysgo
Streamline, Portland
Cloud Nine, Clemmitt's
Tufa, Churnet
Flax Factor, Bourton Combe
Pillar Face, Fisherground
The Flake, Portland
Hanging Crack, Haresfield
Badfinger, Kyloe in the Woods
Mind Trick, Loch Katrine
Speed Trap, Mynydd Dinas
Tier's End, Ramshaw
Central Groove, Bridestones
Joker's Wall Start, Brimham

Banana Finger, Burbage North
Slipperman, Ogmore-by-Sea
Hourglass, Plantation
Monk's Traverse, Pleasley Vale
The Ysgo Flange, Porth Ysgo
Ripples, Portland
Monkey up a Stick, RAC
Ripper, Slipstones
Fisherman's Dyno, St Bees
Pine Buttress, Stone Farm
Undercut Problem, The Barrel
Three Pocket Slab, The Roaches
Joe's Arete, The Roaches
Griddle Groove, Woodwell

// 5+

Sorcerer's Apprentice,
   Back Bowden
The Hoop-La, Frodsham
Fiddler, Goldsborough
Low Pebble Wall, Caley
Moonshot, Beacon Hill
Permutation Rib, Caley
Crystal Arete, Carn Brea
Dark Side Traverse, Bonehill
Cleo's Edge, Burbage North
Sucker's Rib, Caley
Classic Arete, Carn Brea
Left Egg, Cratcliffe
Three Pocket Wall, Curbar
Byte Size, Dinas Rock
Sorcerer, Forest Rock
Hydroponicum, Loch Katrine
Jug U'La, Nesscliffe
Relayer, Beacon Hill
Hanging Flake, Gromlech
Uncle Pete's Arete, Porth Ysgo
The Spine, Robin Hood's Stride
Nu Breed, Portland
Botterill's Mantel, Queens Crag
Dormouse Arete, Harmer's
Braichmelyn Arete, Braichmelyn
Murky Way, Brimham
Jas' Wall, Hartland
Hell's Tooth Start, Helman
Front Crack, Sheep Pen
Pott's Scoop, Simonside
Shark's Fin, Hound Tor
Left Flake, Huntsham
Gorilla Berengii, Hutton Roof
The Pearler, Kyloe in the Woods
Thin Hand Special, Kyloe in
Iron Dish Wall, Frodsham
Thompson Twins, Grinshill
The Crack, Langdale
Quinne Groove, Northcott
Crescent Arete, Plantation
Truth, Porth Ysgo
Slopers Traverse, Rothley
High Traverse, Rubicon
Paul's Arete, Slipstones
Lone Arete, Plantation

AWESOME WALLS
CLIMBING CENTRES
HERE TO MAKE YOU STRONGER!
www.awesomewalls.co.uk
Stockport
0161 494 9949
Liverpool
0151 298 2422
Stoke-on-Trent
01782 341 919

// 5+ (Continued)
Sowden, Slipstones
Rainbow Trail, Tintagel
Dihedral, Warton
Subliminal, Woodwell

// 5
Badger Arete, Badger Rock
Magic Fluting, Shaftoe
Hazelrigg Wall, Back Bowden
Calf Dyno, Ilkley
The Diamond, Fisherground
Super Wall, Frodsham
Active Service, Kyloe Crag
Turtle's Flipper, Shaftoe
Zig Zag, Dumbarton
Crucifix, Almscliff
Fiddler's Arete, Goldsborough
Scoop, Badger Rock
Dartford Runnel,
    Ogmore-by-Sea
The Breathalyser, Reiff
Z'mutt, High Rocks
Jugs, Bridestones
Apiary Arete, St Bees
Crow Man, Burbage North
Pocket Wall, Churnet
Brown's Crack, Cromlech
The Ramp, Cromlech
Erewhon, Dumbarton
Fox Traverse, Fisherground
Last Chance, Harrison's
Anarchy Arete, Lynmouth
Frog Traverse, Pleasley
Nobody Knows, Robin Hood's
Toenail Pie, Rubicon
The Scoop, Simon's Seat
Elephant's Bum, Wimberry
Wiggling Crack, Thorn Crag
Wet Leg Arete, The Breck
Bog Standard, The Roaches
Flake and Chips, The Roaches
Deryn Groove, Woodwell

// 4+
Early Days, Rothley
Uncle Pete's Groove, Porth Ysgo
Pisa Traverse, Pex Hill
The Lemur's Tail, Hutton Roof
Bass Special, Goldsborough
Corner Crack, Godrevy
F.E.A.R., Lynmouth
RAC Arete Left, RAC
Perverted Crack, Brimham
Rabbit Paw Wall, Caley
Snoopy Crack, Carn Brea
Short Crack, Churnet
Pyramid Arete Left,
    Combeshead
Lost Boots, Ilkley
Central Icefall Direct, Longridge
Solitaire, Lord's Seat

Jawa, Clemmitt's
Right-Trending Ramp, Moelfre
Layaways, RAC
Bluebell Crack, The Breck
Whiskey Moon, Tintagel

// 4
Matterhorn Ridge, Almscliff
Steptoe, Dumbarton
The Runnel, Back Bowden
Ash Pit Slab, Brownstones
Friar's Wall, Burbage South
Ledge Crack, Gardom's
Flake Slab, Helman
Swan Wall, Kyloe in the Woods
Climax Wall, Clodgy
Flake and Ramp, Combeshead
Pink Arete, Cratcliffe
Imposter Arete, Dumbarton
Elephant's Ear, Baldstones
Trench Crack, Hartland
Amoeba State, Portland
Inside Crack, Helman
Scar Face, Holmfirth
Flake Crack, Combeshead
Golden Oldie, Shipley Glen
Slanting Flake, Slipstones
Jawbone, Over Owler Tor
Undercut Arete, Mynydd Dinas
Floppy's Arete, Porth Ysgo
The Rammer, Ramshaw
The Funnel, Saddle Tor
Glen Arete, Shipley Glen
Chickenheads, Simon's Seat
Tea Party Slab, Slipstones
Conjoined, Wainstones
Lone Tree Groove, Warton
Back Crack, Langdale
Pablo, Hutton Roof
Shell Shock, Wimberry

// 3+
Alice's Arete, Harmer's
Sandero Luminoso, Hutton Roof
Undercut Flake, Slipstones
Jack in the Box, Beacon Hill
Santa's Claws, Bowles
Verdi Corner, Brownstones
Right Arete, Carn Brea
Lower Wall, Langdale
Crusty, Churnet
Rough Yellow Wall, Clodgy
Diagonal, Curbar
The Beast, Dumbarton
White Slab, Fisherground
Blocky Crack, Haresfield
The Vice, Harrison's
Runnel, Hound Tor
Lower Crack, Langdale
Hazel Barn, Newstones
Joe's Portholes, The Roaches

// 3
Pink Slab, Cratcliffe
Stepped Flake, Back Bowden
Everest Crack, Crookrise
Alfred, High Rocks
Fissure, Badger Rock
Bow Window, Harrison's
3c Crack, Bonehill
Left Edge, Caseg
Serrano Rib, Thorn Crag
Cow Crack, Ilkley
The Negative, Plantation
Stolid, Portland
Primitive Groove, Stone Farm
Quartz Slab, Badger Rock
Crystal Arete, Combeshead
Slab Run, Thorn Crag
Descent Crack, Haresfield
Long Crack, Hepburn
Arsenic Slab, Holmfirth
Mid Rift, Huntsham
Devil's Edge Start, Kyloe Crag
Milk Cap, Mother Cap
Disappointment, Grinshill
Pisa Wall, Pex Hill
JT, Robin Hood's Stride

// 2+
OK Corral, Harrison's
Side Slab, Helman
Slabby Scoop, Moelfre
Fish Slab, Wimberry

// 2
Central Parallel Crack,
    Ravensheugh
Slab, Badger Rock
Y Crack, Goldsborough
Maze Crack, High Rocks
Hörnli Ridge, Wimberry
Scoop Right-Hand, Moelfre
Deadly Sins, Thorn Crag
Prop, Beacon Hill
Morris Minor, Caley
Crag Crack, Carn Brea
Side Slab Arete, Helman
Collywobble Crack, Beacon Hill
Forest Wall, Forest Rock
Amphitheatre, Hobson Moor
Plop Start, Over Owler Tor
Groove and Ledge, Moelfre
JT Crack, Robin Hood's Stride
Gap 2, Stone Farm
Pine Crack, The Roaches
Slabby Arete, Thorn Crag
Passion Play, Bridestones

// 1
Sheep Slab, Burbage South
Shaft, Beacon Hill
Left Ramp, Moelfre
Down Route, Bridestones

The Climbing Academy

The Climbing Academies are high class dedicated bouldering facilities with gourmet coffee, free wifi and good food. They are clean, brightly lit and have efficient chalk extraction coupled with 5 star toilets and showers.

And the climbing is pretty good too!

BRISTOL
Charlton St, Bristol, BS50AE
0117 907 2956 info@theclimbingacademy.com

GLASGOW
Portman St, Kinning Park, Glasgow, G411EJ
0141 429 6331 glasgow@theclimbingacademy.com

ONLINE BOULDERING SHOP
Fingerboards, campus rungs,mats etc
www.tca-climbingshop.com

SCARPA

www.theclimbingacademy.com

The South West

Tom Newberry on Psycho Cowboy, 7C+, Pentire (problem 3, page 55). Photo: Newberry collection.

Dave Westlake on Sharmajection, 7B, Tintagel North (page 57, problem 22). Photo: Mike Adams.

Dave Henderson on the low start to Bjorn Again, 6B+, Saddle Tor (page 72, problem 1). Photo: Carrie Hill.

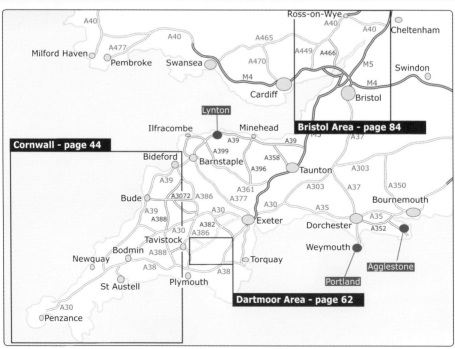

South West / Introduction

Tom Newberry on Supercede, 8A, Hartland Quay (page 61, problem 23).
Photo: Emma Taylor.

The sunny south west, the holiday counties of Devon and Cornwall. Blissful August fortnights that will forever be associated with ice creams, sunburn and floods. It's not somewhere that springs to mind when talking about British bouldering. Yet the past ten or fifteen years has seen a force of development from a small but dedicated band of wreckers, scouring the coastlines and finding tiny bits of treasure.

Northcott Mouth and a few other Culm Coast crags were popular bouldering venues with locals in the 1980s, although they focused mostly on the pumpy traverses as training for routes. Simon Young was the first to develop the harder 'up' problems and certainly the man responsible for promoting the area as the well known bouldering destination it is now. Simon unleashed his biceps on the now classic venues, especially Hartland and Northcott. Simon's up-problems are still classics. In recent years Dave Westlake, Tom Newberry, Barnaby Carver and Andy Whall have added to Simon's original venues as well as developing more themselves.

The other main feature of the south west, Dartmoor granite, is now also a major bouldering area thanks mainly to one person, Dave Henderson. Dave, through several years of dedication to development and his maintaining of the one great info website to the area, javu.co.uk, has put Dartmoor on the boulderer's map.

Where to go? For most people, the bouldering here will be for people who are in the area already on holiday, more than as specific targets. This being so, choice of venue will be decided by where you are and where you can get to. Few of these venues will match the traditional bouldering areas in terms of quantity and quality, but for those in the area they could well be some of the best parts of a holiday.

The north coast venues are mostly tidal which will be the major factor on choosing where to go and when. Hartland and Northcott hold the most classic problems and the best rock although they aren't very concentrated, with a problem here and a problem there, and are generally better for harder stuff. Further south, Clodgy has the best concentration, the best conditions (hardly tidal at all) and the best guarantee of getting climbing. Godrevy is generally acknowledged as the best venue on the coast. However it is fickle. Gwynver is very 'local' and Tintagel, despite some fine problems, is fairly esoteric. Information on many of these areas is hard to come by although Clodgy and Hartland currently have superb online guides.

Portland, perhaps the most popular venue in the region, already has a loyal band of followers. Sunny, non tidal and concentrated, its attractions are obvious.

The granite areas are, of course, more reliable. Conditions are generaly similar across all the venues – rough exposed rock in high prominent situations, quick drying and fun. This is true for Dartmoor, as well as for the odd outcrop that diminish down the spine of the region – Combeshead, Helman and Carn Brea. Combeshead was my favourite. Helman and Carn Brea are most useful as journey-breakers and the Dartmoor venues each have their relative plus points.

Many thanks to all who have helped with this complex section, especially Barnaby Carver (Clodgy), Dan Varian (Godrevy), Dave Henderson (Dartmoor), Dave Westlake (Hartland Quay and Lynmouth), Grant Edwards (Lynmouth), Mike Adams (generally) and Tom Newberry (Northcott and Tintagel).

Andy Whall on Northern Track, 6C+, Clodgy Point, (problem 32, page 46). Photo: Barnaby Carver.

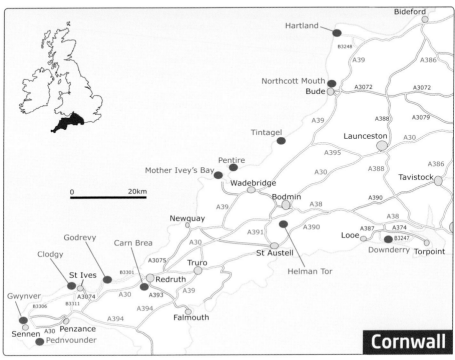

Bideford

Hartland

B3248

A39

A386

Northcott Mouth

Bude

A3072

A3072

A39

A388

A3079

Tintagel

Launceston

A30

A395

Pentire

A30

A388

A386

Mother Ivey's Bay

Tavistock

Wadebridge

Bodmin

A390

A39

A38

Newquay

A38

A30

A390

A391

A390

Looe

A387

A374

Godrevy

Carn Brea

St Austell

B3247

Clodgy

A3075

Downderry

Torpoint

Truro

Helman Tor

St Ives

B3301

Redruth

Gwynver

A3074

A30

A393

A39

B3306

B3311

A394

Sennen

A30

Penzance

A394

Falmouth

Pednvounder

0   20km

Cornwall

44

Gwynver

50.089007
-5.684309

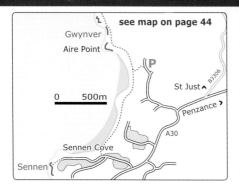

see map on page 44

Gwynver
Aire Point
P
St Just
Penzance >
A30
0   500m
Sennen Cove
Sennen

Some bouldering for the visually enlightened, apparently, although I struggled to see it. What rock there is is nice and people have reported having a good time here.

15 min | 43 probs 4 - 7C+ best from 5 - 7B | slabby | vertical | steep | | tidal

But I'm not one of them. I went here on a couple of visits with the javu guide in my hand looking at something and wondering 'Is this it?' The problems at Aire Point were obvious enough but before and beyond that I struggled a bit. Perhaps it's just that the landings are terrible; the photo on the right isn't typical.

On a related note, there is reputedly good bouldering to be had at Sennen Crag. In fact, that behemoth of reliability, the Jingo Wobbly, states that the more you look the more you start to see. That may well be the case, but after three visits I feel I deserve to see at least one problem! Dave Henderson reports that there are a handful of problems here - the most obvious are found on the short walls below A Swift Flight of Fancy, around the start of Africa Route and the starts of routes near Altar Route. It's not a major boudering venue though!

So, take from this what you will. Folk have found bouldering here, and found it to their liking. Just be prepared not to; then go for a paddle.

// Climbing: Sea-washed granite giving various styles – slabs and walls generally. Landings are generally very bad. The javu guide details 43 problems with everything up to 7C+.

// Approach: Follow the map to paid parking in a layby on the right, opposite a round gate-house. Follow the path beside the gate-house to the coastal path and follow it rightwards. Aire Point is clearly visible. The bouldering is on mini crags stretching between here and a conspicious 12-metre-high outcrop about 250 metres away.

// Conditions: Tidal. Climbable three hours either side of low. Big swells can be an issue. Very clean and quick drying.

// Info: javu.co.uk

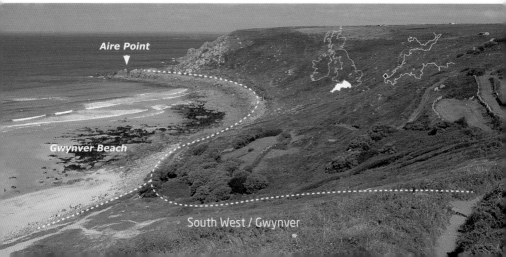

Aire Point
▼

Gwynver Beach

South West / Gwynver

Clodgy

50.214577
-5.48471

Good bouldering and lots of it, within a short walk of the popular holiday resort of St Ives. Loads of steep non-tidal problems across the grades in a friendly seaside location.

The rocks here get reliable conditions and the generally non-tidal nature makes it a good bet if Godrevy is out of nick. The climbing is fingery and powerful and is a good place for some mileage.

The problems are the work of locals, most notably Barnaby Carver and Andy Whall, with further contibutions from Dave Henderson, Mike Adams (with his powerful Groove is in the Heart) and even John Redhead.

// **Climbing:** With only a couple of slabs, the problems here are steep walls or bulges. Generally crimpy. Some highballs, some lowballs, and everything in between. Not many 'lines'. The rock is a bit brittle.

// **Approach:** Park in St Ives. The best parking is at the west end of Porthmeor Beach. Follow the coastal path west past the bowling club then past Man's Head (there is more bouldering in the coastal bays just down and left of this.) Carry on the path for 800m beyond Man's Head to the pointy rocks. The bouldering is on the rocks below this.

// **Conditions:** Generally non-tidal, although very high tides or a large swell can cause some problems. Quick drying and clean. Problems generally face north to north-west and get evening sun. **Family friendly.**

// **Info:** Barnaby Carver's downloadable pdf guide, Bouldering in St Ives, is available for free on **javu.co.uk** It's one of the nicest webguides about.

1 **Face** 5+
2 **Left Slab** 3
3 **Centre of Slab** 5
4 **Right Slab** 3+
5 **Thin Seam** 3
6 **Layback** 3
7 **Arete** 5
8 **Eliminate Wall** 6A+
9 **Climax Wall** 4 *Highball.*
10 **Groovey** 6C+
   From the sitter to The Groove, move left to the arete and up the middle of the wall.
11 **The Groove** 7B+
   Highball. Use the arete to the right, but nothing beyond that.
12 **Groove is in the Heart** 7C+
   Sit start to The Groove.
13 **Slab** 3
14 **Grooved Arete** 3+
15 **Butterfly Wall** 6B
   Start with a sharp pocket for the right hand. Sit start 6B+.
16 **Tortoiseshell** 6A
17 **High Groove** 4+
18 **The Prow** 6C *Dangerous.*
19 **JRA** 6A+
20 **Thin Crack Sitter** 6C+
21 **Vein from Sitter** 6C+
22 **Bloodlust** 7A *From a sitter on the flake.*
23 **Left Fault** 3
24 **Walkabout** 6B
   From a flat hold around the corner, drop down right and traverse the lip into Boomerang.
25 **Boomerang** 7A+
   From a sitter on nasty crimps reach left for a sidepull then up.
26 **Uluru** 7A
   Start sitting 1m left of the crack, climb up into the groove.
27 **Salad Fingers** 7B
   As above, but before the groove move left to the finish of Boomerang.
28 **Layback** 3
29 **Prow** 4
30 **Groove from Sitter** 6A
31 **Crimps to Top** 6A
32 **Northern Track** 6C+
   From 31, traverse the lip up and down to finish up 35.
33 **Victoria** 6C+
   From tiny undercuts climb the wall with the aid of the left side of the crack of 34.
34 **Crack** 5+
35 **Rough Yellow Wall** 3+
36 **Circumnavigation** 7C *Traverse the entire boulder, starting and finishing up number 31.*

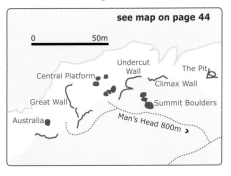

see map on page 44

0   50m

Undercut Wall
The Pit
Central Platform
Climax Wall
Great Wall
Summit Boulders
Australia
Man's Head 800m

180 probs
3 - 7C+
best from
3 - 7A
15 min

The Pit

Climax Wall

Undercut Wall

Cockblock

Australia

Australia

Clodgy

Man's Head

Bowling Club

Porthmeor Beach

Dave Biggs on Providence, 7C+ (problem #). Photo: Biggs' Collection.

Godrevy

50.238669
-5.392967

The finer of the St Ives coastal destinations, with tidal action on steep geology. If you get the conditions right you could well have a great session on brilliant problems.

The super-quick approach and the quality of the problems when in nick make Godrevy worth the risk. If you have time, it's worth checking and if it's skanky then just move on to Clodgy. However, Godrevy is better.

The climbing is tricky to spot even if you're looking at it. Or is that just me? It is divided thus: **The Gullies**, with 12 great problems up to 6C+ on steep walls; **The Cave**, with 18 steeper, more powerful problems mostly 6B to 7C; **The Main Bay** with a dozen roofy problems up to 7C+; **The Bowling Alley** with 15 steep lines in the middle grades. Only a couple of areas are detailed here but those that aren't are just as worthwhile.

// Climbing: The waterwashed slate here has a lot of fans among travelling connoisseurs. About 80 problems up to 7C+. Steep walls or outright overhangs. Lots of smoothness. Landings usually great pebbly sand, but you'll need a mat to keep your feet clean.

// Approach: From Hayle (or the A30) take the B3301 north to and through Gwithian. 500m north of Gwithian turn left toward Godrevy. Follow this road past two car parks to a large grass car park at the very end of the road. Walk seaward from here to arrive at the scene below. The Gully Area is the twin trench on the left. The Cave Area is seen on the right. Round the corner is the Main Bay and beyond that is the Bowling Alley, a trench in the next rocky arm.

// Conditions: Climbable for a couple of hours either side of low tide. Dampness can be a problem in crannies and an onshore wind will help with this. Difficult to get conditions outside the summer months. The level of the beach can vary greatly changing the nature of problems. Seaweed can be an issue. **Family friendly.**

// Info: There are a couple of free guides about on the web but they left me scratching my head a little. Try one on **blocspenwith.blogspot,** or google "Godrevy bouldering suesseals". The place could really do with a good comprehensive guide.

lighthouse
Bowling Alley

Main Bay

The Gullies

Cave Wall Left

Main Bay
1. **Arete** 5+
2. **Virginia** 7A
   From a sitter in slatey slots.
3. **Woolf** 6A+ *Sitter.*
4. **Providence** 7C+ *Sitter.*
5. **Beachball** 7A+
   Sitter. Stick strictly to the arete.
6. **Layback** 5+
7. 6B

Cave Wall Left

8. **Toe Jam** 7A
   Start low and traverse right to gain the crack.
9. **Crack Traverse** 6C+
10. **Upstart** 5+ *Highball. Escape down left to the ledge. A sitter used a glue hold. Now broken and unrepeated.*
11. **Piss Pot** 7A+
    Start hanging small triangular holds.
12. **Low flat holds to Break** 7A

Cave Wall Right

13. **8A Project** *With 8B extension.*
14. **The Sweep** 7A+
    Start from a sitter and finish up the square-cut niche.
15. **Blacking out the Friction** 7C
    Sitter, over bulge and left.
16. **Blacking Right-Hand** 7B
17. 7B
18. **Corner Crack** 4
19. **ur hot** 7B+
    Low start (or better, from a sitter) to the arete then up the nose.
20. **Bruiser** 6C+ *Jump start, then carry on without using the crack.*
21. **Corner Crack** 4+
22. **Crab Crawl** 7A+
23. **French Toast** 7A
    From crimps just down and left of the better crimp of the next problem, spring for the lip and up. Sitter is 7C+.
24. **Crimp Problem** 7A
    Stretch for a crimp just left of the crack and lunge up and left for the finishing holds of 24.
25. **Pocket Dyno** 6B+ *The arete.*
26. **Trigonometry** 7A
    Start in the groove then spring up left.
27. **Perfect Evening Light** 7A+
    From the starting hold of Trigonometry lurch up and right and hand traverse right along the sloping rail.

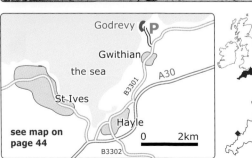

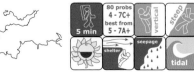

Jamie Maddison on Classic Arête, 5+ (problem 15). Photo: Maddison collection.

Carn Brea

50.221463
-5.246336

A rumble of rounded rocks on an ancient hilltop overlooking Redruth and not far from the A30. Not masses of problems but the quality is high, giving a good hour or two's sharp exercise. A sweet little spot.

Set high on a bracken-covered summit, with remnants of iron age settlement, this is one of those many granite bouldering outbursts with a haunted atmosphere. Think Helman Tor or Combeshead. Woo-woo! A big thanks to Jamie Maddison for all his help with this section.

The nearby castle is a well-recommended restaurant with a unique atmosphere specialising in Middle Eastern food. Open from 6.30pm – 01209 218358, booking essential.

// Climbing: Rounded granite with some terrific aretes. Also steep bulges, the odd crack and some easy slabs. Landings are generally perfect and the problems never become too high. Rough.

// Conditions: Clean, exposed and fairly quick drying. Problems generally face north and west. **Family-tastic.**

// Approach: A bit complicated. The handiest exit from the A30 is the eastern one, sign-

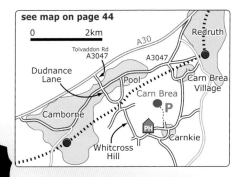

see map on page 44

posted "Cambourne, Portreath, A3047" and NOT the western one, simply signposted "Cambourne". Use the maps, but keep in the direction of Four Lanes and then keep an eye out for the Basset Memorial, a 10-metre obelisk on the summit of the hill. Ask a local for directions, unless you're a bloke in which case drive around the area for hours until you spot the memorial.

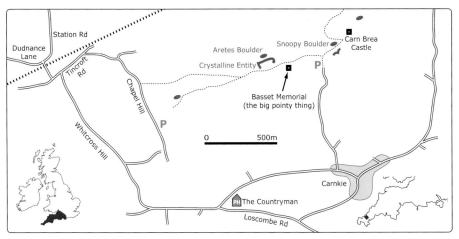

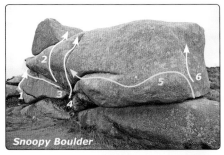

Snoopy Boulder

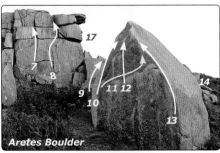

Aretes Boulder

Aretes Boulder

Crystalline Entity

1   **Bulge on Slopers** 6A+
2   **Snoopy** 7A+ *Harder sloper problem just right.*
3   **Traverse** 4+
4   **Snoopy Crack** 4+   *Sitter 6A+.*
5   **Gordon Brown** 6C+
    Traverse from a sitter to finish up the crack.
6   **Snoopy Arete** 6A
7   **Crag Crack** 2
8   **Flakes** 4
9   **Arete on Left** 5+
10   **Arete on Right** 6A
11   **Flake Traverse** 4+   *Finish up arete.*
12   **Wall** 4+

13   **Right Arete** 3+   *Sitter 4+.*
14   **Bloodstone Arete** 7A   *No stacked mats.*
15   **Classic Arete** 5+
    Climbed on the left. No footblock at this grade.
16   **The Wave** 6A
    On a boulder 5 metres up from the Classic Arete
boulder, traverse the lip from a sitter on the right.
17   **Crystal Arete** 5+   *Highball.*
18   **Crystalline Entity** 7A
19   **Power Up** 7A   *Start low.*
20   **Pond Wall** 7A   *On a flat boulder over the*
back, start with left hand on a ramp and a knee bar
in the wide low break and climb direct. Sitter 7A+.

Helman Tor

50.420372
-4.729421

A cromlech of rounded rasping granite with a sacred spread of giant marbles perched high above Bodmin. A few dozen good problems in a great location that will give a great couple of hours of wrist-slashing fun.

If whoever made Cornwall had a nervous practice and put Carn Brea together, then with Helman Tor they got it right. Its setting alone is special, as it's invisible on the approach yet commands a view for miles. It has a very strong feeling of historical significance. You know for damn sure that the ancients got up to something here.

It gives a couple of tiers of seldom visited boulders in a site of interest to high-brow tourists. A great place to bang off ten problems on the way south. A bit sharp for sessioning. Great for families. A cool place, I liked it.

// Climbing: About 30 short problems up to 7B, but mostly concentrated in the lower grades. Usually smeary slabs or rounded walls and aretes. That said, there is a lot of variety. No crimps. The rock is very sharp which may curtail a session. Plenty of other stuff spread out around that described. Lots of grass landings.

// Approach: The tor sits in a warren of hedged-in single-track roads. For the approach here, leave the A30 north onto the A389 towards Bodmin. After 400m turn right under the A30 then left after about 100m towards

Lanhydrock. Follow this road for 0.6 miles then at a staggered five-way junction (by a white pointy stone) turn right and bear left towards Trebell Green. Follow the map below to a car park.

// Conditions: The tor sits on top of a little hill and is very open and catches weather. Most of the problems face south-east to south-west. Quick drying and has no drainage. Can feel cold. The rock is clean. **Family friendly.**

// Info: The out-of-print Cheesewring guide. Another one in the pipeline.

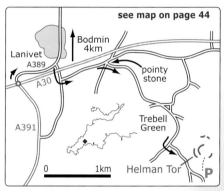

see map on page 44

Lower Tier

1 **Nose** 6A *The rib left of the deep crack.*
2 **Flakes** 4 *In the sidewall.*
3 **Slab Arete** 6B+ *Climb on the left.*
4 **Slab Arete** 6A
5 **Flake Slab** 4
6 **Slabby Arete** 3
7 **Rocking Left** 4
Swing up then rock onto the slab.
8 **Side Slab** 2+

9 **Side Slab Arete** 2
10 **Bloody Helman Start** 6B+
The route to the break: E4 above.
11 **Hell's Tooth Start** 5+
The route to the break: E1 above.

Tim the local 'somewhat engaged' with Bulge, 5 (problem 15); Tristan dwells. Photo: Niall Grimes.

Upper Tier

12 The Grey Face 6C+
The wall above the sloping break on crystals.

13 Arete on Left 4 *Layback runnel at the top.*

14 Arete on Right 4+ *Finish up the runnel.*

15 Bulge 5
Bulge direct to gain a massive hold and up.

16 Inside Crack 4
With a burly reach for a grasping bucket.

17 Left Arete 6A
Finish direct or escape right at 5.

18 Right Arete 6B

19 End Face 6A *Monkey-up-a-stick.*

20 Deep Crack 4

21 Wall without Aretes 6A+

22 Corner 5

23 No Grieving 6B
Move up from breaks via a finger pocket.

On the back, just below the trig point, is a cave formed by three stacked boulders:

24 British East Africa 7A
Come from the back wall to the back of the chockstone and follow the lip all the way to the end. No footlocks against the back wall.

25 Ice Cream Soldiers 6C+
Start at the bottom of the chockstone, come out and up the runnels.

Other Cornish Venues

Downderry

Or, if you're a Prod, Londownderry. A seaside trifle which, while it doesn't have lots to offer, still gets visits from boulderers on holiday by mistake. Tidal, the best feature being The Wave, a pumpy 7A+ traverse. Various other stuff hereabouts, apparently. The walk-in takes one past a small nudist beach so it could most usefully be seen as somewhere to get a bit of forearm fitness combined with a chance to get your tackle out.

// **Climbing:** Basically a steep slopy traverse above the beach. Smooth rock with qartzy crimps and a perfect landing. Various other steep juggy malarky to be rooted out hereabouts. no mats needed.

// **Approach:** Park in Downderry and follow a path down to the right of the school to reach the beach. Turn left (east) and follow the shore for 700m, past a pebble beach, nudists and a tongue of rock to find the traverse just before the most prominent headland. GPS 50.361534, -4.365483

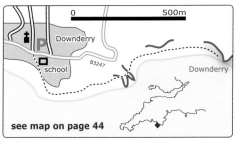

see map on page 44

// **Conditions:** Tidal, climbable a few hours either side of low. Fairly quick drying. **Family friendly.**

Pednvounder

Perhaps the best family bouldering in the land according to Ellis (right) who raved enthusiastically about Pednvounder. A beautiful south-facing nudist beach at the very bell-end of Cornwall. The sand is as nice as sand gets, and is lined with enough pure cornish granite for an hour or two of messing about. No mats required as the landing is so perfectly soft. The thought of doing fun granite problems as the summer sun warms your back and with a fresh salty breeze blowing gently around your balls. Magic!

// **Climbing:** Granite cliff. Essentially messing about on boulders rather than bouldering in an angry-youth style. 3 to 4 metres high, perfect landing.

// **Approach:** For location see map on page 44. Near the village of Treen, easily reached on the B3315 between Penzance and Sennen. A small road runs off the B3315 to a car park in the village. Follow a track past a campsite to the coast, 800m away. Descend a steep path. There you are. GPS 50.050264,-5.641587

// **Conditions:** South facing. Very sunny. **Family friendly.**

Photo: Alice Brockington.

Pentire

A handful of blocks under Great Wall hold some of the best hard problems on the coast. Lots of potential.

Better than Clodgy and Tintagel but maybe not as good as Godrevy. Psycho Cowboy is a coast classic. Thanks to Tom Newberry for the info here.

// Climbing: There are lots of harder problems in close proximity to each other (7 problems 7B+ to 7C+) as well as a few good problems in the low grades. Loads of steep projects. Landings generally good and two pads will be enough for most problems. The seaward face has a few highball up lines between 5C and 6B and a left-to-right traverse at 6C. There are about 15 more problems on the other boulders between 6A and 7B.

// Approach: At the roundabout on the A39 just north of Wadebridge follow the exit towards town centre then immediately signs for Polzeath B3314. Follow this for 4.3 miles than at a right hand go straight on for Polzeath. Follow this and after a mile veer right for Pentireglaze. After half a mile take a little turn right eventually leading to NT parking in Pentire Farm (GPS 50.585253,-4.916897). Follow the track to the coast, walk right for 200m passing a rocky knoll (the summit of Great Wall). Just past this a path leads down to the base of the huge wall. The boulders are below. 20 minutes.

// Conditions: Generally good conditions as it's exposed and dries quickly. It can be hot during the summer when the sun comes round after midday. Tidal but only for a hour each side of high tide, although big swell will severely effect the condition of the boulders. Check magicseaweed.com for sea conditions.

see map on page 44

1 **Rational Bandit**   7C+   *Start sitting at the back of the roof, hands on the undercut.*
2 **Cowboy Junkie**   7C
     Start as for RB and continue direct.
3 **Psycho Cowboy**   7C+   *Start as for RB.*
4 **Cowboy Arete**   7A+   *Sitter.*

Mother Ivey's Bay

Granite beach bouldering in one of the nicest spots on God's green earth. The climbing is nice enough with a handful of problems up to around 7A but you will definitely walk away happy. Family friendly with great beaches, good surf and there's even somewhere nearby called Boobies Bay. What more could you ask for?

Not much bouldering but enough to make you feel you've climbed. Tidal, but not massively so.

To get there follow the B3226 to St Merryn (chippy, cafes, pubs). Follow the road to Harlyn Bay then follow signs for Mother Ivey's Bay. Go past the caravan park then park on the roadside (GPS 50.540749,-5.014679). Follow on to Mother Ivey's than go down the steps to the beach. There's bouldering on the left and right.

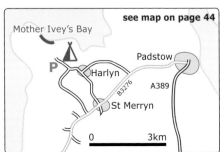

see map on page 44

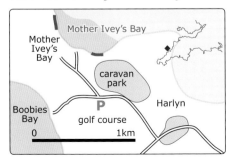

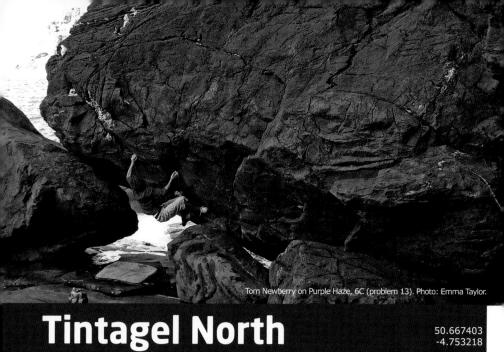

Tom Newberry on Purple Haze, 6C (problem 13). Photo: Emma Taylor.

Tintagel North

50.667403
-4.753218

The latest discovery on the north Corn-wall coast gives a batch of big boulders with a bunch of quality problems in a fine situation. Never destined for the masses, though some of the problems are fine prizes and the place is full of character. Mostly non-tidal.

Tom Newberry's recent find comes highly recommended on the quality stakes. Bouldering on actual boulders, good solid rock and the non-tidal nature are the plus points. Good for a few hour's sessioning. Big thanks to Tom for all the info here.

// **Climbing:** Steep burly action on the undersides of big blocks to sometimes highball finishes or jump dismounts. Bring a few pads – the ground is very hard. Crimpy, and a bit sharp.

// **Approach:** Get to Tintagel and park. Free parking on Atlantic Road. Find King Arthur's Castle Hotel, overlooking Tintagel Head. Go down the path to the right of this and follow the coastal path right (east). Go through a gate in the corner of a field and head for a small rocky outcrop on the skyline, 200m away. At the outcrop, head down bearing slightly right to arrive at the coast and the boulders.

// **Conditions:** Fairly non-tidal, although big swells will interfere. Black Crack can get cut off. Quick drying rock with no seepage. Sometimes greasy in humid conditions. Some of the ground rock can be extremely slippery so be careful, especially if you are carrying a brand new and very expensive camera. Ouch!

20 min | shelter | tidal

30 probs
4 - 7C+
best from
5 - 7B | slabby | steep | roofs

Purple Haze

Black Crack

Kids

Sharmajection

see map on page 44

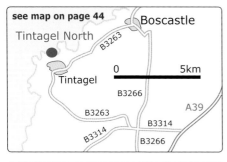

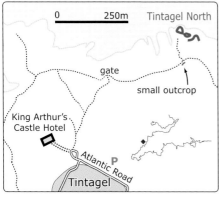

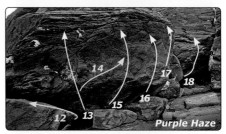

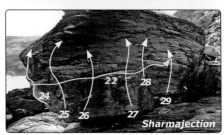

1   Doggers Come Knocking 6B *Sitter.*
2   Black Crack 6A+ *Sitter.*
3   Wall 5+ *Sitter.*   **4   Arete** 4
5   Colorado Dreaming 7C+ *Sitter. On the back of the boulder follow a flake through the roof.*
6   Pink Floyd 7A *Sitter, left hand in pocket, right on low crimp.*
7   The Coppinger 6B+ *Sitter.*
8   Arete 4 *Sitter.*
9   The Groove 5+ *Scary.*
10   Rainbow Trail 5+ *Sitter.*
11   Carnival Girl 6A+ *Sitter from pockets.*
12   Lip Traverse 6A *Sitter.*
13   Purple Haze 6C *Sitter.*
14   All along the Watchtower 7A+ *13 into 15.*
15   The Apprentice 7A *Rampline from sitter.*
16   The Hurler 6C *Sitter.*
17   Green Envy 6A+ *Jump start.*
18   Kids 7B+ *Sitter, hands matched on small flake.*
19   Man O' War 7A *On opposite boulder, climb feint crack from chest-high sidepulls.*
20   Nick's Project 6A+ *Traverse slots.*
21   Le Dopage 6B+ *Sitter.*
22   Sharmajection 7B *Sitter. Long traverse.*
23   Whiskey Moon 4+ *Big.*
24   Hey Joe 6B *Sitter 6C.*
25   Undercut Arete 5+ *Crouch start.*
26   Salad Cream 5 *Groove from crouch start.*
27   Orange Crush 5 *Sitter.*
28   Wall 4   **29   Bulge** 5+ *Sitter.*

Northcott Mouth

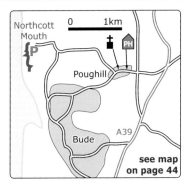

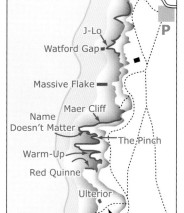

A string of powerful project-style problems smuggled into small caves and nooks along half a mile of mad coastline. High quality and unusual although, as with lots of such seaside venues, you'll need a few factors to come up trumps to get the right conditions. When you do it's good for a full session and some of the problems are the best on the coast. Not great for easier stuff but there is a nice beach.

If it was my job to build the world then I imagine I would make something like the coastline along Northcott Mouth. Full of mad ideas that I never quite got round to finishing, it's tricky from a geological point of view to tell whether it's coming or going. A cool place. Big thank you to Tom Newberry for the info here.

// Climbing: Mostly steep and powerful climbing on wave-smoothed culm rock. Low friction. Landings generally good pebble beach but sometimes bad. You'd likely get away with just one mat.

// Conditions: Tidal, with the problems being accessible for 3 hours either side of low tide. Ulterior is barely tidal and can be accessed from the fisherman's path. Some of the nooks can be slow drying and greasy so sunshine and an onshore wind will help. So too will lots of chalk and a towel. The tides can cause a lot of pebble shift that can vastly change beach levels effecting Warm-Up, Red Quinne and Ulterior more than the others (and thus making things easier). Name Doesn't Matter, Ulterior and The Wafer face south.

// Approach: From Bude, or the A39 just north of it, get to the village of Poughill. Turn north in the middle of the village (phone box and bus stop at the junction) and follow the road to a National Trust car park after 1 mile. Drop down to the beach here and turn left.

Directions: J-Lo – Upon arriving on the beach, turn left and walk to the first fin/outcrop. 70m past this is another fin, with a narrow doorway (Watford Gap). J-Lo is 15m before this gap, hidden on the underside of an arched slab. Through the gap you can see a huge flake in the beach and across this bay is Maer cliff, with numerous E6s. **Name Doesn't Matter** is on the opposite side of this. **The Pinch** is on the next fin, 70m further on. The next two outcrops hold **Warm-Up Wall** and **Red Quinne**. Opposite (before) Red Quinne is a vertical wall with a few easier problems. The next bay has an easy path leading up the slope to the top path. The **Ulterior** boulder is at the base of the path. Around the next headland is the distinctive fin of **The Wafer**.

South West / Northcott Mouth

J-Lo

Name Doesn't Matter

Warm-Up

Red Quinne

Ulterior

The Wafer

Note: In some of these pictures the pebble level is unusually high.

1 J-Lo 7B+ *Steep board-like climbing on pinches and slopers from a sitter. Swing left to finish.*

2 Ben's Traverse 7B

3 Undercut Problem 6C+ *Drop off at jug.*

4 Name Doesn't Matter 7A *Drop off at the flat hold.*

5 Hendo's Wall 7B+ *Crimpy wall to slot. The wall to the right is the start of the route Bodysnatchers: about 6C+ but with a less obvious jumping-off point.*

6 Nameless Arete 6C *Highball arete opposite problem 3. Hard start then easier above.*

7 The Pinch 7A *This sits on a small fin 70m after Name Doesn't Matter area, and facing leftwards towards it. Start sitting, with a low slot and a pinch. The good crimp on the lip out left is out of bounds.*

8 Wall 6A+ *The wall 2m left of The Pinch.*

9 Warm-Up Wall Traverse 6B+

10 The Boy Wonder 7C+ *From sitter on the shelf at the back. Move right on the traverse to finish up the groove.*

11 Captain Crush 7C+ *From the back.*

12 Red Quinne 7C *From sitter on the shelf at the back.*

13 J Dog 6B *From a sitter on an undercut in the middle of the roof.*

14 Red Quinne Traverse 7A

15 Quinne Groove 5+

16 Wall 4 *Sitter. Bad rock.*

17 Arete on Left 6A

18 Ulterior Motive 7B+ *Sitter (hands in ringed slot). 7A from standing.*

19 Wafer Traverse Left 6A+

20 Wafer Traverse Middle 6B

21 Cave's Edge 6C *Jump off.*

22 Wafer Traverse Right 6A+

Gloss Over the Mat

Clinical Edge

Ache Ball

The Trench

North of the hotel

The spiritual home of Culm bouldering with classic testpieces, modern desperates and a bunch of easier stuff stretching along a mad bit of coastline. A stunning location and interesting rock combine to make this the most rewarding of the venues hereabouts.

What a beautiful place. Sitting outside the hotel on a late summer evening as the sun melts into the west, cliffs of an insane beauty ragging off on each side. Content people about. A pint in your hands, your arms and back aching after a great session where you finally ticked that project. Result!

The Quay will give competent boulderers with a whole bunch of mats a full arm-destroying session. Short walks between the areas break the day up nicely. Beach levels can change the nature of some problems. Not covered here is the Hartland Roof area, a cave and a boulder 300m south of Carnage.

Hartland Quay holds some of the south's best ticks: Clinical Edge, Ache Ball, Jas' Wall, Sundance, Supercede and best of all, Carnage. The originals were added by Simon Young and Jason Quinn. Recently Tom Newberry and Dave Westlake have been bringing the area up to date. A great new free webguide to the crag by Dave Westlake should do loads to clear up mysteries of what's what and put the place on the map.

// Climbing: Like Northcott, the climbing is generally on very steep rock with rounded, frictionless holds. Powerful climbing requiring good body tension and technique. Basic strength won't be enough. Better for harder problems. Perhaps best seen as somewhere with a few warm-ups followed by sessioning some harder problems. Landings are rocky so the more mats the better.

// Approach: Follow the map. From Hartland (nice village with shops and pubs), follow signs to Hartland Quay and park at one of the two-level car parks (£2 parking between Easter and October). The two views here are from the lower car park as areas stretch off north and south from the hotel. The **North Area** (on your right as you look out to sea) has a straightforward approach, down the quay and across the beach. For the South Area, (on your left), scramble down the headland below the car park then cut back to the Cave and across the beach to Carnage. For Hartland Roof, follow the coastal path from the upper parking for 400m. On the coast is a prominent pointed hill, St Catherine's Tor. Just right of this, near a stream, a fisherman's rope helps you down a big slab. The bouldering is to the right.

// Conditions: Tidal. Climbable for about three hours either side of low tide. Dampness can linger and some areas don't get much sun or wind. Bring lots of chalk and a towel. Hard to get conditions in winter. Ache Ball, the Trench, Carnage and Hartland Roof face south.

// Info: Dave Westlake has produced a top-class pdf guide with tons more stuff: find it on **javu.co.uk**.

St Catherine's Tor

Carnage

South of the hotel

Hartland Cave

10 min | 52 probs 4 - 8A best from 7A - 8A | steep | roofs | | shelter | seepage | tidal

Hartland Quay

50.99427
-4.534049

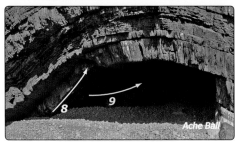

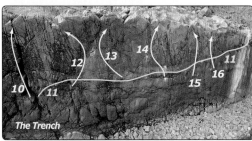

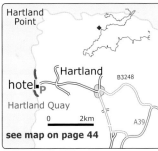

1 Gloss Over the Mat 7C *North-facing slab of free-standing 7-metre pillar. Start on right. Highball.*

2 Arete with Pocket 6A

3 Easy Wall 4

4 Clinical Edge 7B *Sitter.*

5 Egg Nishna 7B

6 One Good Move 5B

7 Ball Ache 7B *Arete on right. Powerful.*

8 Ache Ball 7C *Steep rib from low. Pebble height may vary and change the grade.*

9 Cave Traverse 7B *From blocky undercuts 3m right of AB, traverse inwards to a flake in the roof.*

10 Trench Crack 4

11 Trench Traverse 7B

12 Jas' Left-Hand 5+ *Climb the wall with the prominent slot for the right hand.*

13 Jas' Wall 5+ *Climb the wall from a sidepull using the slot with the left hand.*

14 Trench Eliminate 7A *From a low slot gain crimps above then let rip for the top.*

15 Fingery Wall 6B+

16 Bloody Nora 6C+ *Small crimpy crack.*

17 Sundance 7A+ *Lip traverse then up arete.*

18 Sitter Left-Hand 6B

19 Sitter Right Hand 6B+

20 Carnage Arete 6A

21 Carnage 7B *Sitter to crimp then stretch to undercut. Big move to finish.*

22 Corridors of Power 7C *Link 23 into 21.*

23 Supercede 8A *Sitter from a right hand undercut and sloper for the left. Up on slopers to sidepulls to a big top move. 7C+ from a stand.*

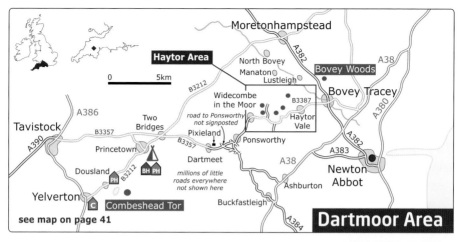

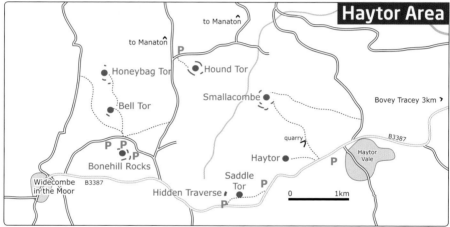

Dartmoor

"Stay off the moors!"

Was there ever a better piece if advice? Dartmoor. A rolling lonesome wilderness of low fogs, driving horizontal rain and howling dark nights. A sanctuary for escaped convicts, werewolves, mysterious big cats, hounds that glow in the dark and raindrenched Duke-of-Edinburgh stragglers, their cheap nylon cagoules flapping in the wind, ill-fitting boots filled to the brim with bog water their wet map shredded many miles ago. Little hungry eyes watch them from the heather, waiting in the off-chance that a smaller one or a weaker one or a wounded one might drop back from the main bunch, stumble, and expose a vascular throat to the moonlight.

It's even worse than that for climbers. The rough granite

crystals can tear at soft skin, sometimes drawing blood or maybe even curtailing a session. Ouch!

The Dartmoor granite has a terrific individual character, with wild high moorland and rough and rounded tors. This section covers a selection of them, enough to shred a week's worth of skin, but there is tons more besides. To explore these, and of course to find out more at the crags covered, visit www.javu.co.uk. Dave Henderson has championed the area for years in his superb website (need I mention that I got all the info here from his webguides? Sssshhhh!) and has truly put the place on the climber's map. Check it out.

Great big thanks to Dave Henderson for his help on this section.

Dave Henderson on Dancing Queen, 7A+, Saddle Tor (page 72, problem 7). Photo: Carrie Hill

Rich mayfield on Sharp Arete, 6A (problem 17). Photo: David Simmonite.

Combeshead Tor

50.506013
-4.019934

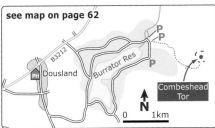

see map on page 62

B3212
Dousland
Burrator Res
PH
P
P
P
Combeshead Tor
N
0   1km

A classy circuit for those who like it rough. A whole session of granite graspers in the lower and mid grades in the sort of setting that makes you want to strip off and howl at the moon.

This was my favourite of the moorland granite areas due not just to the quantity and quality of the problems, but also down to the place. It has an ancient, prehistoric sense about it. Spooky, almost, especially at twilight all alone. I don't mind saying, I scurried back to the car at top speed, looking behind me as I went.

// Climbing: One hundred problems, better for easier ones. Rough, hurty granite with a good variety: cracks, slabs, bulges, aretes, walls and traverses. Mostly good landings but a few significant highballs, especially on Cuckoo Rock and the Hanging Flakes boulder. Sore on the skin.

// Approach: The tor sits on the moor on the east side of Burrator Reservoir. From A386 / Yelverton (shops, pub, cafe), follow the B3212 for 2km to Dousland. Turn right (south) by the pub down Burrator Road. Follow for 1km and turn left. Follow this road for almost 4km, passing the dam and reservoir on your right, to cross a little bridge before the road starts cutting back right. After the bridge is a car park on the left, and after 100m, another. Park in this second car park. Follow the track leading from it to the boulder-covered hillside in 25 / 30 minutes.

// Conditions: Exposed and clean. Quick drying in the right conditions. **Family friendly.**

// Info: javu.co.uk

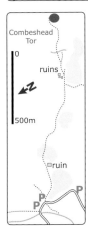

Combeshead Tor
0
ruins
N
500m
ruin
P
P
P

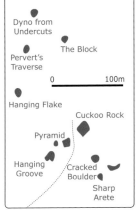

Dyno from Undercuts
The Block
Pervert's Traverse
0   100m
Hanging Flake
Cuckoo Rock
Pyramid
Hanging Groove
Cracked Boulder
Sharp Arete

Hanging Groove

Pyramid

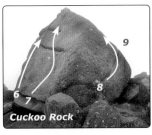

Cuckoo Rock

Cuckoo Rock

Cracked Boulder

Sharp Arete

Hanging Flakes

Hanging Flakes

Pervert's

Undercuts

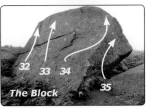

The Block

95 probs
3 - 7A+
best from
4 - 6C+

30 min

slabby / steep

exposed

1	**Flake Crack** 5+	
2	**Hanging Groove** 5+	
3	**Slabby Rib** 4	
4	**Pyramid Arete Left** 4+	
5	**Pyramid Arete Right** 4	
6	**Highball Arete** 4+	
7	**West Face** 6B *E4-ish.*	
8	**Crack and Slab** 6A+	
9	**Back Slab** 3	
10	**East Arete** 6B	
11	6A+ *Trend left through breaks to left arete. Highball.*	
12	**Crack and Arete** 4+	

13	**Slabby Face** 6A *Sitter 7A.*
14	**Cracked Boulder Traverse** 6A+
15	**End Face** 6A+
16	**Sloping Arete** 5+
17	**Sharp Arete** 6A
18	**Arete Right** 5+
19	**Crystal Wall** 6B
20	**Crystal Arete** 3
21	**Crystal Traverse** 6B+ *17 into 20.*
22	**Hanging Flakes** 6C

23	**Flake Crack** 4
24	**Slab** 7A *No crack.*
25	**Arete** 6A
26	**Crack** 5+
27	**Northern Lights** 5+
28	**Slopers Problem** 6B+
29	**Pervert's Traverse** 6C
30	**Undercuts Traverse** 7B
31	**Dyno from Undercut** 6C+
32	**Left of Slab** 3
33	**Central Line** 6A+
34	**Flake and Ramp** 4
35	**Arete from Sitter** 4+

Meilee Rafe on Vague Arete, 6B (problem 7). Photo: David Simmonite.

Bonehill Rocks

50.583128
-3.791614

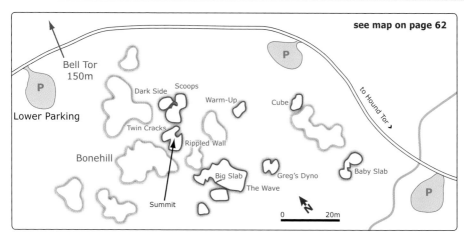

see map on page 62

Bell Tor
150m

P

Lower Parking

Dark Side

Scoops

Warm-Up

Cube

to Hound Tor

Twin Cracks

Rippled Wall

Bonehill

Big Slab

Greg's Dyno

Baby Slab

The Wave

Summit

P

0   20m   N

The epicentre of Dartmoor bouldering with over a hundred blistering problems concentrated into a small and beautiful spot mere seconds from the car park. The rock is rough and unforgiving, so if you're doing any washing up before you go, then wear your Marigolds. Familytastic.

This will be the first port of call for the visiting boulderer. Very convenient, friendly and easy to navigate. The problems follow good lines and have a variety of styles. Not as busy with tourists as Hound Tor but more popular with boulderers. You could easily spend a whole day here, or at least as long as your skin lasts.

Also included here are a few problems at Bell Tor, about 150m from the lower parking and easily included in the circuit. This has the advantage of being a lot quieter on busy weekends.

// **Climbing:** Generally powerful stuff spread across the grades up to 8A but best in the lower and mid grades. The climbing is quite lock-off-y and good footwork is key. The rock is fairly rounded but the problems are still quite crimpy, although usually crimping on big crystals more than edges. Lots of cracks, slopers, traverses, aretes, bulges, walls and slabs. Mostly standard height although there are a few highballs where one mat will be appreciated. Hard on the skin. Good for beginners.

// **Approach:** Park in one of the three spots as shown above. For Bell Tor follow the track opposite the third, lowest parking spot then strike directly towards the tor, 150m away. The bouldering is on an undercut slab, 25m left of the little rocky summit. Also accessibly via the Haytor Hoppa bus route.

// **Conditions:** Problems face in all directions, so always some sun or shade to be had. No seepage and quick drying. Exposed. Climbable all year although the moors can be bleak when the cold wind blows, so best on a nice summer day. **Great for families**.

// **Info:** javu.co.uk.

1 min | 120 probs 3 - 8A best from 4 - 7A+ | slabby | vertical | steep | | exposed

Warm-Up ▶ Summit ▶

Cube ▶ ◀ Scoops

my old Fiat
▼
Lower Parking
▼

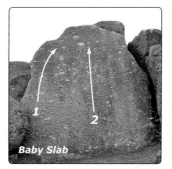

Baby Slab

The Cube

Warm-Up

Scoops

Dark Side

Twin Cracks

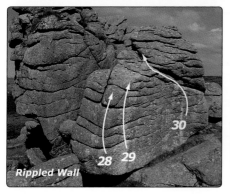

Rippled Wall

Big Slab

The Wave

Greg's Dyno

Bell Tor

1   **Left Edge** 4
2   **Baby Slab** 5+
3   **Prow** 6C
    6C+ from the low break.
4   **Scoop** 6A
5   **Double Dyno** 7A
6   **3c Crack** 3
7   **Vague Arete** 6B
8   6A+ *Start low on crimps near the right side of the wall. Climb to a pocket and finish direct.*
9   **Cube Arete** 6B+
10 **Cube Traverse** 6C+
11 **Slopery Traverse** 6C+
    The right-to-left traverse on the back of the block.
12 **Undercut Nose** 6B
    From a sitter.
13 **Warm-Up Crack** 3
14 **Warm-Up Wall** 4
15 **Warm-Up Traverse** 6A+
16 **Left Scoop** 7A
    From the finger-rail on the lip lock up and left gains a crystal then a scary move to the next break.

17 **Ivory Mountain** 7C
    From the finger-rail of 16 swing up the arete.
18 **Left Arete of Scoop** 7B
    Starting with right hand at th base of the scoop and left on the first sloper on the arete.
19 **The Scoop** 6C
20 **Arete** 4+
21 **Flake** 4
22 **The Dark Side** 7B
    Desperate. Left hand on sidepull pinch, right on poor crystal and step up to break.
23 **Dark Side Traverse** 5+
24 6A *Scary finish.*
25 **Arete from Low** 6C+
26 **Twin Cracks** 5+
27 **Arete** 5 *High: E3.*
28 **Rippled Arete** 6B
29 **Rippled Wall** 6C
30 **Rippled Wall Traverse** 6B
31 **Big Arete** 6A+ *Gets E2.*
32 **You Cannot be Seious**
    6B *Again, E2.*

33 **Wall** 4+
34 **Diff Crack** 4
35 **VS Wall** 5
36 **Innocuous Traverse** 6A
37 **Wave Arete** 6B+
    Finish rocking onto the slab.
38 **The Wave Traverse** 7C
39 **The Wave** 7A+ *Start low and use a 'funny monkey paw hold' to move left to a scary finish.*
40 6A+ *The hanging crack is gained by stretchy moves.*
41 **Slab** 5+
42 **Crack** 5+
43 **Greg's Dyno** 6A+
44 **Right Arete** 6A+
Bell Tor
45 **Flakes** 4+ *Scary.*
46 **Open Groove** 6B
47 **Prow** 6B+
48 **The Famous Grouse**
    7A+ *A highball classic on rounded holds.*
49 6B+
    Reachy moves from the runnel.
50 **Slabby Wall** 4+

Rippled Wall

Big Slab

John Godding on Shark's Fin, 5+ (problem 14). The Top Hat is visible behind and beyond that to the left are the Square Blocks. Way in the distance is Hay Tor. Joyous moorland. Photo: Niall Grimes.

Hound Tor

50.598984
-3.78244

Lots of problems hidden amidst a granite-bestrewed beauty spot. Between problems, scrambling about and the ice cream, Hound Tor will give a good long session.

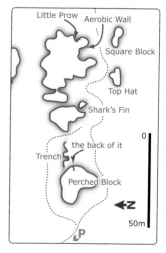

When you arrive in the car park and get the whiff of cheeseburgers wafting from the Hound of the Basketmeals snap wagon, you know you're in for a good time. The tors and boulders, sitting like a beautiful collection of pony shit across a gentle Dartmoor hillside, promise much to the boulderer. However, closer inspection reveals that there is not quite as much as there looks: however, closer inspection will reveal more.

Lots of the stuff takes some finding with many isolated problems. For the full selection download the webguide from javu. To make it managable here the problems detailed are based around the corridor running to the right of the summit, on the outcrops on either side.

// Climbing: Lots of low walls, slabs and bulges as well as a good selection of highballs. The rock is rough on the skin. Landings are generally very good. Good for very easy stuff.
// Conditions: Fairly exposed and catches any weather. The rock is clean and plenty of it is quick drying although some can stay dank. Popular with tourists and climbers. Problems face all directions but mainly south. Best in good weather. **Family friendly.**
// Approach: See the map on page 62. Hound Tor is signposted off the B3387. The Haytor Hoppa bus connects the car park with nearby towns and runs an irregular seasonal service.
// Info: javu.co.uk

Perched Block

Back of the Perched Block

1 2 3 4 5 6 7

The Trench

6 8 10 9

Shark's Fin

12 11 13 14 15

Top Hat

15 16 17 18

Square Blocks

19 20 21

Aerobic Wall

24 22 23

Little Prow

24 25 26 27

1	**Arete** 4	
2	**Easy Wall** 4	
3	**Wall** 3	
4	**Flake** 3+	
5	**Groove** 4	
6	**Wall on Slopers** 6A+ *Sitter 6B.*	
7	**Traverse** 6A+	
8	**Nose** 6A+ *Sitter 6B.*	
9	**Reachy Wall** 6B+ *Sitter.*	
10	**Traverse** 6B	
11	**Left Fin** 5	
12	**Mako** 8A	

Hands following the yellow line. A higher-level traverse, avoiding both aretes and the top, is Shark's Fin Traverse, 7A.

13 **Wish** 6C
14 **Shark's Fin** 5+

15 **Arete** 4+
16 **Wall** 4
17 **Runnel** 3+
18 **High Wall** 5
19 **Arete** 4+
20 **Nose from Sitter** 6B
21 **5c Wall** 6A+
Scary wall.
22 **Limbo Dancer** 6C
Highball bulge: gets E4 as a route.
23 **Aerobic Wall** 6B
Highball flakes: gets E2 as a route.
24 **Little Prow** 6B
E1 to the summit.
25 **Prowed** 7A
Wall on poor holds.
26 **Right Arete** 6A
27 **Little Prow Traverse** 6C+

Saddle Tor

50.571709
-3.769319

A pair of power sapping buttocks of granite giving a roadside thrashing to campus kittens who have good skin and strong forearms. A rampage on the fiercest Dartmoor granite. You'd better be strong.

A tidy venue good for lovers of steep and powerful climbing, and a great place to session something hard. A good contrast to Bonehill, with big up problems and a super-hard endurance traverse with great views. Sharp.

// **Climbing:** A double buttress overhanging by almost fifty degrees at its base means that extreme body tension or the ability to climb footless will be handy, especially on harder climbs. The rock is quite sharp, as is granite's wont. Holds are slopers and crystals. Problems start tough and ease off some as they go but most top out at 5 or 6 metres. Perfect grass landing.

// **Conditions:** Exposed and quick drying. **Family friendly.**

// **Approach:** See map on page 62. Park in the car park 500m east of the junction for Ashburton on the B3387. The tor can be seen from here, 200m away. The Hidden Traverse can be seen from the parking, left of the tor.

// **Info:** javu.co.uk

1	**Bjorn Again**	6A+	*Start from the goodish slot at 2m. Start low at 6B+.*
2	**Foal's Chopper**	7A+	*Go from holds in the vague break. The sit start is 7C.*
3	**Funnel Arete Left**	6A	
4	**The Funnel**	4	
5	**Funnel Arete Right**	6A+	*Gained from The Funnel.*
6	**Super Trouper**	7B	*Lock from the bottom break to a sloper above the roof then on to an easier finish.*
7	**Dancing Queen**	7A+	*Up to a sidepull then up and left to the same finish as for Super Trouper.*
8	**Foul Bite**	6B	*Bewarewolf of the finish.*

9   **Saddle Tor Traverse**   7C+   *Traverse the left hand buttock. Start on the far left and swing along to the jug at the base of Funnel Arete Left. Moving up as per the low start to Bjorn Again is 7C.*

10   **Abba Gold**   8A   *Immense. A traverse of both buttock cheeks. Follow Saddle Tor Traverse to Foal's Chopper; move up this then right to a rest in The Funnel before continuing right along the sloping shelf to finish up Dancing Queen.*

11	**Hidden Traverse**	6B
12	**Hidden Traverse Low**	7A+

Other Dartmoor Bits

If you have visited the Dartmoor venues detailed here then you have definitely earned your granite badge. However, if you are after some more, and in the unlikely event you still have some skin, then here are just a few more venues for you. For all the details see the superb javu website.

Honeybag Tor

This is a remote location spread out on the hillsides north of Bell Tor. Javu details about 80 problems here, best in the lower grades, and spread out on a few buttresses spread along a grassy ridge. The bouldering is not quite as classic as on other venues, nor the problems as obvious, but if you are spending a full day in the Bonehill area, it's only about 10 or 15 minutes stroll from Bell Tor and its quietness will make a nice relaxing end to the day.

To get there follow the well used footpath past Bell Tor, along the ridge for about 900m, to the bouldering. It lies around the second little hilltop you pass. Have a little hunt around. **SX 728787**

Smallacombe

For some, Smallacombe is the best venue on the moor. It has over 120 problems and for boulderers operating up to 6B it's a goldmine. There's also enough harder problems for mid rangers too. Think of it as more spread out Bonehill, placed in a beautiful, more remote location. The rocks sit on a hillside about a kilometre north of Haytor. To get there park in Haytor Vale and follow the road toward Haytor. Before the track to Haytor, follow a good track north to arrive at a quarry after 400m. Continue on, arriving at a granite tramway after 250m. The rocks are spread out on the hillside in the same line, about 300m in front of you. Go explore. **SX 754783**

Bovey Woods

The Woods is one of the favourite venues for the locals where interesting problems on good rock have been unearthed over the last decade. The boulders are strewn throughout the woods, often moss covered, frequently hidden and always shrouded in an air of mystery. Parking is restrictive and access is not too secure. As such there is not much online publicity.

There are over 180 problems up to 7C+. As can be suspected from the name, the Woods are more sheltered, so more slow drying, than other venues.

To keep with the air of mystery, I've not bothered to find any better directions than this: the boulders are in Shaptor Woods, about a mile and a half north of Bovey Tracey and on the east side of the A382. Get to the woods and start snuffling around like a horny pig who's just sniffed some truffles. **SX 805808**

Dartmoor pony with clagnut. Photo: David Simmonite.

Portland

Cuttings   50.539827,-2.431565
Neddyfields 50.531468,-2.437876

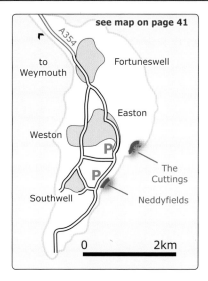

One of the most popular areas in the south with relatively straightforward access from some big cities and very reliable conditions. A couple of hundred smallish problems on the scattered super-scree laying around the base of a populist sport crag.

Covered here is the ever-popular Cuttings with some problems on the crag and loads on a sprawling jumble of boulders scattered twixt crag and sea, as well as the close-by Neddyfields.

// Climbing: The Cuttings boulderfield has loads of problems on smallish boulders usually around 3m high. Sit starts are the norm to make the most of them. Problems on slabs, bulges, aretes, cracks, pockets, crimps and slopers. Landings can be poor, with lots of rocks lying around, so one pad is a necessity, more is better. Rock is fairly smooth and the climbing tends to be fairly powerful. The problems on the crag section are overhanging walls with hard fingery climbing. These need jump descents from 4m so again, at least a couple of pads is nice.

Neddyfields is a long vertical wall covered in small holds and lots of wonderful flowstone giving enjoyable climbs, if maybe a bit samey. Again the problems end at the 4m mark so jump dismounts and/or downclimbs are the order of the day. Pads essential. Thanks to Ben Tyrrell for his help with this section.

Ben Tyrrell on Lightning Strike, 7A+ (problem 17). Photo: Siân Tyrrell.

Ben Tyrrell on Liquid Sunshine, 7B (problem 16). Photo: Siân Tyrrell.

// Conditions: Quick drying, mostly seepage free (Neddyfields gets some) and sheltered with good respite from easterly winds. East facing, getting morning and afternoon sun. All rock is very clean. Climbable year round.

// Approach: The Cuttings: Get to Portland and follow the road through Easton in the direction of Portland Bill. The old landmark, the Mermaid Inn, is closed at the time of writing and is of little use to lost climbers or thirsty quarrymen alike. So, travel through Easton and just as the houses stop there is a little castled gateway at a right-hand bend, and a sign for Portland Museum. Park in Church Ope car park just past this on the right. There is a path just right of the Mermaid, 20m before the bend. Follow this then cut leftwards to gain the quarry road. Follow this for 120m then angle off right under a quarried cliff – the Cuttings. Stomp-

ing with Bez is near the left end of this cliff. For the boulders follow the track overlooking them and just beyond where the cliff veers away from the path a good track leads down. The area is complex so use the map and look around for the boulders.

For **Neddyfields** continue south through Easton. About 900m after the Church Ope parking look out for a big car park (Cheyne Weares) on the left. Stay on the road for another 200m to a small car park on the left at the top of a track. Park here and you can see the Neddyfields ahead. Wander down the track and you are there in one minute.

// Info: Full coverage in the CC **Portland** guide for the Cuttings, Neddyfields and loads of other venues hereabouts.; **Cuttings Boulderfield** (Rockfax).

Crag - Stomping

Boulders– Nu Breed

Anvil

Toll Booth

Southern Soul

Nice Tree

Hermit Hole

Streamline

Cracked Boulder

Lip Boulder

Neddyfields

1   Gunpowder Plot 6c+
The groove just right of the sharp arete from standing.
2   Guy Fawkes 8A
A sit start to Gunpowder Plot, starting with hands in the slots.
3   Stomping With Bez 7A+
Start left of the arete and gain a pocket. Traverse right round the arete to the rib; follow this to the break.
4   Bez Direct 7B
5   Lats, Babes and Bolts 7B   *To the jug.*
6   Blue Skies 5   *Scooped wall. Sitter 6A.*
7   Jo's Arete 4+   *6B sitter.*
8   Nu Breed 5+   *Arete. 6B+ from sitter.*
9   Hammer Time 4+   *Sitter.*
10   The Anvil 5+   *Sitter.*
11   Breaking Rocks 5+   *Sitter.*
12   Sentinel 4+   *Sitter.*
13   Toll Boothe Arete 7A+   *Sitter.*
14   Dominator 6B   *Sitter. No footblock on right.*
15   Southern Soul 6B

16   Liquid Sunshine 7B   *Combine the prow from a sitter (6B+) and the traverse of Liquid Sun (7A+).*
17   Lightning Strike 7A+   *From the back.*
18   Relativity 6B+   *Harder since hold loss.*
19   Streamline 6A   *Sitter.*
20   Lip Traverse 6A   *6B+ from sitting.*
21   Crack 4+   *Sitter.*
22   Arete 6B   *Sitter.*
23   Petty Thief 7A   *Start from the bottom of the hueco at the back of the roof. 6A from the lip.*
24   Split Lip 7A+   *6B+ from the lip.*
25   Cavity Search 7A+   *Cross the roof using a mono then battle up the arete.*
26   The Flake 6A   *Crack and groove.*
27   Stolid 3
28   Savage Traverse 7A+
29   Amoeba State 4
30   Arete 6A+
31   Ripples 6A
32   Razor 6C+   *Sharp crack and pocket.*

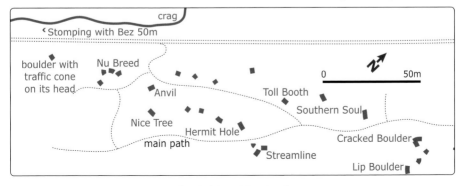

Max and Carl and on the West Face of the Agglestone. Photo: Niall Grimes.

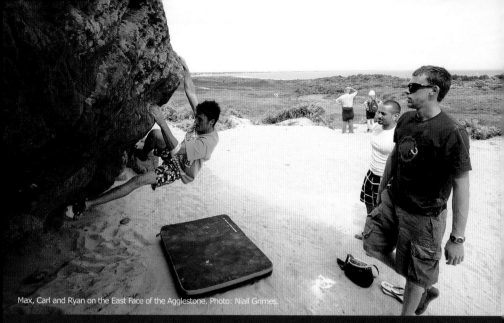
Max, Carl and Ryan on the East Face of the Agglestone. Photo: Niall Grimes.

The Agglestone

50.636656
-1.977239

The Isle of Purbeck's finest erratic. A holiday rock in the middle of nowhere, somewhere to tax the biceps for an hour. Not anywhere that you'd get stressed.

// Climbing: Mostly jugging and slapping around on the deformed logic of twisted bedding planes. Sometimes a bit high but perfect landings. Sandy. No grades are given for erosion purposes. Anyway, the thing's said to be twising, so they'd be worthless.

// Approach: Park in a 5-car layby on the B3351, 300m east of the entrance to Purbeck golf club. Follow a footpath for 200m through the golf course then before a 'Golfers Only' sign, branch left and follow sandy paths to the rock after 700m.

// Conditions: Exposed. Always something in sun or shade. Quick drying but please don't climb damp rock. **Family friendly.**

15 min | 10 problems 3 - 7A best from 4 - 6B | slabby | steep | | exposed

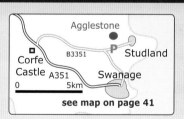

see map on page 41

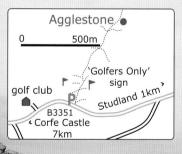

Dave Westlake on the Slopy Traverse, 7B (problem L3). Photo: Westlake Collection

Lynmouth

51.230827
-3.830945

5-20 min | 100 probs 2 - 7C best from 6A - 7B | slabby | vertical | steep | | shelter | seepage / tidal | moon

An esoteric coastal venue with lots of holiday bouldering across a broad spectrum of height, difficulty and quality. Good, but with tricky conditions. Thanks to Dave Westlake and Grant Edwards for this section.

The stretch of coast on the edge of Exmoor is littered with oddly sculpted boulders and giant sea caves. The best concentration lies near the sleepy holiday town of Lynmouth. The second highest tidal range in the world contributes to a wildly varying beach level and means that your project could be here today, buried tomorrow. This also means the rock generally stays wetter than that of the Culm coast, so a visit is always something of a gamble. However, it's a handy venue and when conditions are right those that do make the effort can be rewarded with some unusual and classy gems. The bouldering has been developed since the early 2000s by a small crew of dedicated locals, principally Grant Edwards, Mikey Cleverdon and Neil Blom

with the help of Mike Adams, Joe Harris, Dave Westlake and others.

// Climbing: The rock is well wave washed and smooth slopers are common here. Exquisitely frictionless. Landings range from very good to fairly bad so it is advisable to take a few pads and spotters. Problems also range in quality although there are enough good problems across the grade range for a decent session. There is a wide variety of styles, including several good traverses and highballs. The climbing detailed here is just a taste: you will see boulders everywhere.

Lynmouth East

The Joker

Slopy Traverse

Seventh Wave

Monster Tide

big white boulder (landmark)

to Lynmouth

Chimpanzee

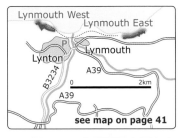

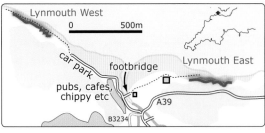

Seventh Wave

Chimpanzee

Monster Tide

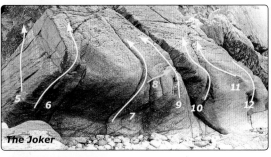

The Joker

Slopy Traverse

Anarchy

1   **Seventh Wave Traverse** 7A+
2   **Chimpanzee Acne** 7A
3   **No More Nails** 7B
4   **Monster Tide** 7A
5   **Face On** 5+
    Avoid big footholds on the left.
6   **Face Off** 7A   *Sitter with left hand on sloper, right in crack.*
7   **Twister** 6A   *Sitter 7C, depending on beach level.*
8   **Cyclone** 7A   *Start up Twister and follow slopers right to Arete Thing.*
9   **Arete Thing** 3+

10   **Slightly Harder Crack** 4+
11   **The Joker and the Thief**
    6C+   *Slopey, A classic eliminate just left is Finger Fury, 7B.*
12   **Easy Crack** 2
13   **Slopy Traverse** 7B
    Starting low and right. The second half is 6A+ while the extended start is a project.
14   **F.E.A.R** 4+
15   **Anarchy Arete** 5 *E3?*
16   **Sid Vicious** 4

// Approach: Park in Lynmouth (pay and display) and walk right (east) along the beach to find the main areas. After about 5 minutes you will reach The Slopy Traverse and The Joker. Further along, past a large white slabby boulder, are the Monster Tide and Chimpanzee boulders. Seventh Wave is in a cave just further again. For the Anarchy block (Lynmouth West) park on the Esplanade (near the cliff railway and a good chip shop), head west and boulder hop for around 15 minutes, passing lots of blocks and problems.

// Conditions: Mostly tidal, accessible for around 3 hours either side of low tide. It is wise to take a towel and plenty of chalk as some problems can stay wet. A strong breeze from west through to north east is ideal. **Family friendly.** Now, heed this warning. If the tide comes in you will be cut off and there is no easy escape. This will not be nice. **SO DO NOT GET CUT OFF BY THE TIDE.**

// Info: Grant Edwards' pdf guide is on **javu.co.uk.**

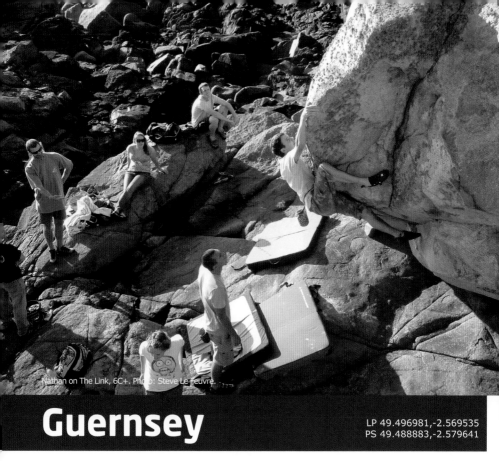
Nathan on The Link, 6C+. Photo: Steve Le Feuvre.

Guernsey

LP 49.496981,-2.569535
PS 49.488883,-2.579641

A Channel Island ringed in fine granite and enough nice bouldering to keep a visitor happy for a few days. Two areas are covered here of interest to a tax exile with good skin. Relaxing venues, good for easier holiday bouldering.

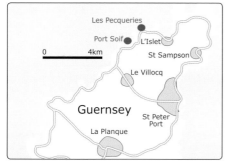

Lots of areas around the coast but these are the two best for a quick hit, and only a kilometre apart. Thanks to Chris Smith for this section. Chris also wanted to say that if anyone is ever visiting the island then get in touch with the Guernsey Mountaineering Club via their website. They will only be too happy to provide all info as well as mats and even spotters if you need them. And me, well I've liked every Guernsey person I've ever met.

// Climbing: Rounded granite boulders and outcrops. Very clean seawashed rock.
// Info: Downloadable topos on **www.gmc.org.gg**

Les Pecqueries
An ideal first venue. There are approximately 23 problems from 3 – 7A with the best routes being in the 6A – 6C+ range. Tides only effect the main boulder on high spring tides although some problems in the area need a low tide. It is climbable year round and the south side is often sheltered from the wind and therefore quite a nice suntrap. Unfortunately overweight men looking to achieve an all-over tan have also discovered this!

Most of the landings are on uneven ground and require a couple of mats and a spotter to be safe. **Great for families.**

// Approach: From Cobo travel north. Going along Route des Pecqueries there is a sharp right-hand bend with a turnoff into some gravel car parks. Take the one furthest from the road. Once on foot head west towards the outcrop of rocks where you will find the main boulder. Walk in is 2 mins.

Port Soif

Another place worth adding and is very close-by. It is right next to a perfect sandy beach, a kiosk and also provides short trad and excellent surfing, A lot of the easier problems here are non-tidal and most don't get wet until a high spring tide. There are currently 27 problems from 4 – 7A. It can be climbed on all year, and most of the landings are good. One or two mats is good. **Great for families.**

// Approach: Travel north along the coast road from Cobo/Grand Rocques (or south from Les Pecqueries) until you see a turning signposted 'Port Soif' on the coastal side. Take this. Drive past the kiosk and park in the left-hand car park. There is bouldering on the crag in front, on the top of it, and also down to the right of the car park.

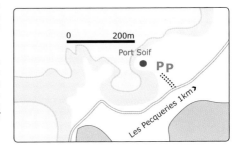

Jersey

Lots of great trad but not tons of bouldering. The main event, the Pinnacle, has a bunch of high quality pump fests on raw granite. As usual for these far flung venues we deputise a man on the ground. Over to you, Ted Kingsnorth:

"I scoured every inch of the coast line and failed to find much other bouldering apart from the Pinnacle."

The bouldering is on the left side, along the severely undercut base of the crag. The sea comes rushing up here (40-foot tidal range on Jersey) so you have to watch where you put your mat sometimes. The best time to visit is in the afternoons as it is north-west facing and

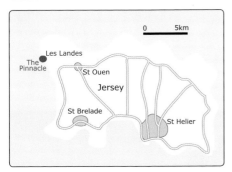

stays greasy and wet from the tide even into summer in the mornings. Also, make sure you go at high- to mid-tide as you won't be able to climb as the sea will be scouring the base of the crag. On a rough sea it can be quite a frightening sight.

The grades really start at about 6C and there are some great steep offerings here. Most problems are above 7A. The traverse is the centerpiece and goes in both directions. TK did it right to left and James Noble did it the other way, a very powerful 8A. There are some pretty nasty 7B+s too on small crimps. The rock quality is very good, not too rough, and makes a change from other rock types on the mainland.

// Approach: Drive to Les Landes on the north western tip of the island. The parking spot is south of Grosnez Castle and the race course. Head south from the hamlet of Les Landes, near the castle, on the minor road running next to the race course. Take the first dirt road on your right which leads to a well used parking area. Head for the coast and a 5-minute walk will lead you past the German gun emplacement and to a spot overlooking the sea. You can see the Pinnacle from here, more a natural 'menhir' i.e. not quite a stack but still joined to the land on one side. There are very old archaeological remains from 5,000 years ago here and a stone circle. Drop down towards the Pinnacle down a steep path, through the stone circle, under the Pinnacle itself and then drop down to the right onto some rock shelves. Turn back left and head to the base of the Pinnacle. You have to do a bad step to pass a boulder choke in a kind of sea chimney and then you are on the sloping platform below the crag. Sounds like fun :-)

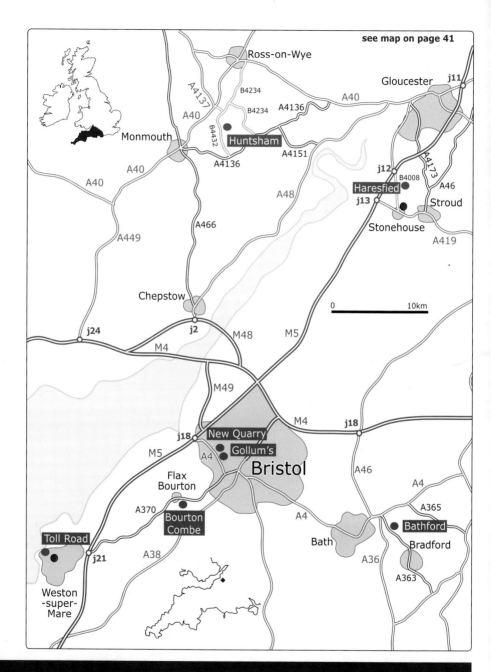

see map on page 41

The Bristol Area

Tom Randall on One Infinity, 8A+ Bathford (page 93). Photo: Mike Hutton.

Rory and Stu passing a slack Monday at the Rift Boulder, here on Rift Wall Traverse, 7A (problem 8). Photo: Niall Grimes.

Huntsham

51.849389
-2.640377

Esoteric? Hell yeah! The best in the area gives a great serving of problems on unusual features, and best suited to people who like a strong taste. A full day of climbing in a reliable climate.

Huntsham is the premier bouldering spot in that Western Front of British sandstone, the Forest of Dean. It is not the hobnob-bedded tot that popular legend will have you believe and some of the problems here would sit proudly in the gallery of any great sandstone area. Still, obscurists will enjoy this more than the straight. The rock is a bit foreign, although anyone used to the Churnet Valley will already speak the language.

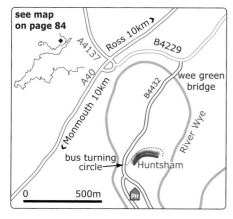

see map on page 84

A4137 Ross 10km →
B4229
A40
B4432
Monmouth 10km
wee green bridge
River Wye
bus turning circle
Huntsham
PH

0   500m

// **Climbing:** Sandstone boulders. Steep and burly, often sitters and sometimes highballs. The rock is not always perfect, but it's often great. Pebbles, pockets, slopers, cracks and aretes. Landings generally okay.

// **Approach:** From A40 / A4137, follow B4229 towards Symonds Yat East, then right on B4432 to same. Continue for a mile to a bus turning circle on the left. Turn around to 3-car spot on left after 25m. Beware double yellows. From the turning circle follow the forestry track. After 200m a small track angles right. For the Dark Side end of the circuit follow this for 280m where a small track breaks left. Follow this up a banking then back left to the path. For the Rift area continue on the forestry track and 45m after the angled track a small, hard-to-spot path leads, after 45m, to the boulder.

// **Conditions:** Sheltered and quick drying. Sunny, most faces getting sun from afternoon. Quite ferny in summer but climbable year round. Fantastic on a sunny winter's day. Sliced Slug is a bit rainproof. Like with all sandstone, avoid if at all damp. The boulders are fairly quick drying and sheltered.

// **Info:** Forest of Dean (CC); **esotericbouldering.co.uk**

// **Access:** The crag might be closed during the winter months because of gamekeeping restrictions, as deer hunting is practiced here. The whole area is an extremely valuable habitat for rare flowers and animals, as well as for herds of deer, wild boar and dormice. Observe any restrictions, be polite, and if you don't want to have your brains blown out, don't be wearing your Christmas antlers.

| 8 min | 80 probs 2 - 7B+ best from 5 - 7A+ | vertical | steep | roofs | | shelter |

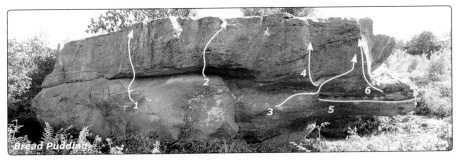

Bread Pudding

Rift

Sliced Slug

Cube

Splasher

1   **Bread Pudding** 5+
     Can be dynoed at 7C.
2   **Pudding Basin** 6C
3   **The Porthole** 7A
     Low start.
4   **Lick the Bowl** 6C
5   **Gnarly Trav** 7B+
     Start along 3, stay low,
continue round back.
6   **Bowl Rim** 6A
7   **Rift Crack** 5+
8   **Rift Wall Traverse**
     7A *6B+ from stand.*
9   **Rift Arete** 6A
     Sitter 6B+.
10   **Mid Rift** 3
11   **The Golden Bicep**
     6C+ *Sitter. 6B+ from*
a standing start.
12   **Left Flake** 5+
     Sitter 6A.
13   **Right Flake** 6A
     Sitter 6A+.
14   **Slugtaste** 6C+
     Very highball.
15   **Ames Low** 7A+
16   **Rocket** 6C+ *Dyno.*
17   **Left Eye** 7A+
18   **Rise and Fall of**
     the Splasher 7A+
19   **The Scoops** 6A
     Sitter.
20   **Arete** 6A+
21   **Traverse** 6B+

Satellite

Dark Side

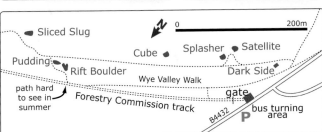

Sliced Slug

Cube   Splasher   Satellite

Pudding   Rift Boulder   Dark Side
Wye Valley Walk
path hard
to see in   Forestry Commission track   gate
summer   B4432   bus turning
area

Haresfield

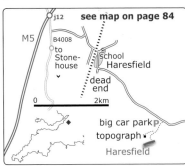

see map on page 84

1	**Finger Crack** 5+	**6**	**Corner** 2+
2	**Hanging Crack** 6A	**7**	**Long wall** 4+
3	**Blunt Arete Right** 5	**8**	**The Hard**
4	**Descent Crack** 3		**Traverse** 6B+
5	**Blocky Crack** 3+	**9**	**Curved Crack** 4

A little cream tea of a crag; polite and well behaved. A lovely place to break a journey.

If I was a rabbit then I'd definitely live at Haresfield. Great views, great grass, great soil and there's nothing to get stressed about. All that and you could be climbing in about 15 minutes from the motorway.

// Climbing: Limestone outcrop. Little tiny trad climbs up wide cracks or brief bulges. Highish, but you wouldn't call it highball. Flatties and cracks. Your biceps will go for a walk but your fingers won't. Easy, good for a mooch.

// Approach: From junction 12 on the M5 take the B4008 towards Stonehouse. After 100m go left direction Haresfield. After 800m at junction go right. After 600m turn right on a bend by a school. Follow for 300m to a dead-end sign then turn left. Follow road uphill for 1.6 miles, passing many parking bays, to a 30-car car park on the right at the summit. Head towards a topograph. What's that? Don't know. When you reach it turn left and after 86m there's a little crag.

// Conditions: Sunny and dry. A good little spot. **Family friendly.**

// Info: Symond's Yat (CC)

Gollum's Cave

Gollums 51.458683,-2.626607
New 51.467353,-2.632411

A little weatherproof den of pinches, crimps and slopers; everything, ironically, except crack. Ugly as sin, but handy.

A limestone hole located usefully near Bristol city centre. First the bad news. If you have ever found that Parisella's Cave offended your sense of the aesthetic, then here's a venue that will have you fumbling for your cyanide tablet. And the good news? Well, if you're a junkie or a wino who has some taste for limestone eliminate bouldering, then there are worse places to crash.

// Climbing: Totally eliminate in nature, with steep moves on polished slopers, crimps and pinches.

// Approach: The cave lies a few hundred metres from Clifton Suspension Bridge. Park on Clifton Down, at the junction with Percival Rd. A tarmac footpath runs parallel with the road. Follow this in the direction of the bridge but immediately take another path that runs into the trees. Follow this and after about 100m there is an old metal fence by the path. 30m from the start of this, it bends. The cave is about 50m directly below the bend. So, from the start of the fence, drop down to a small path below. Follow this for 10m to a concrete block. From here a path runs downhill. Follow this and other vague paths down and left, and just past a white limestone slab is the cave.

// Conditions: Weatherproof, and very sheltered, although it seeps in winter. Gets late afternoon sun. Some sort of ground covering is useful to keep shoes clean.

The New Quarry: Nicer, but still roadside. Located 1km north up the A4 Portway, this is the smaller quarry visible between the two big Avon climbing crags,

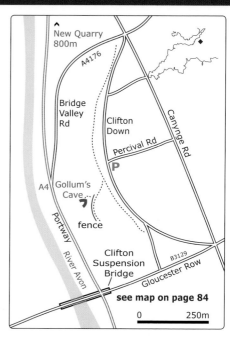

see map on page 84

0   250m

Sea Walls and the Main Wall. Park at the entrance to the quarry. It seeps in winter but when dry gives a great 40m traverse on generally big holds, but with a few hard bits, at a stiff 6B+. Noisy, sunny and pleasant.

James Squire on BC Traverse, 7A+ (problem 3). Photo: James' Mum.

Bourton Combe

51.418265
-2.708044

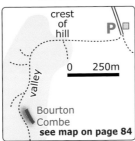

A tiny wee wall of limestone good for pumpy traverses and eliminate link-ups.

// Climbing: Steep and crimpy.

// Approach: From Flax Bourton on the A370, follow Bourton Combe Rd for 200m and park. Follow a country lane up right. The hill crests after 270m. Continue sweeping down and left for 200m to the shallow valley. Follow a path up the valley for 300m. The wall is up scree 30m from the path.

// Conditions: Wooded, sheltered, afternoon sun. Good in winter.

// Info: **esotericbouldering.com**

1	**End of it All** 6A+	*Sitter.*
2	**Full AD Traverse** 7B+	
3	**BC Traverse** 7A+	
4	**Gone for a Bourton** 6B+	*Sitter 6C.*
5	**Soloist** 6A	*To pinch at 5m.*
6	**Cut Throat** 6B	*To pinch at 5m.*
7	**Flax Factor** 6A	*To pocket at 5m.*

James Squire near the Fisherman's Ledge area. Photo: James' Mum.

Toll Road Crags

51.358209
-2.991323

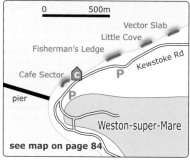

0   500m

Vector Slab
Little Cove
Fisherman's Ledge
Cafe Sector
pier
Kewstoke Rd
Weston-super-Mare

see map on page 84

A collections of coves and caves that give a good number of tough problems. Secluded and exploratory.

The Cafe Sector: Approach from 50m left of the cafe. Ten problems in the 5s and low 6s.

Fisherman's Ledge: The best area perhaps? Park 300m after the cafe by a solar panel. Walk back 50m and scramble down to 15 problems from low-6s to mid-7s, centred around some shallow caves. **The Little Cove** is 250m on, past a couple of headlands. This is a wee 8-metre bay of rounded rock. The traverse, My Religion, is 7B. **Vector Slab** is 200m on. Great topos on esotericbouldering.com.

// Climbing: Limestone crags. Steep and generally crimpy. Good for harder stuff. Landings are rocky so pads needed.
// Approach: From Weston, pass the pier and head north along the sea to Kewstoke Rd. About 200m after the pier there is a cafe on the left. The cafe sector is below this. Try to find somewhere to park or carry on for 300m to the other areas.
// Conditions: A little tidal.
// Info: esotericbouldering.com

10 min   45 probs
4 - 7C
best from
6A - 7A   steep   roofs   shelter   seepage   tidal

Tom Randall on All Elements, 8A. Photo: Mike Hutton.

Bathford

51.382649
-2.29758

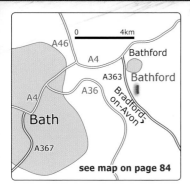

see map on page 84

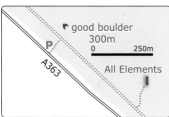

A wooded scattering of local boulders that is now on the map thanks to two desperate roof testpieces.

// Climbing: Lots of smaller blocks with average bouldering. A good boulder sits near the path 300m left of the access point. The All Elements boulder is a quarried head-height roof. All Elements is Tom Randall's 8A roof crack going from the back right-hand corner. The right-to-left lip traverse is 7B. Linking the two is Tom's behemoth of upside-down pump, One Infinity. This gets F8b+ route grade, so somewhere in the 8A+ range. Thanks to Tom for this section.

// Approach: Leave the A4 and go south on the A363 towards Bradford-on-Avon. Drive south for a mile and a half to a 10-car parking spot on the left. Cross the fence on the same side and strike into the woods for 75m to meet the main path. For All Elements turn right and follow this for 400m. The climbing is in a small cave 75m from the path on the left. Access has always been unsure but it seems as if it's actually okay. If asked to leave do so politely.

// Conditions: Wooded, sheltered, afternoon sun. Humid in summer. Best in autumn. Beware of ticks. Seepage free. Quite a spooky place, not very relaxing to be there on your own. Vicars, porn mags, empty bottles: you get the idea.

// Info: **bathbouldering.wikispaces.com**

Tyler Landman on Pac Man Arete, 6C+, at the Pac Man Boulders (page 111, problem 3). Photo: Alex Messenger.

Wales

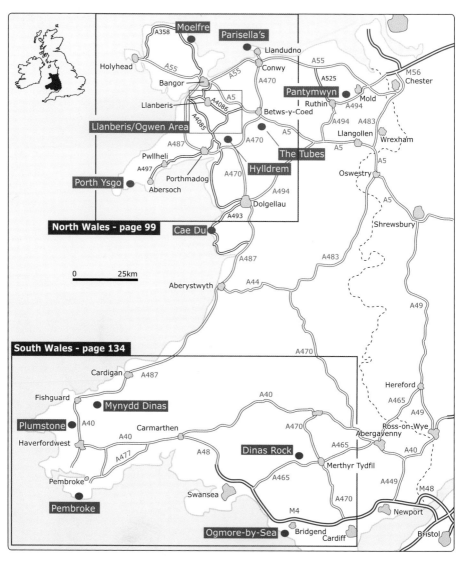

North Wales - page 99

South Wales - page 134

0   25km

Pete Robins on Rock Attrocity, 7C, at Parisella's Cave (page 130, problem 2). Photo: Ray Wood.

Chris Davies on The Gimp, 7B at the Caseg Boulders (page 114, problem 3). Photo: Ray Wood.

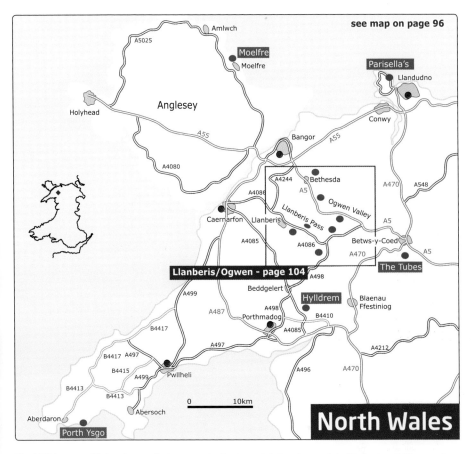

see map on page 96

Amlwch

A5025

Moelfre
Moelfre

Parisella's
Llandudno

Anglesey

Holyhead

Conwy

A55

A55

Bangor

A4080

A4244 Bethesda

A470 A548

A4086

A5

Ogwen Valley

A5

Caernarfon Llanberis

Llanberis Pass

Betws-y-Coed

A5

A4085

A4086

A470

The Tubes

Llanberis/Ogwen - page 104

A498

Beddgelert

Hylldrem

Blaenau
Ffestiniog

A499

A487

A498

Porthmadog

B4410

B4417

A4085

A497

A4212

B4417 A497

A496 A470

B4415

A499 Pwllheli

B4413

B4413

0   10km

Aberdaron

Abersoch

Porth Ysgo

North Wales

North Wales is possibly best known for its mountain circuits, mainly based around the Llanberis and Ogwen valleys, wild, beautiful, wet places filled with wild, beautiful, wet people. Around this are a spread of coastal crags, most notably the holiday favoutite Porth Ysgo and that grot of power-stamina, Parisella's Cave on the Marine Drive.

It has a long bouldering history going back to the ancients and taking in the hard men of the Rock and Ice Club in the 1940s and 50s. In the 60s Martin Boysen and other locals applied their technical skills and in the 70s it was Al Harris and his rabble of friends who carried the torch. The 1980s saw John Redhead really start to work out desperate fingery problems while a younger group including Johnny Dawes and Nick Dixon scoured the mountains and finding hard gems. On the Ormes Jerry Moffatt and friends started to develop Parisella's Cave.

However it was in the 1990s that bouldering in North Wales really kicked off and gained independence from its traditional elder brother. A lull in route development early in the decade led local climbers to root around the slopes for slopers. This led most notably to the Wavelength development in the middle of the decade, led by Paul Pritchard and Simon Panton, and championed in Panton's Northern Soul fanzines.

The ten years that followed saw North Wales bouldering come to maturity. The new phenomen of the era, the Dedicated Boulderer, both locals and incomers, emerged to bring Welsh standards up to that of the rest of the country. Paul Higginson, Mark Katz and Chris Davies stand out as the top players, with Davies in particular doing more than anyone to keep the region up to date for over ten years both in the mountains and on the limestone.

Jim Perrin, Moose Thomas, Martin Crook, Kristian Klemmow, Pete Robins, George Smith, Neil Dyer, Adam Wainwright, Leo Houlding, Gavin Foster, Adam Hocking, John Gaskins, Dave Noden, the Cattells, Will Perrin, Paul Houghoughi, Malcolm Smith and many, many others have also played a major part.

A climber on Ysgo Crack, 5 (problem 23). Photo: Mike Hutton.

Porth Ysgo

52.810414
-4.653997

The best of holiday bouldering. One of the country's favourite bouldering venues where, with enough pads, you can enjoy one of the funnest circuits about. Fantastic setting, tons of superb problems and a weather system more in common with Devon than Llanberis. Of course you're smiling baby.

The approach path, scattered willy nilly with the rusting remnants of an old winding house – cables, axles, frames, housings and other heavy machinery – takes you back in time, somehow not spoiling the ambience, but creating it. The landings are savagely scattered with

ankle-destroying boulders, yet with plenty of pads and friends, tamable, then proudly comforting, like LL Cool J's panther. A place of contradictions. It's Wales, yet the sun is shining!

Ysgo shares the gold-medal spot with St Bees in the coastal bouldering championships. An essential place of pilgrimage for the British boulderer. A fond place.

The nearest fleshpot is Abersoch, the holiday town with more than its share of pubs, ice-cream sellers, shops and outlets for greasy breakfasts. But beware: the village seems to swell with dickheads in naff sports cars and deck shoes over summer weekends.

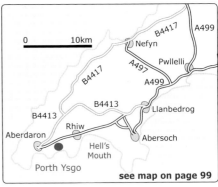

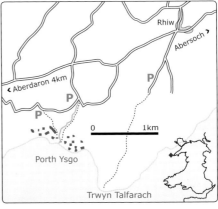

// Climbing: Fantastic climbing on the cleanest gabbro boulders scattered across a bouldery seaside. The rock is solid and well weathered, varying from rasping bubbly bulges to smooth almost slate-frictioned slopers. The boulders give action on all angles from footless steepness to gentle slabs. Aretes, grooves, cracks and bulges all feature, with a good range of grades. There is nothing super-desperate here but it's not the sort of place where you'll be sessioning one problem, rather ticking a bunch of stuff within your grade. As such it will suit everyone. It's worth questing off to Made in Heaven block.

Now for the bad news. The landings don't come any worse than Ysgo landings. Come with a very minimum of two pads and spotters, and the more of both you have the more you will get out of the place. Even with these, some lines will still be intimidating. Surprisingly, this aspect, and the team approach it demands, is one of the things that makes Ysgo special.

// Approach: Follow the maps. The commonest parking, nearest Rhiw, is a small layby near a junction. A sign at the juction points the way. Follow a stream down past lots of industrial architecture to pop out above the beach.

// Conditions: Only some of the bouldering is tidal, so you'll always get something done. That said, lower tides are better. Very quick drying rock in a location that seems to get lots of sun and little rain. Climbable all year, if anything it gets too hot in summer. A brilliant winter crag.

// Info: Full coverage in North Wales Bouldering. Rumours of a Llyn bouldering guide.

Trwyn Talfarach: Those who have visited Ysgo a few times may be interested in this nearby venue offering a smaller chunk of Ysgo's greatness. Fewer problems, maybe not quite as many classics, but a less-good version of Ysgo is still pretty good. The usual caveats about landings apply. See map for approach. Details in the Stone Circle article in Climber magazine, January 2007, and in a forthcoming Llyn Bouldering guide from Ground Up.

Higginson Scar Area

Higginson Scar Area

Beach Boys

Beach Boys

The Ramp

Ysgo Crack

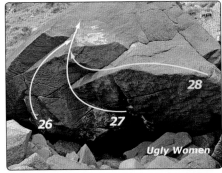

1 **Truth** 5+

2 **Justice** 5+

3 **Really Cool Toys** 7A
Sitter. 4+ from a stand.

4 **The Ysgo Flange** 6A

5 **Ysbeidiau Heulog** 6B+

6 **Higginson Scar** 6B+
From a sitter.

7 **Higginson Right-Hand**
7A *Lip traverse to the groove.*

8 **Wall** 4

9 3

10 **Highball Slab** 5

11 **Arete** 4+

12 **Incredible Shaking
Man** 6B *7B sitter.*

13 **Perrin's Crack** 6A

14 **Uncle Pete's Arete** 5+

15 **Pet Sounds** 7B+

16 **Beach Boys Arete** 6B+

17 **Uncle Pete's Groove** 4+

18 **The Ramp** 6B

19 **Porn Makes Me Horny**
7C+ *From a sitter under the
arete, hands low, gain The Ramp
using the black sidepull slot.*

20 **Unmarked Grave** 6B
*Swing up to the finish of The
Ramp. 7C+ from a sitter as for
Porn..., called Tide of Dreams.*

21 **Floppy's Arete** 4

22 **Johnny's Slab** 6B+

23 **Ysgo Crack** 5

24 **The Smith Route** 6A

25 **Willy's Crack** 6C

26 **Howling Hound** 7A+
*Move up from a sitter to gain
the lip and move right along this to
the finish of Ugly Women.*

27 **Ugly Women** 6B

28 **Early Morning Wigwam**
7A *Lip traverse into Ugly
Women to finish.*

29 **Crack** 5+

30 **Fast Cars** 6C+

31 **Throbber** 7A
Wall to sloping top.

32 5+

33 **Popcorn Party** 7A
*From a sitting start under the
roof bubble up the yellow wall.*

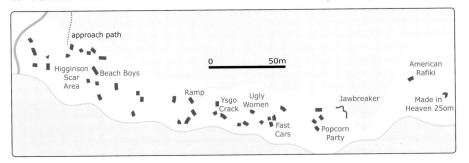

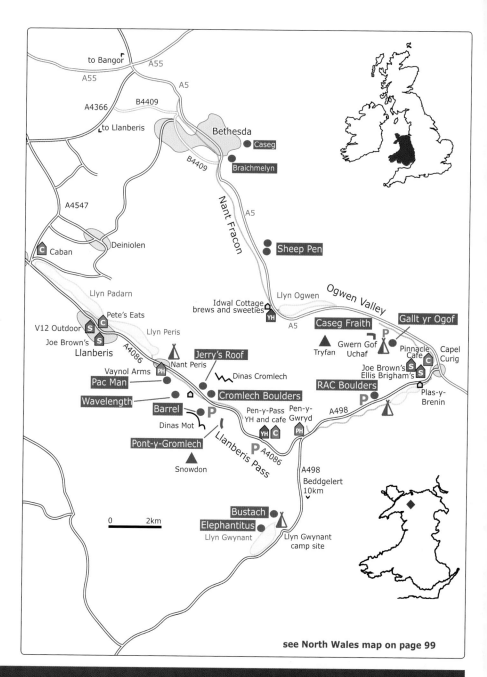

Llanberis-Ogwen Area

see North Wales map on page 99

Johnny Dawes and Andy Cave on the Wavelength Boulder (page 109). Photo: Niall Grimes

Tons of problems in an as-roadside-as-it-gets location, extremely popular due to concentration, accessibility, setting and renown. Everyone's first experience of Welsh bouldering. It doesn't need much selling.

Noel Craine, the Lion of Judah, talks about the 'Hegemony of the Cromlech Boulders'. Well he is a doctor. What he means, I think, is that these are always the first choice when it comes to bouldering in the area. If people want to meet, they meet here. If people want an hour after work, they go here. If people just want to swing around for a bit without thinking too hard they come here. Think of it as a rhyolite version of a reasonable local pub.

I'm not mad about the Cromlech Boulders. Parking can be a pain. The road is busy and noisy and takes away from fully appreciating the amazing setting. The climbing is a bit brutal, I find the holds a bit hurty and the landings annoying. But I know my opinion will count for little and you will go there anyway and you can make up your own mind. Could be I've just not spent enough time here, or maybe I got me arse kicked. Or both.

The nearby Jerry's Roof boulder is included here too.

// Climbing: 120 problems well spread up to 8B. These tend to be very aggressive, fingery and physical. Lots of styles but mainly on pockets, edges, jugs or slopers. Almost everything is steep, from the gently leaning roadside face to nearly footless caves. Some problems are above grass, some are above boggy ground. Others are above boulders or very hard stony ground. A couple of mats will definitely be of use on many problems due to a hard landing although it is easy to find enough that don't need any mats at all. Great for traverses, link-ups and eliminates, all of which means you will never run out of things to do here. Plenty for beginners.

// Approach: See map on page 104. The boulders are obvious by the roadside. Park in one of the nearby bays and away you go. Jerry's Roof lies 100m downhill of the left-hand boulder.

// Conditions: Generally open, friendly and quick drying. Gets lots of sun when it shines but can feel bleak on a grey windy day. Fairly sheltered but can get midge-ridden. The busy road and its noise is a bit of a factor. Climbable year round. **Family friendly.**

// Info: North Wales Bouldering (N-Soul)

1 **Jerry's Roof** 7C
2 **Pool of Bethesda** 8A+ *From high pocket. Malc's start comes from low and left at 8B.*
3 **Mr Fantastic** 8A+ *From good holds on Jerry's Roof drop in and do the next problem.*
4 **Bus Stop** 7C *Start from the undercut.*
5 **Left-Hand Traverse** 6C+ *Finish up 9.*
6 5+ *Up and left from good sidepull.*
7 **Loose Cannon** 6C+ *Dyno.*
8 **Hanging Arete** 6B+ *Start from the crack.*
9 **Brown's Crack** 5 *Sitter.*
10 **Flake** 5+ *Sitter.*
11 **Easy Flake** 3
12 **Ultimate Retro Party** 7B *Sitter, from undercut and sidepull.*
13 **Crouching Start, Hidden Foothold** 7C
14 **The Prow** 6B *Sitter.*
15 **Moose's Problem** 6B+ *Sitter.*
16 **Wall** 5+
17 **Pocket Traverse** 6B
18 **Pull Over** 6A+
19 **Heel Hook Traverse** 6B+

Chris Smith on the Edge Problem, 6C+ (problem 28). Photo: Niall Grimes.

Jerry's Roof

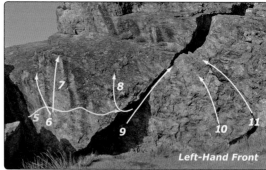

Left-Hand Front

Left-Hand Back

Right-Hand

Right-Hand

20 Diesel Power 8A
21 Roadside Basic 7A+
  Traverse the shelf finishing up The Ramp. Or finish up Roadside Arete at 7A, or the Edge Problem at 7C or Roadside RH at 8A+.
22 Roadside Arete 6C
23 The Ramp 5
24 Ramp Left-Hand 5+
25 Ramp Central 6A
26 Pocket Wall 6A+
27 Johnny's Wall 7A
  Right hand in mono.
28 The Edge Problem 6C+

29 Roadside RH 6A
30 Cromlech Roof Crack
  7A+ *On the back of the boulder is a cave. Traverse the roof crack from right to left finishing up jugs.*
31 Sleep Deprivation 7B
  Direct through the Roof Crack.

Wavelength

53.090687
-4.053311

The Pride of Welsh bouldering. A fantastic mountain circuit with short walks between great blocks winding ever upwards on a beautiful hillside. A variety of styles and problems at all levels will bring a smile to the face of any team of boulderers with a summer day on their hands.

While the Cromlech Boulders will undoubtedly be the first port of call for the first-time visitor to the Pass, it is with a journey up the boulder-strewn hillsides opposite the Grochan that one will truly appreciate the majesty of the Pass. It is best to have a good half day or more to set aside, after which you will be well and truly exercised and aesthetically replete. Bring some sandwiches.

The boulders start with the fabulous Utopia. Above there is Pieshop and Wavelength. Level with these is the Grooves boulder. Above are the Upper Satellites, the Meadow, the Dome and Beyond the Dome. The quality is maintained all the way, although only the lower blocks are detailed here. In general each area is only one or two hundred metres from the last. However, it's worth making a special mention of The Big Smile, a 7C high on the hillside, and the best problem of its type in the land.

	150 probs	
20 min	4 - 8A best from 6A - 7A+	vertical / steep / roofs / ☀ / exposed

// **Climbing:** North Wales Bouldering details almost 150 problems across all grades up to 8A and you will always find something at your grade. Lots of variety with walls, bulges, roofs and the very odd slab. Generally crimpy or slopey and with the odd crack. Sometimes a little highball but the landings are good.

// **Approach:** See map on page 104. Weekend parking in the Pass is an ever-increasing problem, while other options – public transport, parking-and-hitching – are currently imperfect solutions. If you drive, park in one of the roadside bays between the Grochan and the Cromlech Boulders. CC Members can park in Ynys Ettws. You are aiming for the rocky hillside that lies behind Ynys Ettws. Most people start at Utopia. Follow the blocks shown here then for the Upper Satellites, the Meadow, the Dome and Beyond the Dome trend generally 300m up and left from the Grooves boulder.

// **Conditions:** The hillside can feel a bit exposed so it's best enjoyed on a nice day, especially as the circuit is as much about the place and the boulders than ticking something desperate. All the boulders are quick drying. The ground underfoot can be boggy in parts especially on the walks between venues so don't head up there in your best stilettos. Problems face generally south. No sun in winter but still climbably on a nice still day.

// **Info:** North Wales Bouldering (N-Soul)

Utopia Boulder

1 **Utopia Left-Hand** 6C
   Go from the thin break to flake high and left then up. Eliminate.
2 **The Groove** 6A+ *Bold finish.*
3 **Utopia Central** 6B *Pockety seam, avoiding adjacent problems. Sitter 6B+.*
4 **Flake** 4
5 **The Pebble** 7A
6 **Arete** 6C+ *Sitter.*
7 **Crack** 5+
8 **Utopia Right-Hand** 6C+
9 **Utopia Traverse** 7A

Pieshop

10 **Sitdown Flake** 4+
11 **Love Pie** 7C *A one-mover from a crouch start on the hanging rib.*
12 **Humble Pie Disorder** 8A *From a sitter, feet on plinth, traverse left into 11.*
13 **Hanging Nose** 6A+
14 **Kebab Legs** 6B
   Traverse from jug and up the arete.

Wavelength

15 **Scoop Arete** 5+ *Crouch start 7A.*
16 **New Wave** 7C+ *Reachy.*
17 **The Shelf** 6B
18 **The Groove** 6B
19 **Wavelength Central** 6B
   Passing two pockets.
20 **King of Drunks** 6C+
   The topout features the famous golfball hold. 7A from a sitter.
21 **Wavelength** 7B+
   Same start, then right to a flatty and up using thin flake.

Grooves Boulder

22 **Boysen's Groove** 6B+
   With its Great White hold.
23 **The Witch** 7A+
24 **Groove Right-Hand** 6B
25 **Paul's Bulge** 6B
26 **The Ramp** 6A+
27 **The Big Smile** 7C
   The best traverse in Wales, apparently. Quest off to a hanging slab underneath Dinas Mot's Plexus Buttress. Traverse the lip left to right, finishing up the arete.

Utopia

Pieshop

Wavelength

Grooves Boulder

Grooves Boulder

Wales / Wavelength

Other Pass Venues

Three smaller venues to complete the Pass experience, each with its own fine qualities.

Pont y Gromlech Slabs

These are a good place to clear your head if you've been stood by the traffic on the Cromlech Boulders for too long. A clutch of airy highballs on great rock. Necky.

The Barrel

A good spot for power beasts, all of its problems requiring much burl and finger strength. Some classic testpieces for locals and visitors alike.

// Climbing: The Gromlech problems are essentially slabby micro-routes, often with bad landings, so bring a soloing head. The Barrel is fingery and powerful and a good place to session something.

// Approach: These two lie on the hillside opposite the Cromlech Boulders (park as for them: see map on page 104). See the picture below. Cross the river and away you go. Can be boggy.

// Conditions: This side of the valley doesn't get much sun in winter and can be a cold place when the wind blows. However on the right day it is fine. In summer it gets the sun in the morning and evening.

// Info: North Wales Bouldering (N-Soul)

Pont y Gromlech

The Barrel

1	**Scary Rib** 6B	6	**Undercut Problem** 6A
2	**Hanging Flake** 5+	7	**The Minimum** 7A+
3	**Crack** 5	8	**Barrel Groove** 7B+
4	**The Seam** 6A+	9	**Barrel Traverse** 7B+
5	**Cracks** 4+		*Finish up 6.*

Pont y Gromlech ▶

The Pac Man Boulders

These lie on the outskirts of Nant Peris and give a small pocketful of problems across the grades. Although there's not much here the venue distinguishes itself by having very high quality rock, akin to Elephantitus and Caseg no less. Handy for anyone camping in Nant Peris without a car.

// Climbing: Short bulging problems on slopers and aretes mainly.
// Conditions: Quick drying and fairly sheltered.
// Info: North Wales Bouldering (N-Soul)

1	**Karma Sutra**	6C	*Sitter.*
2	**Crack**	4	
3	**Pac Man Arete**	6C+	
4	**Arete**	3	
5	**G Spotting**	7A	*Sitter.*
6	**Arete on Left**	3	
7	**Scoop**	4	

// Approach: See map on page 104. There is a footbridge behind the Vaynol pub in Nant Peris. Either cross this and walk towards the Pass for 650m or, easier, walk up the road until you see the boulders, ford the river and walk up the short hillside. The boulders are recognisable as a big split rock on top of a little hillock. (GPS 53.104177,-4.082923.)

15 min | 11 probs 3 - 8A+ best from 4 - 6C+ | slabby | steep

Si Johns on Left Flake Direct, 6A+ (problem 3). Estelle doesn't seem that impressed.
That's because, at the grade, you're not allowed that right-hand flake. Photo: Niall Grimes.

RAC Boulders

53.095764
-3.94796

A beautiful and relaxed roadside circuit for gentle year-round fun. Popular, but never crowded, and a good alternative for easier stuff when it's too crowded in the Pass.

A superb venue for lower-grade bouldering, in many ways nicer to the more popular hard shoulder that is the Cromlech Boulders. The adjacent road never feels as busy or as oppressive, the valley has a softer feel and the views are magnificent. Parking is always easy and it never seems to get as bitterly cold as it does in the Pass. A great choice any day, especially a sunny winter day.

// Climbing: Many styles of problem on vertical, steep or slabby rock. Generally quite fingery with lots of crimps, flakes, pockets and cracks. The problems are a nice size, and usually above flat grassy landings. Great for beginners and the hungover.

// Approach: See map on page 104. Park in a bay on the north side of the A4086. The boulders are 2 miles from Capel Curig and 2.5 miles from the Pen-y-Gwyrd. There is a small outcrop on the hillside above, and the boulders are visible from the road, only 100m away. The Snowdon Sherpa bus runs below the boulders (01286 678 333).

// Conditions: The boulders get loads of sun, don't seep, are very clean and quick drying. Sometimes a little bit polished. Some of the landings are a little boggy (around the Marsh area, duh!) but mostly dry, usually grassy and always flat. **Family friendly.**

// Info: North Wales Bouldering (N-Soul).

1 **Flake Arete** 5+
2 **Groove** 4+
3 **Left Flake Direct** 6A+ *Sitter.*
4 **Layaways** 4+
5 **Frontside Traverse** 6A+
   From white holds, traverse left to finish up the vague arete.
6 **Steep Wall** 5
7 **Flake** 2
8 **Wide Crack** 2
9 **Scoops** 3
10 **Thin Slab** 3+
11 **Scoops** 4
12 **RAC Arete Left** 4+
   The slabby side.
13 **RAC Arete Right** 4+
   The steep side.
14 **Crack** 5
15 **The Ramp** 6A *Ramp from sitter.*
16 **Corner** 4
17 **Marsh Arete** 6B+ *Sitter.*
18 **Wall** 5+
19 **Monkey up a Stick** 6A
   Crack and arete. 6B from a sitter.
20 **Marsh Dyno** 6C+
   Dyno from the good hold to the top.
21 6B *From the same starting holds as the dyno, swing up powerfully right to good holds.*
22 **Marsh Traverse** 6C+
   Start along the slab, drop around RAC Arete and continue along the steeper face with hands below the top. Continue past The Ramp then use the top of the boulder to gain the next crack (or stay low at 7A), and swing around Marsh Arete and continue to gain the next arete. Swing round this then traverse the next steep face to eventually gain the same easy slab you started on. Finish up RAC Arete.
23 **The Lightning Bolt** 6A
   Perverts, worried that they have enjoyed themselves too much, will love the HVS offwidth crack in the crag behind (visible in the background in the photo left).
24 **Viking Invasion** 6C
   The highball right arete of Lightning Bolt wall, starting left, finishing right. Bad landing: spotters needed. 6C+ from a sitter. The best problem here?

Frontside Boulder

Marsh Boulder

Marsh Boulder

The Lightning Bolt

Frontside Boulder   Marsh Boulder

Caseg Area

C 53.176323,-4.039485
BM 53.176399,-4.051037

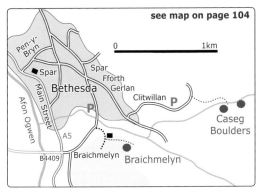

see map on page 104

A pride of proud boulders stashed away in the hillsides above Bethesda will give the discerning boulderer a half day's quality, especially in the middle grades. Great rock, beautiful setting, then a can of Coke and a packet of crisps from the Spar. Mmmmm.

Every now and again mountain rhyolite manages to rouse itself from pedestrian grab-and-pull fodder and mould itself into sublime rounded sculptures. Where jugs and edges are replaced with more sublime, subtler holds that must be thought about as much as pulled on. Where features are climbed, not just the grips that are littered about them. Such sculptures tend to come in small packages and in remote locations with small numbers of problems. In such cases, quality more than makes up for quantity. Caseg is one such venue. Braichmelyn is mighty fine too and a good venue if you have only an hour to spare.

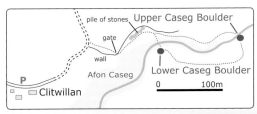

// **Climbing:** The Caseg Boulders feature either gentle slabby problems on smears or harder bulges on big open holds that require a bit of brute action. The Braichmelyn Boulder is a great contrast with a vertical face with technical, (sharp) crimpy problems. Both venues have great landings although a mat or two is nice to have just because of the height.

// **Conditions:** Quick drying and offering year-round climbing. The Caseg problems face all directions but the harder ones on the lower boulder, which are quite conditions-dependent, face north. The Braichmelyn Boulder faces west and gets the sun in evening. It also is amongst the trees giving much shade. Both venues are very sheltered although midges can be a problem beside the river. **Family friendly**.

// **Info:** North Wales Bouldering (N-Soul)

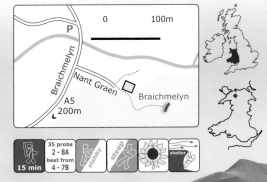

Upper Caseg

Lower Caseg

Lower Caseg

Lower Caseg

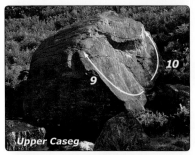

Upper Caseg

Upper Caseg

Braichmelyn

1 **Caseg Groove** 6C+ *Sit start is 8A.*
2 **Main Vein** 7C+
3 **The Gimp** 7B
4 **Nose** 6A+ **5** **Arete** 2
6 **Top Traverse** 3
7 **Groove** 4
8 **Arete** 6A *Layback the right arete.*
9 **Left Edge** 3 *Smear left to climb the arete.*
10 **Right Edge** 2 *Easy right side of slab.*
11 **Arete** 3 **12 Slab** 3
13 **Arete** 4+ *Swing onto the arete from the left.*
14 **Little Sitter** 6A+
15 **Slabby Right Wall** 4+
16 **Braichmelyn Traverse** 7B
17 **The Ramp** 6A *Fun highball finish.*
18 **The Crack** 7A
19 **Central Wall** 6C+
Come in from undercut at 7A.
20 **Braichmelyn Arete** 5+ *Sitter 7A.*

// Approach: Caseg Boulders: From Bethesda, wind up little streets to the village of Gerlan. Park at the end of the tarmac on Clitwillan in Gerlan. Parking here is very sensitive with local residents. If there is not enough space then park in the village below. Walk up the lane for 150m and cross the fourth gate on the right, at the apex of a bend and just past a wall. Head toward a new wooden gate in the corner, 40m away. Go through this and follow the inside of the fence leftwards, past two rows of large stones until the lower boulder comes into view. Either cross the stream here or carry on upstream for 140m to the upper boulder.

Braichmelyn: On the A5 just south of Bethesda, turn up into Braichmelyn (opposite B4409 junction) and continue for 250m and over a bridge. Park down the side-street just after the bridge. Walk back down Braichmelyn towards the A5 and after 50m turn up a small road (Nant Graen). There is a house at the end with a little wall to its right. This wall points to the boulder which is 100m away. So walk down right of the wall and scramble rightwards up a grassy bank then angle left again to reach the boulder, visible only at the last minute.

Andy Scott on The Pinch, 7A+ (problem 19). Photo: Niall Grimes.

Sheep Pen

53.139817
-4.029536

A classic mountain circuit for a nice day giving plenty of action across the grades in a beautiful location. Good burly climbing, and once you've trashed yourself you'll just want to sit down and enjoy the view.

A really beautiful place, especially on a warm summer day, with one of the coolest mountain circuits about. The rock is good and the location feels close to heaven. The quantity of classy problems with fine, strong lines means that Sheep Pen is one of the best mountain circuits about. Essential.

There's easily enough here for a solid half-day session, and once you've done the approach, you'll be in no hurry back down. Get a meathead or a boyfriend to carry up the mats, a picnic, and a bottle of wine, and turn it into a grand day out.

A5

P

Ogwen
2km ↘

P
P
scree
P

Sheep Pen

0   100m

see map on page 104

// Climbing: Generally steep and cranky on edges and slopers. Not high, but landings can be quirky, so bring a couple of mats.

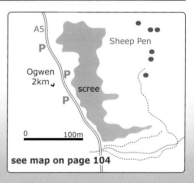

The Pinch ▶

Main Block ↑

◀ Klem's Bulge

Klem's Arete
▽

Klem's Arete

Klem's Bulge

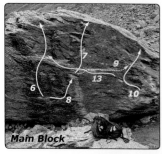

Main Block

Main Block

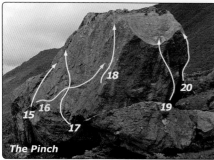

The Pinch

1   Groove 4+

2   Rib 6A+

3   Wall 5

4   Klem's Arete 6A+   *Sitter 6B+.*

5   Klem's Bulge 6C+

6   Jerry's Problem 7C+   *Sitter. Low edge to high left-hand gaston then on to better holds.*

7   Gnasher 7A   *Long shallow pocket to high, sharp pocket and top.*

8   Menace 8A   *Semi-sitter, left hand on Jerry's crimp, up to pod and then follow Gnasher.*

9   Compact Culture 8A+   *Start up Menace to the pod, then along the ramp and finish up Kingdom.*

10   Kingdom of Rain 7A   *From good sidepull pocket (as for Dog Shooter) traverse left and undercut to top.*

11   Dog Shooter 6B+   *From big sidepull pocket.*

12   Toe Dragon 6C+   *Sit start.*

13   Ding Dong's Traverse   *Start at the arete and traverse into and up Toe Dragon at 7B, Dog Shooter at 7B+, Kingdom at 7C. The mega-link, into Jerry's, is Kingdom of Pain, 7C+.*

14   Low Traverse 6A   *Traverse the lip of the low boulder to the right. Rockover at the highest point.*

15   Front Crack 5+

16   Weight Watcher 6C+   *From FC, traverse right on crimps and sidepulls then pull up to better holds and finish at the arete.*

17   Front Face 6B   *Start low in the niche and swing up and leftwards on good holds.*

18   Inch Arete 5+

19   The Pinch 7A+   *From a sit on crimpy edges. 6B from a stand.*

20   Groove 6A   *Groove using the ledge and arete.*

// Approach: Park at one of 3 close-by bays, 2.9 miles from Bethesda, or 1.3 miles from Ogwen Cottage. The boulders are on a plateau directly above, and invisible from below. Stout-trousered monsters of the Comici tradition may take the exquisitely painful direct route through the gorse above. Not recommended. Otherwise, walk along the A5 towards Ogwen. About 25m after the fence on the left ends is a stream. Follow a path on the grassy rib, generally 15m right of the stream. After about 150m (steep) a path breaks off up and left to arrive at the bouldery plateau.

// Conditions: Exposed, clean and quick drying. Some drainage on the Main Block. Would be bleak in bad weather and best enjoyed on a nice day. Very sunny.

// Info: North Wales Bouldering (N-Soul).

20 min | 45 probs 4 - 8A+ best from 6A - 8A | vertical | steep | | exposed

Andy Scott on Problem 12 (6C) on the Ogof Boulder. Photo: Niall Grimes

Caseg Fraith/Ogof

53.123419
-3.966365

A handy, quick-approach, quick-drying venue, with nearly an hour's worth of problems across the grades, and a burlier block ten minutes away for players.

Caseg Fraith is a very useful little venue for those commuting up and down Ogwen with an hour to spend. It is an almost-roadside outcrop of slatey rock (similar to the RAC), giving a few morsels across a spread of grades. It has a few friendly highballs up to 6B+ as well as enough steeper, powerful problems (from 6C+ to 7B) to keep Mongo happy. As well as the problems here, the hillside behind has a scattering of classy 6A – 6C+s (see NWB). 25 problems in total, counting the upper area.

A ten-minute walk away isthe Gallt yr Ogof boulder. This is better suited to session-weasels, with 10 fierce steep, sit-start problems from 6A – 8A+. The problems are a bit small here often with rules and sit starts to make sure you get value from your problem. A mat will keep feet and arse dry. There are other blocks visible on the hillside to the left, under the main crag. These hold the odd highball or obscure sitdown: worth a root around.

// Climbing: Caseg Fraith has a handul of easier, balancy and sometimes highball delights then a fistful of shorter, steeper and more powerful problems. The Fraith highballs are all above good landings, and for here, and the nearby Ogof boulder, you'd get away with just one mat. The problems on the Ogof boulder are short and steep sit-starters, and usually very fingery.

// Approach: Park in the grounds of Gwern Gôf Isaf farm (£2). Caseg Fraith is behind a university club hut. Go up a path leading to a wall to the right of the farm. Cross a steppy A-frame stile and follow the wall to the outcrop. For Gallt yr Ogof, go left to the track. Take the right-hand gate and follow on for 250m where there is a metal gate on the left marking a footpath towards the road and Helyg, the legendary CC Hut. 80m further on, and virtually opposite Helyg, bear directly right through the boggy heather to the rhomboid boulder, 80m back, and well down and right of the outcrops above.

// Conditions: Both quick drying although Caseg Fraith can hold the odd damp section on the steeper bits and can be a bit boggy underfoot. A bleak, drizzly wind, known as the Ogwen Jazz, is prone to trumpeting down the valley. **Family friendly.**

// Info: **North Wales Bouldering** (N-Soul)

3-12 mn | 40 probs 3 - 8A+ best from 4 - 7B | slabby | vertical | steep | exposed

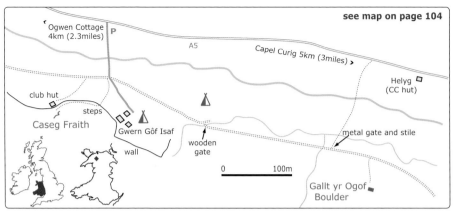

see map on page 104

Ogwen Cottage
4km (2.3miles)

A5

Capel Curig 5km (3miles)

Helyg
(CC hut)

club hut

steps

Caseg Fraith

Gwern Gôf Isaf

wall

wooden
gate

metal gate and stile

0   100m

Gallt yr Ogof
Boulder

Caseg Fraith

Caseg Fraith

1	**Arete** 4	
2	**Wall** 5+	
3	**Tall Wall** 6A+	
4	**Caseg Fraith Arete** 6B	
5	**Twin Aretes** 6A	

Monkey up the twin aretes.

6 **Deep Crack** 3
7 **Ramp** 4
8 **Ogwen Jazz** 6C+
Steep arete from a sitter.
9 **Boneyard** 7B
After the first moves of Ogwen

Jazz, slap along the shelf to do the dyno of the next problem.
10 **Oh Yeah** 6C+
From a sit start on the flake, gain the sloping ledge. A big dyno gains the lip and a still-tricky finish.

Gallt yr Ogof

Gallt yr Ogof

11 **Slab** 6A
12 **Arete** 6C *Sitter.*
13 **The Ramp** 6C+ *Sit start, starting with a left hand on the ramp and right on a low undercut.*
14 **Smackhead** 7C
Sit start. From a left hand

sidepull and little else, bust up to small crimps then finish direct or with the help of The Ramp.
15 **Arete** 6B *Start with left hand high, right hand low.*
16 **Diamond Eyes** 7C
Dyno from head-height holds.

17 **Sway On** 8A
Climb the wall on small sharp holds, starting on very low crimps.
18 **The Parade** 8A+
From a sitter, traverse left on head-height crimps to finish up Diamond Eyes.

Wales / Caseg Fraith

119

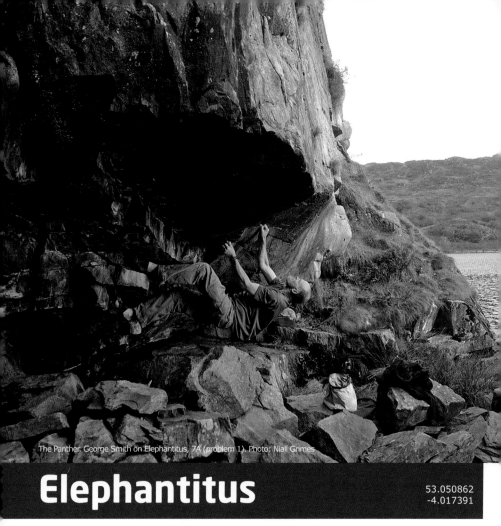

The Panther. George Smith on Elephantitus, 7A (problem 1). Photo: Niall Grimes

Elephantitus

53.050862
-4.017391

A lakeside jewel with a few hard gems for people who know what's what, and a savage boulder for krank-cranks.

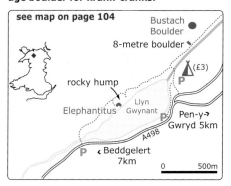

see map on page 104

Bustach Boulder

8-metre boulder

(£3)

rocky hump

Elephantitus

Llyn Gwynant

Pen-y-→
Gwryd 5km

A498

Beddgelert
7km

0   500m

If quality is your thing, then this is the place for you. Quantity merchants, you can piss off. The rock at Elephantitus is among the best rock in Snowdonia, a rough russet stone with high friction and cool rounded features. The cave, lapping on the gentle shores of Llyn Gwynant, holds a little nest of problems that are very much of the quality-over-quantity variety. It would be worth the walk just to do one of the problems, or even not to. The nearby and decidedly hardcore Bustach boulder lacks the charm of Elephantitus, but makes the area into more of a circuit for beasts.

// Climbing: Elephantitus has a royal flush of hard problems springing from a steep, almost roof-like grotto. Burly and slappy with a bullworkey feel. Slopes, flatties and sharp crimps. Not too high (3/4m) but the landings are quirky and a couple of mats are nice. Bustach has a steeper, more fingery, almost limestone feel to it, with six crimpy, pockety problems. All sit starts.

Elephantitus

Bustach

// **Approach:** Park at the beautiful Llyn Gwynant campsite (£3). Free parking out on the road at either end of the lake with a slightly longer walk. Cross the bridge and, for Elephantitus, turn left and follow the rough path for about 500m. After a tiny wooden bridge, branch immediately uphill and follow the path for 100m over the crest of a rocky, grassy dome. Scramble down to a rocky bay just beyond the dome and Elephantitus Cave is on your left. For Bustach, turn right at the first bridge in the campsite and follow the rough path for 400m to a jutting 8m prow of white rock. The Bustach boulder is 100m diagonally right, over a fence in the trees.

// **Conditions:** Both very sheltered. Elephantitus gets lots of sun. Can seep a little but generally gets great conditions. Bustach is tree-sheltered, seeps more and is best after a dry spell. Can be midgy.

// **Info: North Wales Bouldering** (N-Soul).

20 min | 11 probs 7A - 8A+ best from 7A - 8A | steep | roofs | | shelter | seepage

Elephantitus

1 **Elephantitus** 7A   *Finish in the break or carry on.*

2 **Going Down on an Elephant** 7B+
  From the small slot.

3 **Downset** 8A+
  Small slot to crimps and dyno. 8A from the crimps.

4 **Tusk** 7C+   *Prow from slot.*

Bustach

5 **Sick Happy** 7A

6 **Fagin** 7A   *Sitter.*

7 **Bustach Prow** 7B   *From very low jug.*

Elephantitus ▼   *campsite* ▶

Wales / Elephantitus

Old-school eliminate action in a rainproof roadside church where the stale whiff of 1980s testosterone still hangs in the air. Physical, woody-style climbing in an overhanging and overhung location. Sheep friendly. It really comes into its own as a welcome work-out venue on the odd wet Welsh day.

Hylldrem was popular in the 1980s before climbing walls had developed and in many ways is a bad version of a good indoor wall. Climbing-wise it's like an old museum to some mad thing in some old part of Prague that doesn't appear in the Lonely Planet but is all the better for that. The place where Jerry Moffatt started bouldering. Like Heavy Metal, cool, despite itself.

Him again.

Carraeg Hylldrem

52.967445
-4.063557

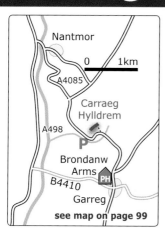

see map on page 99

// Climbing: A small wall of 15-degree-overhanging cellar problems and eliminates on crimps, flatties and undercuts. Natural lines from 6B – 6C and endless eliminates up to 7C are possible (inluding the legendary Six-Inch Dyno). Problems end 4–5m above a hard landing, so mats are needed. The rock is smooth, slatey stuff. Sharp edged but fairly skin friendly. It's not the nicest rock in the world but there's every chance that, given the wrong conditions, you could have a fab day here.

// Approach: Park in the roadside bay just north of a wee bridge, 1.6km (1 mile) from Garreg, 5km (3 miles) from the A498 junction. The bouldering wall is behind the trees above. Skirt the fence on the right, by the track, and wander left to the wall. The Snowdon Sherpa 97 bus runs from Porthmadog to Betws, via the road below the crag (0870 6082608).

// Conditions: South-east facing, getting the morning and early afternoon sun. Almost totally rainproof. No seepage.

Crispin's mate Matt. Photo: George Smith.

The Tubes

53.068806,
-3.790208

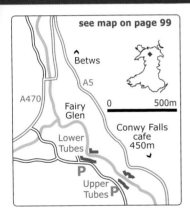

see map on page 99

Betws

A5

A470

Fairy
Glen

0   500m

Conwy Falls
cafe
450m

Lower
Tubes

P

Upper
Tubes P

**A genuine goldmine of Welsh esote-
ria. A parade of catacombs, S-bends
and watery graves hewn by a wild
river into a frictionless nightmare of
climbable spouts. Is it bouldering?
Is it hell, but it's in the book.**

I have been here. I might have seen it but
I'm not sure. I certainly didn't understand
it but have been bullied into including it in
this book. As a Philistine I didn't feel quali-
fied to describe the Tubes so a believer has
been delegated to tell you about it. Take it
away, the one, the only, Mr George Smith.

Upper Fairy Glen, or the Tubes, spend most of their time under water,
subject to the whims of the Afon Conwy. Lost in dense conifers, the
river thunders by, stones on the bed turning, slowly drilling their way
through the soft but perfect bedrock hereabouts. So only during the
hottest driest spells can we admire this aesthetic work in progress, as a
queer collection of scoops are revealed, with their unique smoothness.

At first this seasonal and textural inconvenience may put people off, as
everything is effectively much trickier than it looks. But some folk will
doubtless develop the same extreme passion for this peaceful place as
earlier pioneers like Crispin Waddy, Nick Dixon and Johnny Dawes.

The Tubes are mostly wider than one can bridge, requiring a whole
gamut of techniques. It all takes a bit to get used to. The exceptional
glassiness calls for a degree of power which due to the absence of wear
to fingertips, will kind of creep up and take you by surprise. Bare feet
or wet-suit booties may provide results on some stuff. Many problems
merit a top-rope though some tubes have gravel bases in a sustained dry
spell. There are also a number of lengthy traverses over the most beautiful pools. Encountering new levels of insecurity makes for a memorable
experience, especially when you are poised just above the deep dark
waters. A degree of coolness is guaranteed any which way!

// Approach: From Betws follow the A5 south towards Llangollen
then A470 towards Dolgellau. Follow the A470 for 1km and take an
unsignposted left turn down a single-track road (about 500m after
a bridge) which immediately crosses a bridge. Follow this for about
500m to a two-car parking spot on the right (150m after some cottages). The Lower Tubes are below, centred around a right-angled bend in
the river. For the Upper Tubes continue for 450m to a small pull-in on
the left, 30m before a crash barrier. The climbing lies below the pull-in
and the barrier. Good luck.   **// Info: Merionnydd** (CC).

Cae Du

52.632412
-4.115539

A seaside stretch of smoothness giving 70 problems mainly in the lower and middle grades. Not somewhere you'd travel for but a bit of holiday bouldering if you're at all in the area. Accepted, but not madly loved.

I've not made my mind up about Cae Du. The first time I went there it rained but I remember being impressed by the place and had it at the bottom of the same division that St Bees and Ysgo were in. The second time I went I was much less excited about it. It was raining even harder that day. See the topos, where the rocks are obviously streaming with water and the lens specked in raindrops. All very realistic.

The campsite's really cool – wet day by the shore with goldfish nets and yellow wellies-style of place – with a rough and woolly feel and is a nice place to stay if you're in the area. I think one of those Christmas-present-style books about cool campsites mentions it. If you are staying here, the boulders are without a doubt worth a visit.

// Climbing: The action of the sea has rounded off all the edges from Cae Du leaving lots of bulging problems, often following grooves, cracks and bulges with the help of lots of slopers. Powerful. Low friction rock. Lots of highball/easy soloing topouts, although the problems themselves feel small. Landings are flat but with big pebbles, so mats are a necessity.

// Approach: About 2 miles south of Llwyrgwril the A493 swings inland. On the apex of the bend take a little road off down to Cae Du Campsite. Pay here for parking (a civilised £1) then continue under the railway bridge and park. Gain the beach and follow it left (south) for 300m to the crag. Lots of train stations nearby.

// Conditions: Tidal, climbable a few hours around low tide. Very clean and solid. Often too hot in summer and damp in winter. West facing. **Family friendly.**

// Info: North Wales Bouldering (Ground Up)

1	**Arete** 3
2	**Arete** 6A
3	**Arete** 5+
4	**Traverse** 6B+ *Finish up 5.*
5	**Crack** 5
6	**Bulge and Groove** 4
7	**Groove** 3+
8	**Groove** 5+
9	**Hanging Arete** 7A
10	**Groove Layback** 6A+
11	**Traverse** 7A
12	**Gully** 5+
13	**Groove** 5
14	**Grooved Nose** 4
15	**Flake** 5+
16	**Arete** 6A+
17	**Hanging Arete** 6A
18	**Crack** 5+
19	**Roof** 6A
20	**Corner** 2
21	**Crack** 6A+
22	**Cae Du Crack** 6B *Sitter 7A+.*
23	**Teeter** 6B
24	**Groove** 6A
25	**Groove** 3
26	**Mantel** 7A
27	**Bulge** 5+ *From a sitter in the niche.*

Dolgellau
A493
A487
0   5km
Llwyngwril
Rhoslefain
B4405
Cae Du
Tal-y-Llyn Railway
A493
Tywyn
A487
see map on page 99

70 probs
3 - 7A+
best from
5 - 6B
6 min
slabby
steep
seepage
shelter
tidal

boulders ▶

campsite

railway line

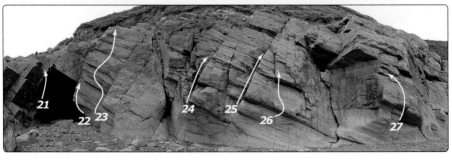

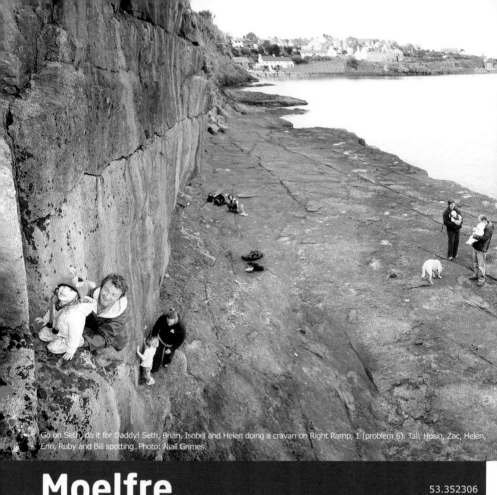

Go on Seth, do it for Daddy! Seth, Brian, Isobel and Helen doing a cravan on Right Ramp, 1 (problem 6). Tali, Hosin, Zac, Helen, Erin, Ruby and Bill spotting. Photo: Niall Grimes.

Moelfre

53.352306
-4.236367

A little wall of limestone on the outskirts of a pretty seaside village. A good holiday venue where, even if the kids can't climb very hard, they can still get into great danger. A happy place, and while the bouldering isn't the best in the world, it's still worth a visit if you're trapped on Anglesey.

Moelfre doesn't demand much from visitors and consequently it easily rewards a visit. Think of it as a place to have a day out with the chance of getting some climbing in. The problems give highballs across the grade all above a flat but hard landing.

The nearby village scores very high on the holiday front too, with a cracking cafe, a good pub, an ice cream man and a hamburger hatch. Add to this a lovely little pebble beach and a bunch of wee boats and you have a venue to ease the blood pressure.

// **Climbing:** Natural limestone outcrop. All the climbing is on a 6-metre high wall giving mostly vertical problems and a couple of slabs. Quite fingery on the steeper stuff and a wee bit sharp. Technically interesting. All the problems are highballs but the area still feels very friendly. The landing is flat rock but you wouldn't want to fall on it from any height without a bouldering mat, although one pad would be enough. A good place for a bit of a mooch about.

// **Approach:** Get to Moelfre (see map on page 99). Follow the coastal path east from just in front of the cafe for 100m then scramble down to the wall.

// **Conditions:** East facing and gets morning sun. Quick drying and doesn't seep much. High tides will affect the climbing. **Family friendly.**

4 min

14 probs
1 - 7A
best from
2 - 6B+

slabby

vertical

shelter

tidal

126   Wales / Moelfre

1	**Slabby Scoop** 2+	*6*	**Right Ramp** 1	*11*	**Groove and Ledge** 2
2	**Scoop Right-Hand** 2	*7*	**Slab with Borehole** 4	*12*	**Seams** 6B
3	**Vertical Groove** 3+	*8*	**Right-Trending Ramp** 4+	*13*	**Crack Layback** 6B+
4	**Rattly Arete** 2+	*9*	**Little Holds** 7A	*14*	**Fingery Ramp** 6C
5	**Left Ramp** 1	*10*	**Main Overhang** 6A		

bouldering

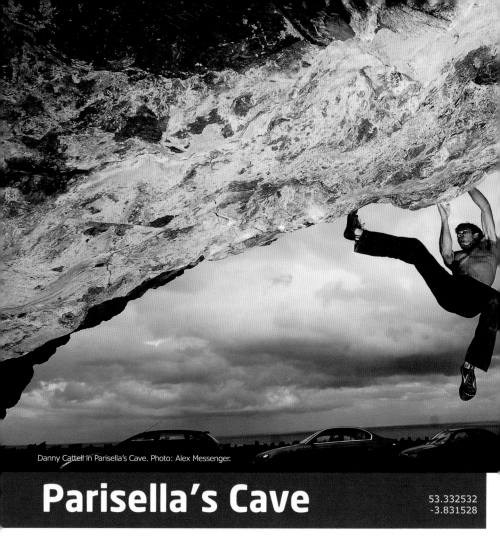

Danny Cattell in Parisella's Cave. Photo: Alex Messenger.

Parisella's Cave

53.332532
-3.831528

All hail the polished, slippery, dank, ugly, dusty, goat-shitted, wee-smelling Mecca of power-stamina. A rainproof grotto, heaven or hell, depending on how you feel about glassy pinches. A venue with fiercely loyal devotees who would have this alone on their desert island yet which will cause the heart of the holiday boulderer to sink when they pull back the curtains to see horizontal rain and realise to their dismay that there is only one option: the Cave. Again.

The best climbing in Wales some say, with the highest concentration of hard steep problems in the country. Endless lines, eliminates and link-ups giving a lifetime of climbing for the hardcore. Love it or hate it: I know I do.

A bit uninviting on first acquaintance, but by your twentieth visit it doesn't seem too bad, I hear. Initially it will feel depressingly desperate. But persevere; get the knack, the power and the fitness and the Cave will yield some great problems. Britain isn't overendowed with steep climbing and so this is a place of pilgrimage for roof monsters. Split Infinity is the smaller cave just behind Parisella's. Pillbox Wall is a less steep section of cliff along the road, with desperates of a more crimpy nature.

For refreshments Parisella's Cafe does crisps, coffee and ice cream while Llandudno has plenty of fleshpots and, on weekend evenings, flesh. The best pub is the Kings Head at the bottom of the tramway (chippy opposite).

// Approach: The crags lie along the Marine Drive, a scenic toll road that runs along the headland of the Great Orme. Follow signs from the A55 to Llandudno, then towards the town centre and head for the seafront. Go in the direction of the pier, past the Grand Hotel, and continue to the start of the toll road. Most parking in Llandudno is paying, so climbers generally pay the £2.50 toll and park considerably right beside the cave which is about 150m after the tollgate. For Pillbox, contine for another 500m. Going round a headland the road starts to dip and about 70m after this is a ruined concrete shelter, about the size of a posh person's fridge. The bouldering is behind this. Please note, the Marine Drive is one-way, so you must continue around the headland when you're finished. Train station in Llandudno.

// Conditions: Parisella's is almost totally rainproof. However condensation and seepage can leave damp patches that might make problems unclimbable. It can all feel a bit stoic on cold wet blustery days when you have come here because you can't climb anywhere else and you find yourself struggling with some hellish sit start as the wind blows up your hole. Having said that it most often enjoys good conditions and can be a saviour when the weather turns a bit Cymru or when it's too hot. Gets summer sun till 11am. Pillbox is also fairly rainproof and sits on a more exposed point of the headland making it a bit fresher but still with very reliable conditions.

// Info: North Wales Bouldering (N-Soul);
Parisella's Cave (Ground Up).

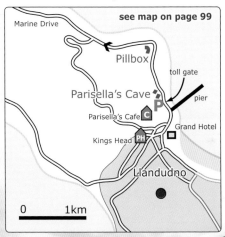

// Climbing: The Cave is a quarried limestone niche covered in crimps, pinches, sidepulls and undercuts. The grips are big, but seldom feel like jugs. As such they demand a dynamic style and tons of body-tension to make them work. Moves are desperate on first tries and often depend on clever footwork, funky positions and getting everything exactly right. Problems are sustained and it makes a great training venue. Sometimes a bit highball and your body can be horizontal resulting in bone-shaking falls. A few pads are useful. Best for hard sessioning. It's worth noting that problems are not really eliminates as they follow the lines shown using whatever holds or sequences work best. Polished and skin friendly.

The Pillbox area is a twenty-degree-overhanging wall of white limestone with a good bunch of natural lines and link-ups. Again, it is fairly hardcore.

Parisella's Cave Left

Split Infinity

Pillbox

Wales / Parisella's Cave

Parisella's Cave Right

Parisella's Cave

1 Left Wall Traverse 7B
From a low sitter. Can be done from the horizontal shothole at 7A.

2 Rock Attrocity 7C
From good a diagonal hold follow a line past drilled pockets to a juggy slot.

3 Bonnie 8A+
A highball line starting from the finishing slot of RA.

4 The Incredible Bulk (Part II) 7C+
From the juggy slot. Start up Lou Ferrino at 8B.

5 Cave Life 8A
Go left from a low jug, passing under Rock Attrocity then left to gain and finish along LWT.

6 Lou Ferrino 7C+
The hanging ramp, and holds out left, from a sitter to the RA finishing slot.

7 Trigger Cut 7C+
Start at an obvious slot with left and poor pinch with right. Start up Lou at 8B: Director's Cut.

8 Parisella's Roof 7A+ *The break to jugs.*

9 Beaver Cleaver 7B
From the rail, swing right to a sloper on the lip then continue up and left.

10 Clever Beaver 7A+
Rail, into undercuts, out to big sloper then press on for square jug.

11 Beaver Right-Hand 6C
From sitdown jugs move out and climb direct.

12 Cave Right-Hand 6B+
From a sitter, follow bad holds to good holds.

13 Pilgrimage 8B+
Monster. Reverse Left Wall Traverse, reverse Cave Life to gain Rock Attricity and follow this. Traverse right and finish up Beaver Cleaver.

Split Infinity

14 Split Traverse 6A+ *Left from the corner.*

15 Pillar Finish 6B
Alternative finish from hands on the sloping ledge.

16 Slim 7A+ *From the juggy break reach to the lip then gain the next break above.*

17 Bellpig 7C *Finish on jug on left.*

18 Pump Traverse 6B
Start in the corner then come out to gain the high line and come down easier ground. Link into a reverse of Split Traverse at 6B+.

19 Split Youth 7B+
From a bunched sitter gain the lip then press on leftwards, passing another slot. Move leftwards into the corner via the horizontal crack.

20 Lickety Split 7B *Gain the lip as per Split Youth then climb to the break.*

21 Rock Bottom 7A
From the same start traverse right then cross the roof on poor holds leading to an easier rightwards finish.

Pillbox

22 Whisky Bitch 7B
Crank up right to edges (from standing) then right to gain and follow the horizontal crack then jump off or downclimb. 7B+ from a sitter on crimps.

23 The Greek 7A
After the first move of Whisky Bitch go back left to follow the crack to better holds.

24 Gaskins Problem 8B *Sitter.*

25 Pillbox Original 7A
Sit start on flake. 6C+ from a stand.

26 Drink Driving 8A+
Start up 24 and finish on easy ground on far left.

27 Chocolate Wall 7B *To the Whippy flake.*

28 Mr Whippy 7A+ *Direct to the juggy flake.*

Byron Orde on Be Ruthless, 7C (problem 6). Photo: Matt West.

A hell-hole of power for Mold-based roof-monsters. An everdry suntrap with a fistful of desperates, on solid, good quality limestone. Hardcore, but a pretty spot.

A small chapel of power, useful for worshippers without the time to make it to the Mecca that is Parisella's Cave. A bunch of brutal, fingery and arm-busting projects for crazed young men. The setting is rather pleasant, nestled beside a river in a little country park, but you'll hardly notice it. A short approach will ensure your legs don't develop. Big up to Sam Cattell who has done most development. Thanks to Matt West for info here.

// Climbing: Limestone roof. Slopers, pinches and crimps. Problems end at 3-4 metres and need jumping off. Landing is flat but hard. You'll need a mat.
// Approach: Follow the A494 south from Mold. 800m south of the Rainbow Inn turn right towards Pantymwyn (good bus service). Follow this road for a mile to a crossroads with a church and pub (the Hand). Turn left and after 800m, as the road bends right, turn down Cefn Bychan Road and park courteously on the right. Take a tarmac track straight on (green walking sign), past a cattle grid, and as it swings left after 120m, take a small footpath straight on over a stile. This leads directly to the top of a deep Gorge belonging to The Devil. Skirt this on the right and follow the path to the floor of the gorge. The climbing is in the gorge, on the Robert Duval wall 20m right and the main cave, 35m right.
// Conditions: Sharply overhanging, staying dry in most rain. Some seepage after rain but climbing possible year round. Very sunny. Great for bad weather, or for a bit of winter action. **Family friendly.**
// Info: **Clwyd Limestone** (Rockfax); loads of info on new developments on **northwalesbouldering.com**.

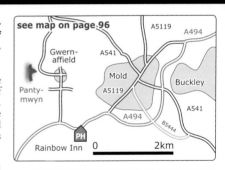

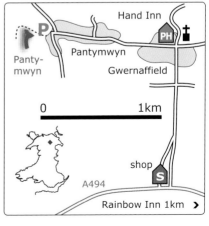

Pantymwyn

53.173068
-3.209295

1 Under The Bridge 7B+
On the steep, right wall of Devil's Gorge, just at the entrance, and under the bridge, is a head-height roof. Start from undercuts, cross the roof and follow the bulging rib to jugs.

2 Robert Duval 7A *Sitter.*

3 July Rain 7A
Start on a couple of pockets and traverse left just above ground level.

4 Faith Healer Variant 7A
Sitter.

5 Under Pressure 8A *Sitter.*

6 Be Ruthless 7C
Use undercuts in the big hole to reach a good pocket with the right hand. Move left to the lip then back right to match a triangular flake to finish.

7 Pantys Down 7A+
The opposite of Be Ruthless, getting the good pocket with the left hand, moving right then back left to the finishing flake.

8 Pantys Down Sitter 7B
Move up and join the original from jugs at the bottom of the hole. Come from undercuts lower, on the lip of the hole, at 7C+.

9 Thug Mentality 7B+
Start as for Panty's Down and continue traversing along the lip to finish matched on a big flat jug.

10 Mental Extension 7B
Starting from the flat finishing jug of Thug Mentality, traverse right to the finishing holds of Sparks.

11 Thug Mental 7C+
Link Thug Mentality into Mental Extension.

12 Gasoline Straight Up 7B+
Sitter. The original version, Gasoline (D'ya know what I mean?) starts as for Firestarter/Sparks and is also 7B+. 7A+ from a standing start.

13 Sparks 7C+
Sitter. Move up on jugs to get a chipped three-finger slot with the right hand. Traverse the lip leftwards and move up and right to finish matched in the break. 7B from stand.

14 Firestarter Variant 7A+
Start as for Firestarter then move up and left to the finishing holds of Gasoline.

15 Firestarter 7A
Sitter. Start as for Sparks to the chipped slot then continue up and exit right.

16 Burnt Ember 6C+ *Sitter.*

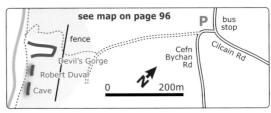

see map on page 96

P bus stop

fence

Devil's Gorge

Robert Duval

Cave

Cefn Bychan Rd

Cilcain Rd

0   200m

35 probs
6C - 8A
best from
7A - 8A

12 min

steep

roofs

shelter

seepage

rain proof

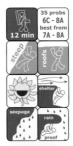

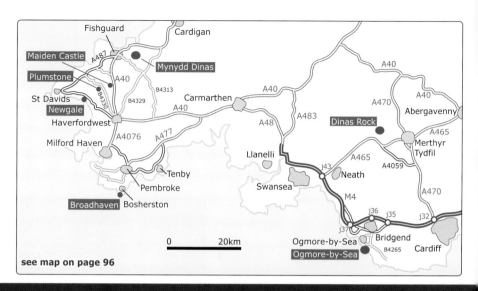

Fishguard
Cardigan
Maiden Castle
A487
Plumstone
Mynydd Dinas
A40
B4313
St Davids
B4329
B4330
Carmarthen
A40
A40
Newgale
A40
Haverfordwest
A48
A483
Dinas Rock
A470
A40
Abergavenny
A465
Milford Haven
A4076
A477
Merthyr
Tydfil
A465
Llanelli
A465
A4059
A470
Tenby
Pembroke
j43
Neath
Swansea
M4
Broadhaven
Bosherston
j36
j35
j32
j37
Bridgend
Ogmore-by-Sea
B4265
Cardiff
Ogmore-by-Sea

0   20km

see map on page 96

South Wales

Huw Gilbert highballing in the Trench, Ogmore-by-Sea (page 143). Photo: Jo Gilbert.

James Squire at Dinas Rock (page 140). Photo: James' Mum.

Mynydd Dinas

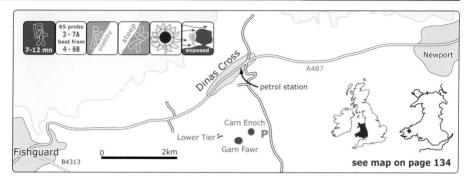

65 probs
3 - 7A
best from
4 - 6B

7-12 mn

slabby

steep

exposed

Newport

Dinas Cross

A487

petrol station

Carn Enoch

P

Lower Tier

Garn Fawr

Fishguard

0   2km

B4313

see map on page 134

An obscure little gem in a remote, yet handy, location with lonely exposure and enough at your grade to justify a day off for nut-placers. A lovely place. Be nice to it.

Two bluffs of heavily weathered mountain rock that deliver a half-day session across most grades. A lower outcrop gives a good bunch of warm-ups. The main crag has a powerful spiritual presence with a good circuit of problems as well as a couple of harder tests. Magic. And guess what. This is where they got the rock for Stonehenge.

The setting is grand and surprisingly remote, high above Cardigan Bay. The rock is good mountain rock and gives a great range of styles from paddy slabs to crimpy highballs. The crag is not well known so has an unspoiled nostalgia; bring an open mind and a soft brush. Thanks to Steve Quinton for help and info.

While the crag is far away from centres of population, it's a great place to go when on a long tradding trip to Pembroke. For those wanting a change of scene for half a day, the car park is about 40-45 minutes from Bosherton and the walk-in is short. Its moorland wildness will be a nice change from vertical limestone and makes a great place for a family picnic.

// Climbing: Quite fine-grained mountain rock giving some slabby, some steep, climbing. The place is little-documented but there's probably about 65 problems from the easiest up to about 7A. All styles, including slabs, aretes, bulges and overhanging walls. Good grassy landings generally and one pad and a spotter would suffice. Even the crag's most impressive feature, a 6-metre-high overhanging wall, undercut at its base, is hardest at the start and above a sweet little pitch. Natural lines run steadily up to about 6C then, with only a little discipline, a few 7A-ish crankers. Below Garn Fawr is a sweet lower tier with a dozen easier problems and an awesome view of the sun setting.

// Approach: From Fishguard take the A487 east towards Newport to reach Dinas Cross. Fifty metres past the filling station (about 1.3 miles from the first sign for Dinas Cross and about 2 miles from Newport), turn south, away from the sea, down a road signposted 'Cwm Gwaun and viewpoint'. Wind up and along this for 1.5 miles. 200m after passing a white-painted stone inscribed 'Crug Las', park on the right. The lower outcrop (Carn Enoch, meaning 'the snoozing hippos') can be seen here. The main crag (Garn Fawr) can be seen from that, about 7 minutes away.

Diagonals

Big Wall

Lip Traverse

The Cave

Garn Fawr

// **Conditions:** The crag is high and exposed with all the good and bad that brings: it will catch any weather going, especially the wind. Sometimes a little dirty and on bleak days can be slow drying. Bring a soft brush, but be very gentle with it. Best on a nice summer day. Problems face all directions so there will usually be something in the sun, the shade or the shelter. **Great for families.**

// **Info:** See the Pembrokeshire Bouldering Guide at **climbers-club.co.uk**. Steve Quinton is working on a comprehensive guide for the CC.

// **Access:** Don't take dogs on the moor.

1	**Little Boulder Arete** 5+		**11**	**Wall** 6A
2	**The Nose** 6A		**12**	**Swing in the Groove** 4
3	**The Ramp** 4		**13**	**Rememberance** 4
4	**Freddie's Nightmare** 6B		**14**	**Thin Wall** 6B
5	**Pete's Slab** 6A+		**15**	**Cave Left** 6A
6	**Easy Crack** 5		**16**	**Thrutch** 5+
7	**Crack** 4+		**17**	**Death Wall** B1
8	**The Rail** 6A+		**18**	**Offwidth** 5+
9	**Lip Traverse** 6B		**19**	**Face Route** 6A+
	Sitter. Finish up arete.		**20**	**Sam's Arete** 6C+
10	**Undercut Arete** 4		**21**	**Speed Trap** 6A
	Step in from the boulder or go or direct at 6A+.		**22**	**Gargoyle** 6B
			23	**Offwidth Roof** 6B
				Sit start.

Carn Enoch

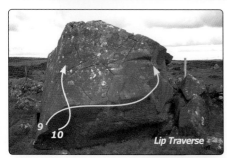

Lip Traverse

Diagonals

The Cave

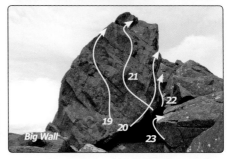

Big Wall

Plumstone/Maiden

MC 51.888028,-4.971871
PS 51.870059,-5.024625

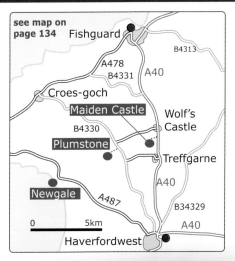

see map on page 134

Plumstone

Possible venues for Pembroke visitors desperate to get a bit of scrambling and easy bouldering in. Quick easy access belies the remote and commanding situation. Nice places to be although from a pure bouldering point of view they're not much cop.

The nearby outcrops of Maiden Castle and Plumstone are best seen as somewhere to go for a couple of hours away from Pembroke limestone. Think family picnics with a bit of scrambling and bouldering thrown in. I didn't think much of the bouldering but the writer of the CC webguide to the area (climbers-club.co.uk) is very keen on it so maybe I just didn't get it. The two venues are very similar and of the two I preferred Maiden Castle.

// **Climbing:** The heavily featured quartzy rhyolite is not a natural bouldering medium. Jagged walls, aretes and cracks give positive crimpy climbing above generally alright landings. Probably good for a relaxing low-grade exploratory circuit with a bit of easy soloing thrown in. With this approach each venue probably holds about 25 problems.

// **Approach: Plumstone:** From Haverfordwest take the B4330 for 5.5 miles. At the summit of the moor a bridalway on the western side leads to an open car park. The rocks are 100m from here. **Maiden Castle:** Half a mile south of Wolf's Castle (a mile north of Treffgarn) there is a car park on the west side of the road with a mill. At the south of this a small dead-end road curls uphill. Follow this for 200m then park on the right at the end of the public road. Follow the footpath on the opposite side of the road for 30m then break right up a smaller path to reach the crag after 25m.

// **Conditions:** The rocks are in an exposed situation. They are very clean and quick drying but can feel windy. Rocks face all directions, giving sun, shade or shelter somewhere on the crag.

// **Info:** See the Pembroke Bouldering Guide at **climbers-club.co.uk**

5 min | range 3 - 6C+ best from 4 - 6A | vertical | steep | | exposed

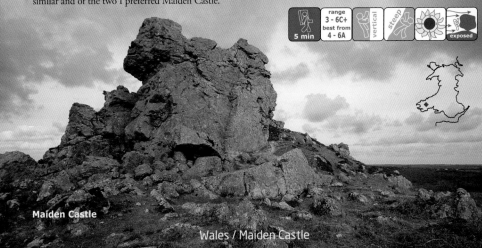

Maiden Castle

Pembroke

The artwork below is entitled 'Broadhaven: The despair of the boulderer'. Why? Well basically, Pembroke is not a great spot for bouldering. No doubt you're here for the top-quality tradding but if you did have a pad where would you go?

There were reports of sport to be had on the super-scree at the base of Trevallen crag. However, the thought of leading out on Barbarella with a bouldering mat on your shoulder might make this one for a limited market.

And so to Broadhaven, the Fontainebleau of east Tenby. As you go down the steps, the rocky ridge on the opposite side has a few nubbins. A shallow cave on the left could give a few desperate eliminates up to 6C. A bigger cave to the right is deeper and steeper and if it dried out would give more of the same. A roof to the right is curious. The whole place is best seen as a way to justify a bit of a paddle.

There's no need for any approach maps. Broadhaven is just outside Bosherston and Trevallan is where Barbarella is.

A bit further away, but more in keeping with this section than the next Maiden Castle area, is **Newgale Beach** (see map on the left). At the far north end of the beach, and just out of sight, are four caves that hold about ten problems based around rising, sloping, undercut ramps. These give problems up to about 7A/B. Climbing is possible here for 3 hours either side of low tide. The approach is under water before the climbing so keep an eye on the tide. The caves seep a lot and a towel is useful. The landings are stony so bring a pad.

Also rated here is Dolph's Boulder, a sandstone block at the south end of the beach with a half dozen problems from 6A to 7B. To find it walk south along the beach past the prominent headland and into the maze of small zawns that point out to sea from that point on. The bouldering is hidden away amongst this jumble. You may walk around and think there is nothing there, however persistence reaps rewards.

For both these venues google 'redclimbing blogspot newgale' for topos.

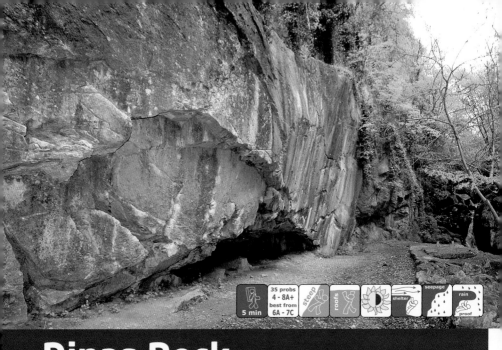

Dinas Rock

51.759394
-3.578711

Bring your burl. The powerhouse of South Wales bouldering with a rabble of hard forceful problems on superb rock. Great place, and it stays dry in the rain. One of the best limestone venues in the country.

A little venue with a looming, impressive and foreboding character. One of those places that when you see it, you think 'Oh wow!' It provides the local who has spent the winter hanging off that one-inch edge a chance to see if it has all paid off; it is also worth bearing it in mind if you are on your way home from a wet weekend in Pembroke and your biceps don't feel that they have had a chance to express themselves. If this is the case, and you are heading back to the M50, the detour via Merthyr Tydfil and Abergavenny is only 20 minutes longer than the M4 way. Thanks to Kev Hughes in this section.

Dinas Rock, or more particularly Kenelgarth Wall, is top ten as far as UK limestone bouldering is concerned. The rock is high quality with solid, interesting holds that aren't even too badly polished. Gymnastic and burly in a nice setting, it's well worth the detour. Problems are mostly the work of locals Kev Hughes, Liam Fyfe and a once-resident German, Thomas Stark.

// Climbing: Powerful and gymnastic climbing, very much toward the sterner end of the spectrum. Problems are sit starts under a roof leading onto a 15-degree wall. Finish at obvious good holds at 4 – 5 metres. Lots of burly stuff on crimps and sidepulls and the ability to jam won't hurt either. Good strong lines and the possibility for lots of eliminates. Brilliant for power-sapping traverses. The landings are good but you'll definitely want a pad or two to take the sting out of the hard ground.

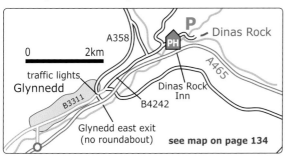

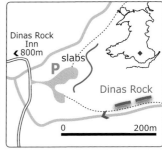

// **Approach:** On the A465, the village of Glynnedd (Glynneath) has two exits: a western one, with a roundabout and an eastern one, with a slip road. Take the eastern one and follow for 150m to traffic lights. Turn right and after 200m take a left turn onto the B4242 (signposted Pont-Nedd-Fechan). Follow this for a mile then, as the 4242 bends left up a steep hill by a pub, go straight on a smaller road through houses. After 700m the road turns right over a bridge and after this park in

the car park on the left. Head to the right of the wire-covered slabs and walk upstream for 300m to see the wall on your left.

// **Conditions:** The wall faces south-east and gets sun till late afternoon. It can get hot on summer days although a chilly wind can blow down the valley. It can get midge-ridden in the summer. **Family friendly.**

// **Info:** See <u>swbg.co.uk</u> for full topos and a great collection of YouTube movies by Kev Hughes.

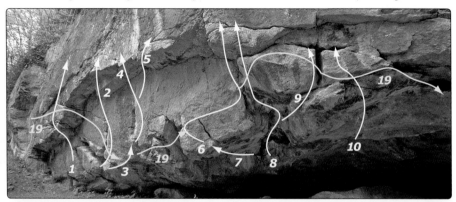

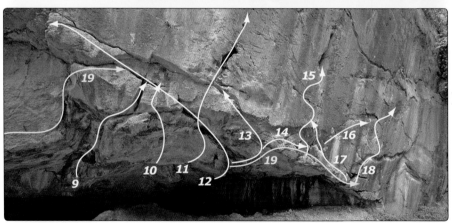

1	**Achilles** 6B+		**11**	**Great White Stark** 6A+
2	**Byte Size** 5+			*Undercuts to big polished sloper and up to a very high finish.*
3	**Banana Boy** 7A		**12**	**Poodle Traverse** 6A
	Low traverse into Monkey Boy.		**13**	**Riding Hannah** 7A
4	**Monkey Boy** 6B			*From the big hold to a delta of small crimps, moving up then left to good holds.*
	The crack and jugs on right.		**14**	**Fat Cat Roof** 7C
5	**Puppy Love** 6A+			*Move right from the crimps on Riding Hannah and finish up Honey Pot. Finish up Launch Pad at 7C+: The Riot.*
6	**Gentle Jess** 6C+		**15**	**Honey Pot** 6C+
7	**Gentle Jess Sitter** 7A			
8	**The Groove** 7A+			
9	**Infidel** 7A			
10	**The Mongrel Mob** 7A+			
	Move out from the big hole via small crimps.			

16 **Carpenter's Apprentice** 8A+ *Follow Fat Cat Roof then go diagonally up to the finish of Launch Pad.*

17 **The Blessing** 7A *From holds on the lip just left of 18. Sitter is Life of Fife, 7C.*

18 **Launch Pad** 7A *Finish at a good hold near a bolt.*

19 **Wife of Fyfe** 8A+ *Liam Fyfe's awesome power-endurance traverse taking in most of the hard climbing on the wall; F8b+ route grade.*

Tim Wilkinson on Daylight Robbery, 7B (problem 2). Photo: Dave Ripley.

Ogmore-by-Sea

51.460612
-3.631411

A unique parade of seawashed limestone that, if it's to your taste, might well give you a great session. Sometimes lowball, sometimes highball. Tidal, and well worth it if you're in the area.

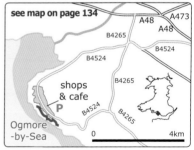

see map on page 134

Big thanks to Tim Wilkinson and Rob Sanderson in this section. Below the surf-happy village of Ogmore-by-Sea lies some of the lowest-friction bouldering you will find. The Daylight Robbery area has its neo-classic lowball slope-shuffle as well as a few up problems through it. The wall opposite holds a bunch of steep, 5-metre high problems in the 4 – 6B range. Go right (north) along the coast for 50m to find Hardy's Bay, 15 problems, 4 – 7A. Four hundred metres left (south) is the Trench, a box canyon of sloping holds and groovy fissures on the slipperiest rock in the union. Here, the barnacle is your friend, sometimes your only friend. Treat my grades here with suspicion. It's a very hard venue to get info on. There is a scattering of other easier stuff, including juggy traverses, between Daylight Robbery and the Trench.

// Climbing: A variety. Some harder slope tests around Daylight Robbery and some easy overhanging walls on jugs, as well as another area 50 metres north. The Trench itself gives 6-metre highballs. The starts are steep, the holds are imaginary slopers and the rock is like a frictionless version of slate. Be prepared not to get up anything. The landings are perfect – just as well. The lowballs need pads because of a rocky landing.

// Approach: Get to Ogmore-by-Sea. From Franklin's Cafe (01656 880661), cross the road and head straight for the sea along an old wall. Daylight Robbery is directly below. For the Trench, head left (south) from here on the path along the wall. 300 me-

tres after the wall ends there is a wood and stone bench on the right. The Trench is directly below.

// Conditions: Daylight Robbery has tricky conditions. Tidal, and accessible an hour before and three hours after low tide. Can be dank under the roof and a towel would be a good idea to dry holds. A low sun and breeze help. West facing. The Trench is tricky too but not as bad. Tidal, walls face north-west and south-east. Can be damp. Sand levels vary. **Family friendly.**

// Info: swbg.co.uk

1   Robbed Arete 6B+ *From semi-sitting on sloper and sideways crimp. Super-low start goes from a slot at the back of the roof at 7B+.*

2   Daylight Robbery 7B
From the start of 1 to finish up 6.

3   Hooby's Roof 7A
From jugs at the back of the roof.

62 probs
3 - 7B
best from
6A - 7B

5-10 min

vertical | roofs | seepage | shelter | tidal

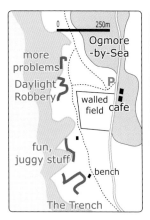

Daylight Robbery

Trench West Wall

Trench East Wall

4 Hooby's Special 7B
Start up 3 then traverse left to finish up 1. The best problem here?

5 Hip Hop Paperboi Scandal 7A+ *From back of the roof, up to the pocket on lip with the right, and then up the groove.*

6 Achilles Heel Hook 6B+
Sit start with incut edge for left, sloper for right.

7 Arete 5

8 Corner 5

9 Move Right 5+

10 Blunt Arete 6C

11 Scoop Dragon 6C
Or maybe 7C?

12 Sandy 6B *Crack.*

13 Slipperman 6A
Exit the groove of 14 to climb the arete on the left.

14 Groove 5+

15 Descent Route 2

16 Oyster 6C

17 Arete 6C

18 Rib 6C

19 Wall 4

20 Easy Way 3

21 Dartford Runnel 5

22 Crack 6A+

23 Arete 6B

The North West

Martin Boysen on Super Wall, 5, Frodsham (problem 6, page 181). Photo: Niall Grimes.

The bouldering in the North West doesn't appear on many scorecards. Let's have a look at what's on offer to understand why. Grotty, loose, dark, midge-ridden holes in the ground that allow rough scrambling; horrific finger-rippers on sandstone sumps overlooking 2000AD hellscapes of combustion and pipeage; remote gritstone at the end of a long uphill slog; small limestone huffs that often contain some of the defining events in human achievement.

So you may not have climbed in Lancashire and the Cheshire area. It's all easy to dismiss. But ask yourself this: how come these two areas have produced some of the best climbers in the land? Hank Pasquill, Joe Healey, Al Rouse, Mark Leach, Paul Pritch, Tony Mitchell, Ian Vickers, Gaz Parry, Jamie Cassidy, Naomi and Jordan, Pete Hurley, all the Smittonses and your man, Ryan. There's something going on over there. Perhaps Lancashire is to British bouldering what Slovenia is to high-altitude mountaineering: if you can survive day-to-day life, then being on the north face at 8,000 metres isn't that bad.

The sandstone around the Mersey Estuary is a conoisseur's delight with lots of fingery, technical highballs very much there to be savoured. An area with a long and rich bouldering heritage. Hugh Banner, Martin Boysen, Tom Leppert, Al Rouse, Tim Carruthers, Mike Collins, Phil Davidson, Joe and Gaz Healey, Stevie Haston, Mick Adams, Richard Hessian, Ben Farley, Pete Chadwick and Andy Popp are some of the names to thank for development there.

The South Lakes Limestone around Silverdale is the ultimate, if dusty, museum to the abilities of John Gaskins. Gaskins, the John Gill figure of British bouldering, totally dominated the area around the turn of the century. He added a good number of problems and some of them, while not always appealing in aesthetic terms and sometimes quite eliminate, remain even today the hardest bits of climbing done in the world. All hail.

Greg Chapman has explored and added numerous problems to the South Lakes area that, while not quite the same level of difficulty as Gaskins' (what is?) are the match in terms of quality. However, as much as his development, his championing the area in the form of his Lakesbloc website has done more than anything to put the area on the map. It has been a big help in making this book.

Below that you're into Lancashire proper with its dark satanic quarries, with Longridge being especially appealing to pump-heads. Generations of locals who have performed centre-stage on the big Yorkshire limestone crags – Dave Kenyon, Mark Leach, Tony Mitchell, Ian Vickers, Neil Carson, Gaz Parry and others – dutifully spent their time at Longridge, back and forth, back and forth, getting what they needed to hang on steep limestone forever.

Brownstones, where Hank Pasquill and his cronies worked out their eliminates, Thorn Crag, a beautiful upland grit crag, and Heysham Head (seaside grit) complete the Lancashire scene.

Adam Lincoln on Texas Hold 'Em, 7B+, at Trowbarrow (problem 3, page 155). Photo: Adam Lincoln collection.

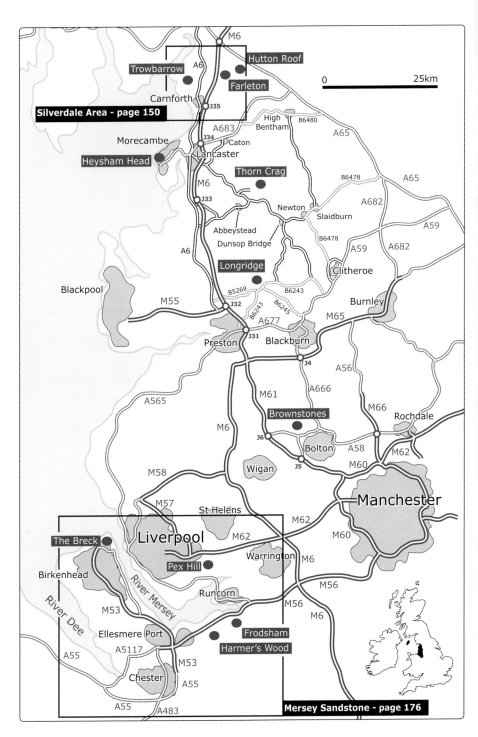

0   25km

Silverdale Area – page 150

Trowbarrow
Hutton Roof
A6
Farleton
Carnforth
J35

Morecambe
A683
High Bentham
B6480
A65
J34
Caton
Lancaster
Heysham Head
Thorn Crag
B6478
A65
M6
J33
Newton
Slaidburn
A682
Abbeystead
Dunsop Bridge
B6478
A59
A682
A6
A59
Longridge
Clitheroe
Blackpool
B5269
M55
B6243
A677
Burnley
J32
B6243
B6245
Preston
J31
Blackburn
M65
J4
A56
A565
M61
A666
M66
Rochdale
Brownstones
M6
J6
Bolton
A58
M62
M58
J5
Wigan
M60
M57
St Helens
Manchester
The Breck
Liverpool
M62
M62
M60
Birkenhead
Pex Hill
Warrington
M6
River Mersey
Runcorn
M56
River Dee
M53
M56
M6
Ellesmere Port
Frodsham
A5117
Harmer's Wood
M53
Chester
A55
A55
A55
A483

Mersey Sandstone – page 176

148

Gill Peet on Push to ythe Prolapse, 6C+, at Craig-y-Longridge (page 172, problem 13). Photo: David Simmonite.

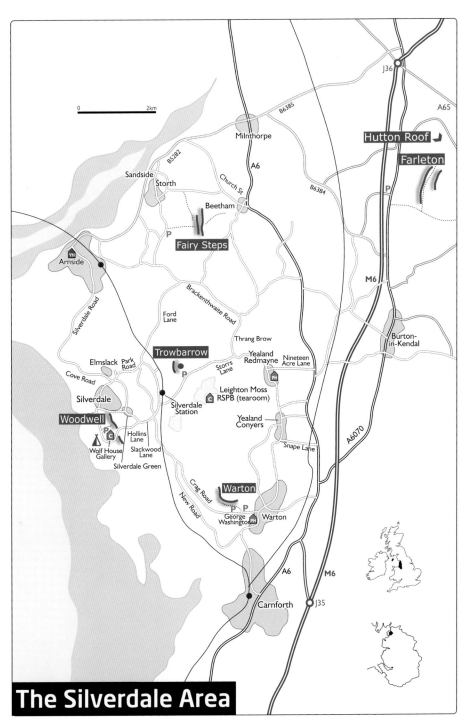

The Silverdale Area

Fairy Steps

54.20214
-2.803059

A two-tiered escarpment in the trees with good, vertical, natural limestone giving over a hundred problems mainly in the lower grades. Usually tiny solos, there are also a fewer harder problems including one of the hardest vertical climbs anywhere. A great little place for a whole evening. Some access issues of late. Please check crag access on the BMC website ahead of a visit.

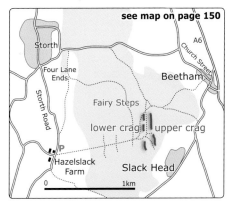

see map on page 150

The Fairy Steps are flights of rugged risers that cut through two levels of limestone escarpment and, as legend has it, are on an old 'coffin route' where the dead were led from rural outposts across the fields to the parish church in Beetham. The upper flight is particularly narrow and it is said that if you can pass down it without touching the rock on either side, then the fairies will grant you a wish. That may or may not be true. However, the same test could be used to decide whether you are here to try one of Gaskins' hardest problems or whether you should stick to enjoying the 4s and 5s.

The left side of the upper tier itself has 80 documented problems, mostly 3 to 6A, and if you go to its very end you'll find Gaskins' concept piece, Walk Away Sit Start: 8C. The other three areas, the upper right and lower left and right, have another 50 problems and micro-routes spread along little buttresses. There's a pleasant and relaxing air about the place, and only a fraction of the problems are documented here. Check out the Les Ainsworths' Lancashire guide or Greg Chapman's online guide, or just go for an explore.

// Climbing: Nice natural limestone giving positive climbing. A hundred problems mainly in the lower grades but with enough significant harder problems to satisfy all tastes. Mostly vertical climbing on cracks, walls and aretes. Some low roof action on some of the harder problems. For the easier stuff, the problems can be interspersed with a few micro-routes to give a fuller day. Landings are often blocky so a mat is good.

// **Approach:** Can be approached on footpaths from Beetham or Storth but the usual one is from Hazelslack Farm. Follow the path opposite the farm through a yard and fields to reach the woods. Continue slightly uphill for 600m to reach the first steps. Problems to the left and right here. Carry on in the same line to reach the upper steps. Problems stretch left and right here too. The upper left extends for about 300m with Walk Away be- ing at the very far end. To easily reach this, follow the good track below the crag for 300m. About 6m from the track on the right is a low flat rock. Walk Away is set back from here.

// **Conditions:** West facing, getting the sun from early afternoon. Very sheltered. Can be weepy in winter.

// **Info: Lancashire Rock** (BMC), is good for the micro-routes; **lakesbloc.co.uk** for the bouldering.

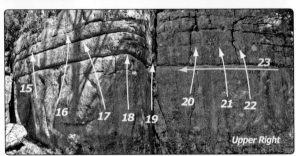

Walk Away – *300m left of track:*
1   **Send Me No Flowers** 6A+
2   **Intellect** 6C+ *Sitter 7C.*
3   **Walk Away** 8B *Sitter 8C from very low undercuts.*
4   **Axiom** 7C+ *Sitter 8A+.*
5   **Rigger** 4+
6   6B
7   **Crack** 5+
Crucifixion - *120m right:*
8   **Roadtrip** 6C+ *Highball*
9   **Landmark Corner** 4+
10   **Arete** 4
11   **Groove Direct** 6C+

12   **Crucifixion** 6A+
    Sitter 6C+.
Upper Right - *45m right of steps:*
13   **Tower Crack** 5+ *Highball*
14   **Tower Arete** 4 *Highball.*
15   **Talesin** 4+
16   **Merlin** 4+
17   **Diagonal Crack** 4
18   **Rheaed** 6A
19   **Woodbind** 4+
20   **The Mole of Mark** 5+
21   **Crack** 6B+ *Sitter 7A+.*
22   **Caerliol** 5+
23   **Down the Edifice** 6B

Lower Left - *Walk 200m, passing Aeon, then about the same again to:*
24   **Democracy** 7A
25   **Sharpville** 6A+
26   **The Cultural Elite Signup Sheet** 6B
27   **Cullinan** 6A
Aeon – *200m right of Cullinan:*
28   **Aeon** 7C+
29   **Aeon Crack** 6B+
30   **Aeon Dyno** 7B
31   **Prow without juggy sidepull** 7C+

John Gausden on Ramp Traverse, 6C+ (problem 7). Photo: Niall Grimes.

Trowbarrow

54.171981
-2.796471

A boulder of hard and very hard power-crazers and a pumpy eliminate training wall to satisfy the slack-jawed. Set functionally in an arid quarry, it is sheltered and offers over 30 hard problems, some of them weatherproof. Not somewhere to bring your new girlfriend.

Many years ago an asteroid from the planet Krank pierced the Earth's nanosphere and exploded into an old north-Lancs lime workings. Over the years many have applied themselves to it until John Gaskins hatched from its depths and levitated up its south face to give Il Pirata.

To a certain type of boulderer, the type who will love lists and deadhanging, this is the most inspiring piece of climbing they can imagine. To me it looked like a hard, dirty little thing. But I am too far away to understand.

The Shelter Stone is a place of pilgrimage for the UK's ultra-power punters. With 17 problems from 6C+ to 8C, it suits a session-testpiece approach. Nearby, the Red Wall is a wrong-by-ten-degrees wall of polished, featured limestone. This has pumpy traverses and loads of ups, and stays dry in solid rain (although it can seep).

There's a tearoom in the nearby bird reserve.

// **Climbing:** Very powerful, fingery, body-tension junk on the Shelter Stone. The Red Wall is steep with roundy jugs. Good for the arm-centric.
// **Approach:** Follow the maps. If you get lost, find Silverdale station, drive south towards Warton for 100m then go left. Drive for about 1km and park in the bay on the left. From the parking area walk up short steps and follow the path through a gate. Take the right fork and after 60m go straight on through a gate to reach the quarry. Soon you will see the Shelter Stone. Red Wall is just beyond, on the left.
// **Conditions:** Very sheltered. Both Red Wall and the Shelter Stone seep some in wet periods. Once dry Red Wall offers rainproof climbing as can parts of the Shelter Stone. Red Wall gets morning sun. It can suffer from condensation when leaves are on the trees. The Shelter Stone is 360 so gets sun all day on some face.
// **Info:** lakesbloc.co.uk

Silverdale
1km

Red Wall
Shelter Stone

Red Bridge Lane

gate

gate

P

Yealand Storrs
1.5km

Leighton Moss

Silverdale
Station

Storrs Lane

0   500m

see map on page 150

Shelter Stone

1. **Wamdue Project** 6B+
   Rock left to finish.
2. **Funk Phenomena** 7A
   Vague prow
3. **Texas Hold 'Em** 7B+
   Start with the left hand in the slot and climb up and right. Knacky, especially on the knees.
4. **Sloper** 6B+
   Jump to sloper and a highball finish.
5. **Isla de Encanta** 8B
   From a low start on a big undercut, pinch up the prow then swing right to the shelf to finish.
6. **Shallow Groove** 8A+
   Scooped wall.
7. **Ramp Traverse** 6C+
8. **Various Slab Bimbles** 4 – 5
9. **Il Pirata** 8C
   From very far down in the gap, climb to the lip, and up.
10. **Pit Problem** 7B+
    Slot to diagonal edge and top.
11. **The Groove** 6C+
12. **Vitruvian Man** 7C
    From opposing edges slap up right for a better hold then move back left to a hard finish.

Red Wall

13. **Shallow Grave** 7A+
14. **The Crack** 5
15. **The Groove** 3
16. **American Express** 5
17. **Greg's Dyno** 7B
18. **Classic Rockover** 5+
19. **Red Wall Traverse** 7A
    Traverse the wall in either direction. Very pumpy, more like F7b+ route grade.

Barrow locals on What's This For, 6C+ (problem 7). Photo: Niall Grimes.

Woodwell

54.16266
-2.821426

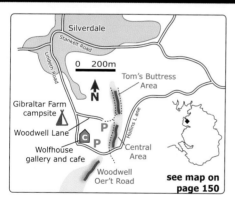

A great venue with lots of hard, sometimes very hard, and sometimes even harder than that, cellar-style cranking. A row of mini-buttresses in a pretty, woody setting. Short outcrops of natural limestone with mostly lowball action in the harder grades, climbing out or across roofs, as well as some easier higher stuff. A winter weeper. Very sheltered, and best from 6C upwards.

Perhaps the best of the South Lakes limestone crags, especially as far as hard bouldering is concerned. Tons of problems in a beautiful, gentle setting featuring minimal walk in. The first problems were climbed in the 1970s by locals, especially Tom Walkington who went on to point out the crag's potential with his traverse. The additions of Gaskins sent the standards here skywards in the 1990s. It is now a must-visit crag for the serious boulderer.

The thing that struck me first about Woodwell is how pretty it is. I visited there first in early spring. The air was pungent with the smell of wild garlic that grew in plumes all along the edge of the crag. Young mothers were playing with tiny children by the pond. The spring that fed the pond gurgled from the cliff, the rock below wreathed in decades of moss. Horses gambolled in the field by the crag and birdsong filled the air. Glory.

A gentle stroll took me leftwards, past some vertical walls to Tom's Buttress. Just beyond is a nice wall than past that another low roof holding Gaskins' Anasthesia. If you are one of those people who think that difficulty and quality are the same thing, then this is one of the best problems in the area.

Right of the spring is the central area where a load more walls and more broken buttresses string out for a hundred metres or so. At the right end is the best of the buttresses, most appealing in the higher grades. This ends just before the road. Across this road is, surprisingly, Woodwell O'ert Road. We're not allowed to climb here. That's a shame, because it looked brilliant. Problems here go up to 8B+, all recorded on Lakesbloc.

Katie Mills on Not Bad Dave, 6B (problem 28). Photo: David Simmonite.

Anasthesia

The Question

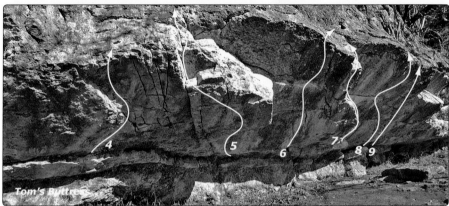

Tom's Buttress

Tom's Buttress

1   **Anasthesia**   8B   *Start sitting on the flat block on the far left. The second half, going right from the flat hold, is Anna, 7B.*

2   **Slanting Crack**   5

3   **The Question**   6A+

4   **The Beauty of Being Numb**   7B   *Low slot to gaston crimp to lip.*

5   **Sanctified**   6B+   *Flake, undercut then left.*

6   **The Art of Self Destruction**   8A

7   **What's This For**   6C+

8   **Kaizen**   8B+   *Cross the roof on crimps and a high right-hand gaston starting from the blob and avoiding the crack on the right (feet go on the ramp of 13).*

9   **Memories of Tomorrow**   8A   *Crack only for the hands - no prow.*

10   **Screaming Slave**   7A   *Venerable left-hand and right-hand eliminate versions use roof crimps with only left or only right hand (both 7B+/C).*

11   **Nothing to Say**   6A

12   **Subliminal**   5+

13   **Got a Lot to Say**   6A+

14   **Tom's Reverse**   6C+

// Climbing: Problems are spread throughout the grades although it is definitely the harder stuff that has given the crag its reputation. Low roofy stuff on edges, giving dynamic and burly power problems where finger strength and body tension are the weapons of choice. It is worth bearing in mind that there are often rules about what holds can and cannot be used, starting positions, etc. Usually, no problem uses holds on an adjacent problem. The easier stuff is mini-highball cracks and walls. Pads useful. A mat is definitely useful on the lowballs also as the thought of slamming your heels into the embedded limestone floor is enough to make you wince.

// Approach: Best located from the Wolfhouse Gallery and Cafe (01524 701405), perhaps somewhere to sooth your beast after a savage session on Tom's Buttress. Follow the maps onto Woodwell Lane and park at the end of this by a pond. The crag is just ahead with the Tom's Buttress area (and Anesthesia) off to the left (keep below the crag line, all the buttresses are fairly obvious) and the Central Area to the right. For the buttresses detailed here follow the crag rightwards for 80 – 100m to find the more continuous rock.

// Conditions: The curse of most limestone bouldering, Woodwell seeps for some of the winter and after periods of rain. In fact, it can be quite fickle at any time, so be prepared to be flexible. Very sheltered and gets sun from mid afternoon. **Family friendly.**

// Info: lakesbloc has a superb free guide to the crag detailing all problems as well as tons of videos.

// Access: No climbing on Woodwell O'ert Road.

Central Area: Rosie

Deryn Groove

Whistler

Griddle Groove

Central Area - Rosie (these walls start about 80m right of the well):
15 **Pussycat** 4
16 **Rosie** 5+
17 **Tree Arete** 3+
18 **Flake Crack** 3
19 **Deryn Groove** 5
20 **Paws for Thought** 5+
21 **Long Crack** 3+
22 **Whistler** 7A *No holds in the cracks.*
23 **Cannon Crack** 5+

24 **Tew Hoo** 5
25 **Honcho's Poncho** 5
26 **Creative Urge** 5
27 **Not Bad Nige** 8A *From a flat hold, traverse right to gain the low start of NBD and finish up this.*
28 **Not Bad Dave Standup** 6B
29 **Not Bad Dave** 7C *Starting from undercuts at the back of the roof, climb into the standup.*
30 **Griddle Groove** 6A
31 **Spicy Parsnip** 7B+ *Traverse, starting from a sitter at the base of a crack right of the tree.*

North West / Woodwell

Hana Edwards-Lihocka on Lone Tree Groove, 4 (problem 7). Photo: Jon Bassindale.

Warton

54.145049
-2.772009

More top quality Lancashire limestone with a long-strung string of buttresses high overlooking the overlooked beauties of Morecambe Bay. A fine location for 50 powerful problems in the 5 - 8A+ range.

The area is a nature reserve, famous for flowers and birds, and as you slog up the hill from the parking quickly gaining height, a feeling of freshness overcomes one, the world around swollen with natural joy. Airy views over the bay, the sheer loftiness of it all. Great.

All this talk of natural wonder aside, you're still going to have to pull like a total bastard when you get here. As with so much of the crags hereabouts, Warton offers superb steep, physical and fingery brutes of problems that seem to get better towards the higher grades. Quelle surprise!

There's a good lot of climbing beyond what's covered here and between the two areas detailed is a virtually continuous string of problems and micro-routes. Dave Bates, Nick Clement, Greg Chapman and of course John Gaskins are responsible for the action.

// Climbing: 50 problems across the grades, but good for hard stuff. High-quality natural limestone. Plum Buttress' character comes from its generally undercut start. Most problems struggle over this on slopers, crimps or cracks. Optional stand- or sit-starts. Powerful. Fairly highball. Rocky landings, problems that finish by jumping off at high holds and the sheer difficulty mean that several pads are required. The other buttresses are more vertical or slightly overhanging, again on cracks, slopers and crimps.
// Approach: Follow the map. The climbing is set about 200m back from the edge of the quarry and below the summit of the hill. Plumb Buttress is the first rock you come to. Black Buttress is hard to find. The easiest way for first-timers is to follow the cragline all the way, climbing as you go, till you find it.
// Conditions: Very clean and quick drying with little seepage. Gets evening sun, which won't help on those slopers. One word of warning – after one visit here I removed 14 ticks from my body. Take precautions.
// Info: **lakesbloc** gives superb coverage of the bouldering and **Lancashire Rock** (BMC) gives loads more micro-routes.

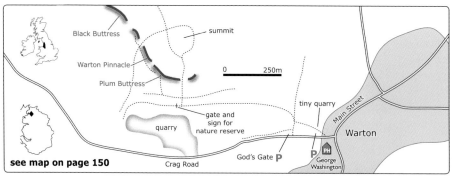

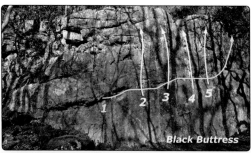

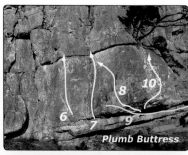

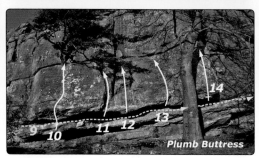

1   **Labyrinth** 6C

2   **Black Jack** 6A

3   **Black Magic** 6A+ *The wall a metre left of the crack on pockets.*

4   **Black Sheep** 4+ *The crack.*

5   **Black Light** 7A *The wall on flowstone.*

6   **Blunt Prow** 6B *With the help of the diogonal crack.*

7   **Lone Tree Groove** 4 *Sit start.*

8   **Hoodoo People** 6C *From a sit start under the prow (same place as Voodoo People), trend left to gain the disgonal flake and use this to pull round to the groove above.*

9   **The Full Traverse** 8A+ *The long traverse of the buttress following the yellow line to finish up 17.*

10   **Voodoo People** 7B *Classic. From a sitter climb to the right end of the break over the roof and up the wall. 7A+ from standing.*

11   **Sugarfix** 6C+ *Layback the flake.*

12   **Big Plum** 6A

13   **Plumline** 7A *From hands in the jug in the break, climb the wall and flake.*

14   **Original Debaser** 8A *The blunt prow.*

15   **Debaser** 7A+ *From a low sit start get the jug in the break left of the groove then bust on for the features in the prow to finish at the tree.*

16   **Dihedral** 5+

17   **The Vine Line** 6A

18   **The Prow** 5 *6B from a sitter.*

19   **Plumline Traverse** 7A *Traverse the break rightwards from the jug below Plumline to finish up 17. This is the final section of The Full Traverse.*

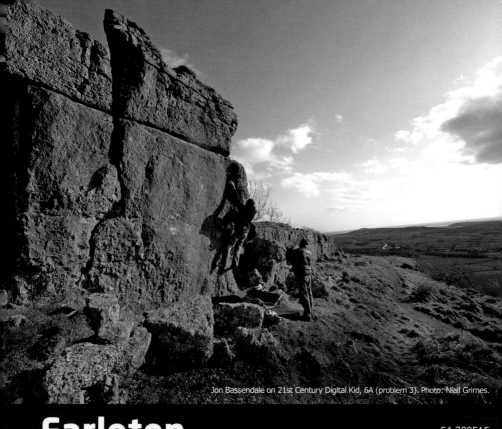

Jon Bassendale on 21st Century Digital Kid, 6A (problem 3). Photo: Niall Grimes.

Farleton

54.208515
-2.722163

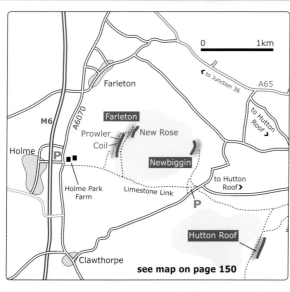

A prominent limestone hillside with unrivalled views across the M6 and the fish farms beyond. The main area offers two tiers of low escarpment that sometimes muster themselves into reasonable bouldering. Geologically interesting.

This is the big grey hill of bare rock you see on the east of the M6 when travelling towrds Kendal. Lovers of clints and grikes will find much here to their liking, although it has something of a local feel as far as bouldering is concerned. Still, the rock is good where it's good.

Three walls are described here: one on the upper level and two below. Also described is Newbiggin Crag which is the back side of the escarpment. This has a bunch of very low walls giving some sport in a lovely picnic-style setting as well as one fine boulder.

// **Climbing:** **Lancashire Rock** records about 60 easy and mid-grade highballs/micro-routes following cracks, grooves and walls and lakesbloc covers the bouldering shown here plus about 15 more problems. The bouldering gives harder fingery wall-climbs, often on small sharp holds. Sometimes highball, and some problems (eg New Rose) have awful landings, so a couple of pads are useful. Eliminate rules often apply, generally no touching holds on neighbouring problems.

// **Approach:** Park around the little road opposite Holme Park Farm. Walk south along the A6070. Just south of the farm, follow a bridleway (signposted 'Limestone Link') through the farm and on through fields for about 500m. Go through a gate and continue uphill for about 150m, roughly in the same line, then turn left along a wide grassy plateau and follow this. There is a low broken escarpment on the right and another below, on the left, which eventually form the upper and lower tiers. Continue for about 450m to find New Rose on the right. The other areas are on the lower tier, about 100 – 150m back towards the farm. Drop down and head back the way you came. Pass along a handful of lovely little buttresses of micro-routes (mostly HS – E1) to find Prowler, then, just right, The Coil.

// **Conditions:** Farleton is west-facing getting sun from the afternoon and evening. Exposed and quick drying. It takes little seepage. Newbiggin faces west (morning and afternoon sun) and is similarly dry.

// **Info:** <u>lakesbloc</u> for the bouldering; **Lancashire Rock** (BMC) for the micro-routes.

Newbiggin Crag: Follow the map and park in a layby on the north side of the road. Walk east to arrive at a gate with a sign saying "Public Bridleway Holme Park Limestone Link". (This can be followed to Farleton in 25 minutes.) Follow the path for about 100m then contour right for about 400m to see the boulder and the crag (only 2 – 3m high) behind. Great for a relaxing hour.

New Rose

Prowler

The Coil

20 min	40 probs 3 - 7C+ best from 5 - 7B	vertical			

1	J Crack 3	13	The Coil 7A+
2	New Rose 7B	14	The Final
3	21st Century		Frontier 6C+
	Digital Kid 6A	15	Arete 3
4	The Arete 3		
5	Prowler Left 6B		*Newbiggin:*
6	Prowler Right 6A	16	Arete from
7	Cracker 4+		Sitter 6A
8	Pandemonium	17	5+ *Swing up to*
	7C+ *Hard at top.*		*the traverse line and left*
9	Flakier 3+		*along this to the arete.*
10	The Family Way	18	Cracks 5
	4 *Crack.*		*From a sitter.*
11	Coil Traverse 7A	19	Whiteout Roof
12	Undiscovered		7A+
	Country 7C		

Newbiggen

Hutton Roof

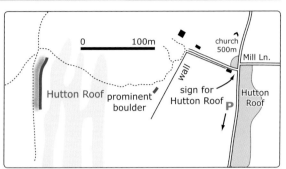

see map on page 150

A little limestone gem with boundless easier powerfests jugging over low roofs and classy highballs and microroutes for airheads. A great fresh setting, good rock and lush grassy surroundings complete the picture. Some desperate low sit starts too for those that need such things. This was my favourite of the north Lancashire limestone venues (although I think it might be in Yorkshire!).

Hutton Roof has been a favourite with locals for years, a great place to get some mileage in a beautiful setting. A fairly short, yet uphill, approach gets the blood going and leaves you on an isolated limestone ridge. The first view of the crag will bring a smile to the face of all but the most ardent fans of dead-hanging, with lush grass sweeping to the base of a bunch of clean mini-buttresses. Time to break out the picnic.

// Climbing: The climbing comes in several forms. The left section holds a good number of highballs on fine, just-off-vertical walls. The rock here is very good and rough and the problems tend to be hardest near the bottom. The juggier upper sections can be traversed off if you're not in the mood and are often led. The landings are generally good and a couple of mats will usually suf-

fice, as long as you don't fall off. Ape Buttress, the heavily featured roof at the right end, holds more burly fare. The natural lines can be done from standing or logical lower starts to give about 10 great problems in the 4 to 6B range. Again, these can feel high near the top, but become very easy. Some have been done from desperate, very low starts to give problems in the 6B – 7B range. The rocky base of this section means that a mat is needed to save your heels and coccyx.

// Approach: Follow signs from the A65 to Hutton Roof village. The most considerate parking is at the south end of the village. From the centre of the village follow a lane opposite the junction (signed for Hutton Roof) then the footpath that trends left uphill, to the right of a prominent boulder on the skyline. The path goes over the crest of the hill and the crag is on the left just after this.

// Conditions: The crag faces west and gets sun from afternoon. The rock is clean, solid and very quick drying and doesn't seep much. It is a little polished in places but not desperately so. The bouldering sits high on a ridge, so it is fairly exposed. Good all year round. **Family friendly.**

// Info: lakesbloc and **Lancashire Rock (BMC).**

South America Buttress - *Solo to the top or traverse off at mid-height. Mats are useful:*

1   Sandero Luminoso   3+
2   Sandanista   5
3   American Dream   6C+
4   San Miguel   4+
5   Pablo   4

The Cave:

6   Upper Traverse   5
7   Roof Traverse   5+
8   Roof One   5+
9   Roof Three   6A
10 Roof Four   4+

Ronson Kirkby Wall - *Solo to the top on steep, fun jugs or traverse off:*

11 Wings   3+   *The easy crack.*
12 Wings Traverse   5+
13 The Scoop   6B+
14 Cyclops   6A+
15 Serpent   4

Ape Buttress – *Once again a buttress with hard starts and fun, though high, finishes. The problems are usually made more satisfying by carrying on to the top, and harder by adding low starts:*

16   4+
17 Primate   5+
18 Swamp Fever   6A   *Go direct from the hand ledge. Start down and left from the undercut at 6A+.*
19 Primark   6B   *From the hand ledge at the base of Primate, rock up to the pinchy cracks. Start down and left from the undercut for more action.*
20 The Lemur's Tail   4+   *The thin crack.*
21 Nick's Traverse   7A   *A historical eliminate going either way along the buttress using only the holds marked with (now fading) red dots. F7c route grade.*
22 Gibbon Take   5+
23 Chimp   4+   *The bulge and right-slanting crack. Start at the back of the roof at 7A+.*
24 Gorilla Berengii   5+   *The flake and wall.*
25 Gorilla, Gorilla   6A+   *Start with hands on the low jug and crank up to the flake cracks above. Start at the back of the roof at 7A.*
26 Pithecanthropus Indirectus   6A   *Start low with hands on the lip then up to the diagonal crack and right.*
27 Traverse   6B+   *Start on the lip as for 26 and traverse left to climb 24.*

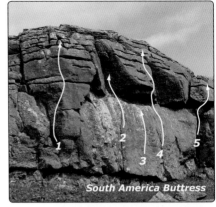

South America Buttress

The Cave

Ronson Kirkby Wall

Ape Buttress

Ape Buttress

Isle of Man

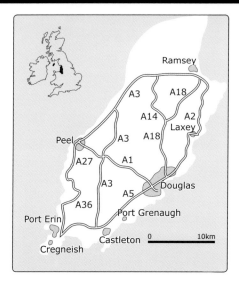

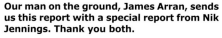
Laxey. Photo: Nik Jennings.

Our man on the ground, James Arran, sends us this report with a special report from Nik Jennings. Thank you both.

The bouldering is poorly documented, conditions are a little fickle and venues are often tidal so finding a local to show you the areas is the best bet. Failing that, the areas worth checking out are:

Peel: Good, steep wave polished sandstone on the beach 300m north of the skatepark on the promenade. There are good areas in the cave and on the beach but the pebbles rise and fall with storms. This is James Arran's favourite area.

Also limited DWS 'bouldering' around the back of the castle: weird but fun on a nice calm evening.

Laxey: 300m south of the promenade there's a nice cluster of boulders. Nik Jennings has documented these and there's a topo available on the UKBouldering Vimeo site. Just google that.

This collection of boulders give about a dozen or so problems from 4 to 8A, some of reasonable quality, some less so. They are located about halfway along the beach. Park at the prom and head south (away from the harbour) along the beach. The Piano boulder is easily recognisable. The boulders are climbable except at high tide and will dry pretty quickly on the open faces (especially with a breeze) but some of the more sheltered corners can remain damp. Note: The height of the pebbles below the

problems can vary significantly, and as such can affect the difficulty of the problems. Also the pebble landing means that a mat is pretty much essential.

Douglas, Marine Drive: There's a dead-end road heading south down the coast from Douglas. On the beach below it (you'll have to park up and walk where the road is closed) is a wrecked boat. On the beach, 300m north of the wreck is some good bouldering. It's tidal but dries ok in a breeze. Approach carefully down the steep scree.

Chasms Beach: This one is a little hard to find. From Cregneish, walk down toward the old Chasms cafe then turn right and follow the coastal path for about 500m until it opens out into a patch of bracken on the left. Battle through that then pick your way carefully down the slabs to the sea. There's a couple of isolated boulders and a huge wave of steep slate.

Santon: Park at Port Grenaugh and follow the coastal path for 1km until you get to a small bridge over a stream. There's a grassy rake on your right leading down to an isolated boulder and a wrecked marine engine. There's also a hidden gully full of short routes with bouldery starts just a few metres to the south. Tidal and fickle but worth a look if you fancy a walk.

Bradda: There's a good area on the beach behind Bradda (Port Erin) but it requires seasonal cleaning.

You'll want a pad at all the venues listed.

Heysham Head

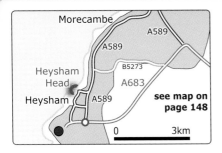

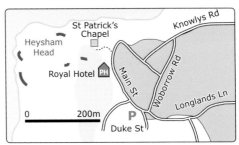

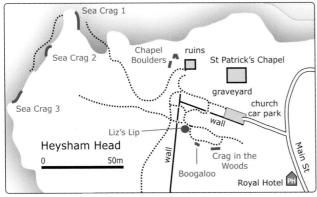

Obscure seaside sandstone. It gets slated but there have been good times had here. Just follow the maps to the boulders and see what you find. Popular with gentle tourists but not climbers. Only one of the seven areas is covered here. See Lakesbloc.

// Climbing: A variety of styles. Some soft sandstone boulders; some hard things by the sea. Some wooded walls. Please avoid climbing on the Chapel Boulders.

// Approach: At the junction of the A683 and A589 is a roundabout. Go north on the A589 for 800m then left on Longlands Lane, signposted for St Patrick's Chapel. This leads to Heysham Village. Park in the large pay and display and walk up Main St, past the Royal Hotel pub, and follow the map.

// Conditions: If the rock is damp don't climb on it. Mostly clean but some surfaces are a bit crunchy. Stuff in the trees can be slow drying. **Great for families.**

// Info: lakesbloc.co.uk

1 **Full Intention** 6C+
2 **Dyno** 5+
3 **Wall Brawl** 4
4 **Groovy** 4
5 **Atomic Garden** 8A
6 **Above the Royal Flake** 5
7 **Wall** 6C+
   Flake for left hand.
8 **The Mean Green** 3+

The Clitheroe scene. Alice on Slab Run, 3 (problem 31), Joe on Burnt Heather, 6B (problem 33) and Ben, who seems to be missing a chair. Photo: Niall Grimes.

Thorn Crag

53.995236
-2.629547

Gritstone with a sea view. A mega-session of top quality problems overlooking one of the more pristine wildernesses of northern England. A beautiful and majestic spot with great lines to match. Remote and exposed it is best enjoyed on a long sunny day. Superb.

The majority of the bouldering is on three small boulder-clumps that lie a few minute's walk from each other. The approach is a bit of a slog for a boulderer's legs but once the golden contour is reached these clumps lie just off a good track. A flask and sandwiches would be a good way to celebrate each new venue. Family friendly.

40 min | 100 probs 2 - 8A best from 4 - 7B | slabby | vertical | steep | | exposed

// Climbing: Natural gritstone boulders. Good range of stuff will give a full day out for most. Problems are a nice relaxed height with the odd friendly highball. One or two mats is enough. Lots of slopers, aretes, bulges and slabs. Great lines. Great for easy stuff and beginners.

The surface has a vaguely scrittly feel. Excessive brushing will destroy it so best just to accept any surface issues as part of the experience. Ride on!

◄ *Seaview Boulders*

Trackside Boulders ◄

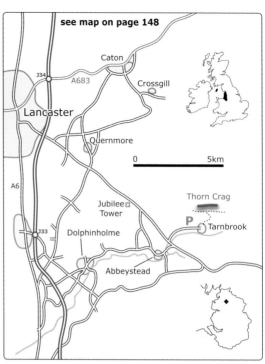

see map on page 148

Caton

A683

J34

Crossgill

Lancaster

Quernmore

A6

0   5km

Thorn Crag

Jubilee
Tower

P

Tarnbrook

J33   Dolphinholme

Abbeystead

// **Conditions:** Exposed and probably best enjoyed on a nice day to get full spiritual nourishment. The climbing faces south and gets loads of sun. The rock is very fine grained but it is not as super-hard as some gritstone. Quick drying and good all year round if you get the weather right. **Family friendly.**

// **Approach:** The crag lies above the tiny hamlet of Tarnbrook which is on a dead-end of a road amidst the wild Trough of Bowland. I reached this by coming off the M6 at junction 33, then following signs for Dolphinholme then Abbeystead. Go through Abbeystead bearing left after the river and 1km later, at a T-junction, bear left downhill. In 500m and after the river, follow the signed road to Tarnbrook.

Alternatively, Lakesbloc recommends coming off the M6 at junction 34, then coming off the A683 at Caton. Follow Quernmore Rd and Postern Gate Rd to the village of Quernmore. Continue to reach the long straight road from Lancaster. Go right along this passing the monument (Jubilee Tower) to reach the same small road to Tarnbrook. Parking is very limited in the village. In the centre is a small green with a 'No Parking' sign. Don't park here. There's room for a couple of cars just before the village, otherwise drive back out until you find a sensible spot and walk back.

From the green go through the gate and follow Land Rover tracks uphill for about half an hour. This is eventually crossed by more good tracks and the boulders and crag are easily visible off to the left and right.

// **Info:** As usual **lakesbloc.co.uk** has all the answers. Also covered in the **Yorkshire Bouldering Guide Volume 2** (Total Climbing).

// **Access Issues:** Generally good access but it can be banned at the owner's discretion for hunting or bird-nesting reasons (mainly April to June). **Dogs are banned at all times.**

Thorn Crag

*Crag
Boulders*

Sea View Boulders

Sea View Boulders

Sea View Boulders

1	**One-Eyed Willy** 6A	**7**	**Slab** 3	**14**	**Little Wall** 3
	Sitter.	**8**	**Scoop** 3	**15**	**Groove** 2
2	**Seam** 4+	**9**	**Chilica** 5+ *Scary.*	**16**	**Serrano** 3 *Flake.*
3	**Wall** 3+	**10**	**Mothership Reconnection** 7A+	**17**	**Serrano Rib** 3
4	**Edge** 3		*row from sitter: finish left.*	**18**	**Bulge** 3+
5	**Jalapeno Arete** 6A	**11**	**Slab** 3	**19**	**Rib** 2
6	**Endangered Species** 8A	**12**	**Slabby Arete** 2	**20**	**Deadly Sins** 2
	From a sitter in the hollow.	**13**	**Chilli Billy** 3+	**21**	**Wall** 3+

Sea View Boulders

Trackside Boulders

Crag Boulders

Diamond Slab

Split Rocks

22	**Rib** 4	**33**	**Burnt Heather** 6B
23	**Resistance is Futile** 7A	**34**	**Easy Karma** 5+
24	**Elemental** 6C	**35**	**And For My Next Trick** 7A
	Traverse from sitter.	**36**	**Here I am Again** 6B
25	**2001 A Grit Odyssey** 4+	**37**	**Diamond Crack** 5 *Sitter.*
26	**Gritasaurus** 3	**38**	**Ouzel Thorn** 6B
27	**Arete** 2	**39**	**Jam Roof** 5 *Sitter.*
28	**Wiggling Crack** 5	**40**	**Bad Moon Rising** 7B+
29	**Rising Smoke** 4+		*High prow from low flake.*
30	**Perving Arete** 5	**41**	**Slice of Life** 7A
31	**Slab Run** 3		*Highball line, flake.*
32	**Neil's Thorny Arete** 5		

Slice of Life

◄ Split Rocks ► Thorn Crag

Diamond Slab ►

◄ Slice of Life

Crag Boulders

Adam Lincoln on Super Submarine, 8A+ (problem 12). Photo: Lincoln collection.

Craig-y-Longridge

53.839171
-2.583311

A coal face of pump for Lancastrians who come to mine for stamina. A workmanlike crag where you clock in and go to work in the hope of getting some fitness in your paycheque at the end of the month. Nice legs, shame about the face.

Wars are not won or lost when one side kills all of the other. What happens is that when such level of pain – casualties, moral or financial anguish – is inflicted on one player, they capitulate. In the same way do climbers fall off at Longridge. Watch them, see their faces after they drop off, a scene of horror and agony stretched across the face, the look a mixture of disappointment and phenomenal relief. Were it a war then Longridge will always be the one who drops the atomic bomb on the Hiroshima of your forearms.

// Climbing: Almost a hundred recorded up-problems and one monster traverse which is conveniently broken into six or seven fairly natural sections of varying degrees of desperation. Despite a huge number of up-problems, they are not so popular and for the first-time visitor, a few will usually suffice. Once you are up-sated then you get to work on a traverse section of your choice. The full

traverse is F8b+ route grade. The holds are mainly big flat slopers or small flat crimps with a variety of sidepulls, undercuts, cracks and flakes thrown in too. Can be a bit wearing on the skin. The up-problems are often quite highball, as are some sections of the traverse but the landings are perfect. Still, bring lots of pads. The bottom line is that you are here to get fit and fit you will get.

// Conditions: Longridge is almost limestone-like in its fickleness. Seepage comes through in winter and after spells of heavy rain at other times. However when it is dry it does offer weatherproof climbing. It gets the morning sun, is very sheltered, but it can feel humid. The setting is odd, with an estate of holiday cottages within spotting distance of the climbing.

// Approach: Follow the maps. The entrance is through a wooden gate 65m up from the entrance to the Green Bank Park holiday village.

// Access: Longridge has had troubles in the past as far as access goes. Since the BMC purchased the strip of land below the situation has settled. However it is important that there is **no music, no dogs and no climbing before 10am or after sunset.**

// Info: Lancashire Rock (BMC) has traditional English tech grades for almost all the problems here best referenced to their numbers.

Left End

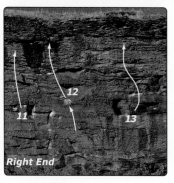

Right End

1	**Kiss the Razor's Edge** 7A	
2	**Black Jake** 4+ *(18)*	
3	**Timothy's Route** 6A *(19)*	
4	**Wobblebottom** 5+ *(20)*	
5	**Bomb Squad** 6B	
6	**Central Icefall Direct** 4+ *(23)*	
7	**Tarot Plane** 6C	
8	**Thirty Feet of Pain** 6C+ *(26)*	
9	**Pump Til You Jump** 6A+ *(29)*	
10	**Cruel Country** 6C+ *(28)*	
11	**Smeg City** 6A *(52)*	
12	**Big Marine** 7B *(54)*	
	Sit start off crimps is Super Submarine 8A+	
13	**Push to Prolapse** 6C+ *(56)*	

14 **Pot of Gold** 8A *Dyno to Rainbow's starting jug.*
15 **Bend in the Rainbow** 7A
The high starting hold is gained from the ladder.
16 **Rug Thug** 6A+ *(58)*
17 **In Excess** 6A+ *(59)* *Sit start 7B+.*
18 **Fertile Delta** 7A
19 **Porridge Gun** 6C *(60)*
20 **New Stone Age** 6A *(63)*
21 **Unknown Arete** 5 *(64)*

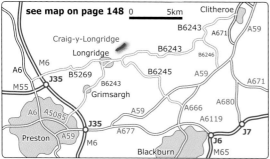

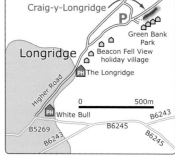

Nick Colton on Ash Pit Slab, 4 (problem 7). Photo: Me!

Brownstones

53.607066
-2.482798

The pride of Lancashire bouldering with endless technical and fingery eliminates in a friendly, sunny and sheltered quarry close to the road. A happy place for happy people.

This little suntrap is justifiably one of the area's most popular climbing venues. Endless eliminates exist on these short walls and slabs on polished holds and smears where local rules often apply. Good landings, if sometimes a little highball, and clean rock make it a fun venue.

// Climbing: About 125 main problems and many eliminates. Generally technical and fingery on quarried vertical walls, where finger strength and good technique are required, or slabs that will repay a sense of balance; cracks, slabs, wall and traverses. Some slabs are a little high but landings are good flat and grassy.

// Approach: Follow maps. Park along the road near a row of cottages (Colliers Row). Cross the wall at a bridleway sign and follow a track for 100m to the first short walls (Pool Area). The more highball Ash Pit Slabs are 100m further on.

// Conditions: West facing. Quick drying and sheltered; climbing possible all year. Gets sun from late afternoon. Can be muggy on hot summer evenings when midges can also be a problem. Great in winter. **Family friendly.**

// Info: Lancashire Rock (BMC) has the whole script, and **Western Grit** (Rockfax) has a best-of.

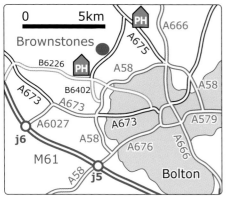

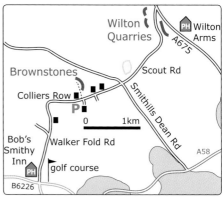

Ash Pit Slab

Pool Area

1	**Corn Mantel** 5+	**8**	**Parabola Direct** 6B	**16**	**Brownstones Crack** 4+
2	**Degree Crack** 4	**9**	**Pigswill** 7A	**17**	**Moss Wall** 4
3	**Directissima** 6A	**10**	**Parr's Crack** 6A	**18**	**Verdi Ramp** 4
4	**Digitation** 6A+	**11**	**Hank's Wall** 7A+	**19**	**Verdi Corner** 3+
5	**Ash Pit Slab Direct** 4		*Avoid the cracks.*	**20**	**Verdinand** 6B+
6	**Ash Pit Traverse**	**12**	**Layback** 5+	**21**	**Verdigris** 6B
	4+ *Traverse the line with your*	**13**	**Dragnet** 4+	**22**	**Twostep Left** 6A
feet. Using it for your hands is 6A+.		**14**	**Hernia** 3	**23**	**Pond Traverse** 6B
7	**Ash Pit Slab** 4	**15**	**Slimer** 5+		

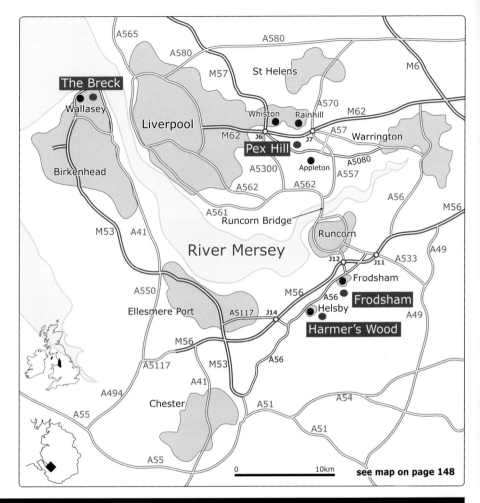

Mersey Sandstone

What can I say about Mersey sandstone that won't lead me to getting my head kicked in next time I go to Pex Hill?

Okay, here goes. I rank Merseyside sandstone alongside things like mussels, country music and my mate Richard. These were things that, while on first acquaintance were far from my liking, I'm glad I persevered because I later became very fond of them. If you're all about jelly babies, The X Factor and nice clean T-shirts than this handful of craglets might not be suited to you.

The crags are big on character. Pex Hill is the main bouldering crag giving lots of finger-searing testpieces and a myriad of eliminates. If you climb to be in beautiful places then best keep driving but if you enjoy staunch wall climbs then check it out. The crag has trained a long list of great climbers.

Frodsham is a much prettier location. It is mainly a classy highballing venue, sometimes a bit scary if you're in the wrong mood. Harmer's Wood has got locals very excited over the past couple of years and now has a great evening's worth of fingery frolocking.

The Breck is the true test of how immune you are to location. A historically significant, seldom visited quarry of most use to locals or unemployed tunnellers. Still, it is legendary and a visit here is worth boasting about.

Emily Huzzard on Pisa Traverse, 4+. at Pex Hill (page 179, problem 9). Photo: Paul Evans

Pex Hill

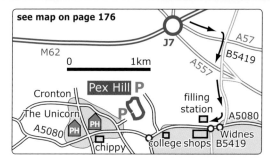

see map on page 176

The true heart of Merseyside finger strength. A square-cut hole of vertical sandstone dressed with tiny holds that give stern tests of old-school vertical nous up to that tendon-popping level – English 7a. Urban, and not to everyone's taste.

The Mecca of Merseyside, a legendary venue that in the 1980s trained up Phil Davidson and Joe Healey, two of the strongest crimpers in the country. Lots of walls around the quarry but covered here is the friendly Pisa Wall with lots of great little highballs and some well-explored eliminates, and to its right the Lady Jane Wall. This has lots of more testing problems, many of them highball classics of the grade. An essential sandstone venue.

The quarry is popular with kids and has a reputation for broken glass, stone throwing and petty crime. However such incidents are few and far between and is probably down more to climbers' suspicions of the urban youth of Merseyside. Still, watch your wallet.

// Climbing: Quite a tough venue with lots to go at. Vertical quarried walls give fingertip cranking across the grades. The climbing can often feel a bit 'ouch!' Often quite high: for Pisa Wall a mat is very useful. Lady Jane Wall starts okay but soon becomes quite highball, turning into routes by halfway along. Lots of problems are the starts of routes: jump off at logical heights or press on to solo to the top. Very technical and balancy. Lots of savage crimps but also some cracks and lots of pockets. Good for traverses. A good training crag.

// Conditions: The walls covered here face west and get morning sun. Lady Jane Wall can be damp after wet weather but Pisa Wall is much drier. Very sheltered and can get muggy in warm weather. Pisa Wall is climbable year round, Lady Jane often damp in winter.

// Approach: From M62, junction 7, follow the A57 towards Warrington for 700m. At intersection go right on B5419 direction Widnes. At junction go right on A5080 direction Cronton. Cross two mini-roundabouts following towards Cronton. Continue on A5080. After 1km, and 300m after a new roundabout, go right on Hall Lane then right on Mill Lane. Park at the bend after 100m and follow the little lane to steps that lead one between Pisa Wall and Lady Jane Wall. Also parking and approach via Cronton Lane. Good bus service to Cronton Rd, Widnes.

// Info: Sandstone (BMC); **Western Grit** (Rockfax)

Pisa Traverse, 4+ (problem 9).
The full version continues to below the two 'eyes',
the twin square pockets in the bottom left, at 6B. Photo: Niall Grimes.

Pisa Wall

Lady Jane left

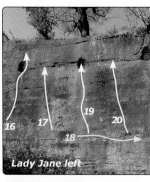

Lady Jane left

Lady Jane right

1	**Handshake** 5+	
2	**Pisa Wall** 3	
3	**Straight Crack** 3+	
4	**Mankey Road** 6A *Crack.*	
5	**Monkey Grip** 5+	
6	**Fingers** 6B *Climb to and past the big pebble in the break.*	
7	**Bushy Tail** 5+ *With a long reach to a vertical slot.*	
8	**Commando** 6A+	
9	**Pisa Traverse** 4+ *Start up the arete and follow the line. Continue just above ground level*	

for 15m to below two 'eyes' (10m right of the corner) at 6B, or stop in a tiny groove 5m earlier at 6A.

10	**Too Bold for Steve Boot** 6A
11	**Traverse** 6B+
12	**Set Square Direct** 6A
13	**Tequila Sunrise** 6A+
14	**Harvey Wallbanger** 6A
15	**Lew's Leap** 5+
16	**Bermuda Triangle** 6C
17	**Breakaway** 7B
18	**Traverse** 3+ *Feet in break to end up on ledges 20m right.*

19	**Catalepsy** 7A+
20	**Monoblock** 7C+
21	**Unicorn** 4+ *E3 to top.*
22	**Hart's Traverse** 6C+
23	**Ladytron** 3+ *E4 to top.*
24	**Hart's Arete** 6C *E4 to top.*
25	**Crack and Up** 5 *E1 to top.*
26	**McArthur Park** 6A+ *E3 to top.*
27	**The Abort** 3+ *E1 to top.*
28	**One Step** 5 *E1 to top.*
29	**The Web** 4 *E1 to top.*

Frodsham

Big scary highballing on a lovely woody hillside. The juggiest of roofs, guaranteed to get the juices flowing. Historic: an essential sandstone venue.

A great little crag to waken the arms up after a winter of rest and a sunny spring evening spent here, working along from buttress to buttress, will leave a long fond memory for some time to come.

// Climbing: Sandstone edge. The climbing is best seen as highball/micro-route crossovers. As such you better be confident at height to really get anything out of it. It varies from Hoop-La Buttress which is basically bouldering height (albeit with a funny landing) up to Great Wall, which is 10m high. Landings are okay, but sloping. The climbing is almost always roofs, mostly juggy.

// Approach: Leave the A56 on the A5393 opposite the Netherton Hall pub. Continue for a mile to farmhouses and a post box on the right. Room for 2 or 3 tidily-parked cars or continue for 200m to more parking. From the farm follow the track opposite, go through the gate and go right and immediately left up the steep hillside. Just below the top drop down left and follow a little path under all the climbing.

// Conditions: Sheltered and very tree-shrouded. Climbable year round but best on spring and autumn evenings. In summer leaves can keep the crag humid or damp after rain. Never climb here if the rock is remotely damp. West facing and gets evening sun.

// Info: Sandstone (BMC); **Western Grit** (Rockfax).

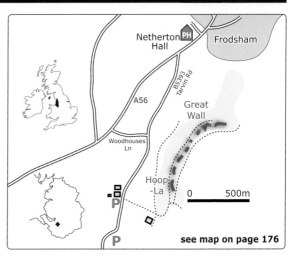

1	**Iron Dish Wall** 5+		**10**	**Pullover** 6A+
	Route E1. If the top is dirty		**11**	**Thin Crack** 4+
escape left into the tree.			**12**	**Left-Hand Crack** 3+
2	**Frodsham Crack** 4		**13**	**Low Traverse** 6B
	Route VS.		**14**	**Middle Traverse** 6A
3	**Cinema Arete** 4		**15**	**Intermediate Route** 5
4	**Arete Route** 5+		**16**	**Direct Route** 6A
5	**Crew's Arete** 6A		**17**	**Colton's Crack** 7A
6	**Super Wall** 5		**18**	**The Hoop-La** 5+
7	**Hobart** 6A+		**19**	**Boysen's Route** 6B
8	**Jimmy's Crack** 6A+		**20**	**Banner's Route** 6A+
9	**Direct Route** +			

Great Wall

Cinema Screen

Cave Buttress

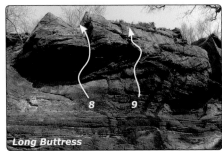

Long Buttress

Long Buttress

Double Overhang

Neb Buttress

Hoop-La

Tom Leppert on The Traverse, 6C (problem 2). Photo: Niall Grimes.

Harmer's Wood

53.269782
-2.757311

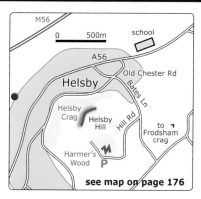

M56
school
0   500m
A56
Old Chester Rd
Helsby
Bates Ln
Helsby Crag
Helsby Hill
Hill Rd
to Frodsham crag
Harmer's Wood
P

see map on page 176

1 min | 42 probs 7 - 7A+ best from 4 - 6C+ | vertical | | shelter | seepage

A wee quarry in a nice woody setting with a good handful of highball aretes, corners and walls. Some harder fingery walls too, set amidst reassuring Cheshire affluence.

If Pex Hill was a boyfriend, being brought home to meet mother for the first time, then the in-laws would certainly have their reservations. Rough and tough, with a whiff of glue. But if daughter brought Harmer's Wood home then mother would breath an approving sigh of relief. Tea would be served in china cups.

Harmer's Wood is another little local venue which will give a fun hour. The land hereabouts is owned by locals and are friendly to climbers. Please have your behaviour levels turned up to 11, and don't put chalk everywhere. Helsby Crag lies just over the hill.

// Climbing: Quarried sandstone. Vertical walls ranging from 4 to 7 metres. Perfect landings, but it still helps to have a bit of bottle. Good for aretes, corners, pockets and walls, some juggy, some hard and fingery. Good for traverses and eliminates.

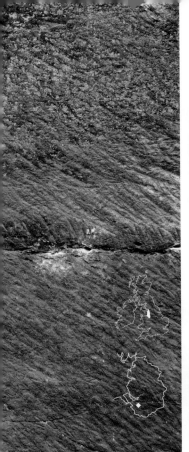

// **Approach:** On the east, Frodsham side, of Helsby Village, turn onto Old Chester Rd, just west of a school. Turn left onto Bates Lane and after 300m right up Hill Rd. Follow this for 350m and park on bays on the right. Refuse Quarry is visible from the upper parking bay (check for access restrictions). The Main Quarry is 40m right of this and 70m back from the lower parking.

// **Conditions:** Very sheltered. A hole with trees, so condensation and dampness can be a problem and it takes a couple of days to dry properly after rain. Best in spring and autumn when there are no leaves on the trees. Climbable year round if the conditions are right. Can be gopping. Do not climb if at all damp.

// **Info: Sandstone** (BMC).

1	**Through the Looking**	**4**	**Little Groove** 4	**10**	**March Hare** 6A+
	Glass 4+	**5**	**Alice's Arete** 3+	**11**	**Letter Box Wall** 5
2	**The Traverse** 6C	**6**	**Layaway** 6B+	**12**	**Thin Crack** 4
	The last section, from the cor-	**7**	**Cheshire Cat** 6A *Corner.*	**13**	**Bex** 6A
ner of 10 to finish up 14, is 6B.		**8**	**White Rabbit** 4+	**14**	**Dormouse Arete** 5+
3	**Martin's Wall** 6C	**9**	**High Heaven** 6C+		*Climbed on its right is 6A.*

No Rebate, 6A (problem 4). Photo: Niall Grimes.

The Breck

53.419124
-3.060336

The ultimate Merseyside quarry, a mythical venue with underground kudos. The holy grail of graffiti and urban chic with highball crimping and ghosts of old heroes. Ugly as sin, but well loved by lovers. An esoteric tick for a certain trainspottery type.

A very local venue, much loved in its day, enough to bring a tear to the eye of a certain generation of Scouser. This little quarry once meant a lot and in the 1970s and 80s it produced some very strong climbers. Just check out Al Rouse's Overhanging Wall Direct or Stevie Haston's dyno, a relic from the days of rules-based testpieces.

// Climbing: Sandstone quarry. Fingery highball wall climbs and eliminates. Walls up to 6m. Hard flat landing. Bluebell Wall is certainly highball, Overhanging Wall even more so. You'll feel as if you're trying hard at the Breck and if you wind up here while visiting rellies on the Wirral you may well go away feeling like you've had your arse slapped. Many problems end up at private gardens meaning a traverse off or jumped dismounts: pads almost essential. Lots of eliminates on Granny Rock.

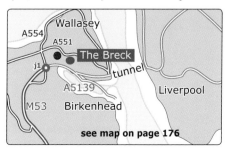

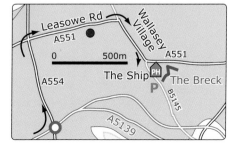

Bluebell Wall

// **Approach:** Leave the M53 at junction 1 onto A554. Left at roundabout (A554). After 600m go right for Wallasey (A551), passing the Wallasey train station. Go right at roundabout after 500m (A551). After 500m go right at mini roundabout onto B5145. Park just after The Ship pub. Good bus service to here (Breck Rd/Hillside Rd stop). The quarry is just behind the pub. All the walls are within a 150m-distance.

// **Conditions:** Walls face north, west and south. Lots of sun and shade. Very sheltered. Can have some wet streaks after heavy rainfall. Can feel unused although it is cared for by locals. Stories of broken glass and dog poo are much exaggerated although graffiti is part of the ambience.

// **Info:** Sandstone (BMC)

Granny Rock

1	**Bluebell Crack** 4+	13	**Arete** 3+
2	**Fagan** 4+	14	**The Overlap** 4
3	**Melancholy** 6A	15	**Central Wall** 6A+
4	**No Rebate** 6A	16	**Adam's Traverse** 5+
5	**Lightning Crack** 6A		
6	**Armlock Crack** 6B	17	**Wet Leg Arete** 5
7	**Ant Crack** 6A+	18	**The Breckfast Lane** 7A+
8	**Bluebell Traverse** 6C+	19	**Overhanging Wall Direct** 7B+
9	**Left Arete** 2	20	**Haston Dyno** 7C+
10	**Ledge Climb** 5+		*Mythical eliminate dyno.*
11	**Positron Traverse** 6B	21	**Greasy Cobweb Crack** 6A+
12	**High Traverse** 5		

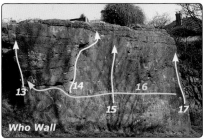

Who Wall

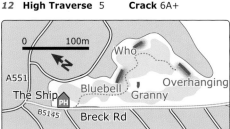

Overhanging Wall

The Lakes

Jon Bassindale on The Overhang, 6C+, Langdale Boulders (page 207, problem 2). Photo: Himself

Helen Keane on Fisherman's Dyno, 6A, St Bees (page 195, problem 39), with Siobhan, Jenny and Joan spotting.
Photo: Niall Grimes

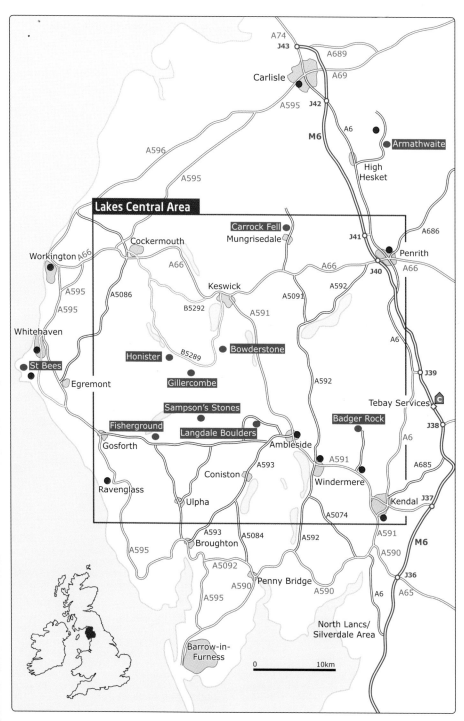

Lakes / Area Map

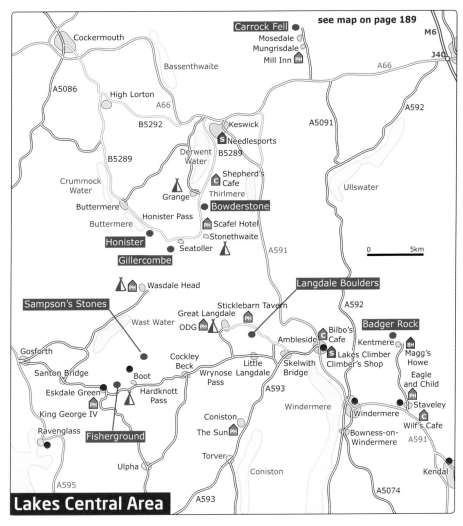

Carrock Fell
Mosedale
Mungrisdale
Mill Inn PH

Cockermouth

M6
J40

A66

A5086

High Lorton

A66

B5292

Keswick

A5091

A592

Needlesports

Derwent
Water

B5289

Ullswater

B5289

Shepherd's
Cafe

Crummock
Water

Grange

Thirlmere

Bowderstone

Buttermere

Honister Pass

Scafel Hotel

Buttermere

Stonethwaite

Honister

Seatoller

A591

Gillercombe

0   5km

Wasdale Head

Langdale Boulders

A592

Sampson's Stones

Sticklebarn Tavern

Great Langdale

Wast Water

ODG

Badger Rock

Bilbo's
Cafe

Kentmere

Ambleside

Magg's
Howe

Gosforth

Cockley
Beck

Lakes Climber
Climber's Shop

Eagle
and Child

Santon Bridge

Boot

Little
Langdale

Skelwith
Bridge

Eskdale Green

Wrynose
Pass

A593

Staveley

King George IV

Hardknott
Pass

Windermere

Windermere

Wilf's
Cafe

Ravenglass

Coniston

Fisherground

The Sun

Bowness-on-
Windermere

A591

Torver

Ulpha

Kendal

Coniston

A595

A593

A5074

Lakes Central Area

The Lakes is becoming ever more popular as a bouldering destination as the quality of what's on offer becomes better known. Due to its geographical location, further away from larger areas of population than the Peak or Yorkshire, it is essentially somewhere for travelling climbers. But, as one of the most beautiful parts of the country, these travellers are many. Every year they flock along the M6 and get herded obediently into the gift shops and expensive tea houses. Well the good news is that if you have a pad in the back of the car you are in for a treat.

St Bees is rightly recognised as one of the best locations in the country, well worth the effort (it's MILES away). The Bowderstone, the best single boulder in the land, perhaps, is a place of pilgrimage for power-weasels.

Smart rocks such as the Langdale Boulders, Badger Rock and Fisherground continue to bring a handy smile to holidaymakers while big days out on venues such as Carrock Fell, Gillercombe, Honister and, best of all, Sampson's Stones will give special days out to the mountain lover in us all.

Popularity has also spread as the area is very well served by guides. The Rockfax Lake District Bouldering from 2006 is still pretty up to date and will fill in all the blanks left by the following few pages. However for all info, news reports, lots of great videos and a seemingly constant stream of new and updated guides (some of the best webguides about) Greg Chapman's site **lakesbloc.co.uk** is a tremendous resource. This section relied heavily on it.

Scoop, 5, Badger Rock (problem 3, page 209)

Lakes / Crags

St Bees

54.515801
-3.626261

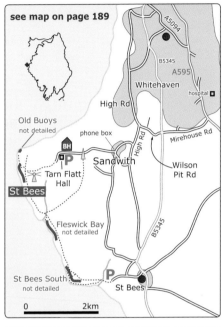

see map on page 189

A5094
B5345
A595
Whitehaven
hospital
High Rd
Old Buoys
not detailed
phone box
Mirehouse Rd
High Rd
BH
P
Sandwith
Tarn Flatt
Hall
Wilson
Pit Rd
St Bees
Fleswick Bay
not detailed
B5345
St Bees South
not detailed
P
St Bees

0   2km

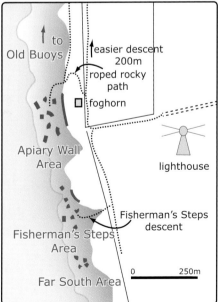

↑ to
Old Buoys

↑easier descent
200m
roped rocky
path

☐ foghorn

Apiary Wall
Area

lighthouse

Fisherman's Steps
descent

Fisherman's Steps
Area

Far South Area

0   250m

One of the nicest bouldering venues in the country. A seaside suntrap with over 60 problems of all grades on magical sandstone boulders. Generally non-tidal and quick drying. A bit out of the way so if you go, plan to spend the entire day. It will be one of those great days.

One of the essential bouldering areas in the country, rating along with Porth Ysgo as the best coastal bouldering spots. The approach, through grey concrete housing estates, is contrasted perfectly with the splendid isolation of the venue. Stunning, guano-bedashed rock walls tower behind, the deep blues of the Irish Sea below. Scattered betwixt are dozens of perfectly-sculpted boulders all fielding a great collection of fine problems on strong lines above usually perfectly flat landings. A magical place.

Detailed here are the Apiary Wall and Fisherman's Steps areas. For the Far South area head south for 50m from the Fisherman's area for 35 more problems on boulders and the crag ranging from 4 to 7C+.

20 min | 90 probs 3 - 8A best from 4 - 7C | vertical | steep | | shelter | tidal

Tom Peckitt on Clash of the Titans, 7A+ (problem 8). Photo: Dave Gator.

// Climbing: Tons of variety. Walls, cracks, aretes, traverses, slopers, pockets, pinches and crimps. The very odd slab. Many problems with optional sit starts. All grades, and low to medium-grade boulderers will have a field day. Problems are seldom high, although one mat is needed to take the sting out of the hard rock platform.

// Approach: From Whitehaven, follow signs for St Bees Village then look out for easily-missable signs for the village of Sandwith. From Sandwith, a private road turns off by a phone box. Follow this to Tarn Flatt Hall Farm, and pay £2 for parking. (There is a camping barn at the farm too - 01946 692162.)

Take the track towards the lighthouse. Continue to the fence and follow the coastal path right for 25m then cross the fence just past the foghorn. A scrambly and worrying descent, with hand-ropes on the steepest sections, gains the base of the cliff just by the Apiary Wall area. For the Fisherman's Steps area, continue for 300m, passing awkward, tidal rock steps along the way. The path above these boulders, the Fisherman's Steps, is another possible approach but is spooky and not for the feint-hearted. If the Apiary descent is too awkward for you, or if you have kids or dogs then stay on the upper path at the foghorn. After about 200m, and just after a stile, cross the fence and follow an easy winding path down to the base from where some boulder hopping brings you to the boulders.

// Conditions: Gets sun from midday till sunset. Very quick drying, although, as with all sandstone, don't climb if the rock is damp. A sheltered sun-trap. Generally the bouldering isn't too badly effected by tides but avoid at high tide if the sea is rough. Access between the Apiary and Fisherman's area is blocked at high tide. Although climbing is possible year-round, during the winter the rocky base can be trecherously slippery making climbing virtually impossible.

// Restrictions: The Fisherman's Steps (the descent path, not the boulders), should be avoided at nesting times (Feb 1 to July 31), as should the Far South area.

// Info: Brilliantly served by a free pdf guide on lakesbloc.co.uk, with all the newer stuff, as well as by Lakes Bouldering (Rockfax).

Old Buoys: Boulder hop north from Apiary Wall for 250m to just before the coast swings round. 28 smaller problems from 4 to 7C.

Fleswick Bay: Follow the coastal path then drop down to the big cliff for 50 problems from 4 to 6C+ along the base of the cliff then 20 problems 3 to 7C on free-standing boulders at the south end of the beach. (Bird restrictions.)

St Bees South: Park as for the beach in St Bees and follow the beach (at low tide) for 600m for 70 problems from 4 to 7C.

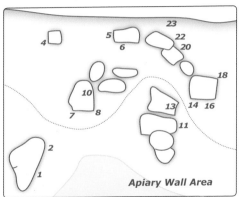

Apiary Wall Area

Apiary Wall Area

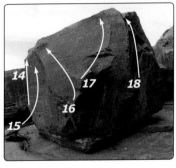

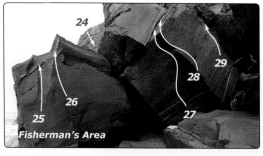

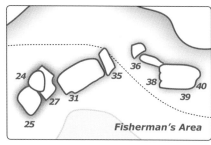

1   **Wave Wash Traverse** 6A+
2   **Undercooke** 7A *Sitter.*
3   **Yellow Desert Wall** 7C
     Direct from pockets. No arete.
4   **Yellow Desert Scream** 7A+ *Highball.*
5   **Headbanger** 7A
6   **Red Snapper** 7C
     Traverse from below corner to climb wall on crimps.
7   **Clash of the Titans** 7A+ *Sitter 8A.*
8   **Apiary Arete** 5
9   **Scoop** 6A
10   **Pockety Crack** 5 *Sitter.*
11   **Wall** 4+ *Sitter.*
12   **Arete from Sit** 6c+
13   **Honeycombe Way** 5+ *Sitter.*
14   **Arete** 5+
15   **Chipper's Wall** 7A+ *Run and jump.*
16   **The Rail** 6B
17   **Arete** 6A
18   **Groove** 2
19   **Kiss Kiss Bang Bang** 7C *Sitter (no block
     on left). Lip traverse then trend to drilled pocket.*
20   4+
21   **Lip Traverse** 6B+

22   **Slopey Arete** 6C+ *From sitter.*
23   **The Power of RAAA** 7C+
     The seam and scoop to finish mantelling the ledge.
24   **Bow Wow Prow** 7B
     *The steep prow, at the back of the boulder from 34,
     from a sitter to a rightwards finish.*
25   **Whaling Wall** 4+
26   **Baby Rib** 5
27   **Floating Points** 7C
     Sitter, hands below tramlines. No arete.
28   **Drop Off** 7A
29   **Groove** 6B
30   **The Other Arete** 7A+ *Sitter 7C.*
31   **Arete** 6C+ *Sitter 7B.*
32   **Groove** 3
33   **Crimper's Wall** 6C
34   **Crimper's Way** 6B
35   **Fruits de Mer** 7B *Arete on right from sit.*
36   **Flake** 4+
37   **Arete** 4
38   **Hueco Crack** 6C+ *Sitter 7A+.*
39   **Fisherman's Dyno** 6A *Not a dyno.*
40   **Tim's Crack** 7C
     The roof crack from a low sitter deep in the cave.

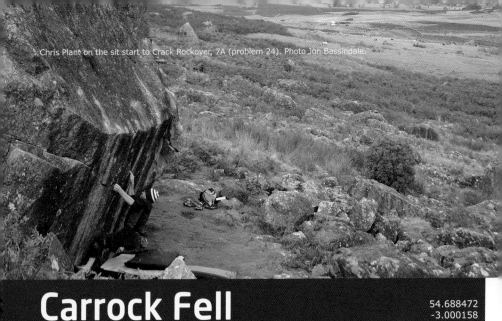
Chris Plant on the sit start to Crack Rockover, 7A (problem 24). Photo Jon Bassindale.

Carrock Fell

54.688472
-3.000158

A supermarket of roadside cranking. Big on quantity, big on setting, just not big on bigness. Loads of powerful problems in a nice quiet valley with superb views. Morning sun, quick drying and not too exposed. And all the little horses.

The gentle bracken-covered hillside of Carrock Fell, only 6km north of the A66, has over 35 bouldered-on boulders strewn along a few hundred metres of hillside. Many of these are quite small, some are highball and, like Baby Bear's porridge, many are jussssst right. The rock is rough gabbro, and where this venue really scores high is in the quantity stakes. Good for a full day of exploring. Good for families. Only a small fraction of the boulders are detailed here. See the definitive guides for tons more.

// Climbing: Usually steep and aggressive climbing on crimps, cracks and slopers. Some slabs and walls. Lots of sit starts, lowballs and some highballs, these more due to landings than altitude. Can be sore on the tips.

// Approach: Follow the small road from the A66 through Mosedale. About 1km past Mosedale the boulders will be seen on the left. The first, large angular block seen is The Kirk Stone. The first boulder described, Lean-To, is 200m north of this. From here, keep your eyes peeled to recognise the described boulders.

By Bus: The Caldbeck Rambler runs from Keswick to Carlisle via Mosedale in the summer, and every Saturday (0870 608 2608).

// Conditions: The boulders are on an east-facing hillside and get morning sun. Many boulders are quick drying and mostly clean. Sometimes boggy underfoot. Some parts are very brackeny in the summer. **Family friendly.**

// Info: lakesbloc.co.uk; **Lakes Bouldering** (Rockfax)

1   **Cave Route**   7B
     Sit start hanging an edge and undercut out to join 2.
2   **Lean-To**   6A+
3   **Bulge from Sitter**   6B+
4   **Next Bulge**   5   *Sitter.*
5   **Undercut Arete**   6B+   *Sitter.*
6   **Ground Force**   7B   *Lip traverse.*
7   **Vicicle Graffiti**   6B
8   **No Pain No Gain**   6B
9   **Via Dolorosa**   6B
10   **Traverse**   6C+
11   **Punk's Life**   7A+   *Dyno from sloper.*
12   **Little Groove**   6B
13   **Sitdown Arete**   6C+
14   **Lip Traverse**   7A+
15   **Sing a Rainbow**   7A   *Sitter.*
16   **I Can, I Can't**   6C+
17   **Mile High Guy**   7B
18   **I Can See for Miles**   6B   *A bit loose.*
19   **Lip Traverse**   6C+
20   **Bulging Wall**   6A
21   **Slopy Arete**   7A   *Sitter.*
22   6B+   *From the good low hold, or lower at 7A.*
23   **McHaffie's Crack**   6B+   *Sitter 7A+.*
24   **Crack Rockover**   6A   *Sitter 7A.*
25   **Traverse**   6C+
26   **Boardman's Arete**   6B+   *Sitter 6C+.*
27   **Rouse's Wall**   6C+

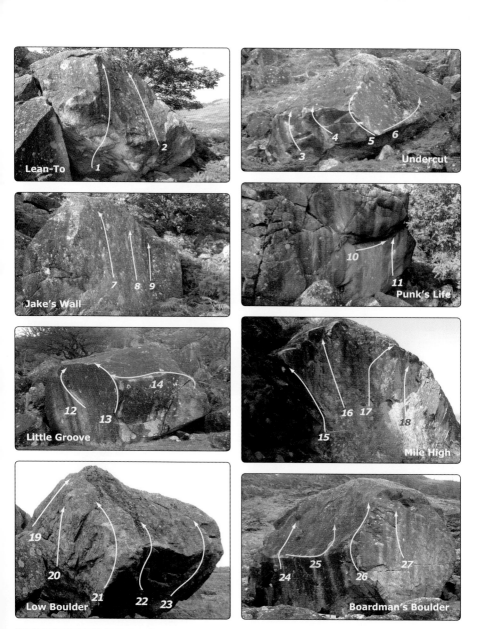

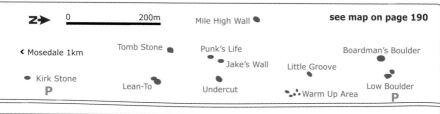

Gillercombe

54.511341
-3.199875

Awesome Arete

Mike's

Dirty Face

The Arete

1   **Gillercombing** 5
2   **Awesome Arete** 6C
    Scary.
3   **Neil's Wall** 7A   *Scary.*
4   **Traverse** 6B   *Sitter.*
5   **Mike's Problem** 6B
    Sitter.
6   6A+
7   **Left Arete** 6A   *Sitter.*
8   6A+   *Sitter.*
9   **Arete on Left** 4+
    Sitter.
10 3+
11 **Dirty Face** 4+
12 **Arete from Sit** 6A+
13 **Slab** 3
14 **The Arete** 7B+
    6C+ from a stand.
15 **The Arete Right-
    Hand** 7B
16 **The World's
    Hardest V3** 6B
17 **The Groove** 3
18 **Lip Traverse** 5+
19 **The Crack** 6A+

A nice little venue. Not tons here but a lovely location and the problems and rock are
good enough. A steep walk gives access to
half a dozen blocks of the usual mountain
rock with problems across the grades.

// **Climbing:** Sitty problems on edges and aretes. The
Arete is a classic of its 7B+.
// **Approach:** Park at the slate mine and follow the
steep footpath to the ridge. Follow the ridge left then
strike ahead to the boulders which lie under the big dark
crag. A bit boggy: 25 minutes.
// **Conditions:** This is a rainy part of the world.
When it's not raining the rock dries quickly. Exposed. A
wee bit boggy. **Family friendly.**
// **Info:** lakesbloc.co.uk: **Lakes Bouldering**
(Rockfax)

see map on
page 190

Honister Pass

P

B5289

Honister Boulders
2km

Slate Mine

YH

Gillercombe Buttress
(big dark crag)

Gillercombe Boulders

0   500m

47 probs
3 - 7B+
best from
4 - 7B

25 min

slabby   vertical   steep   exposed

Awesome Arete

Dirty Face

Mike's Problem

The Arete

Honister Boulders

North Boulder

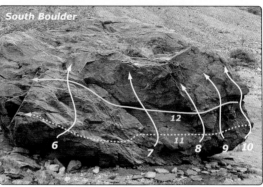

South Boulder

Nothing special in some ways but a great spot for a family and it will give daddy an hour of swinging around on rounded jugs which will ease the tension a bit for the afternoon. Two blocks sit either side of a popular, friendly river at the bottom of a really nice valley. Approach in seconds.

"Genuinely rubbish," said one commentator. "A nice little spot," said another. Whatever. It is, as an American might say, a low-investment venue. Have a look.

This venue doesn't ask much and won't offend anyone. A handful of stuff around 6A to 7A with nice landings. Good for beginners. The sun shines. Why don't you just chill out? If you can't then High Rock, 500m south, has a classic 7C right-to-left lip traverse called Ian's Lip.

// **Climbing:** About 10 problems in low and mid grades. Sit starts are the norm.
// **Approach:** See map on page 190. Both blocks are roadside.
// **Conditions:** Sunny and quick drying. Not too exposed. **Family friendly.**
// **Info:** lakesbloc.co.uk: Lakes Bouldering (Rockfax)

North Boulder
1   **Traverse** 6A   **2 Wall** 4
3   **Arete** 6A+   **4 Groove from Sitter** 7A
5   **Lip Traverse** 6C+

South Boulder
6   5+   7   6A   8   **Flake** 5+
9   **Eliminate** 6C+   *Avoid flake and arete.*
10   **Arete** 6A+   11   **Low Traverse** 6C+
12   **High Traverse** 6A

High Rock

South Boulder   parking

North Boulder

Bowderstone

54.541688
-3.155458

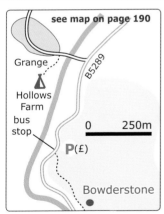

see map on page 190

Grange

B5289

Hollows
Farm
bus
stop

0   250m

P(£)

Bowderstone

An asteroid of power for those who like to have tourists admire their crimp-strength. A hardcore gallery of power-stamina that will satisfy the most basic and brutal of tastes. Weatherproof, sunless but slow drying. Perhaps the best single boulder in Britain. Also not far from Shepherd's Cafe, the best in the shire.

An axis of evil could be drawn from the Bowderstone in the Lakes to Parisella's Cave in the Wales, along which many power-Nazis would happily spend their lives travelling. A church of 45-degree slope and crimpfests. Not for the weak hearted. Rarr!

It's a bit limited for easy stuff and warm ups. Best seen as somewhere to go in the vain hope of actually getting up something. Absolutely tons to go at, but your session might only last for an hour or two before your tendons beg for the fleshpots of Keswick.

Developers include Jerry Moffatt, Pete Kirton, John Gaskins, Dave Birkett, Adam Hocking, Ryan Pasquil, Steve Dunning and Dan Turner.

// **Climbing:** Rhyolite boulder. The problems are hardcore; overhangs or roofs on crimps and slopers. Can feel sharp if you're feeling soft. Generally flat but hard landings, and a few mats are useful.
// **Approach:** The paying parking is 1km south of Grange. From the road just below this follow the path to arrive at the boulder in 10 minutes. The Borrowdale Rambler bus runs from Keswick to Seatoller.
// **Conditions:** Gets hardly any sun. Climbable year round. Conditions can be fickle. Many faces stay dry in the rain. Seepage can be a problem after rain, as too can condensation. Can be very midge-ridden. **Family friendly.**
// **Info:** lakesbloc.co.uk: **Lakes Bouldering** (Rockfax); **Borrowdale** (FRCC)

1 Ears of Perception 7B
From sat in the niche, pull out and climb leftwards to the prow and continue into the hanging scoop.

2 The Crack 6C

3 Crack Direct 6C+

4 Coming Up For Air 7A+ *Go left from the start of Bowderiser to finish up Crack Direct.*

5 Bowderiser 7A *Crack from a low jug.*

6 Inaudible Vaudeville 7B+ *Eliminate. Start with a pinchy pocket for the left and good edge for the right. Slap a good hold then on to the ladder.*

7 Picnic Sarcastic 7A+ *Follow the rampline then pass a pocket and carry on to a big jug. Sitter 7B.*

8 Phantom of the Opera 7C+
Ramp, razor crimps then right to lip.

9 Improper Opera 7B+
From flat hold, passing a poor pinch.

10 Opera Right Hand 7B+ *Starting to the right, use the circled hold to reach the same finish.*

11 Power Pinch 7A+ *Move up from edges, using a sidepull, a gaston then some crimps. Using the ringed hold is a more natural 6C+.*

12 Slapstick 7A *Climb from the rail to the sloper then the ramp above. Historically recorded as an eliminate going to the sloper with no intermediates at 7C.*

13 The Rib 6B+ *The line of least resistance.*

14 Lateral Gruntings 7B

15 XXXX 8A *The centre of the big overhang on the back side, from a stand.*

Lakes / Bowderstone

Jams on Pillar Face, 6A (problem 4). Photo: Niall Grimes.

Fisherground

54.387111
-3.316905

A beautiful spot with a couple of finger-trashing hours of superb granite action. Friendly atmosphere, quick access, clean and easy to find. Mmmmm. Go there.

A reclusive little Lake District gem, the Fisherground offers a finite but fine clutch of great problems on good, rough, clean granite. The problems are all a nice height, with maybe one or two higher ones above good landings. Great for a couple of hours, very family friendly and good for beginners. A happy place.

The King George is perfect for beers and meals, while Gosforth has cafes and shops. Fisherground Campsite (open March to September), 1km on the road towards the Hardknott Pass, has an adventure playground (01946 723 349). The La'al Ratty narrow-gauge railway, which puffs out of Ravenglass, is guaranteed steam-powered fun (01229 717171).

// Climbing: Burly, powerful moves are the order of the day, mainly on nice rounded holds, aretes, cracks and the odd crimp. Plenty of slabs too. Rough on the skin. A couple of friendly highballs but generally just about the right height. About 40 problems in the main area. The Rockfax and lakesbloc detail more climbing on granite boulders and outcrops, spread over a few different areas: about 50 more problems from 4 to 7C.

// Approach: Park either on the verge near the pub, or in the car park for Eskdale Green station. Follow a track over the little railway and, just before the house, turn left. The boulders are now about 100m ahead, and all lie within about a 60m radius.

// Conditions: They are quick drying, and get lots of sun. Climbable year round although can feel very hot in summer. Fairly sheltered. **Family friendly.**

// Info: lakesbloc.co.uk: **Lakes Bouldering** (Rockfax)

Foxes' Den and Wall Boulder ◄

White Slab

Gem

The Cave

Diamond

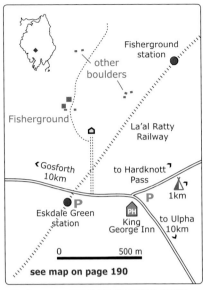

Diamond

The Cave

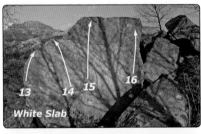

White Slab

Gem

Wall Boulder

Foxes' Den

1	**Left Crack** 4+	**8**	**Cave Crack** 4	**14**	2	**21**	**Rob's Crack**
2	**Rob's Wall** 7A+	**9**	**Crimpy Face**	**15**	**White Slab** 3+		6B+ *Sitter.*
	7C *from sitter.*		6B+	**16**	3	**22**	**Slab** 4 *The face*
3	**Classic Arete** 7A	**10**	**Strong Arete**	**17**	**Phil's Traverse**	*right of the arete.*	
4	**Pillar Face** 6A		6A+ *Sitter 7A+.*		6B+	**23**	**Fox Traverse** 5
5	**Crack** 3+	**11**	5+	**18**	**Flake** 4	**24**	5+
6	**The Diamond** 5	**12**	**Face** 6B+	**19**	**Light Fantastic**	**25**	**Overhang** 6A+
7	**Juggy Traverse**	**13**	**White Slab**		7A *Sitter.*	**26**	**Lip Traverse**
	4+ *Right-to-left.*		**Left** 4+	**20**	**Lip Traverse** 4		6A+

Sampson's Stones

Bouldering heaven with one hell of a walk. Among the best of Britain's mountain circuits, six megaliths scattered over Great Moss, the Belgian Congo of Lake District upland. Loads of problems, the first one being the walk in.

Carlsberg don't do bouldering venues, but if they did, then they'd put them a lot closer to the road than Sampson's Stones. Now, a tale of woe. In my many missions across the land while researching this volume my policy was to spare no effort in research. You wouldn't believe the crap I've visited. But twice I set off to the Sampson's. Once a biblical rain shower drove me away. A second time I set off but my spirits were low and as time passed I didn't seem to be getting any closer. The sight of the Heron Stones broke me and I scurried down again. So, dear reader, I must confess I haven't visited the Sampson's. Hence the crap pics.

However, perhaps we should persevere. I once asked Ray Wood who, along with Simon Panton, travelled the land visiting bouldering areas for their iconic Stone Circles articles in Climber, which of the venues they visited he was most impressed with. The Sampson's, he responded. Now that's a recommendation.

// Climbing: Climbing on great boulders ranging from smallish to 5 metres. Steep powerful climbing on crimps. slopers and aretes. Problems are a good size and one mat is usually enough. Lots of sit starts.Good across all grades, especially lower ones.

// Approach: Right. Deep breath. The parking is just as the Hardknott Pass levels off on its western side. Park in a large car park 1½ miles from the Hardknott summit. This is about 100m above a cattle grid on the road. A hundred metres west of the cattle grid, a small track, with a phone box at the corner, leads off to Brotherilkeld Farm. Take this track. Either follow the paths up the right side of the River Esk or, just before the farm, go left over a metal bridge and follow the left side. In lakesbloc (and Greg should know), it is recommended to take the left side then fork off left again after a little bridge (marked 'upper approach' on map). I'd take his advice on the matter as he has forced most of the development here. It might take one hour. Prepare for two.

// Conditions: Loads of sun but the altitude and setting mean they're best in nice summer days, but amazing on any sunny settled day. Generally very clean.

// Info: lakesbloc.co.uk: **Lakes Bouldering** (Rockfax)

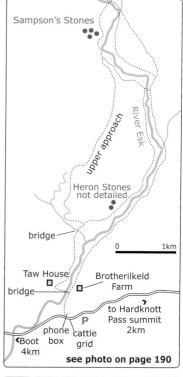

Hana Edwards-Lihocka on The Crack, 5+ (problem 3). Photo: Jon Bassindale.

Langdale Boulders

54.443824
-3.05907

Rhyolite doesn't come much better than this. Two roadside boulders with tons of powerful, quick-drying problems at all grades with perfect landings. Very friendly. Pure magic.

It was a tale of simple farming folk, many, many years ago. They lived in their mountainous lands, and they were happy, and their gods were happy. On dry days they would climb on their mountain crags. On wet days, they watched the flock. They were satisfied.

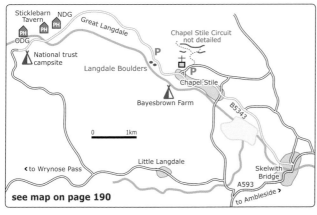

Then one spring day one of the little people was sent to Derbyshire to sell a cow, and when he came back he was full of tales of wonderment and magical small stones, Stanage, Cratcliffe, the Roaches, and big groups of happy people having a laugh and getting strong. The simple farming folk thought, "Why can we not climb so?" and they petitioned their gods.

Their gods were kind and they were merciful, and on the Seventh Day there was a mighty karate chop and some boulders were made in a field just west of Ambleside. The simple people saw them and they were happy, and lo, they tried the sit-down start. A tribal elder, in his joy, got out his chisel and hammer and inscribed in his native cup-and-ring markings on the stone, his message to the future – "Sucks to be You, Peakie!"

Lakes / Langdale Boulders

Upper Boulder

// **Climbing:** Slabby, vertical and slightly overhanging problems mainly on crimps, slopers and cracks. Often powerful. Good for traverses and sitting starts. One mat is usually enough.

// **Conditions:** Very clean and quick drying. Problems face all directions. Sheltered. **Family friendly.**

// **Approach:** From the A593, turn up Langdale. Pass through the village of Chapel Stile, and a few hundred metres after the village, the boulders can be seen in a field on the left. Park in a lay-by just beyond on the right. The Stagecoach 516 bus from Ambleside (0871 2002233) stops in Chapel Stile.

// **Info: lakesbloc.o.uk**: **Lakes Bouldering** (Rockfax)

// **Access:** Dogs on a lead if stock is in the field. Avoid the prehistoric cup-and-ring markings on the lower boulder.

Upper Boulder

Upper Boulder

1   **Stefan Grossman** 7C *8A sitter.*
2   **The Overhang** 6C+
3   **The Crack** 5+
4   **The Traverse** 7A *7C if done from the wall under Stefan Grossman.*
5   **The Pocket** 6C+
6   **Blunt Arete** 7A
7   **The Scoop** 3+
8   **Wall and Crack** 6A+
9   **Easy Wall** 3+
10 **Arete Mantel** 6B+ *Sitter.*
11 **Groove** 4+
12 **Wall to Mantel** 6B
13 **Nose on Slopers** 6A+
14 **Back Crack** 4

Lower Boulder

15 **Triple Dyno** *From low edges, dyno to the shelf (6A+), to the nose up and left (6C+) or to the top of the boulder (7B).*
16 **Mantel from sitter** 6C
17 **Sitdown Flake** 4
18 **Lower Crack** 3+
19 **Lower Wall** 3+ *Sitter 6B.*
20 **Wall** 5
21 **Blunt Arete** 4
22 **Rising Traverse** 7A+
23 **Top Traverse** 6C+

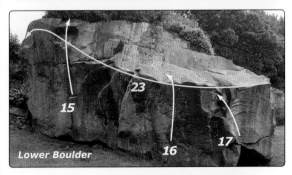

Lower Boulder

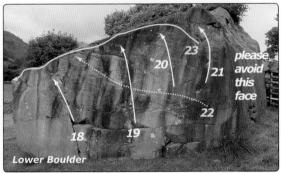

please avoid this face

Lower Boulder

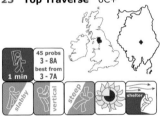

45 probs
3 - 8A
best from
3 - 7A

1 min

slabby   vertical   steep   shelter

Badger Rock

54.429263
-2.839864

Roll up! Roll up! A beautiful Lakeland valley peppered with bouldering. A variety of venues, some popular, some not. Best known for Badger Rock, a good block for a couple of steep, fingery hours' fun. Good landings, sometimes a little high. Easy walk in, beautiful views, and lots of harder stuff just over the wall.

Good climbing in a great location, within easy shooting distance of Kendal and Windermere. Lots of other bouldering in the vicinity, although none attracts the same attention as Badger Rock. It's not hard to see why. It is ringed with quality, fun bouldering on clean solid rock, above a nice grassy landing with an easy walk-in. 25 problems, 3 – 7C.

Just beside is Little Font (emphasis on the 'Little') has a further 40 problems from 3 to 8C. Yes, *8C*. Pilgrims of the Possible may wish to prostrate themselves below Shadowplay and make love to the little holds.

Beyond these, a further 15 minute's walk will bring you to the Garburn Boulder and Valley of the Kings. The casual visitor won't get this far and neither of these are detailed. The Garburn Boulder is a fine block with 18 problems, 5 – 7C, the best being a bunch of steep sitters in the 7A – 7C range. Very good. The

Valley of the Kings is a grand name for a bracken-covered hillside holding nine scattered blocks of alright mountain rock: 30 problems, 4 – 7B.

// Climbing: Badger Rock: Lots of steep and fingery climbing on positive edges, as well as some easier-angled stuff. About 25 problems, best from 4 to 7A. Perfect landings, although many problems are high enough to warrant mats.
Little Font: The problems are generally smaller, sit starts being the norm. Steep and crimpy.

// Approach: Turn off the A591 at Staveley and follow the Kentmere Valley to Kentmere Village. Park at the church, and pay at the honesty box. Keep following the road, around a left-hand bend, to some houses. At the far end of these, a signed path leads off to the Garburn Pass. Follow this for 150m to Badger Rock. Little Font lies in the trees just over the wall. The other areas are 500m further up towards the Garburn Pass. There is a train station in Staveley.

Shadowplay is near the back of Little Font.

// Conditions: Badger Rock is very sunny and quick drying, and is fairly sheltered. So too is the Garburn Boulder. Little Font mostly lies in trees so it is very sheltered and shady but is a wee bit green in places and will stay damp after a wet spell. Valley of the Kings is very brackeny so avoid in summer. **Family friendly.**

// Info: <u>lakesbloc.co.uk</u>: Lakes Bouldering

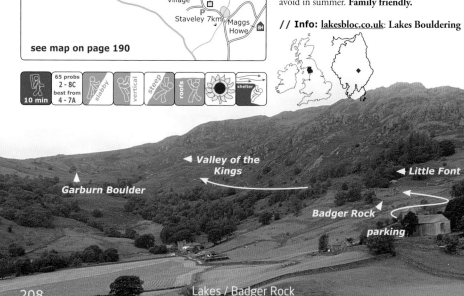

1	**Badger Arete** 5	*15*	**Wall** 5 *Sitter.*
	6C+ from a sit.	*16*	**Wall Left of**
2	**Left Traverse** 7A		**Arete** 6A *Sitter.*
3	**Scoop** 5	*17*	**Arete** 3+
4	**Wall** 5	*18*	**Slab** 3
5	**Groove** 4	*19*	**Fissure** 3
6	**Arch** 6B	*20*	**Slab** 2
7	**High Finish** 6B	*21*	**Flake** 3
8	**Right-Hand**		
	Traverse 7A+		

Link in with problem 2 for
a very tough 7B.

Little Font

9	**Brock Stone**	*22*	**Little Women**
	Wall 7A		8A+ *Low start,*
10	**Quartz Groove**		*right to left line.*
	6A	*23*	**Shadowplay** 8C
11	**Quartz Slab** 3		*Steep line of most re-*
12	**West Traverse**		*sistance.*
	6B+	*24*	**Tourniquet** 8A+
13	**Wall** 4+		*Sitter, then along*
14	**Arete** 4		*slopes to the groove.*
		25	**Supercalafrajal-**
			istic 7A *Sitter*

Little Font

Armathwaite

54.806399
-2.767138

A peach beach with a butch clutch of harder eliminates in a lovely, weatherproof setting, only a short detour off the M6.

Here's a tranquil little spot, just perfect for frustrated Lancastrian men driving south, having been rained out of Scotland once again. There are about ten obvious eliminates, 6A – 7A+, but that's probably enough. It's just one of those places for locals, or for fortunate passers-by. Lots of afternoon sun. The wall overhangs and the bouldering is very rainproof. A lovely pastoral setting amid some well-off farmland and a perfect sandy landing on a tranquil cove complete the picture.

// Climbing: The problems are slightly eliminate, but you can easily forgive that. Mostly crimps and flatties, and the odd sloper. Perfect sandy landing.

// Approach: Armathwaite is signposted from the A6, just south of High Hesket. In Armathwaite, pass the Dukes Head, and park just over the bridge. Gain the riverside path and follow it for about 800m. About 100m after some rapids, the path forks by a fence. Take the right fork, and 100m later, drop down right to the bay. By Train: Armathwaite has a train station. Perfect.

// Conditions: The small bouldering wall remains dry in the rain and doesn't seep very much and is quick drying making this a great venue on a bad day. Very sheltered. Afternoon and evening sun. Climbable year-round. **Family friendly.**

// Info: lakesbloc.co.uk

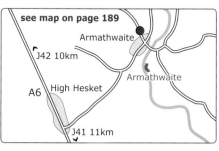

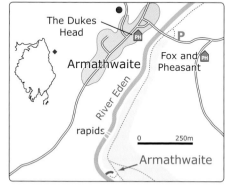

1   6B+   *From a low slot trend left to a diagonal crack then go direct.*
2   6C+   *From the same low slot, move left then go direct.*
3   7A+   *From the same low slot again, move up and right to climb the prow.*
4   **Prow** 7A

5   6C
6   6C
7   6B   *Sitter, from hands in low slot.*
8   **Exocet Start** 6A   *Sitter, avoiding the ramp for the feet.*
9   **Traverse** 7A+   *Low traverse to finish up Problem 1.*

Jams on problem 5, 6C. Photo: Niall Grimes.

Lakes / Armathwaite

Northumberland

Dan Varian on Queen Kong, 8A, at Queens Crag (page 241, problem 6). Photo: Mark Savage.

Andy Earl on Bad Company, 6A, at Kyloe in the Woods (page 221, problem 8). Photo: David Simmonite.

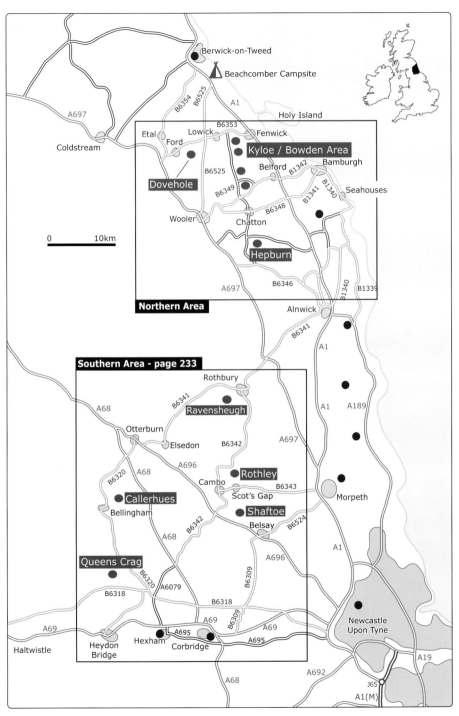

Berwick-on-Tweed

Beachcomber Campsite

Holy Island

A697

Coldstream

B6354
B6525
A1

Etal
Lowick
B6353
Fenwick

Ford

Kyloe / Bowden Area

Belford
Bamburgh

B6525
B1342

Dovehole

B6349
B1341
B1340
Seahouses

Wooler

B6348

Chatton

0   10km

Hepburn

A697
B6346

B1340
B1339

Northern Area

Alnwick

B6341

A1

Southern Area - page 233

A1
A189

Rothbury

B6341

A68

Ravensheugh

Otterburn

Elsedon
B6342

A697

A696

Rothley

B6320
A68

Cambo
B6343

Scot's Gap

Callerhues

Bellingham

Morpeth

B6342

Shaftoe

Belsay
B6524

A696

Queens Crag

A68

B6320
A6079

B6318
B6309

B6318

B6309
A69

A69

Newcastle
Upon Tyne

A69

A695

Haltwistle

Heydon
Bridge

Hexham
A695
Corbridge

A19

A68

A692

J65
A1(M)

I still find it hard to believe when I meet a boulderer and it turns out that they haven't climbed in Northumberland. The quiet golden Mecca of British sandstone, it ranks along with the Peak and Yorkshire as one of the original homes of British bouldering.

The place has a great pedigree. The seventies and early eighties were dominated by a no-nonsense band of Newcastle hard men including Bob Hutchinson, John Earl, Tommy Smith, Steve Blake, and chief among them the great Bob Smith. Smith, always at the head of the pack, led the area in terms of routes and, what the area is best at, mega-highball bouldering. Pete Kirton, that early example of the pure boulderer, also cut his teeth here in the early 80s. The hardest problems in the area today are mainly thanks to Geordie local Andy Earl with some super-hard additions from Scottish bedroom rocker Malcolm Smith. Standards have been consolidated by Dan Varian, Chris Graham and others.

Just to say, sandstone is a very delicate rock and due to erosion concerns the Bowden Doors and Henhole sections have no problem details given here. Just go there.

In this section it's really difficult to pick out what the really good crags are. Everytime I visited one of them I would think: this *has* to be the best crag in Northumberland. The showroom of Northumberland, or The County as locals call it, has to be the area around Belford. Boulderers could have endless visits to the Bowden and Kyloe crags; in fact many visitors don't get any further than these. But even in the northern area there are other great crags to explore, Dovehole or Raven Crag perhaps, or Hepburn for a great day out.

The crags in the south aren't so concentrated but give more varied and individual experiences. Callerhues has that killer combo of beautiful place, great problems and a long walk. South of this Queens Crag is home to a host of hardcore testpieces that will be of interest to bouncy players. Rothley is a pert little roadside scamp that suits a quick hit if you're after a bit of concentrated fun. Nearby the sprawling acres of Shaftoe contain friendly bouldering across the quality spectrum and gives, at best, a whole day of varied and fine climbing.

Andy Earl on The Bitch, 8A+ at Back Bowden (page 224, problem 14). Photo: Mark Savage

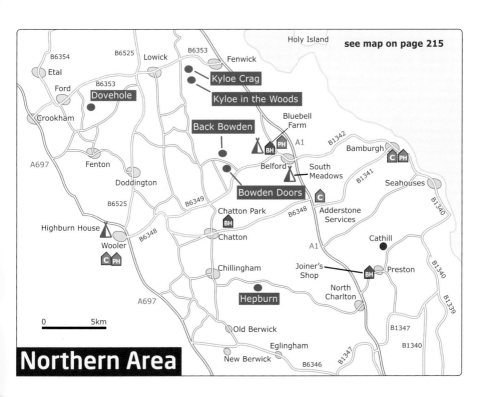

see map on page 215

Holy Island

Fenwick

Kyloe Crag

Kyloe in the Woods

Back Bowden

Bluebell
Farm

Dovehole

Bamburgh

Belford

South
Meadows

Bowden Doors

Adderstone
Services

Chatton Park

Cathill

Highburn House

Chatton

Wooler

Joiner's
Shop

Preston

Chillingham

North
Charlton

Hepburn

Old Berwick

Eglingham

New Berwick

0   5km

Northern Area

I call this image 'Evolution'. Sarah Daniels on Roof Left-Hand, 6C (problem 8). Photo: Niall Grimes.

Kyloe Crag

55.65222
-1.945133

A classy venue for a relaxed day with about 45 problems, mostly steep, 4 – 7C+. Great rock, quick drying, afternoon and evening sunshine. There is a God.

Kyloe Crag is the regal elder brother of the more popular Kyloe in the Woods, and offers both your fingers and your senses a pleasant contrast to it. While trees are still a motif, it has a more open, sunnier aspect. The bouldering is less concentrated and the atmosphere less intense. On weekends, the sounds of childrens chatter and the clinking of large hexes – ahhh... traditional music – reverberate around the gentle trees. The rock is superb, and the crag encourages a relaxed, contemplative day out.

// Climbing: Vertical and fingery, steep and fingery, or overhanging and fingery. Can you see a pattern? A wee bit highball.

// Approach: See map opposite. Park near the broad track, just north of a farm, and 400m south of the B6353. The crag is visible from the road. Park sensibly and approach the crag in 12 minutes. It is possible to approach from Kyloe in the Woods, but for some reason, this never seems as easy as it should, and you'll get lost and never be found.

// Conditions: It is climbable year-round, and especially beautiful on a sunny winter's day. Quick drying but never climb on damp sandstone. **Family friendly.**

// Info: Northumberland Bouldering Guide (NMC)

The Quarry

The Quarry

Overhanging Buttress

Fir Tree

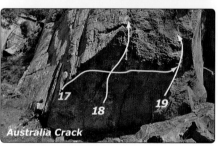

Australia Crack

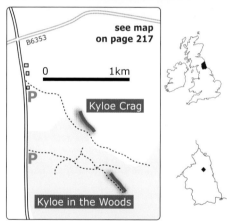

see map on page 217

B6353

Kyloe Crag

Kyloe in the Woods

1   **Quarry Arete** 7A   *Arete on left.*
2   **Active Service** 5   *Arete on right.*
3   **The Fat Lady Sang** 6B+
4   **Dirty** 4+
5   **Quarry Slab Traverse** 6A+
6   **Devil's Edge Start** 3   *Reverse from the break.*
7   **Learning to Fly** 7C   *Dyno up the overlap.*
8   **Roof Left-Hand** 6C
9   **Albatross** 7A+
10 **Traverse** 5+
11 **Green Greeny** 5+
12 **Wide** 3+
13 **Moment of Glory** 6A
14 **Rib** 3   15   3+
16 **The Crack** 4
17 **Posh Traverse** 7A+   *Start up the left arete
and cross the wall to finish in the groove on the right.*
18 **Prime Time** 7B+   *Sitter, up to slot then flake
on the slab.*
19 **Northern Territory** 7C   *Arete from a sit.*

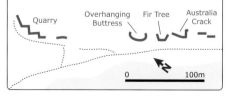

| Quarry | Overhanging Buttress | Fir Tree | Australia Crack |

45 probs
3 – 7C+
best from
5 – 7A+

12 min

slabby   steep   roofs   shelter

Andi Turner on Bad Company, 6A (problem 8). Photo: Niall Grimes.

Kyloe in the Woods

55.644395
-1.945674

A County treasure, and one of the country's essential venues. A top-notch crag in a magical wooded setting. Fierce, fingery and steep climbing on pockets and crimps. Be a tiger: kittens will not prosper here.

Hushed and spooky, it looms from the wooded approach like an unlikely Mare Celeste, only becoming real on close quarters. Mysterious and magical, feel the other-worldly atmosphere, an atmosphere where hobbits, unicorns and maidens wouldn't necessarily raise an eyebrow. Beguiling and bewitching, were it not for the blood spurting from your ravaged tips on the way home, you might well wonder: "Was I really there?"

The problems have been added through the years by the cream of local bouldering talent and by raiding Jocks. Bob Smith, John Earl, Dave Cuthbertson, Murray Hamilton, Jason Myers, Andy Earl, Chris Graham and Malc Smith have all set the standard here over the years.

// Climbing: Brilliantly brutal. Mostly steep, powerful and very fingery, requiring an aggressive and steely approach. Lots of traverses, stand-ups and sit-starts. The climbing is intense, problems are often sessioned and require lots of slapping and cranking. All but the fittest climbers will flail after an hour or two. The landings are good, but some mats will be appreciated for the up-problems, as many involve jumping off at the break at 4 or 5 metres.

// Conditions: Fickle. Very sheltered by trees. Faces south/southwest. Some afternoon sun can filter through. Not much wind and can be muggy on hot summer days and at any time of the year can be prone to condensation. Due its steep nature, some bits can stay dry in the rain. Climbable year round given the conditions although it can be dank in winter. Do not climb if it's at all damp.

// Approach: Park by a gated forestry track, 900m south of the Kyloe Crag parking, and 1.3km south of the B6353. Go over the gate and follow this track for 500m to a right fork. Take this and after 300m turn right at a T-junction, and the crag is on the left after 150m.

// Info: Northumberland Bouldering Guide (NMC); **Northern England** (Rockfax).

1 **Swan Wall Direct** 5+
  Escape down the crack to the right of 2.
2 **Swan Wall** 4
3 **Marmoset** 4
4 **Pink Gin** 6B+
5 **Red Rum** 6B
6 **Elf Direct** 6A
7 **Badfinger** 6A
  The wall just right of the arete. Sitter 6B.
8 **Bad Company** 6A
  Flake.
9 **Catapult** 8A+
  Dyno.
10 **Monk Life** 8B+
11 **Monty Python's Direct** 6C+ *Sitter 7A+.*
12 **Monty Python's Flying Circus** 7A+
13 **Bad Company Traverse** 6C *Start by stepping off the boulder.*
14 **Monty Python's Traverse** 7B *From a good hold at the end of 13, traverse all the way to the corner.*
15 **Cubby's Lip** 7B+
  Start with hands in the corner crack and finish up The Pearler. Or stay low and finish up The Yorkshireman at 8A.
16 **The Pearler** 5+
17 **Jocks and Geordies** 6C+ *Sitter 7A.*
18 **The Yorkshireman** 7B+ *Sitter 7C+.*
19 **Thin Hand Special** 5+
20 **Hitchhiker's Direct** 7B+ *Sitter 7C+.*
21 **Hitchhiker's Guide to the Galaxy** 7A+
  Gain the flake by stepping off the buried block.
22 **Rack Direct** 7C+
23 **Rack Left-Hand** 5+
24 **Leviathan** 8B+
  Malcolm Smith's epic, un-repeated, traverse. Link 13, 14, 15, and continue all the way to finish up Rack Direct. At the grade avoid resting-jams in the main cracks and the footledges under Monty Python's.

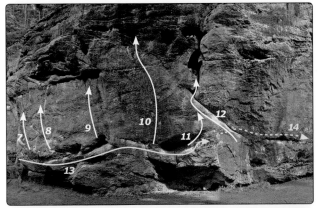

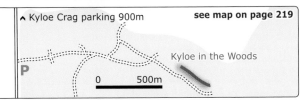

^ Kyloe Crag parking 900m

see map on page 219

Kyloe in the Woods

P

0   500m

Northumberland / Kyloe in the Woods

Bowden Doors

55.583475
-1.88452

A rolling wave of the finest County sandstone cresting over the yawning Cheviot moorland. Delicate and perfectly-sculpted, with endless steep problems that soon have you too high off the ground. A treasury of problems, highballs and solos, guaranteed to satisfy the soul and the senses. The colour of gold, but even more precious; it brings a tear to my eye just thinking about it.

As I lie here upon my sickbed (bloody Bubonic Plague), I keep my cockles warm with thoughts of what I call 'Sunset Crags'. Those places where, at the end of a great day climbing, the sun's last rages cast a magical spell of gold over the rock and transform it into an emotional gallery of memories and possibilities. A time to stop, stare, and thank whoever your god might be that you are a climber and you are there. There's something about the West that the East can never match.

The Roaches, Stanage, Almscliff, St Bees, Ysgo, Mynydd Dynas and Hartland Quay are all Sunset Crags. But chief among its peers, in my opinion, is Bowden Doors. Invariably with trashed tips and bulging biceps, with both fear and footwork satisfied, with a group of friends and usually with a long homeward drive ahead, for this is where you will want to end any trip to the County. Sit down for a few moments in silence. These moments are special.

Bowden Doors is the essential crag for any visit to Northumberland whether you are a boulderer or a route-fiend. It's not necessarily the best crag for bouldering, nor even, perhaps, the best for routes. However, it's the place that's special. The setting, the rock, the history. The mix of sit starts and terror-ridden topouts and everything in between.

Note: No problem details given. Due to concern about the delicate nature of the rock at Bowden Doors, and to avoid extra pressure falling on a selection of problems, there are no problem details given here. Just go and have an explore or check out the local guides.

// Climbing: Mostly steep or slightly overhanging wall climbs but with lots of properly steep stuff too. Technical, burly and slappy. Some very sharp crimps. Lots of problems become routes so use your sense: jump off or press on for the full buzz. The more mats the better.
// Approach: Go west out of Belford on the B6349. About 2½ miles from the village there is a turnoff (signed Hazelrigg and Lowick, leading to the Back Bowden parking). Stay on the B6349 for 600m and the crag lies on the right (invisible when going west). Park in bays on the left (south) side. A stile leads over the fence to the crag. Alternatively park as for Back Bowden and heather-bash your way to the left end (more awkward).
// Conditions: West facing and gets the sun from early afternoon. Fairly exposed. Quick drying but please don't climb here if the rock is at all damp as the delicate rock is weakened. On a related note, the hard surface of the rock is very thin. Once this goes the rock erodes and problems are destroyed, a fate that has happened to a few classics here. Don't brush at loose rock, just leave the problem be. If you feel your actions are damaging the rock in any way then err on the side of caution. **Family friendly.**
// Info: Northumberland Bouldering Guide (NMC); **Northern England** (Rockfax).

Raven's Crag: For much the same ambience, albeit much quieter and with easier, less frequented climbing, stroll away from Bowden Doors for 200m to find 75 problems, mainly 4 – 6C, mainly walls and slabs, often enjoyably highball. See NBG.

Climbers on Cave Left-Hand, 6B.
Photo: Niall Grimes

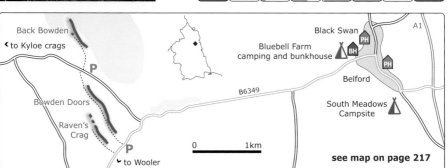

see map on page 217

Back Bowden

55.591345
-1.892384

Yet another star on the Northumbrian crown. A brooding and very sheltered crag that sometimes offers an option on a bad day. However, while it lacks on setting, the climbing is as classic as on any crag and will give a whole day of burly bat-finking.

Now, no offence to the locals, but if I had been given Bowden Doors, then I would have said 'No thanks' when I was offered seconds. Not so the Geordies, and for their boldness they were served up another huge dollop of sandstone as fine as any in the country. This is what Southern Sandstone dreams of becoming. It almost seems like a waste to have two such good crags next to each other.

But no, it's not a waste, it's an indulgence. Shier, and a bit uglier, it nestles behind it's prettier brother, but once you get to know it, you'll like the personality.

Andi Turner showed me a really cool hold at the top of Hazelrigg Wall. Go find it.

// Climbing: Tons, all across the grades. The easier problems that tackle the steep sections are demanding on strength and might feel ugly if you haven't got it. From here, the climbing becomes sublime as it moves up the grades. Physical and fingery climbing that's also fairly demanding on technique. Similar to, but a little more subtle, than Kyloe in the Woods. It's also got a sweet vertical wall and, as if you needed it, another roof section as well as a handful of small, quality boulders. A couple of mats are useful despite good landings. Good for a full session.

// Approach: See map in the Bowden Doors section (previous page). Follow the approach shown, taking the B6349 out of Belford, then the Hazelrigg turn after 2½ miles. Park on a verge after almost a mile, just over the crest, near a gate. Also parking for Bowden Doors. There has been a lot of trouble here when the farmer has had his gate blocked. Be very careful not to. The crag is not visible but lies 120m behind a wee outcrop visible on the skyline. Go over the gate and follow muddy paths.

// Conditions: South-west facing. The sunny bits get sun from the afternoon while other bits in the trees get little sun. Very sheltered. Many sections are rainproof but some also have a tendency to stay damp. Don't climb on any rock that's at all damp.

// Info: Northumberland Bouldering Guide (NMC); **Northern England** (Rockfax).

The Arches – *Halfway along the roof section.*
1   **Arches Start**   6A   *From the low jug.*
2   **Roof and Wall**   7A+   *Make a hard move to the lip then continue on tiny holds.*
3   **Hard Reign**   6A   *From the jug at the back.*
4   **Weird Sisters Two**   7A
5   **Weird Sisters Three**   6C+

The Sorcerer
6   **The Young Warlords**   6C   *Classic traverse from left end to the right end.*
7   **Harry Potter**   7A+   *From the big pocket.*
8   **Black Magic**   6B   *Big line to the good hold on the lip.*
9   **Intermediate Traverse**   6C+   *Holds below the break into The Sorcerer.*
10   **Pockets Traverse**   7C
11   **Sorcerer's Apprentice**   5+
12   **The Sorcerer**   6A

Tube Boulders – *The boulders below the classic E4 traverse.*
13   **The Bitch**   8A+   *Out on crimps from the back of the roof enter and finish up the scoop.*
14   **Mantel Misery**   6A+   *Traverse into mantel.*
15   **Mantel Masterclass**   6C
16   **The Runnel**   4
17   **Super Slab**   4+
18   **Rib**   3
19   **Warm-Up Arete**   3
20   **South Wall**   6A+

The Arches

The Sorcerer

Tube Boulders

Bat Cave

Hazelrigg Wall

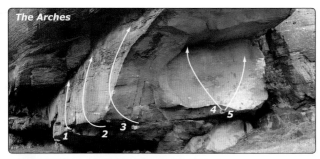

The Arches

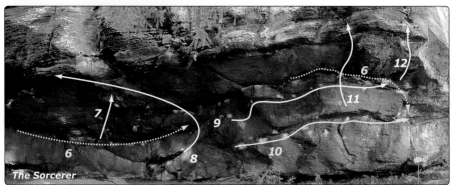

The Sorcerer

Tube Boulders

Tube Boulders

Hazelrigg Wall

Bat Cave

Hazelrigg Wall – Highball wall up and right.
21 Four Mats Wall 7B
22 Stepped Flake 3
23 Hazelrigg Wall 5
24 Risk and Hope 6A+ *The hanging corner.*

Bat Cave – Come on arms, do your stuff.
25 Barbastelle 7A *Start from the back and gain Dwarf's Nightmare on the lip.*
26 Bechstien 6C *Diagonal to the lip.*
27 Brandt 6B+ *Bish, bash, bosh.*

Dovehole

55.622581
-2.056332

A herd of slightly soft boulders that are perfect for a slightly soft day. A dozen blocks set amidst a forest clearing that give the sort of place where you'll go to chill out. A good place for a family picnic and a bit of scrambling/bouldering. Cute.

Not a heavyweight crag by any means but it is gentle and might just be what you need. A funny location, nestled in a clearing in a pine wood. Or they might be cedar. Or larch. The rock's not perfect but you'll have a nice time anyway. A bit of rock-hopping, a bit of bouldering then a bit of a scramble. What's wrong with that?

I'm pulling the Joker here. There's no grades for any of the problems because if I singled some out I'd worry the soft sandstone would get trashed. Ha! As if anyone's going to buy this stupid book. Anyway the rock's delicate. These are like some little part of Font where the baker didn't leave the rocks in the oven long enough. But still, they're there to be enjoyed.

// Climbing: The climbing here is gently boring, in the nicest possible way. The rock is blobby and problems are often sit starts that lead into bulging middles followed by sloping tops. As well as blobs there are some vertical walls, the very odd slab and one speleological tube. Holds are horizontal breaks, slopers, pockets and sometimes a fabulous honeycomb. Landings are generally flat grass. The rock is soft and the surface can be a wee bit sandy so don't climb if the rock is at all damp and don't go brushing it. About 90 problems in the easier and middle grades. Great for beginners.

// Approach: Follow the map. The boulders can be seen in a clearing in the woods on the approach. Visitors must ask permission to climb at Ford Woodhouse Farm: the owner is very gracious. Go back and park below the boulders and slog uphill for 100m to the clearing.

// Conditions: The boulders are on a south-facing hillside. Problems face all directions and there is plenty of sun to be had. The setting, in a wooded clearing, ensures plenty of shelter from the wind. Fairly quick drying but please don't climb on damp sandstone. **Family friendly.**

// Info: Northumberland Bouldering Guide (NMC).

Goat's Crag: Nearby is a more hardwearing outcrop. I went to Goat's Crag but to me it lacked the charm of Dovehole. It was a bit mundane. A few good things, for sure. If you're up for it follow the map and park at the junction with the farmer's lane. Follow this and ask permission at the house to visit the crag. For the info see the Northumberland Bouldering Guide.

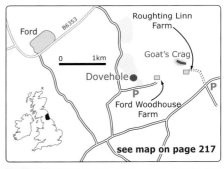

see map on page 217

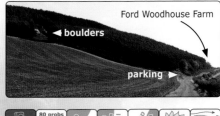

80 probs
4 - 7A+
best from
4 - 6C

2 min

Rachael Barlow grasps Dovehole sloper with Ali spotting. Photo: Pete Robins.

Craig Marshall on A Northern Soul, 7A+, at Hepburn (page 231, problem 23). Photo: Jenny Randall.

The Magician's Nephew, 6B+, on the Rabbit Stone at Queens Crag (page 241, problem 22). Photo: Ray Wood

A bit of an unsung gem among the Northumbrian heavyweights but which still gives a swell day out. A fine ridgeline ferries a load of great little problems best suited to the 4 to 7A climber from where, if you are up to a 7A+ highball, you can continue to do one of the best rides about. A fine spot giving a good few hours if you have already ticked the more pumped-up crags or for those seeking a quieter experience.

Driving across Hepburn Moor you are struck that here is a genuinely remote and unspoiled patch of the world, yet only a few miles from the A1. Lots of birds and big skies and double-barrelled countrymen. The climbing lies on the scarped edge of the moor where a ridge of blocks overlooks forestry below. A great little venue.

// Climbing: The problems range from the very small to the rather big and the landings range from perfect to fairly gash: but don't let that put you off. There's plenty of sport to be had no matter how you feel about green-sticking your tibia. The problems along the ridge, usually just-beyond-vertical walls and aretes, come in a range of height and you could easily enjoy a couple of sketchy highballs before doing a load of less threatening stuff (problems 1 to 8 are highballs). A few boulders lie just below the ridge giving nice powerful sit-start type stuff. Cracks and rounded holds are the order of the day. Further on, in the trees, are a few very small blocks and below this is the Hepburn Crag area with a couple of big boulders and the wonderful A Northern Soul. A few pads are very useful here.

There are more problems on the moor behind, with west- and north-facing blocks. See the map for locations and the Northumberland Bouldering Guide for all info.

// Approach: Park in the Forestry Commission car park and follow the land rover track into the trees. 30m after a wooden gate strike left up the hill on a path. A short steep approach (6 minutes) leads to the ridge. The climbing here starts with a few scattered boulders on the

left then gathering itself into a mini-edge on the right after about 60m. The Ridge Boulders lie just 25m below.

For the Hepburn Crag area, be prepared to hunt. A wire fence runs from below the Ridge Boulders and passes just above the crag, essentially a little dirty outcrop, after about 200m. So, from just past problem 15, carry on along the hillside and slightly downhill into the trees to eventually meet the fence. Follow this, keeping your eye open for boulders on the right. Cross the fence and you are there. The problems are obvious here, with Titanic lying level with the crag about 30m through the trees. Allow 10 minutes from the boulder ridge.

// Conditions: Problems face south-west and get loads of afternoon and evening sun. The ridge is in a fairly exposed position so catches the wind. However blocks below the ridge get surprising shelter. Stuff out of the trees is quick drying but can be a wee bit scrittly. There's some moss around the Crag Boulders. A bit brackeny in high summer but climbable year round.

// Info: Northumberland Bouldering Guide (NMC)

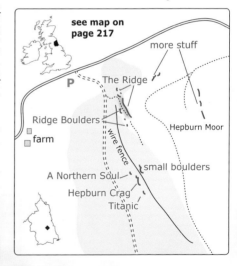

8 min	90 probs 3 - 8A best from 4 - 7A+	slabby	vertical	steep		shelter

1	**Prow** 6C *Sitter.*
2	**Crack Problem** 5+
3	**Photo Opportunity** 5
4	**Orthopaedia** 7A+
5	**IF** 7B
6	**Rheumatology** 7A
7	**Orthopaedic Arete** 6B
8	**Trauma Arete** 6A

    Crack and arete on the right end of the boulder.

9	**The Sidewall** 7C
	Wall left of arete from sitter.
10	**Arete** 6A
11	**Short Crack** 3
12	**Long Crack** 3
13	**Hard** 6B
14	**Ramped Arete** 4
15	**Tricky Wall** 4+
16	**Another Arete** 6B+
17	**Another Flake** 6C

18	**Sandy Arete** 4+
19	**Roof Left-Hand** 6B
20	**Roof Right-Hand** 6B
21	**Substantial** 5
22	**Preparation H** 8A
	Standing start.
23	**A Northern Soul** 7A+
	Awesome highball arete.
24	**Titanic Flutes** 5+
25	**Titanic** 7A

Stu Campbell on Eyes of Silence, 7C+ at Callerhues (page 239, problem 13). Photo: Mark Savage.

Southern Area

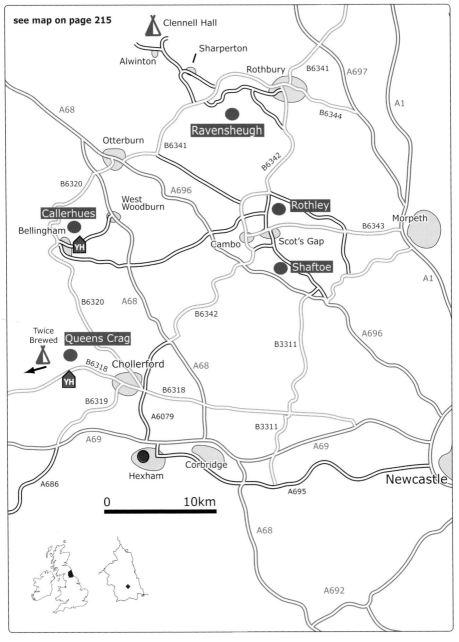

see map on page 215

Clennell Hall

Sharperton

Alwinton

Rothbury

B6341

A697

A68

Ravensheugh

B6344

A1

Otterburn

B6341

B6342

B6320

A696

West Woodburn

Callerhues

Rothley

Bellingham

YH

Cambo

Scot's Gap

B6343

Morpeth

Shaftoe

A1

B6320

A68

B6342

A696

Twice Brewed

Queens Crag

B3311

B6318

Chollerford

A68

YH

B6318

B6319

A6079

B3311

A69

A69

Hexham

Corbridge

Newcastle

A686

A695

0   10km

A68

A692

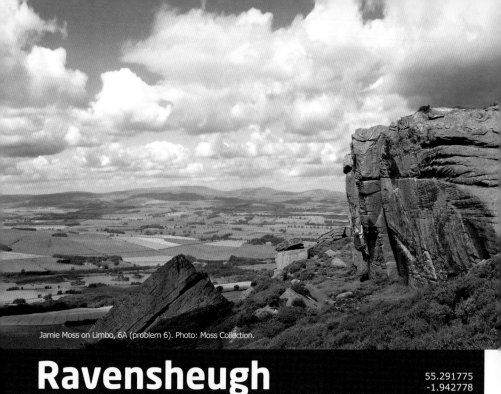
Jamie Moss on Limbo, 6A (problem 6). Photo: Moss Collection.

Ravensheugh

55.291775
-1.942778

The summer retreat for Northumbian gnarlers. A fantastic bastion set amid faraway moorland with a score of sublime lines that often claw their way into highball territory, and beyond. A north-western aspect and lofty altitude mean that it will enjoy perfect conditions when Bowden slopers will be buttery bumps. A special crag.

Not a crag for the masses mainly due to feisty climbing and a longish, albeit beautiful, walk in. This is a good thing as that means more magic for those who make it up: the fairies still live at Ravensheugh. This is a crag you will remember. Best suited to good climbers: lowballers won't be happy here.

The other venues listed here spread over the Simonside hills provide tons more challenges, generally much less highball. A great day can be had exploring them all.

// Climbing: Sandstone crag. Burly climbing on roofs and steep bulges on well weathered holds. Problems are often highball, sometimes alarmingly so. Bring lots of pads and a good team.

// Approach: Turn south in Rothbury down Bridge Street (B6342), signposted towards the hospital. Cross the river and turn right, signposted Great Tosson. Follow for 700m then go right at the junction again for Great Tosson. After 2 miles go left (Great Tosson) and

upon reaching the village, after 50m, turn left. Park in a large car park in the trees on the right after 800m. Follow the map to Ravensheugh or other areas. The walk is uphill, long but relaxing.

// Conditions: North-west facing and best visited on a nice summer day. Lots of shade. Quite exposed. The rock can be dirty in parts so a soft brush and a short ab rope might allow some problems to be brought into condition. Go easy with the brush as the rock is quite soft. Parts can be slow drying. Best after a few dry days and never climb on any damp sandstone.

// Info: Northumberland Bouldering Guide (NMC)

Other Simonside Venues
Simonside Woods: A handful of excellent hard lines lurk in the woods. Awooga, 7C (sitter 8A), a prow just right of a slot-cave, is a neo classic. Well worth hunting out. As are the problems above the track.
Dove Crag: 26 problems on small north-facing craglets. Generally sit starts, best from 4 to 6B.
Old Steall Crag: 23 problems with a friendly aspect, facing all directions. Best 4 to 7A+ (Dulcinea is the classic 7A+).
Potts Buttress: 25 problems, mostly 4s and 5s but with some tough 7s.
Simonside North Face: The impressive crag has a dozen problems scattered about its base, mainly 4s and 5s. See the Northumberland Bouldering Guide for all these venues and more besides.

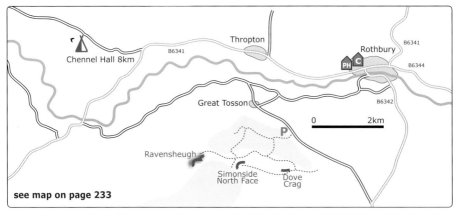

see map on page 233

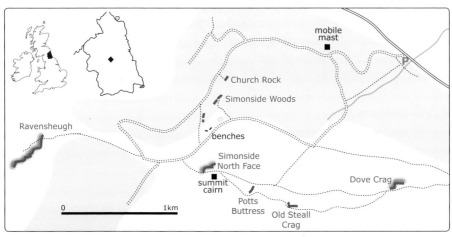

Parallel Cracks

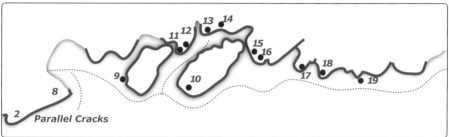

Parallel Cracks

1   Low Level Traverse 7A   *Finish up Big Daddy. An easier finish hand traverses down the ramp right of the third wide crack then moves up and left and uses a hollow flake to gain the break at 6B for the whole traverse.*

2   Incident 5   *HVS.*

3   Rubberneck 5+   *HVS.*

4   The Wall 5+   *Wall with the aid of the left arete.*

5   Central Parallel Crack 2   *VDiff.*

6   Limbo 6A   *E1.*

7   Arete-shun 6A   *The left arete of the third wide crack.*

8   Big Daddy 6C+   *Vague flake.*

9   Lupino Lane   *An ungradeable classic of the County. Leg it down the hill in a flurry of leg kicks and you may end up heading towards some opposing holds high up near the right arete (top out once gained). Most likely you will end up heading towards a 5m landing radius of boulders and grass. The grass is preferable.*

10   Ivan Dobsky 8A+   *Starting from a jug on the left at the back of the huge roof, head slightly rightwards to the blunt keel. Squeeze your way out this and round some hard lip moves. Jump off at the break or ideally top out.*

11   Flake Roof 7A   *From a sitter at the back of the short roof head out direct via some nice holds.*

12   Flake Roof Right 7A+   *From the same start as Flake Roof head out rightwards through the roof and up the blunt arete.*

13   Octopus 7A   *A total classic but beware the grade. Eight long arms are advised for it to feel 7A.*

14   Reiver 7B+   *Highball bouldering perfection up the blunt arete. Sublime. Can get dirty.*

15   Check oot me Tyres 7C+   *This lies just right of Ravensheugh Crack and under the roof. From a sitter at the back on the shelf head out the crimpy pods to the lip. Cunning your way righwards to slightly near the very blunt rib and finish direct up to the ledge.*

16   Check oot me Pipes 7C+   *Lean backwards from the ledge. Kiss bicep. Fire to hold on the lip and top out.*

17   Penfold 7B+   *The classic high arete. The right wall is out all the way.*

18   Underpowered 7A+   *From a sitter near the corner follow the lip rightwards and under the prow to the poor ledge. finish up the crack above (E1).*

19   The Duergar 7A+   *The high arete is climbed on its right with the aid of a flake high on the wall for the right hand to a crux topout.*

20   Debbie McGee 7A+   *100m right is a buttress with some aretes. This climbs the smaller blunt arete 5m left of the taller steeper one (The Magician).*

21   The Magician 7C+   *The taller overhanging prow to the right with a jump start to prominent horizontal slopers. E7 7a. The wall immediately right is The Plumber, 7B.*

Kev Gibson on Pott's Scoop, 5+, Pott's Buttress. Photo: Fraser Harle.

Pete Michal on Dulcinea, 7A+, Old Steall Crag. Photo: Fraser Harle.

Callerhues

55.153349
-2.238679

An escarpment of fine bouldering in a lonely and beautiful setting that will easily reward aesthetes who don't mind a little bit of a walk or a little bit of fear. A natury paradise with either tough highballs or lowballs. A venue that's good for the soul. Good for a full day out.

Another one of those 'best crags in Northumberland' type of places. However, like many such venues it will never become busy, protected from the hoards by the horror of a thirty-minute walk-in. Which is, of course, a good thing: this is one of the special places. Lying amidst wild moorland and not far from the Pennine Way the crag is a paradise of unspoilt wilderness. The fact that it holds good bouldering is a bonus.

The older highballs are the work of the usual County gnarlers, Bob and Tommy Smith and the like. Dan Varian realised the crag's true bouldering potential in more recent years and it is he who is responsible for most of the modern problems.

// Climbing: Great variety of styles on fine-grained sandstone. The problems are based along an escarpment that ranges from 3 – 7 metres high. As such it gives everything from sitters to lowballs to mad E-worthy highballs. Coupled with this is a good variety of holds: slopers, cracks, perfect pockets, aretes and an agglomeration of obscure bubbly snakes means that you won't get bored. Lots of stuff that isn't very high but you'll really feel you're missing out if you're not into highballing (on the Footpath area or around Crouching the Mahogany – which, and I never knew this, is slang for taking a shite, giving a clue to the style of the crux move) in which case a few mats will be a good idea. Landings are generally soft. Conversely, the grades are quite hard.

// Conditions: An exposed crag that's best in good weather. It faces south-west and gets sun from early afternoon till sunset. The rock is quite clean but will be more scrittly in the winter months, something you won't appreciate when 7 metres up. As with all sandstone, please don't climb for a couple of days after rain as it becomes brittle. If, like me, you hate bracken more than anything else made by God or man in this damned world, you'll find it hard going in summer. Therefore best in spring and autumn.

// Approach: Take the road from Bellingham to West Woodburn then take the private road to Blakelaw Farm. Here you must go to the farm and ask permission to park. Far from a chore, this is one of the great things about climbing in Northumberland, these little interactions with really nice farmers. However, the farmer requests that large groups and dogs avoid the crag. Follow the Pennine Way as far as a copse of trees (the obvious more direct approach is boggy) then strike off to the crag. A bracing thirty-minute yomp.

// Info: Northumberland Bouldering Guide (NMC)

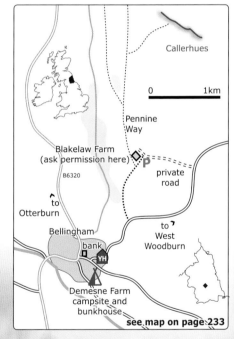

Left-Hand   Boulevard   Crouching

Northumberland / Callerhues

Left-Hand

The Crag: Boulevard

The Crag: Crouching

Right-Hand

Right-Hand

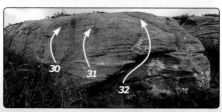

1 **On The Mark** 4 *7A+ from opposing chest-height sidepulls.*
2 **Bracken Black** 4
3 **Colour Bruise** 4+
4 **Smile** 7C+ *Prow from sit.*
5 **Cloud Nine** 6A+ *Flake.*
6 **Love Handles** 6A+
7 **Air** 7A+
8 **Postal Service** 6B
9 **Wall** 4+
10 **Iron Pirate** 5+
11 **Boulevard** 6C+ *E3.*

12 **Footpath** 6B *E2.*
13 **Eyes of Silence** 7C+
14 **Crouching the Mahogany** 7A+ *E4+.*
15 **Weeping Fingers** 6B *E2.*
16 **The Storyteller** 6C *E5.*
17 **Task Master** 5+ *HVS.*
18 **Binary Choice** 6A
19 **Softly Softly** 7A
20 **Soft Touch** 7B+
21 **In The Clouds** 5
22 **Vittel Movement** 6B

23 **Golf War** 6B+
24 **Microbe** 5+
25 **Blue Caix** 6A *Sitter.*
26 **Dot to Dot** 5+
27 **Fone Call** 6B
28 **Happy Slapping** 6A *7A from sitter on ramp.*
29 **Daisy Chained** 5+
30 **Pasty Face** 5
31 **O Zone** 5
32 **Factor 15** 6B

Queens Crag

A dark battlement of problems of the highest order lying in the lee of Hadrian's Wall. However no Roman governer could ever have come up with defences to match those of this crag. A tough paradise for good climbers with a full day's worth of bouldering and a good place to session a hard problem.

A cold kitchen for people who can take the heat. A stout crag where you'll need to bring a load of psyche and as such it is a venue for good climbers. It might not be to everybody's taste, however, as it feels tough and tall and is not a great crag for messing around on. There are loads of easier problems but these don't quite have the charisma of the harder ones and are often highball.

The crag has become a bit of a forcing ground of late too since the new millennium thanks to climbers such as Dan Varian, Chris Graham, Ned Feehally and Andy Earl. The Magician's Nephew, Worldline, Red Dragon, Queen Kong and Ark Royal are as good as anything their grade in the country.

Queens Crag also has a great sense of historical depth about it. On the approach as you walk over old ditches and random hummocks it's easy to think of ancient Roman earthworks designed to keep marauding Scotchmen away from Northumbrian maidenhood. And have sympathy too for poor Roman soldiers taken from the comforts of the capital – lions, the baths and a bit of nookie – and stationed here in this godforsaken outpost of the known world. Feel that wind, Christian.

// **Climbing:** Fairly stout, whatever the grade: be prepared to clench. Lots of highballs. The rock is an unusual dark sandstone with a very fine grain demanding fairly aggressive climbing on edges, slopers, cracks and aretes. There are a few slabs. Lots of sit starts and lots of highballs, some being what the over-40s refer to as E7s. Bring a lot of pads.

// **Conditions:** A crag in a wild setting overlooking a beautifully bleak moor. It faces north-west and is generally pretty shady although with its serrated nature lots of west-facing sidewalls get sun on summer evenings. Lots of dank corners although this dankness doesn't affect the climbing too much. Best on nicer days in the nicer months: on cold grey blustery days it can feel a bit austere.

// **Approach:** The crag is on the north side of the B6318 Military Road, 1.4 miles from Housesteads Fort and 3 miles from Bricolita car park. There is a house by the road and a gated farm track to its left. Go through the gate and follow the track that passes in front of the farm. Ask permission to climb at the farm (and you may be asked for a £2 parking charge) and continue along the road to park by a cattle grid. Driving beyond here goes onto another farmer's land and might cause hassle. Continue along the track following it to the lower cattle grid at the bottom of the hill. The crag can be seen on the skyline from here. (Careful not to confuse it with the chossy Sewingshields crag.) Approach direct across the fields (15 to 20 minutes from the lower cattle grid), keeping always to the right of the wall. This can be boggy. Drier, more direct approaches are possible but for well-shod first-time visitors the approach described is the most straightforward.

// **Info: Northumberland Bouldering Guide** (NMC)

see map on page 233

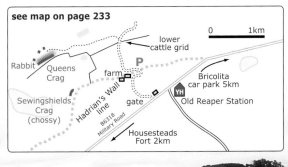

Left End

Middle

Right End

Rabbit Boulder

1 First Problem 4+ *Flake from sitter.*
2 Worldline 7B
Double aretes from a sitter at the back.
3 Prow One 5
4 Steve's Layback 4+
5 Prow Two 5 *Sitter 7A.*
6 Queen Kong 8A *Highball. Sitter 8A.*
7 Cinderella 7B *Seam in the broad groove.*
8 Border Reiver 6C *Highball arete.*
9 Stell Green Groove 4 *Highball.*
10 Feet of Strength 7C+ *Layback the arete on its right.*
11 The Crack in the Shadows 8A
Blank wall to set of cracks. Very ballsy.
12 Glorious 7A+ *Very highball arete on left.*
13 Groove 5
14 Scooped Arete 6A
15 Botterill's Mantel 5+

16 Wall 5+
17 The Queen is Dead 7A+ *Highball. An indirect sitter starts from down and left, following the tiny arete then moving right to QID at 7B+.*
18 How Soon is Now 7C+ *True sitter to 18.*
19 Ark Royal 8A+ *Highball. An easier escape, dubbed Ark Royearl, moves right near the top to the finish of 21 at 8A.*
20 QE2 8A+ *Sit start to AR that escapes into 21. Not yet linked into the original.*
21 Hat Full of Hollows 7B *Highball.*
Rabbit Stone: *Tricky scary descent. Scope it out beforehand.*
22 Magician's Nephew 6B+ *Prow.*
23 Rabbitstone Crack 6A+
24 Red Dragon 8A *Arete on its right.*
25 Mxymatosis 7A
26 Descent Route 5

Liz and Helen watching Rich Cross on Thin Edge Wall, 6B (problem 14). Photo: Niall Grimes.

Rothley

55.201063
-1.931233

A generous little roadside bluff, perfect for a quick hour for passers-by but also giving a longer session to those with a bit of time to spare. Great for the mid-grade climber. A good bunch of clean sunny problems taking fun lines and sure to bring a smile to your face.

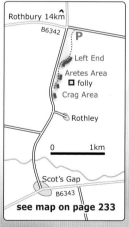

Rothbury 14km
B6342
P
Left End
Aretes Area
□ folly
Crag Area
Rothley
0   1km
Scot's Gap
B6343

see map on page 233

110 probs
4 - 7A+
best from
5 - 6C
10 min
exposed
slabby
vertical
steep

You can see what you're in for as you drive along the adjacent road. A scattering of little blocks near the trees on the left are good for warming up: over fifty problems, mostly easy up to 7A. To the right of this is the Aretes Area, a great series of aretes, corners and short walls which are the centrepiece of the crag: twenty five problems from 6A to 7A. To the right the impressive main crag gives a handful problems to those with some energy left. Beyond this the boulders continue all along the hillside for another couple of hundred metres with a further hundred problems up to 7A.

// Climbing: Good and varied problems on slabs, aretes, pockets, overhangs, slopers and traverses. The more popular problems, and most of those detailed here, are usually stand-ups following good lines to a nice height, but never too high. As well as these there are lots of highballs, sometimes with bad landings. The rock is fine-grained sandstone. It is a tiny bit scratchy on the left-hand problems, while those in the aretes area are clean and have a well used feel.

// Conditions: Perfect for a relaxing evening. Faces west getting evening sun. A little exposed. Some stuff on the left takes a while to dry but the best stuff, around the aretes, is quick drying, but please avoid if it is at all damp. In summer bracken can be a pain in the hole but generally climbable all year round. **Family friendly**.

// Approach: The crag lies about 2 miles north of Scot's Gap. Follow the maps taking the minor road that passes the crag then take a small turning and park north of the crag. Please don't use the more obvious parking on the road in front of the crag. From the parking take a track down along the trees to the bouldering in under 10 minutes. Can be a wee bit boggy.

// Info: Northumberland Bouldering Guide (NMC)

Aretes Area

Roof   *Yorkshire 8A*

1	**Roof Crack** 6A	
	Start low. Solo up and right	
or jump off.		
2	**Roof Highball** 6A	
3	**Scooped Wall** 6A	
	Highball.	
4	**Andrew's Arete** 6B	
	From a sitter on the right.	
5	**Another Arete** 6A	
6	**Yorkshire 8A** 7A	
	Get it?	
7	**Bulge** 6A+ *Left of centre.*	

8	**Amphetamine** 6A+
	Right of centre.
9	**Sloper Traverse** 6B
10	**Hanging Arete** 6B
11	**Faint Edge** 6B+
12	**Groove** 4
13	**Rounded Arete** 6A+
14	**Thin Edge Wall** 6B
15	**Warm Up**
	Traverse 5+
16	**Slopers Traverse** 5+
17	**The Crack** 4

18	**Low Spirit** 6A
	Sitter. Escape right at the
break.	
19	**AB's Problem** 7A *Sitter.*
20	**Long Reach** 6C+
	Sitter.
21	**Noel's Arete** 6B
22	**Nails** 6A
23	**Brave Face** 5+
24	**Early Days** 4+
	Highball.

Folly

The Crag

The Face

loads more problems

Shaftoe

55.135077
-1.903467

The **Fontainebleau of Northumberland** for those who have never been to Fontainebleau. A whole mess of boulders scattered across mild moorland with 300 steep problems through the grades. Proximity to Newcastle and a friendly nature ensures its popularity. Non-threatening.

Shaftoe is a bit of a love it/hate it place and first-time visitors may well scratch their heads in disappointment. However, a lot of people hate it simply because it is a bit hard to navigate and if you miss the best stuff you will most likely find a load of problems that take lowballing to new depths, naff sandy shuffles along horizontal breaks and tedious juggy roofs on rock that deserve to be left alone. But find the bigger, better stuff and you will have a much better impression of Shaftoe.

The problems listed here are designed to give the first-time visitor a sample of the better stuff and generally confines itself to the more easily navigated central section. However there are lots of great problems not covered here: the Northumberland Bouldering Guide reveals the area in all its glory.

// Climbing: The climbing is usually on low outcrops of gritty sandstone that have nudged their way out of grassy hillocks to give short steep problems. Sit starts are common to help make the most of the height. Lots of very lowball problems but also loads at proper bouldering height. A few highballs but the landings are generally flat and grassy. Lots of walls, bulges, roofs, cracks and aretes. Not many slabs. Holds are generally rounded breaks, slopers or nice open pockets. Not very crimpy. The rock varies from good to soft. Please treat it with care.

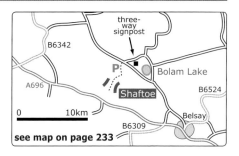

see map on page 233

// Conditions: Problems face all directions but those covered here face west or north. A sunny venue. Low level and quite sheltered. Climbable year round although it can be a bit boggy in winter and bracken-infested in summer, but never too bad. Avoid climbing on any damp rock. **Family friendly.**

// Approach: Follow the map to the junction west of Bolam Lake. By a signpost (Scotsgap 3½, Bolam 1½, Belsay 3) and 100m from The Stable coffee shop. Here drive down a track down past some houses. Follow this, strictly observing a 5mph speed limit and continue for a few hundred metres along rough track and a huge autoxylophone and into a field just past a cattle grid. Park here. Follow a track along the left side of the lake that takes you through a gate in the wall. Carry on in this direction to arrive at the areas covered here. Best go all the way to the far wall and use the photo below.

// Info: Northumberland Bouldering Guide (NMC)

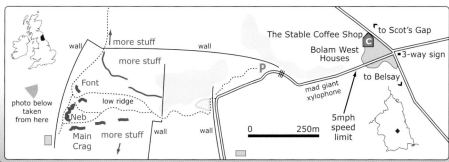

Font Boulder

Smith's Rock

Turtle Rock

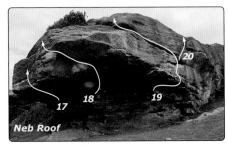

Neb Roof

Main Crag

The Cob

1	**Bleaustard**	6A+
2	**Purely Belter**	7C
3	**Surprising Solution**	7A
4	**Incipient Crack**	6A
5	**Font Traverse**	6C
6	**Bulge**	6B
7	**Short Crack**	4+
8	**The Lip**	7A
9	**Classic Arete**	4
10	**The Clamp**	5+ *Low start.*
11	**Proposal**	6C *Low start.*
12	**Turtle's Flipper**	5
13	**Boody Gold**	6C

Jump start.

14 Blood Sport 8A+
Come from the back to large pocket on the lip then past another pocket to the break and mantel. A great 7C from the big pocket.

15 Soft Centre 6A *Stretch for jugs then mantel direct.*

16 Hard Shell 6C

17 Broken Hearts are for Assholes 7A+

18 The Neb Roof 6C

19 The Original 6A *Sitter.*

20 Sloper Masterclass 5+
Direct finish to 19.

21 Left Arete 5+

22 Viagra Plus 6B+

23 Central Wall 7B+
High starting holds. Sitter is Vorsprung Durch Technik, 8A.

24 Main Wall 6C

25 Timmy Tip Toes 6B
Sitter 7A+.

26 Magic Fluting 5

27 Cob Arete 5

28 Honeycomb Wall Traverse 6C

29 Killer Queen 6C

30 Hip Hop 6A

approach

Main Crag   The Cob

Smith's Rock

Turtle Rock   Neb Roof

Yorkshire

Naomi Buys on Ringpiece, 7B+, Ilkley (page 279, problem 18). Photo: Alex Messenger.

Steve Dunning on Jason's Roof, 7C+, Crookrise (page 275, problem 23). Photo: John Coefield.

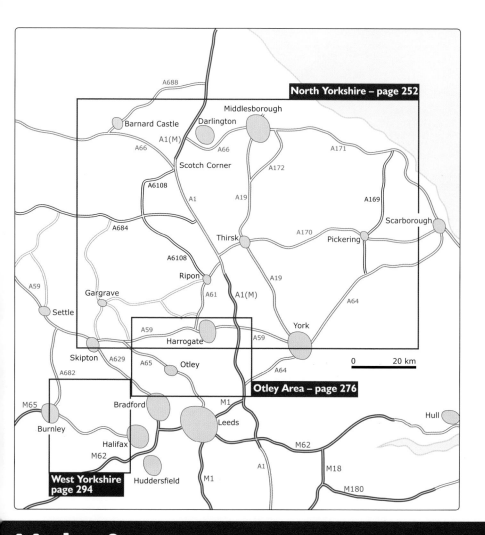

North Yorkshire – page 252

A688

Middlesborough

Barnard Castle   Darlington

A1(M)

A66   A66

Scotch Corner   A171

A6108   A172

A1   A19   A169

A684   Scarborough

Thirsk   Pickering

A6108   A170

Ripon   A19

A59   A61   A1(M)   A64

Settle   Gargrave

A59   A59

Harrogate   York

Skipton   A629   A65   Otley

A682   A64

Otley Area – page 276

M65   M1

Burnley   Bradford   Leeds

Halifax   M62

M62   A1   M18

West Yorkshire
page 294   Huddersfield   M1   M180

Hull

0   20 km

Main Area

Yorkshire / Introduction

Lee Robinson on Liberate, 6C, at Clemmitt's Wood (page 261, problem 16). Photo: Robinson collection.

Yorkshire is one of the original homes of bouldering where the pioneers would naturally practice their art on the blocks that surrounded their great crags. Claude E Benson climbed Matterhorn Ridge in the early years of the 20th century. In the 1950s Arthur Dolphin and Allan Austin (mucho respect) were the masters. Later, in the 1960s, the Barley brothers took the baton and ran.

However it was in the 1970s that Yorkshire bouldering really took off. A hardcore band of talented technicians coalesced around Leeds university. Allan Manson, Pete Livesey, John Syrett, Mike Hammill, Ken Wood, Bernard Newman, Steve Bancroft and Jerry Peel set standards sizzling much the way John Allen and the Stokes brothers did on Peak gritstone. Many of the classic lines at Caley, Almscliff, Shipley Glen, Brimham, Bridestones, Widdop and Ilkley fell to this good-time crew, under the influence of a healthy sense of competition. Later these teams were joined by a talented youth, Ron Fawcett.

Later this era was quite rightly known as the Golden Age of Yorkshire gritstone.

In the 1980s standards soared across the nation as training and application gave rise to new levels of power. Climbers such as John Dunne, Andy Swann, Andy Brown, Ian Cummings and Paul Ingham joined in with the evergreen players of the last generation such as Peel and Fawcett, whose prime seemed to go on and on. The technical and bold challenges of the 1970s were replaced by burlier and more powerful fare and problems of the highest order continued to tumble.

The 1990s and 2000s saw further development, with bouldering pads aiding in the addition of some fantastic big lines. Jason Myers' Jason's Roof, Ben Moon's Cypher and Steve Dunning's High Fidelity must surely top the quality stakes in the county while problems like Tim Clifford's Cherry Falls at Almscliff were at the cutting edge of short power problems.

Today Steve Dunning continues to force many of the new harder lines often in beautiful, remote settings. Tom Peckitt also keeps the county up to date, most notably with his mighty Bulb Haul link up. Great stuff.

James Ibbertson prospecting at Caley Roadside (page 280). Photo: Niall Grimes.

Jon Pearson on a tough up-problem on Brimham's Joker's Wall (problem 31, 6C, page 269). Andi 'Tex' Turner spotting. "Now what do you boys want around here?"

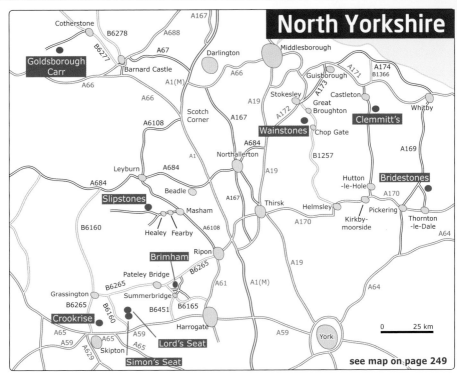

North Yorkshire

Cotherstone

B6278

A688

A167

B6277

Goldsborough Carr

Barnard Castle

A67

Darlington

A66

Middlesborough

A174

B1366

A171

Guisborough

A173

Castleton

Whitby

A66

A1(M)

A66

Scotch Corner

A6108

A167

A19

Stokesley

Great Broughton

A172

Clemmitt's

A169

A684

Northallerton

Wainstones

Chop Gate

Leyburn

A684

A1

A19

B1257

Hutton -le-Hole

Bridestones

A684

Beadle

A167

Thirsk

Helmsley

A170

Pickering

Thornton -le-Dale

Slipstones

Masham

Healey Fearby

A6108

Kirkby-moorside

A170

A64

B6160

Brimham

Ripon

Pateley Bridge

B6265

B6265

Summerbridge

B6451

B6165

A61

A1(M)

A19

A64

Grassington

B6265

B6160

Crookrise

Harrogate

A59

York

A65

A59

A629

A65

A59

Skipton

Lord's Seat

Simon's Seat

0   25 km

see map on page 249

see map on page 249

North Yorkshire Map / Yorkshire

Charlotte Telfer on Jumping Jack Flash, 6A+, Goldsborough Carr (problem 21, page 262). Photo: Tom Peckitt.

Jugs, 5 (problem 12). Photo: Niall Grimes.

Bridestones

54.302409
-0.652699

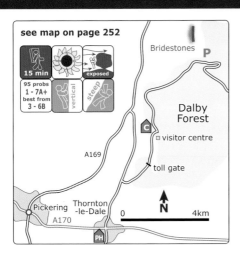

see map on page 252

15 min

95 probs
1 - 7A+
best from
3 - 6B

exposed

vertical

steep

Bridestones   P

Dalby
Forest

C

visitor centre

A169

toll gate

Pickering   Thornton
-le-Dale
A170

N

0   4km

PH

Buttress One
Buttress Four

0   250m

shallow valley

Pepperpot
Fourth Pinnacle

First Pinnacle

Bridestones
gate   car park
P

toll gate 6km

The less famous Bridestones give a couple of hour's fun for competent climbers who value situation as much as power. Not the most interesting climbing but unique formations in a lovely place. Plenty of pump and pinnacle ticks. A fun venue.

// **Climbing:** Sandstone pinnacles and outcrops. Steep climbing mainly on rounded jugs. Not very technical. Can be sandy. Often a bit high, around 5 – 6 metres, but perfect landings and lots of traverses. Tons in the 3 – 5 range (NE England guide lists over 80). Good for getting pumped. A place for a relaxed day out.

First Pinnacle

Second Pinnacle

Fourth Pinnacle

Pepperpot

Buttress One

Buttress Two

Buttress Three

Buttress Four

1	**Down Route** 1	**8**	**Crack** 2+	**14**	**Going Up North** 5
2	**Passion Play** 2	**9**	**Descent Crack** 4	**15**	**Griff's Traverse** 6B
3	**Guano Wall** 4+		*The crack at the back.*	**16**	**Nürburgring** 7A
4	**Crack** 4+	**10**	**Mr Pepperpot** 7A	**17**	**Turbo Charged** 5+
5	**Scoop** 5	**11**	**Central Groove** 6A	**18**	**Standard Traverse** 6B+
6	**Bulge** 3+	**12**	**Jugs** 5	**19**	**Wind Up** 5
7	**Roof** 3+	**13**	**Dingley Dell** 5	**20**	**Traverse** 6A+

// Conditions: Quite high and open. Exposed. Quick drying but avoid if the rock is at all damp. Always something in the sun on the lower pinnacles and the four upper buttresses come into sun about midday until sunset. Brilliant for picnics. **Family friendly.**

// Approach: From Thornton-le-Dale follow signs for Dalby Forest. Pay at the toll gate (£7) and drive 4 miles to Bridestones car park. Follow maps to the rocks.
// Info: North East England (SBP/CMC); <u>climbon-line.co.uk</u> (full free guide)

Wainstones

54.423025
-1.118846

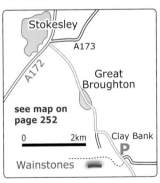

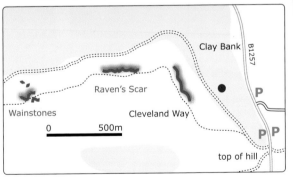

Located in a dip on Hasty Bank The Wainstones has a nice circuit on fine rock, great on a hot breezy day and the views are amazing. Big up Lee from betaguides.com for this section.

// Climbing: Sandstone boulders. Varied climbing, delicate slabs traverses and roofs. Blocks up to 6m. Grades from 2 – 7C.

// Conditions: Catches the midday sun and enjoys the breeze in summer avoiding the midges, drys quickly. **Family friendly.**

// Approach: As the B1257 heads south from Great Broughton the road climbs up a long hill called Clay Bank. Near the summit is plentiful roadside parking. At the summit there is a gravel road beside some steps leading into the trees and the Cleveland Way. Follow the steps and the paths sticking to the lower one which leads under the crags just alongside the treeline. Follow this for 30 minutes to reach the lower boulders over a stile.

// Info: www.betaguides.com

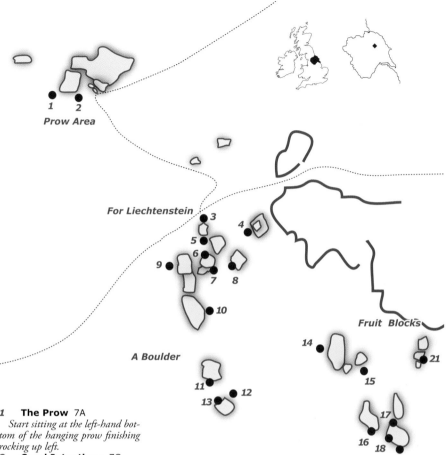

Prow Area

1   2

For Liechtenstein

3

4

5

6

9

7   8

10

Fruit Blocks

A Boulder

14

21

15

11   12

13

17

16   18

20

1   The Prow 7A
Start sitting at the left-hand bottom of the hanging prow finishing rocking up left.
2   Cruel Intentions 7C
Right arete from a sitter. Strict: no pockets.
3   For Liechtenstein 7B
From a left hand crimp and a right hand pinch, swing up right for the top.
4   West Face Direct 7A
The centre of the wall to a groove and a crimp; bold.
5   Frogs Legs 5+
The left arete. Sitter 6B.
6   Rock On 6A
Follow the overlap and finish up the arete (without chipped footholds).
7   Hand to Hand Combat 5+
Exit the crack using the left arete. Sitter 7A+.
8   No Hands 4+
Up the slab, without hands. Can be hopped at 7A.

9   The Groove 5+
A hard start into some great moves. Sitter 6B+.
10   The Finger 7C
Put your finger in the hole and pull for the top.
11   Readheads Roof 6C
Over the bulge direct.
12   Pebble Climb 6A
The right arete is a delight.
13   The Crack 5+
From a sit start follow the crack.
14   Jet Set 5+
The centre of the slab.
15   Conjoined 4   *Steep slab.*
16   Fade to Grey 7A
Sitter. A right to left traverse of the lip, rocking up on the face to finish.
17   Use Your Loaf 6B
The right arete from a sitter.

18   Breadline 5+
The groove at the left end of the boulder.
19   Beneath the Breadline
6C+   *From a sitter, pull over the slab finish direct. 5+ from standing.*
20   Loaf Traverse 4+
Start at the right end and traverse across the left end.
21   Fruit of the Gods 6C+
From a sitter, on the second block (use the small block for feet). From a right hand undercut and with left hand on small features, work your way across rightwards via the crack and slopers, better holds lead to a bold finish.

Steve Ramsden on The Prow, 7A, Wainstones (problem 1). Photo: Lee Robinson.

Clemmitt's Wood

54.423075
-0.914226

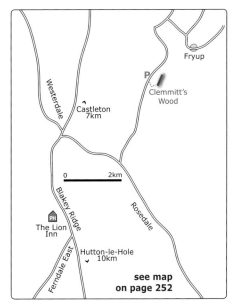

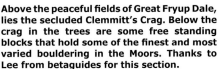

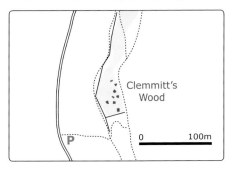

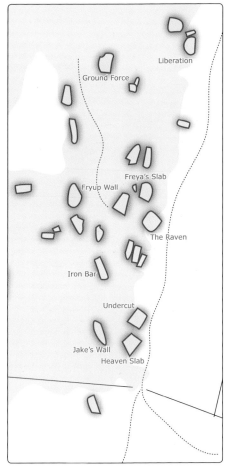

Above the peaceful fields of Great Fryup Dale, lies the secluded Clemmitt's Crag. Below the crag in the trees are some free standing blocks that hold some of the finest and most varied bouldering in the Moors. Thanks to Lee from betaguides for this section.

// Climbing: Sandstone boulders. Varied climbing from delicate slabs to dynos, sustained traverses and roofs. Blocks up to 5m. Grades from 4-7B+ with harder projects not yet climbed.

// Conditions: Catches the sun until 4pm and is sheltered from the wind. The bracken gets high in summer as do the amount of biting insects, take your insect repellent.

// Approach: The area is a bit of a warren. Get out your road atlas. Blakey Ridge is a broad moorland ridge 8 miles north of Hutton-le-Hole. It can also be gained from Castleton, which is signposted south from the A171 west of Guisborough. From Blakey Ridge, turning to Rosedale at Rosedale Head, take the next left and follow this road until Camp Hill Crag appears on your left, park in the lay by near a grouse butt and head east down to the woods, via a gate next to a sheep pen.

// Info: www.betaguides.com

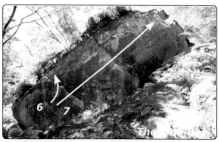

1	**Cloud Nine** 6A		*11*	**Princess Leia's Golden Bikini** 4+
2	**Stairway to Heaven** 5+		*12*	**Jawa** 4+
3	**Arrogance of Youth** 6C+ *Sitter.*		*13*	**Full Breakfast** 6C *Sitter.*
4	**Jake's Wall** 5+		*14*	**Plum Tomato** 7B *Sitter.*
5	**Dyno Saw** 6B+		*15*	**The Lip** 7B *Sitter.*
6	**Iron Bru** 7A *Sitter.*		*16*	**Liberate** 6C *Sitter.*
7	**The Iron Bar** 7B *Sitter.*		*17*	**Paradise** 7A *Sitter.*
8	**The Wave** 5+		*18*	**Spotless** 7A *Sitter.*
9	**Sam's Slab** 5+		*19*	**Little Ewoks** 6A
10	**The Raven** 6A+			

Rupert McBain on Bass Special 4+ (problem 24). Photo: Niall Grimes.

Goldsborough Carr

54.557431
-2.077618

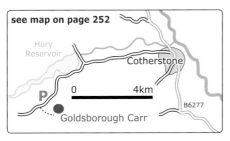
see map on page 252

Hury Reservoir

Cotherstone

P

0   4km

B6277

Goldsborough Carr

10 min | 130 probs 2 - 8B best from 4 - 7B+ | vertical | steep | roofs | | exposed

A little gem of a crag, a crown of gritstone sitting loftily over wild moorland. It gives meatheads a great session, with solid chunky climbing over hefty overhangs and airy highball finishes to follow. A lovely wild spot.

Good for problems across a wide spread of grades. Most of the climbing is on the south and south-east side, away from the road, but there is a lot more stuff along the north, road-facing side too. Harder problems here are the work of Steve Dunning and Ian Cummings.

// Climbing: Mainly natural gritstone outcrop (some quarried). Loads of problems and micro-routes. Typically steep starts lead into highball, easier finishes. Several mats useful. Plenty of lowball stuff too. Strenuous and fingery.

// Approach: From Barnard Castle take the B6277, direction Stockton, to the village of Cotherstone. Just north of the village follow a small road signposted East Briscoe. Follow this road for about 5 miles, passing Hury Reservoir on your right, and park in bays on the right. A footpath leads to the crag.

// Conditions: Exposed and quick drying. Climbable year round. **Family friendly.**

// Info: **Yorkshire Gritstone Bouldering Volume II** (TC); **North East England** (SBP/CMC); **climbonline. co.uk** (full free guide)

approach

the climbing

1	**Y Crack** 2
2	**Finger Crack** 4
3	**Enigma Direct** 6B
4	**Old Moss** 5+
5	**Flake and Crack** 3+
6	**Hubris** 6A
7	**Saturnaila** 5
8	**Ian's Arete** 7A
9	**Mawman** 3
10	**Yoke Sike** 4
11	**Motivation** 5+

12	**The Obsessed** 6B
13	**George's Roof** 7C
	Finish up The Obsessed.
14	**Fiddler on the Roof** 5+
15	**The Long Reach** 6C
	Escape at the break.
16	**Fiddler's Arete** 5
17	**Fiddler** 5+
18	**The Scoop** 6B
19	**Low Level Traverse** 7A
	Finish up 21.

20	**Jumping Jack Flash** 6A+
21	**Beth's Traverse** 7B+
22	**Plagarist** 6A
23	**This One's for Bill** 7A
24	**Bass Special** 4+
25	**Diagonal Crack** 3
26	**Diagonal Direct** 3
27	**Milk Snatcher** 5
28	**Kel's Problem** 5+
29	**Ricochet** 4 *The arete.*

Dan Varian on Cypher, 8B (problem 32). Photo: Mark Savage.

Slipstones

54.228163
-1.777167

A remote edge of finest-grained gritstone that's guaranteed to warm your golden cockles. Everybody likes Slipstones. A perfect venue for a full day out, especially a sunny day where you will get the full magic of the place.

The location is absolutely three-star, with yawning remote moorland disappearing into the sunset giving a real sense of wilderness. The rock is best-quality fine-grained sandstone-grit and makes for great moves. Now for the heresy bit – in terms of pure bouldering Slipstones isn't all that amazing. For the length of the edge there isn't all that much of it. What there is is very good but to get the most from it it would be best combined with a bit of HVS-style soloing. For this reason I've given lots of straight bouldering as well as some highballs / solos. Some of these will feel pretty high and the landings are not always perfect. See the grades included. If you don't know what these mean then you should learn.

Having said this if you speak to people who won't highball or solo, they'll still say that this is one of their favourite places. It's just that kind of special crag. The nearby village of Masham is home to Black Sheep beer. Mmmmm.

Slipstones was one of those venues that bouldering discovered at the turn of the millenium. It had been a very local crag loved by gnarly technicians. Its first true heroes were Paul Ingham and Ian Cummings, initially active in the 1980s, who added a lot of lines that are, even today, some of the best ticks on the edge. It remained an obscure crag until the widespread use of mats by the year 2000 ripened it. Steve Dunning's article about it in On The Edge mag awoke interest in his first ascents including Super Furry Animal, an 8B body-length dyno. This interest culminated in Cypher, Ben Moon's noble arete, named after his pants, that really is 8B royalty. Today it is now a cliff for both Everyman and the A-list.

// Climbing: Gritstone edge. Good strong up-lines give quality across all grades up to 8B. The climbing tends to be very technical and balancey but also requires a lot of power. Not many sit starts or traverses, and a lot of the better lines feel a bit highball. Mostly good landings but a couple of pads are recommended. Good for aretes and steep fingery walls.

Those happy to highball will have more to choose from than those who don't but even those who don't will have a swell time.

// Approach: From the village of Masham (lots of pubs) follow a small road towards the villages of Fearby and Healey. Follow this road, passing the Black Swan and a campsite in Fearby. Half a mile past Healey there is a fork. Take the right fork and continue for one and a half miles to a tight wriggle. A hundred metres after this there is a layby on the right at the entrance to West Agra Farm. Park here, being very careful not to obstruct the track.

From here follow the track until it turns right towards the farm. Continue on smaller tracks until you go through a gate. Angle right from here to the right end of the crag or stay on the track for easier access to the left end.

// Conditions: Very clean, exposed and quick drying. Quite high (300m) so a bit bleak on a dirty winter day but great on a still sunny one. Hot in summer. South-south-west facing. Very sunny. **Family friendly.**

// Info: **Yorkshire Gritstone Bouldering** (TC); North East England (SBP/CMC); **Northern England** (Rockfax); **yorkshiregrit.com**

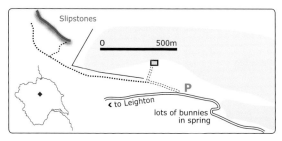

Paul's Arete

Beldin

Seven Up

Sowden

Ripper

Twins

1	**Paul's Arete** 5+ *HVS.*	*12*	**Dennis in Darlo** 6A *E1.*
2	**Beldin Direct** 4+ *To break. HVS to finish.*	*13*	**Sowden** 5+ *HVS*
3	**Original Route** 4+ *To break. HVS to finish.*	*14*	**Space Plucks** 6B *E3.*
4	**Timeless Divide** 6A+	*15*	**Leany Meany** 5+ *E1.*
	Twin aretes. The arete on its right is 6C+.	*16*	**Killer** 6C *E4.*
5	**Agra** 5 *HVS.*	*17*	**Ripper** 6A *E1.*
6	**Wisecrack** 6A+ *Gain the hanging crack*	*18*	**Sunday the Twentieth** 6B+
	from the right. E1. Direct start 6B+.	*19*	**Right Hand Twin** 6A *Arete on its left.*
7	**Impregnable** 6A+ *E2.*		*Climbed on its steep right side is Leaning Wall, 6C+.*
8	**Squak's Arete** 5 *HVS.*	*20*	**Strictly Personal** 6B+
9	**Undercut Flake** 3+ *HS.*	*21*	**Lay-By Arete** 7B+
10	**Flakeout Arete** 4+ *HVS.*		*Finish on the left or stay on the right at 7C.*
11	**Seven Up** 6A *E2.*	*22*	**Lay-By** 6A

Paul's Arete   Beldin   Seven Up   Sowden   Ripper   Twins

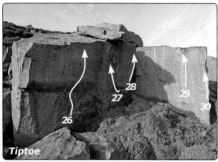

23 Rock On 6A
24 Twenty Something 4
25 Flaky Wall Traverse 6C
26 Super Furry Animal 8B
Sitter; move up to left-hand sidepull and dyno to top.
27 Sidewinder 7B+ *From sitter on undercuts.*
28 Curving Crack Arete 6A *Sitter.*
29 Steptoe 6A
30 Tiptoe 5+
31 Davies' Ramp 6B+ *Step off the boulder and climb the high, tricky ramp. A direct start avoiding the block and arete is Simple Sally, 7A+.*

32 Cypher 8B
33 Sulky Little Boys 7A+
34 Slanting Flake 4
35 Stereo Android 4
36 Tea Party Slab 4
37 A Question of Balance 5+
38 Ramp 2
39 Flakes 3
40 Arete 2
41 Slab 3

Brimham

A gritstone wonderland with a whole mess of boulders. Quality varies from great to soft so there's much less bouldering than there is rock. Find the good stuff and you'll love it. A fun place, very family friendly.

There's a shit load of rock here but I have often struggled a bit. Perhaps there's just too much of it. The very complex layout makes it easy to miss the better stuff and I often wish they would just get rid of all the crap and just leave the good stuff. However, persevere, because the good stuff is very good. This is Dave Birkett's favourite bouldering.

// Climbing: Climbing on small well-weathered and sometimes eroded craglets. Often steep and strenuous. Some highballs, but lots of everything and landings are generally good. Can be rounded. Good for traverses.
// Approach: Follow the maps and signs for Brimham Rocks to the NT car park (£4/5). Crag layout is complex and I have only given a small section to give a flavour. See the map and photo below.
// Conditions: The pinnacles get lots of sun and the edges face mainly southwest getting sun from the afternoon. Sheltered but sometimes can remain damp. Joker's Wall is quite rainproof. **Family friendly.**
// Info: Yorkshire Gritstone Bouldering (Total Climbing); **yorkshiregrit.com; Yorkshire Gritstone** (YMC)

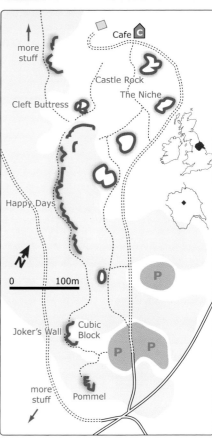

	230 probs 3 - 8A+ best from 4 - 7B	vertical	steep	roofs		shelter
5 min						

see map on page 252

Pateley Bridge
B6265
B6265
Brimham Rocks
Smelthouses
Wilsill
Brimham Rocks Rd
Brimham Rocks Rd
B6165
Summerbridge

0   2km

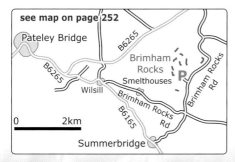

photo taken somewhere above Happy Days

cafe

Castle Rock

Cleft Buttress

more tourists

tourist

Yorkshire / Brimham

1 **Niche Arete** 6C *Sitter.*
2 7A+ *Sitter.*
3 **Left Flake** 6A
4 **Niche Dyno** 7C
   From the low flatty to the top.
5 **Right Flake** 6A
6 **Corner** 6B+
7 **Niche Roof** 6B
8 **Long Haul** 7B
9 **Clingon** 6C *The arete.*
10 **Jumper's Traverse** 7A
   Traverse right from the arete and
finish along 14. Extend the start along
the initial break at 7B.
11 **Murky Way** 5+ *The crack.*
12 **Dyno** 6C
   From sloper in the break just right
of the crack, dyno to the shelf above.
13 **Murky Rib** 6B *Sitter 7A.*
14 **Break Traverse** 6A
15 **High Steppa** 6A
   Pockets right of the arete.
16 **Green Arete** 5+
17 **Perverted Crack** 4+
18 **Pair in a Cubicle** 7A
19 **Thelma** 7B+
20 **Traverse** 7B
21 **Arete** 3+
22 **Ian's Traverse** 7C
   Lip traverse into 23.
23 **Happy Days** 6B+
24 **Happy Days Sitter** 7B
25 **The Fonz** 8A
   Link 24 into 26, or start along
22 at 8A+.
26 **Bilge Pump** 6C
27 **Joker's Traverse** 7A
28 **Joker's Wall Start** 6A
29 **Joker's Wall Right** 5+
30 **Slapstick** 8A
31 6C
32 **Minion's Way** 5
33 **Flake** 6C+ *Sitter 7A+.*
34 **Arete** 4+ *Sitter 7A+.*
35 **Flake** 3+
36 **Pommel** 6C+
37 **Low Traverse** 6A
38 **Benchmark** 7B
39 **Arete** 6C+
40 **Pocket Wall** 6C
41 **Wall** 5+ *Sitter.*

The Niche

Cleft Buttress

Happy Days

Joker's Wall

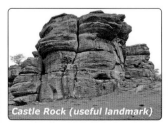

Castle Rock (useful landmark)

Pommel

Yorkshire / Brimham

Amongst the finest moorland bouldering in the country, a remote collection of gargoyle-ridden rocks in a lofty and superior position overlooking a quiet corner of Yorkshire. A full day of cranking, highballing, soloing and exploring will easily reward the walk on a fine summer day. Bring a good packed lunch.

Barden Fell is to remote moorland gritstone what Catalunya is to limestone 9a. There are little pimples of grit everywhere, it seems. The two venues here are the best starting point and a visit will thoroughly nourish your soul, that is if you have one.

It's a brilliant surprise as Simon's Seat pops into view. This has lots of problems and great frolicking solos. Both are covered here. It's worth noting that there are probably 50 further, undocumented problems from 2 to 5 scattered everywhere, taking fine little lines. Great for exploring, great for beginners, great for families. Just great.

Lord's Seat lacked the impact, in my opinion, as my senses had already been tickled by Simon's. It has perhaps more straight bouldering but perhaps less standout lines (although it still has a lot).

// Climbing: Gritstone outcrop and boulders. Big rounded blocks and buttresses with aretes, cracks, crimps, slopers and a myriad of unusual sculptural holds. Lots of standard bouldering but maximum value will be had from doing some soloing. Good lines. Some bad landings, some good landings.

// Conditions: High (460m) moorland setting meaning that it is best enjoyed on a good summer day where other venues are too hot. Very exposed, meaning a breeze will probably keep midges at bay. Boulders very quick drying and while the surface does have some scrittle when compared to Almscliff, it is still amazingly clean. **Family friendly.**

Dave Barrans on Whaleback, 7A+ (problem 22).
Photo: Alex Messenger.

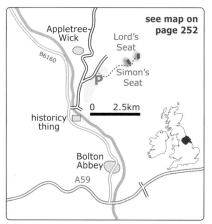

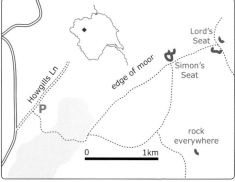

Yorkshire / Simon's Seat

Simon's Seat Area

54.028318
-1.904669

// Approach: From the A59 follow B6160 direction Bolton Bridge. Continue for 3.7 miles then turn right direction Appletreewick. Cross a bridge and follow the road for 1 mile to a right turn to Howgill Farm. Follow this for 300m to a four-car parking spot on your right. Signs indicate this is a private road but parking seems tolerated. However if the spaces are full don't park in the lane: get back out on the road and find somewhere else.

From the right of the parking a land-rover track runs steeply up into the trees. This is all very much first-gear yomping for 700m. About 300m after a gate the path splits. The main one heads off towards an outcrop, but take the left branch along the edge of the moor. This leads after 1km to Simon's Seat. Continue for 500m to Lord's Seat.

// Info: Yorkshire Gritstone Bouldering Vol 2 (TC); **yorkshiregrit.com; Yorkshire Gritstone** (YMC)

Lower Face

Lower Face

Lower Face

Drift Wall

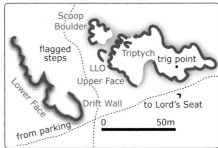

Scoop Boulder
flagged steps
Triptych
trig point
LLO
Upper Face
Lower Face
Drift Wall
from parking
to Lord's Seat
0   50m

16

Scoop Boulder

behind Scoop Boulder

Triptych

Simon Says

LLO

Whaleback

Triptych
trig point
Scoop Boulder
Upper Face
LLO
Simon Says
Drift Wall
Lower Face

Yorkshire / Simon's Seat

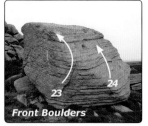

Front Boulders

Front Boulders

Front Boulders

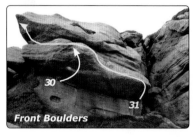

Front Boulders

Front Face Right

Front Bay

Front Bay

Front Bay

Front Face

Lord's Seat

Front Boulders

Crookrise

A Yorkshire gem. Tons of problems taking fine, classic lines on great rock in a sunny, heavenly setting. Often highball, frequently legendary, always great. A must-visit crag.

The most classic of the string of wild crags that rim the moorland north of Skipton, including Rylstone, Crookstones and Eastby (check out the local guides for these beauties). Not surpisingly it attracted the attention of a young Embsay lad, Ron Fawcett. Ron wandered the fells here and climbed not one, but two cracks.

Be prepared for the odd bumrush: there are some highball classics here as well as a good few uneven landings. The climbing is best enjoyed with a good bunch of people and pads.

The circuit here centres around the Hovis area at the left side of the crag but the Everest boulder is worth a visit too. The crag is covered with problems and great solos.

// Climbing: Generally burly problems a little on either side of vertical and with a great variety; slopers, crimps, pebbles, slabs, walls, aretes, grooves, cracks and traverses. Problems on the crag and on boulders. Lots of highball/micro route type things, and some easy topouts go into pure soloing territory. Perhaps that's what makes it so good. Plenty too that are not highball.
// Approach: Follow maps to parking at Embsay Reservoir. From here follow the track along the reservoir then cross the fence by a stile at the end. Follow left to gain tracks that run somewhat steeply up the edge of the moor, as it runs along a wall. As the path levels out a stile leads to the Everest boulder. For the Hovis area continue to 120m before the trig point. A stile beside a boulder in the wall leads to the area.
// Conditions: The crag sits in an exposed situation at 400m on the edge of a moor. South-west facing and gets the sun from early afternoon. Can be too hot in summer, and annoyingly ferny. Great in winter on still days. Very clean and quick drying. Popular. **NO DOGS**
// Info: Yorkshire Gritstone Bouldering Vol 2 (TC); **yorkshiregrit.com; Yorkshire Gritstone** (YMC)

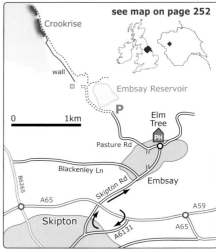

see map on page 252

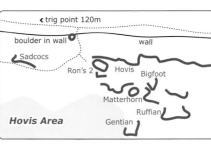

Hovis Area

Crookrise

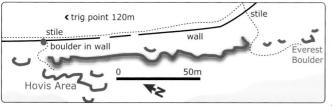

1 **Left-Hand Rib** 5
2 **Hanging Flake** 6B
3 **Sadcocs Wall** 6B+
4 **Crack** 5
5 **Sadcocs Traverse** 5+
6 **Barry Kingsize** 7A *Steep face past a flake. The sitter, from down and left, is 7A+.*
7 **Ramp** 5+
8 **Strange Albanian Genius** 7B+
9 **Ron's Crack 2** 6C+

Hovis Buttress: All these problems require soloing easier, higher (10m) tops, traversing off or jumping dismounts.
10 **Crease Direct** 6A *Groove; escape left.*
11 **The Fly** 7B *Slab.*
12 **Small Brown** 7A *The left arete of the face. Escape right or continue for E4 tick.*
13 **Hovis Superdirect** 6C
14 **Hovis Direct** 6B+
15 **Arete** 6A
16 **Flake** 4
17 **Slab** 3
18 **Footprint Arete** 4+
19 **Steep Wall** 7A *Sketchy topout.*
20 **Ruffian** 6A
21 **Flake Problem** 6C *Sitter.*
22 **The Urchin** 5
23 **Jason's Roof** 7C+ *Start with hands at the back of the roof.*

Everest Boulder: The bigger problems here are fairly high and bold.
24 **Ron's Crack 1** 6C *Sitter 7A.*
25 **Palm Gem** 6B+ *Sloping arete from a sitter.*
26 **Everest Crack** 3
27 **Groove** 6A
28 **Left Centre** 6A *Pass a pocket aiming for the high undercut.*
29 **Right Centre** 7A *Pass a chickenhead and a shallow dish.*

Sadcocs

Ron's 2

Hovis

Matterhorn

Bigfoot

Ruffian

Gentian

Everest

Yorkshire / Crookrise

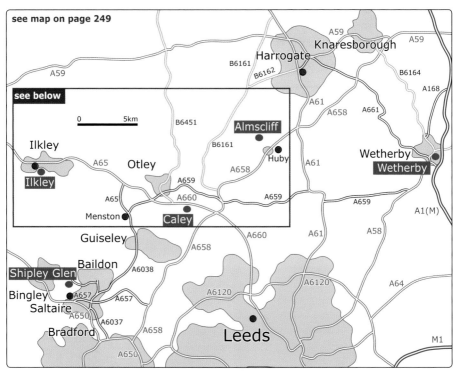

see map on page 249

see below

0   5km

Ilkley

Ilkley

A65   Otley

A659

A65   A660

Menston

Caley

Guiseley

Baildon

Shipley Glen

A6038

Bingley   A657

Saltaire   A657

A650   A6037

Bradford   A658

A650

B6451

B6161

Almscliff

Huby

A658

A659

A659

A61

A58

A660

A658

A6120

A6120

A64

Leeds

M1

A59

B6161

B6162

Harrogate

Knaresborough

A59

A59

A61

A658   A661

B6164

A168

Wetherby

Wetherby

A659

A1(M)

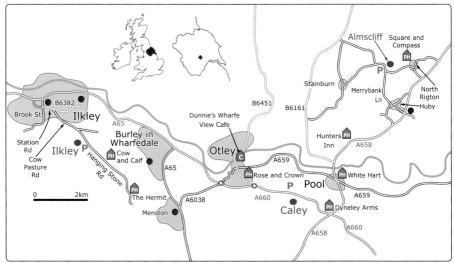

Almscliff   Square and Compass

PH

Stainburn

Merrybank Ln

North Rigton

Huby

B6382

Brook St

Ilkley

Station Rd

Cow Pasture Rd

Ilkley   P

Hanging Stone Rd

Burley in Wharfedale

Cow and Calf

PH

A65

The Hermit

PH

Menston

A6038

B6451

B6161

Dunnie's Wharfe View Cafe

Otley

C

Rose and Crown

PH

A659

Pool   White Hart

P

PH

A660

Caley

Dyneley Arms

PH

A659

A658   A660

Hunters Inn

PH

A658

0   2km

The Otley Area

Adam Long on Terry, 7C, at Caley Roadside (page 285, problem 11). Photo: John Coefield.

Be careful, little chavs, you've just projected the descent route.

Ilkley

53.916475
-1.800202

A cold shoulder overlooking a superficially-attractive tweetown on the edge of the Yorkshire moors. A fairly steely venue demanding good skin, limestone strength, not to mention a stout pair of long-johns. A classic but well-used venue, very popular with tourists. Great for a classy power-sapping session in the right conditions. A bit bleak and brutal for some tastes.

John Dunne's home crag: it's not hard to see where he got his burl from. Lots of big bullying lines and eliminates generally requiring strong fingers. Can feel a bit austere but the walk-in is minimal and there's a tea shop in the car park.

// Climbing: Good across the grades, but better in the higher grades. Some highballs, especially on the Calf. Lots of very crimpy, training-style problems. The steep face on the Calf is home to a myriad of desperate weatherproof eliminates.

// Approach: From the traffic lights at Ilkley town / A65, follow Brook St, go left along Station Rd (for 100m), right up Cow Pasture Rd (for 500m), right up Hanging Stone Rd for 500m to see the crag on the right.

// Conditions: It's as windy as hell up here and will be insufferable on colder days. You wouldn't want to be up there baht 'at. Much of the rock in north- and east-facing and can be green after rain. As such it's better in the warmer months. For the same reason it can be a great escape from the heat and midges in summer. The steep face on the Calf can stay dry in the rain. Often very littered but still fairly **family friendly**.

// Info: Yorkshire Gritstone Bouldering (TC), **yorkshiregrit.com**, Yorkshire Gritstone (YMC)

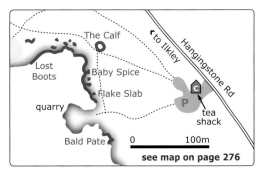

see map on page 276

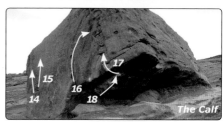

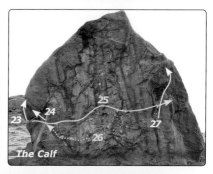

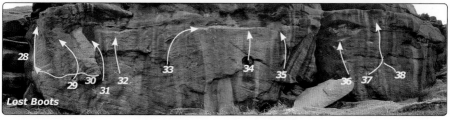

1 Doris Direct 7B+	**10 Baby Spice** 7B	**19 Facet Wall** 6B+	**29 Rib from Hole** 6C
Get pocket from crimp and chip.	**11 Ron's Traverse** 7A *Feet in lowest break.*	**20 Super Set** 7B+	**30 Traverse** 7A+
2 Bald Pate Superdirect 7B	**12 Slopers** 5	**21 Car Park Crack** 5	**31 Patience** 5+
3 Arete 4+	**13 Cow Crack** 3	**22 Crack Trav** 7A	**32 Waiting Room** 6A
4 Slab Direct 6A	**14 Pebble Groove** 5+ *Highball.*	**23 Bonington's Book Problem** 5+	**33 Little Hole** 7A
5 Flake Indirect 5	**15 Pebbledash** 8A *Highball.*	**24 Calf Dyno** 5	**34 Big Hole** 5+
6 Arete 6C+ *Sitter, no jug out right.*	**16 Early Starter** 6B+ *Highball.*	**25 Calf Traverse** 7B+	**35 Doing the Business** 6C
7 Gully Wall 6B+	**17 The Ring** 6A	**26 Almost Pleasant** 6C+	**36 First Arete** 7A+
8 Slab 4	**18 Ringpiece** 7B+	**27 Gnome** 6B+	**37 I Am Curious Yellow** 7C+ *Sitter 8A.*
9 Old Spice 5		**28 Lost Boots** 4+ *From low start in hole.*	**38 Right-Hand Start** 8A+

Caley Roadside

53.896942
-1.65031

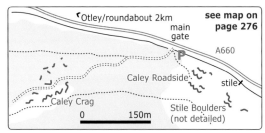

Otley/roundabout 2km
main gate

see map on page 276

A660

Caley Roadside
stile

Caley Crag

0   150m

Stile Boulders
(not detailed)

Caley. Hell Yeah! An exotic zoo of brilliant boulders nestling across a ferny hillside. Problems at every grade. As good as it gets. Technical, fierce, bold and legendary. The essence of gritstone: feel it.

"The best bouldering in England" declares Alan Cameron-Duff's old Rockfax guide. Quite possibly. Enough projects, circuits, highballs and eliminates for a lifetime at a venue that just oozes quality. Trashed skin, twisted ankles, a bloody shin, screaming fingers, bloated biceps, scared shitless – but let's just do one more.

Caley has always been a forcing ground for Yorkshire standards, and Allen Manson, John Syrett, Ron Fawcett, Ben Moon, and Steve Dunning have all left significant calling cards here.

// Climbing: Everything: slabs, walls, bulges and overhangs. Crimps, slopers, aretes, pebbles, jugs and chickenheads. Sitters, highballs and everything in between. Some of the highballs are in fact routes. The more pads you bring the more possibilities you will have but you can get by without any. Problems demand a brain and good footwork as well as strong fingers. Good lines and interesting holds and moves. Can be sore on the skin.

// Conditions: Problems face in all directions, but generally north. Can be green and damp in winter. In summer can be hot, midgeridden and brackeny. Best in spring and autumn. Sheltered. **Family friendly**, but near a busy, noisy road (seperated by a wall).

// Approach: Caley lies beside the busy A660 Leeds – Otley Rd. Roadside parking by the wall under the roadside boulders (visible from here). Go through the main gate then angle back left over a stile. Wriggle up little tracks for a hundred metres to the boulders. There's a bus stop on the road below the crag (Pool Rd, Otley).

// Info: Yorkshire Gritstone Bouldering (TC); **yorkshiregrit.com;Yorkshire Gritstone** (YMC)

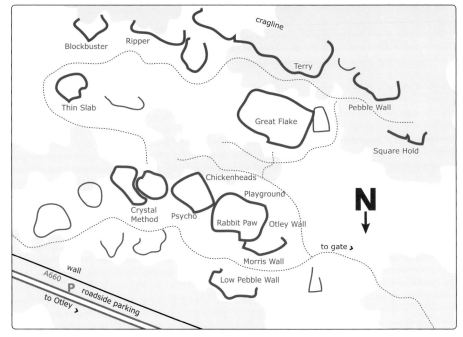

James Ibbertson on Forked Lightning Crack, 6B (problem 40). Niall Grimes.

Thin Slab

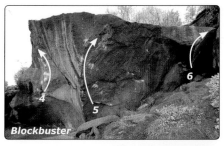

Blockbuster

Ripper

Terry

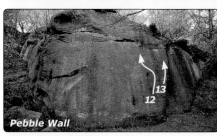

Pebble Wall

Square Hold

Great Flake

1   **Groove**   4

2   **Thin Slab**   6A
Aim for the shallow groove.

3   **Wall**   6B+

4   **Blockbuster**   7C
7B with jump start. 7C+ from sitter from crack down and left.

5   **Zoo York**   8A   *Sitter.*

6   **Ju Ju Club**   7B+   *Sitter.*

7   **Ripper Traverse**   6B   *Scary.*

8   **Ben's Groove**   7B   *Sitter 7C+.*

9   **Secret Seventh**   7B+

10   **Chocolate Orange**   7A

11   **Terry**   7C   *Highball.*

12   **Pebble Wall**   7B

13   **MBKC Arete**   6C   *Slabby arete.*

14   **Wall**   6A   *Sitter.*

15   **Square Hold Arete**   5+   *Sitter.*

16   **Great Flake Start**   5+
Jump off at break. Sitter 6C+. Come in from the undercut out right at 6A+.

17   **High Fidelity**   8B   *Highball.*

18   **Nothing's Safe**   7C   *Highball.*

19   **Bob's Bastard**   6A
Mantel direct using a pocket.

20   **Lip Traverse**   6B+

21   7A+
Sitter. Slap the lip from pocket and poor edge.

22   **Arete from a Sitter**   6C+

23   **Crystal Method**   7B+

24   **Psycho**   7A
Highball: E5. Step right off the boulder and climb the slab on chickenheads. If you don't know what a chickenhead is, you will by the time you get to the top. 7B direct start.

25   **Permutation Rib**   5+
Highball: E1. Gain the arete from the left.

Crystal Method

Rabbit Paw Wall

Otley Wall

The Playground

26 Waite 7C
27 Rabbit Paw Wall 4+ *Highball.*
28 Chips 4+
29 Otley Wall 6A *Gain the crack from 28.*
30 Courser Edge 5+ *Arete on left.*
31 Playground Traverse 5+
    Keeping hands below the top.
32 Slab 2 *Avoiding chips is 4.*
33 Chipped Slab 2
34 Playground Crack 2
35 Chipped Slab 3
36 Stretcher 6B+ *Reachy.*
37 Chickenheads 6A
38 Morris Minor 2
39 Maurice Chevalier 6A *Scary.*
40 Forked Lightning Crack 6B
41 Low Pebble Wall 5+
42 Cruel Crack 5
43 Cruel Arete 5+ *Using arete and pinches.*
44 New Jerusalem 6C+
    Start matched on long edge.

Chickenheads

Morris Wall

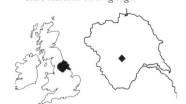

Low Pebble Wall

Yorkshire / Caley Roadside

Mike Stacey on Flapjack Traverse, 7A+ (problem 23). Photo: Andrew Poland.

Caley Crag

53.896942
-1.65031

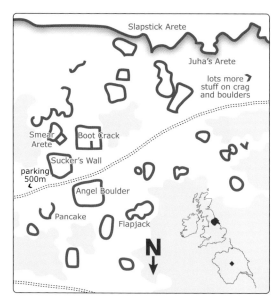

Slapstick Arete

Juha's Arete

lots more
stuff on crag
and boulders

Smear Arete

Boot Crack

Sucker's Wall

parking 500m

Angel Boulder

Pancake

Flapjack

N

More Caley class tucked away among the trees. A lot more sheltered and hidden than the Roadside area and with a magical ambience. Well lovable.

You'll be climbing among the mushrooms in this bouldering Hobbitland. Plenty of gnarly blockbusters on the left side of the path, high hard lines with 'landing issues', while on the right lies a dozen friendly low-slung, high-quality boulders. The circuit here covers only some of the boulders (see map for the rest) and there's more along the crag.

// Climbing: In many ways similar to the Roadside Boulders, being technical, fingery, footwork and powerful. Stuff on the left side of the path is not a good place for beginners as there are a lot of highballs, plenty of bad landings and sometimes both. Bring lots of pads. Also some problems need a bit of skill just to get off. The boulders on the right of the path are friendly and less threatening. Famous testpieces across the grades.

Sucker's Wall

Boot Crack

Smear Arete

Slapstick Arete

Juha's Arete

Pancake

Flapjack

1	**Twin Pockets** 5+	**9**	**Smear Arete** 5	**19**	**Ranieri's Reach** 8A
	Step off boulder; 6B+ direct.	**10**	**Arete Right** 5 *Sitter 7A.*	**20**	**Juha's Arete** 7C
2	**Front Traverse** 7A+	**11**	**Lip Traverse** 6C+	**21**	**Mr Smooth** 6A+
3	**Scary Canary** 7B+	**12**	**Nose** 6A *Finish up slab.*	**22**	**Pancake Arete** 4+
4	**Sucker's Rib** 5+	**13**	**Arete on Right** 5	**23**	**Flapjack Traverse** 7A+
5	**Sucker's Wall** 4+	**14**	**Slapstick Arete** 7A+	**24**	**Flapjack Groove** 5+
6	**Pocket Rock** 6A+		*From sitter on hold down left.*		*Sitter 6C.*
	The arete on left. Sitter is Pocket Knife, 7A+.	**15**	**Left Arete** 4+	**25**	**Flapjack Mantel** 5
		16	**Double Rib Traverse** 6A	**26**	**Flapjack Pockets** 3+
7	**Back Stabber** 6B	**17**	**Scooped Wall** 6A	**27**	**Flapjack Slab** 5+
8	**Rick's Rock** 6C	**18**	**Right Arete** 4+	**28**	**Flapjack Scoop** 5

// **Approach:** See map on page 280. Park as for Caley Roadside and continue up the bridalway for 400m to arrive at Sucker's Wall. The edge has problems all along and there are loads of boulders in the trees. Loads more, have a hunt around.

// **Conditions:** Mainly north-facing. It is very sheltered, not that sunny so is slow drying and can be very green for a lot of the winter. Best in spring and autumn, when it is particularly beautiful and the woods come into their full glory.

// **Info**: Yorkshire Gritstone Bouldering (TC); **yorkshiregrit.com**, Yorkshire Gritstone (YMC)

Almscliff

53.93761
-1.597427

The spiritual home of Yorkshire bouldering and the brainstem venue for locals. An exposed mini-mountain with lovely views and endless lines and eliminates. Generally burly climbing across all grades and with a great supply of testpieces of the highest historical value. An essential venue.

Hang on. Let me check whether there are any Yorkshire people listening: no, we're okay. The truth is Almscliff leaves me a wee bit cold. For a long time I didn't see what all the fuss was about. The climbing seemed a bit basic and unnecessarily brutal and the rock and landings had a very well-used feel about them. It was only when I was taken around by someone who knew it well did my opinion of it improve.

But whatever you think of Almscliff, you *have* to go there. Make no mistake about that. If you want to get your Level 1 Bouldering Badge, the most basic qualification, then you must at least do Matterhorn Ridge (as well as something at Stanage).

Almscliff has pedigree: the greats have walked this way. Cecil Slingsby, Claude Benson, Joe Brown, Arthur Dolphin, Allan Austin, Al Manson, John Syrett, Jerry Peel, Andy Swan, John Gaskins and Steve Dunning. Locals have always loved it, thanks in some way to its proximity to Leeds and easy access. It also dries very quickly. But perhaps its best draw to a local is the way it can give endless quality eliminates on old classics. There is always something to do at Almscliff, and for the up-and-coming Yorkshire boulderer the classic problems are a true measure of one's progress. Have it!

// **Climbing:** Great for people who think with their biceps. Steep, sometimes very steep, and fairly brutal. Climbing on boulders and crag. Sometimes highball (especially on the Virgin Boulder) and landings are hard and stoney. Bring a lot of pads. Plenty of lowball stuff too. Great across all grades and good for beginners. Aretes, cracks, walls and some easier slabs. Lots of crimps and slopers and some pockets. Brilliant for traverses, eliminates and link-ups.

// **Approach:** Follow the maps and park by a sharp left-hand bend. A footpath leads to the crag (please stick to it and don't cross any walls).

// **Conditions:** Very clean and exposed. Drys instantly. Can be extremely windy and cold. Gets loads of sun. Has a slightly worn feel and the rock is a bit polished in parts. Lovely location amidst rolling farmland. The field can get a bit cow-shitty. Popular with tourists. **Family friendly.**

// **Info**: **Yorkshire Gritstone Bouldering** (TC); **yorkshiregrit.com, Yorkshire Gritstone** (YMC); **Northern England** (Rockfax).

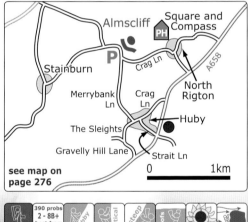

see map on page 276

Andi Turner on The Gypsy, 6B (problem 24). Photo: Niall Grimes.

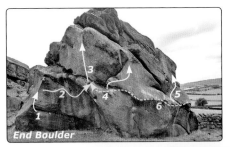

End Boulder

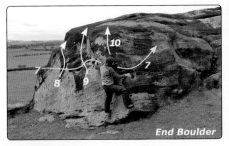

End Boulder

First Area

The Virgin

The Keel

1   **Arete Sitter**   6A
2   **Traverse**   7A   *From 1 swing right on pockets and up 3.*
3   **Morrell's Wall**   6A
4   **End Wall**   4
5   **Ramp**   4
6   **Slopy Traverse**   7B+
7   **Traverse**   3+
8   2   **9**   3   **10**   3+
11   **West Cave Wall**   3+   *Highball.*
12   **Roof and Slab**   4+   *Highball.*
13   **Three Swings Traverse**   5+
14   **Hanging Rib**   6A
15   **Rib from Sit**   5+
16   **Pork Chop Slab**   5+
17   **North Ridge**   6C   *Scary.*

18   **Flying Arete**   6A+
19   **Top Cat Traverse**   7B+
     Traverse pockets just above the lip from right to left finishing around arete then up into the groove.
20   **Virgin Traverse**   6B+
21   **Gaskins' Problem**   8A
22   **Cherry Falls**   8A+   *Using small high crimp for right hand and dish/pocket for left.*
23   **Crusis**   7B   *From low sitter.*
24   **The Gypsy**   6B   *Scary top.*
25   **Magnum Opus Direct**   7C   *To the break.*
26   **Arete**   6A
27   **Bulbhaul**   8B+   *From 26 swing into 28 on pockets, down to the keel (without using the block at the back), follow The Keel and finish as for The Bulb. Chip used.*

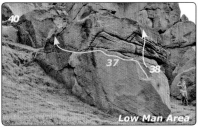

28 Keel Crack 6B+ *Sitter.*
29 The Keel 7C *From a sitter on block. 7C+ without the chip on the slab (The Real Keel).*
30 The Bulb 7C+ *Start as for The Keel then move right using a bulb-shaped hold to finish (without the pocket used by The Keel).*
31 Sloper Patrol 6C+ *Traverse the lip of the Keel boulder, downwards, to a belly-flop finish.*
32 Groove 3   **33 Slab** 3+
34 Crack 3   **35 Arete** 3
36 Wall 3+
37 Traverse 6C+
38 5+
39 Wall 5
40 Matterhorn Ridge 5
41 Patta's Arete 7A

42 Upper Traverse 6C+ *Finish up 44.*
43 Dyno 7A
44 Arete 6A+
45 South Cave Traverse 7A+
46 Crack 4
47 Stu's Roof 7C+ *Climb directly out to crimps on the lip then up via sharp crimps.*
48 Demon Wall Roof 7A+
49 Dolphin Belly Slap 7A
  Right arete and holds to the left.
50 Traverse 6C+
51 Traverse 6B+ *Keep going to the wall.*
52 Crucifix 5
53 Crucifix Arete 6A
54 Pebble Wall 6C+

Ceri Katz On Mouse Wall, 6A+ (problem 32), with Mark Katz spotting. Photo: Kevin Avery.

Shipley Glen

53.847501
-1.802541

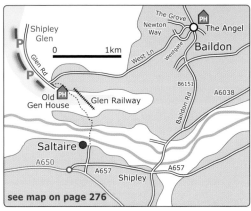

see map on page 276

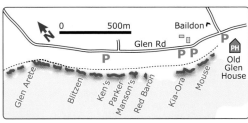

Seventies-style bouldering in a tree-lined urban playground. Mainly big vertical lines that quickly feel like soloing. A good mileage venue for the confident. Unlovely, yet loved.

In the 1970s, bouldering meant climbing where it wasn't worth putting a rope on. Such is Shipley. Not loads of bouldering in the modern idiom: you won't want to do lots of falling off. Problems are high and landings sometimes bad. Yet this has always been a favourite spot for an evening's exercise for locals, both human and canine.

// Climbing: Tall, angular and vertical mini-buttresses. Lots of aretes, horizontal breaks and cracks. Some sit starts under roofs. Bold. Bring a lot of mats. The rock can feel a bit slippery.
// Conditions: Very sheltered. Tree covered giving lots of shade. Lots of nooks (and, I suspect, nooky). Can be green in winter or after wet periods. Fairly urban and a bit messy.
// Approach: Follow the map to the big roundabout in Baildon (Angel pub on right). Take second exit (The Grove) then after 60m fork left into Newton Way. Follow this (becomes West Lane after 80m, then Lucy Hall Drive) for 1.4 miles to a junction with Glen Rd. The cragline is straight ahead. Turn right and park. Also a half-hour walk from Saltaire train station. Buttresses stretch all along the rim and the topos here offer a sporadic selection.
// Info: YGB (TC): **yorkshiregrit.com**

Glen Arete

Blitzen

Ken's Arete

Parker

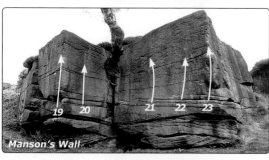

Manson's Wall

Red Baron

Kia-Ora

Mouse Wall

1	**Glen Arete** 4	**11**	**Ken's Arete** 6A	**19**	**DAZ** 6B	*of far arete. No ledge for feet.*
2	**Groovy** 4+	**12**	**Mike's Mantel** 6A+	**20**	**Off Stump Wall** 4	**26** **Step Down** 6A
3	**Faint Heart** 4+	**13**	**Green Wall** 4+	**21**	**Manson's Wall**	**27** **Interstellar**
4	**The Hole** 4	**14**	**Green Arete** 4		6C	**Overdrive** 6B
5	**Golden Oldie** 4	**15**	**Honey I Shrunk**	**22**	**Phil's Wall** 7A+	**28** **Echinococcus** 6C+
6	**Adolph** 6A		**the Kids** 7B *Sitter.*	**23**	**Vim** 6A+	**29** **Pirouette** 5+
7	**Donner** 6A	**16**	**Why Crack** 4+	**24**	**Red Baron** 7A+	**30** **Woolman** 5+
8	**Rudolph** 6C	**17**	**Parker** 7A+		*Sitter 7C+*	**31** **Woolman**
9	**Millstone Grit** 7B		*Sitter 7B+.*	**25**	**Dead Baron** 8A	**Right** 6B+
10	**Blitzen** 5+	**18**	**Nosey** 5+		*Start from a jug right*	**32** **Mouse Wall** 6A+

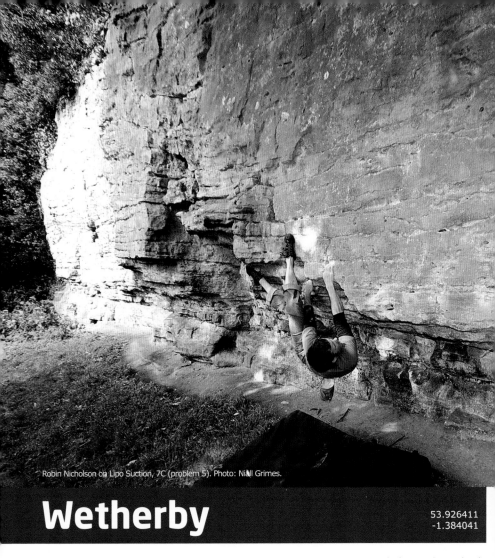
Robin Nicholson on Lipo Suction, 7C (problem 5). Photo: Niall Grimes.

Wetherby

53.926411
-1.384041

A local pump for local people. A long flat wall of limestone, lovingly-polished by generations of aerobic Yorkies. Easy access, reliable conditions and only a few minutes off the A1.

Essentially a training crag. The climbing is not the most interesting but it is certainly worthwhile and the crag has lots of devotees. The Al Manson training ground where he reputedly traversed with pocketfuls of brass.

// Climbing: A long wall of limestone with lots of cracks, flatties, crimps and pockets. Mostly vertical with a steep base. Lots of up-problems but these have tiresome topouts or else jump dismounts so are not massively popular. Most folk are here for the traverses. These are pumpy and refreshingly brainless.

// Approach: Get to Wetherby. On the south side of town, just north of where Main Street / A661 crosses the River Wharfe, is a mini-roundabout (the third one if coming north into town from the A1). An inconspicuous exit from this roundabout (beware bad tempered commuters who don't see it) leads down to a large car park beside the river. Park here. Carry on a footpath for 100m to the crag. Good public transport to Wetherby.

// Conditions: Sheltered and good year round. Some winter seepage but not too bad. Good on summer evenings but can get sweaty. **Family friendly** but mind the dog shit.

1	**First Traverse** 5+	
2	**Second Crack** 4+	
3	**Third Crack** 4+	
4	**Groove** 4	
5	**Lipo Suction** 7C	

Lip traverse, hands on lowest holds, feet at hand level. Finish up problem 12.

6	**Wall to Ledge** 4	
7	**Lip Traverse** 6B	

Reverse Lipo Suction but with feet on rock below.

8	**Arete** 5	*Sitter.*
9	**Traverse** 6B	
10	**Cracks** 4	
11	**Sit Start Crack** 5+	
12	**Steepness** 6A	
13	**Prow** 6A+	
14	**Crack** 2+	
15	**Arete** 6C+	
16	**Mega Traverse** 7A	*Link all the sections but continue*

all the way to the bivvy cave on the far right.

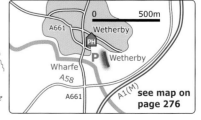

see map on page 276

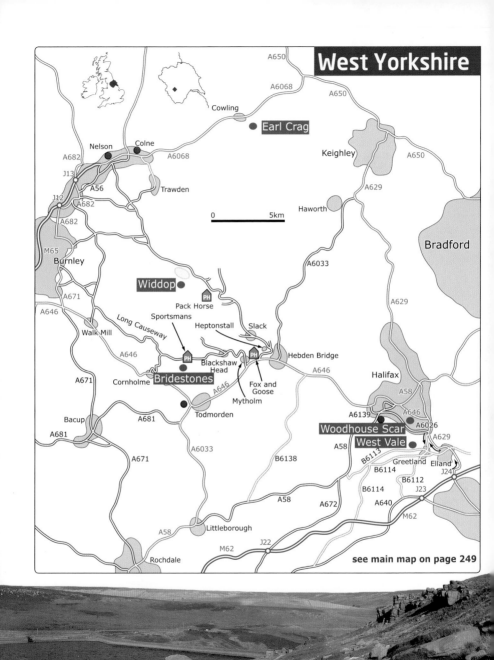

West Yorkshire

A650
A6068
A650
A650

Cowling
Earl Crag
Keighley
Nelson
Colne
A682
J13
A6068
A56
Trawden
A682
J12
A682
A682
A629
Haworth

0   5km

Bradford

M65
Burnley
A671
A646
Widdop
A6033
A629

Long Causeway
Walk Mill
A646
Sportsmans
PH Pack Horse
Heptonstall
Slack
A629

Heptonstall
A671
PH Bridestones
Blackshaw Head
Cornholme
A646
Fox and Goose
Mytholm
Hebden Bridge
A646
Halifax
A58

Bacup
A681
Todmorden
A6139
Woodhouse Scar
A646
A6026
West Vale
A681
A671
A6033
B6138
A58
B6113
Greetland
Elland
B6114
J24
B6112
J23
B6114
A58
A672
A640
M62

A58
Littleborough
M62
J22
Rochdale

see main map on page 249

Jerry Peel on Big Top, 6A, at Widdop (page 301, prpblem 12). Photo: Mike Hutton.

Matthew Chambers on Problem Rib, 5+ (problem 4). Photo: Niall Grimes.

Earl Crag

53.879301
-2.021484

A shaded and burly beauty of a crag, a well hung gallery of testpieces across all grades. A great place to escape summer heat if you have a good supply of pads. Hard travelling on great lines, a true boulderer's crag but be prepared for a scrap 'cos you're sure going to get one. A real A-lister.

Caley might be the finest bouldering in England but this might be the best crag in Yorkshire. How do you think that ranks? A special crag, a favourite amongst strong connoisseurs who have a good sense of being in the right place at the right time. And how comes that crags that face north are always hard? Queens Crag, Burbage South, Wimberry. Why can't they just relax?

// Climbing: Gritstone edge. Big strong lines, many originally done with E-grades. Lots of pads will ensure that your knees and ankles will have a good day even if that compromises your E-tally. Often grassy landings but these are sometimes sloping. Even problems that are not high have a bold feel about them, perhaps because you are trying so hard you feel as though you'll pop off at any second. All in all not a great beginner's crag. There's lots of standard-height problems too, perfectly safe, but if you haven't gone home without at least one major wobble you will feel you missed out.

Lots and lots of aretes. Plenty of crimps and slopers and lovely rounded flakes. Good lines. Powerful, technical and fingery, often just over vertical.

The crag has a great historic feel about it too and climbers such as Jerry Peel, Ron Fawcett, John Dunne, Ben Moon and Dave Buchanan have left their mark here.

// Approach: Get to Cowling on the A6068. Now, two choices. At the south end of town Old Lane runs up then left to a large car park behind Wainman's Pinnacle. Alternatively, at the north end of town, Dick Lane winds up below the crag passing a parking bay near the top of the slope or continue round to the Wainman's parking.

The Pinnacle Area is directly below the large car park. The Kipper area is more quickly approached from the Dick Lane parking. Most of the problems are on blocks above the main section of crag and are generally friendly with good landings.

For Butterfly Wall find a good track that cuts down along the crag from a stone wall on the crag-top path, just right of the Kipper Area. This quickly leads to it. Desert Island Arete is a bit further on.

// Conditions: Gets sun on summer evenings. Fairly shady otherwise. Gets good conditions in summer but can be cold in winter. Quick drying on the popular, cleaner stuff although its aspect means that some corners will get licheny. The busy road, while some way away, makes its presence felt, so you don't quite have the wilderness vibe. **Good for families and doggys.**

// Info: Yorkshire Gritstone Bouldering (Total Climbing); **yorkshiregrit.com; Yorkshire Gritstone** (YMC)

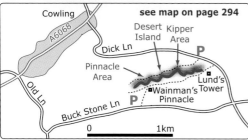

Kipper

Problem Rib

Hanging Groove

Trick Arete

Small Block

Cool Hand

Butterfly Wall

Desert Island

1 **Kipper** 6B+ *HVS.*	**10** **Slab** 5	**18** **Superfly** 7B
2 **Erasor Slab** 4+ *HVS.*	**11** **Trick Arete** 6B	**19** **Desert Island**
3 **Edge of Darkness** 7C	**12** **Arete** 5	**Arete Start** 7A *Sitter 7A+.*
Crack with hard start: E5.	**13** **Arete** 6B *Sitter.*	**20** **Mousehole Slab** 3+ *VS.*
4 **Problem Rib** 5+	**14** **Cool Hand Wall** 5	**21** **Undercut Arete** 6A
5 **Rubber Arete** 6A	**15** **Cool Hand** 6A	**22** **Rat au Van** 6A
6 **Grey Wall** 4+	**16** **Green Rib** 6B	**23** **Layback** 4
7 **Hanging Groove** 6B+	*Arete and wall.*	**24** **Sour Grapes** 6C
Sitter.	**17** **Slim Shady** 7C+	*E3 crack.*
8 **Vanishing Point** 8A	*Wall to break.*	
9 **Sloping Beauty** 7B		

Problem Rib

Hanging Groove

Trick Arete

Cool Hand

Kipper

Kipper Area

Yorkshire / Earl Crag

Rat au Van

20 21 22 23

Grape Nut

24 25 26 27 28

Pinnacle Area

29 30 31 32 33

Pinnacle Area

34

Pinnacle Area

35 36 37 38

Pinnacle Area

39 40

25 The Boundary 6C
26 Grape Nut 7A+
27 Wall 6A
28 Scoop 4
29 Rib 4
30 Arete 4+
31 Arete 5+
32 Handy Andy's 7A+
33 Arete 5+
34 Underworld 7C+
35 Rib 3+
36 Arete 5 *Sitter 6A.*
37 Groove 5+ *Sitter 6B.*
38 Weight Gain 5+
     Sitter 6B+.
39 Hanging Arete 6B+
40 Scoop 4+
41 The Gimp 6C
42 Lager, Lager, Lager
     7C
43 Ron's Slab 6C+
44 Ron's Arete 6C
45 Crack 5
46 John Dunne Slap
     6B+

The Gimp

41 42

Ron's Slab

43 44 45 46

Wainman's Pinnacle

Pinnacle Area

Desert Island

Rat au Van Grape Nut

The Gimp Ron's Slab

Butterfly Wall

Pinnacle Area

Yorkshire / Earl Crag

Widdop

53.791323
-2.096243

Widdop, wild and woolly, with one of the best circuits about. Best suited to technicians, pebble-heads or beginners.

A really fantastic spot with lots of quality problems and enough for a full day out. An easy approach, good landings and a beautiful setting make this a very friendly spot, great for families.

The problems detailed here centre around the boulders by the reservoir. There is also bouldering on the crag and a load on the mini-buttresses that stretch off rightwards along the hillside. These are greener in winter. There is a lot more great bouldering at other venues in the immediate area (see map); check out the Total Climbing guidebook for the lowdown.

// Climbing: Technical and fingery problems on slabs, aretes and walls. Mainly on slopers, crimps and pebbles. Harder problems hurty on the skin. A few highballs above good landings. Good lines. Lots for beginners.

// Approach: Follow maps and park in the large layby. Car break-ins are a problem here.

// Conditions: A bleak, beautiful moorland setting best enjoyed on a nice day, although it can be sheltered from prevailing westerly winds. Boulders sometimes green in winter but generally climbable. Boggy in winter. There is a lot of bouldering on the edge which is north facing and can be dirtier than the boulders. Midges on still summer days: sheer hell! **Family friendly.**

// Info: YGB (Total Climbing); <u>yorkshiregrit.com</u>; Yorkshire Gritstone (YMC)

1 **The Boss** 5+
2 **Bruce** 6A
3 **Iggy Pop** 5+
4 **Ernie** 2
5 **Hallo Little Lady** 2
6 **Splashdown** 6B *Arete.*
7 **Pot Black** 6C
8 **Fight on the Black** 7B *Arete.*
9 **The Traverse** 6B+
10 **The Shelf** 6B
11 **Pool Traverse** 6B+ *Traverse right from the hole then up into the scoop.*
12 **Big Top** 6A *Lip traverse.*
13 **Pickpocket's Crack** 6A+
14 **Fagin's Ridge** 5 *On the left.*
15 **Fagin's Ridge Right** 3
16 **Traverse** 3
17 **Mild** 3 *Left flake.*
18 **Bitter** 3+ *Right flake.*
19 **Stout** 5+
   Avoid the chips out right.
20 **Chips** 4+ *The chipped slab.*
21 **Flake** 2
22 **Panic** 7B+
23 **Four Square** 6A
24 **Get Shorty** 5+
25 **Spice** 3+
26 **Red Edge Right** 6A
   The arete on its right. Just as good, and the same grade, on the left.
27 **Traverse** 4+
28 **Ronnie** 3
29 **Fortune Cookie** 3+
30 **Pebble Wall** 6C+
31 **The Hurt Locker** 4+ *Offwidth.*
32 **Umpleby's Arete** 4+ *Highball.*
33 **The Big Crack** 4+ *Highball.*
34 **North Face** 5+
35 **Runnel for your Life** 5+
36 **Bod** 7A+ *From a sitter, hands in the low pod, slap left and up the arete.*

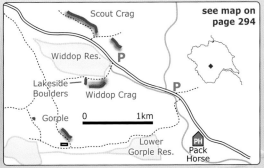

Scout Crag
Widdop Res.
Lakeside Boulders
Widdop Crag
Gorple
Lower Gorple Res.
Pack Horse

see map on page 294

0   1km

10 min | 75 probs 2 - 7B+ best from 4 - 7A | slabby | vertical | exposed

Scout Crag   The Crag

P

Four Square

Splashdown

Pickpocket   Red Edge   to Umpleby's

First Boulder

First Boulder

Splashdown

Pickpocket

Pickpocket

Four Square

Red Edge

Umpleby's

Umpleby's

One of the original homes of Yorkshire bouldering with a strong and venerable history. Endless gritstone eggs, mini-buttresses and rocky erections create a wild wonderland of bouldering in an exposed landscape. In recent years it has become victim of it's own quality and erosion has rendered the place a sad reminder of how we can destroy that which we love most.

The rock at the Bridestones has always been delicate. The hard protective crust is quite thin and the grit below not as strong as in other areas. Consequently when the crust has worn the rock below has crumbled away. Several classics are now destroyed. To save further destruction the latest Total Climbing guide doesn't cover the crag. Here there are no problems detailed. If you like the sound of undocumented classics is a wild setting, check it out. But please be gentle. Don't climb on any delicate holds, don't climb on damp rock and don't brush any problems. **Also, no climbing on The Bridestone, the tall, narrow-based egg at the right end of the crag.**

// Climbing: Climbing on natural edges or smaller boulder-like mini-towers. Mostly vertical, or a bit either side. Climbing is on strong lines and generally quite forceful. Sometimes highball: perfect landings. Mats useful. Good for aretes and slopers.

// Conditions: Very open and exposed. The Bridestones sit high on a wild moor and are very exposed, especially to prevailing westerly winds and liable to cold shrouds of mist. If this is the story then the nearby Widdop boulders, lower down and sheltered from westerlies, would be a better idea. On nice days however, the Bridestones are fantastic. The wind is good for keeping midges away. Climbable year round. Climb very gently here and don't climb on any loose rock. Avoid any brushing. **Family friendly.**

Matt Kilner on Horror Arete, 6C. Photo: Jamie Moss.

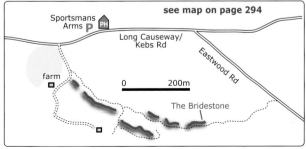

Bridestones

53.741871
-2.109439

// Approach: Approach from Walk Mill or Corn-holme via the Long Causeway (Kebs Rd). If coming from Hebden Bridge go towards Todmorden on the A646. About 400m out of town, about 100m after Heptonstall Rd, turn right towards Mytholm (not signposted) along Church Lane (by a bus stop). Wind ever uphill (Glenview Rd, Rawtonstall Bank, Badger Lane) to reach Blackshaw Head after a mile. All these ways lead to the Sportsmans Arms. Park here and follow the map to the rocks.

// Info: ACD's old **Yorkshire Gritstone Bouldering** (Rockfax); **Yorkshire Gritstone** (YMC)

5 min | 120 probs 3 - 7C best from 4 - 7A+ | slabby | vertical | steep | | exposed

Climber on Centipede, 3+ (problem 17). Photo: Niall Grimes.

Woodhouse Scar

53.707707
-1.876388

A dark edge of problems and highballs with a certain dirty, littered charm. Urban as hell, but still, the climbing is quite good.

// Climbing: Gritstone edge with climbing on buttresses big and small. Heights from small to highball. Good landings. Aretes, slabs, cracks, roofs and walls.

// Approach: From the major roundabout in the centre of Halifax follow A58 direction Rochdale. After a mile turn left onto A646 (Skircoat Moor Rd) direction Huddersfield (a large tower / monument is visible on the right). Follow this for 350m and turn right onto Albert Promenade. Follow this and park on the right before some bollards. The crag is below.

// Conditions: Faces south-west getting evening sun. Very sheltered. Tree cover means not much breeze so can stay damp after wet weather or a bit humid in summer.

// Info: **Yorkshire Gritstone Bouldering** (TC); **yorkshiregrit.com**: **Yorkshire Gritstone** (YMC); **Yorkshire Gritstone** (YMC)

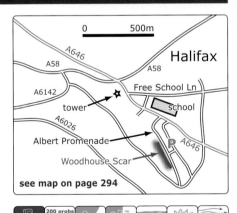

see map on page 294

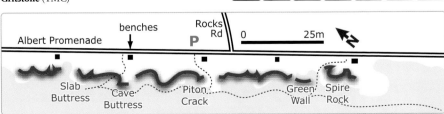

Slab Buttress

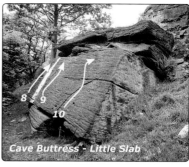

Cave Buttress - Little Slab

Cave Buttress

Piton Crack

Green Wall

Spire Rock

lots of weather-proof eliminates

1	**Slab** 3	**13**	**Basin Crack** 3 *Sitter 4+.*	**23**	**Close to the Edge** 7A
2	**Crack** 2+	**14**	**Groove** 5+	**24**	**Radium Arete** 6A
3	**Corner** 3	**15**	**Chryophorous** 5	**25**	**Bear Down** 7C *Sitter.*
4	**Ledges** 1		*Sitter 6B+*	**26**	**Wall** 7B *Sitter.*
5	**Pockets** 3+	**16**	**Johnny One Time** 6A+	**27**	**Arete** 6A
6	**Slab** 4	**17**	**Centipede** 3+	**28**	**Crack** 6A
7	**Crack** 2+	**18**	**Arete** 2+	**29**	**Arete** 6A *Escape at break.*
8	**Paint Arete** 6A *Sitter.*	**19**	**Piton Crack** 6C	**30**	**Chipped Wall** 4
9	**Crack** 4 *Sitter.*		*Highball crack on left of buttress.*		*VS to top.*
10	**Crack** 4+ *Sitter.*	**20**	**Arete on Left** 6A+	**31**	**Spigolo** 5 *HVS to top.*
11	**Arete** 4	**21**	**Houdini** 7B+	**32**	**Wall** 6C+
12	**Done Years Ago** 6C+	**22**	**Ian's Roof** 7C		*A scary highball.*

Mark Boulton spotting Caitlin Lister on Traverse of the Gods, 6C+ (problem 20). Niall Grimes.

West Vale

53.689255
-1.860144

A harmless place. A little urban quarry with an easy approach and a relaxed nature. A few up-problems but best for traversing with a long old-school marathon. Despite the usual graffiti and urban setting it retains a natury feel.

// Climbing: Quarried gritstone. Vertical or slightly overhanging walls. Climbing on flatties, crimps and cracks. Some problems a bit high but landings are perfect. Good for traversing. The area around the Overhanging Face has lots of well-developed eliminates, accounting for most of the harder problems in the quarry.
// Approach: From M62 take exit 24 and follow A629 direction Halifax. Continue for 3 miles and turn off, signposted Stainland B6112 (where the A6026 meets the A629). Follow the B6112 towards Stainland. After 900m there is a crossroads in the village of Greetland. Turn right on the B6113 Rochdale Rd. After 300m The Star pub can be seen up a little sidestreet on the right. Park courteously near this. Walk up the right side of the pub and 30m after it, and before the road bends right, take a lane on the right. Follow past some houses and continue along a track leading to the quarry.
// Conditions: South facing, getting the sun for most of the day. Very sheltered and quick drying. Maybe some seepage after lots of rain. Reliable: a good winter venue. **Family friendly.**
// Info: Yorkshire Gritstone Bouldering (TC); **yorkshiregrit.com**; Yorkshire Gritstone (YMC)

Overhanging Wall

Scott is Bent Wall

Buddy Holly Bay

Madness Wall

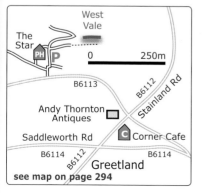

West Vale

The Star

0   250m

B6113

Stainland Rd

B6112

Andy Thornton Antiques

Saddleworth Rd

Corner Cafe

B6114

B6112

B6114

Greetland

see map on page 294

1	**Low Traverse** 6C	12	**Traverse** 6A
2	**Crack** 3	13	**Crack** 4
3	**Low Traverse** 6B+	14	**Flaky Crack** 2+
4	**Crack to Slot** 6A	15	**Arete** 5+
5	**Rampline** 6A	16	**Traverse** 6C+
6	**Niche** 4+	17	**Traverse** 5+
7	**Triangular Hold** 6C	18	**The Ramp** 6C+
8	**Arete on Left** 6A	19	**Crack** 2
9	**Arete on Right** 7A	20	**Traverse of the**
10	**Traverse** 6A		**Gods** 6C+ *Traverse the*
	Start in corner.		*entire quarry by the easiest*
11	**Wall** 5+		*line, sometimes going high.*

Yorkshire / West Vale

John Roberts on Technical Master, 6B, Millstone (page 333, problem 35). Photo: Alex Messenger.

The Peak

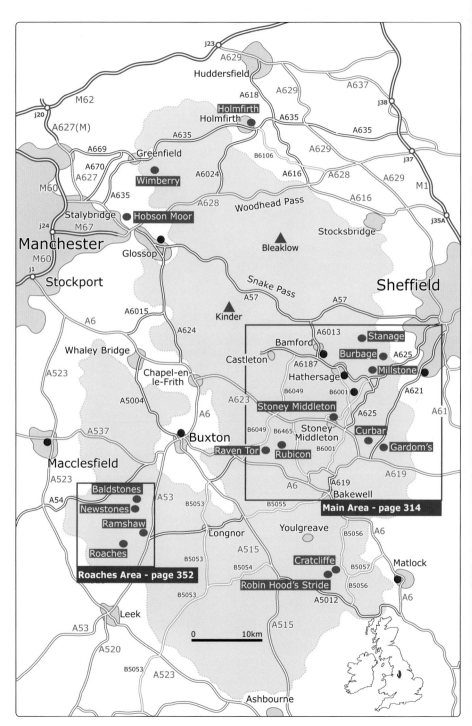

Peak / Introduction

Laura Evans on Razor Roof, 6C+, at Cratcliffe (page 351, problem 29). Photo: John Coefield.

The history of bouldering in the Peak stretches back as far as the history of rock climbing itself, to James Puttrell who, in the late-1800s, wandered the edges and scrambled on blocks and boulders with a boulderer's mindset.

The post-war years saw the Rock and Ice club take to gritstone, both big and small, with gusto. Joe Brown and Don Whillans bouldered extensively at the Roaches and Stanage accounting for some of today's mid-grade classics.

However it was the 1970s that saw the real surge in bouldering. Just as in Northumberland and Yorkshire, the technical standards in the Peak rocketed, led by a youthful band of bold boulderers. John Allen led the way, ably assisted by Gabe Regan, Steve Bancroft and the Stokes brothers, Mark, Neil and Nicky. They rode the bus from Sheffield and scoured the eastern edges, hurling standards well into the 7A level. At the same time the Woodward brothers, Jonny and Andy, applied themselves in the Roaches area.

In the 1980s a dedicated and able band of full-timers carried standards on. Ben Moon, Jerry Moffatt, Johnny Dawes, Dougie Hall, Rob Gawthorpe, Martin Veale, Al Williams, Simon Nadin, Nick Dixon, Pete Kirton, Chris Hamper, Quentin Fisher and Mark Leach all upped the ante and quality on gritstone boulders as grades inched into the upper 7s.

Limestone saw a real surge in really hard problems in this era too. Again it was Moffatt, Moon, Leach, Fisher and Kirton who pushed levels way beyond what was being done on grit.

In many ways the 1990s and early 2000s saw Peak bouldering mature. The big lines were Ron Fawcett's Careless Torque, Jason Myers' Brad Pit, Jerry Moffatt's The Joker and The Ace, Ben Moon's 8 Ball and Voyager. Since then James Pearson, Dan Varian, Steve McClure and Steve Dunning have filled out the top grades.

The Peak District is very well served by guidebooks - full coverage is in the new series of BMC guides and Peak District Bouldering guide from Vertebrate. A new Rockfax guide is in the pipeline too. This builds on the older Rockfax guide, still available, and still a great book. The history of guides also stretches back to Al Williams' Peak Bouldering Guide published by On The Edge, the UK's first bouldering guide.

Another great resource, and getting better all the time, is **peakbouldering.info**, great for photos, videos and comments. Log on, tune in and drop out.

Below: Fran Santos on Trackside, 7A, at Curbar (page 335, problem 9). Photo: Niall Grimes.

James Hilliard on Fish Arete, 6C+, at Wimberry (page 365, problem 28). Photo: David Simmonite.

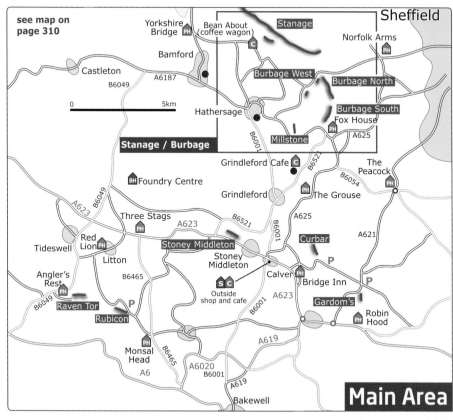

see map on page 310

Yorkshire Bridge
Bean About (coffee wagon)
Stanage
Sheffield
Norfolk Arms
Bamford
Burbage West
Burbage North
Castleton
A6187
B6049
Burbage South
Fox House
Hathersage
A625
0   5km
Stanage / Burbage
Millstone
Grindleford Cafe
The Peacock
B6521
Foundry Centre
B6054
A623
B6049
Grindleford
The Grouse
A625
Three Stags
A623
B6521
B6001
Curbar
A621
Tideswell
Red Lion
Stoney Middleton
A625
Litton
Stoney Middleton
Calver
Robin Hood
Angler's Rest
B6465
Outside shop and cafe
Bridge Inn
Gardom's
B6049
Raven Tor
A623
B6001
Rubicon
Monsal Head
B6465
A619
A6020
B6001
A6
A619
Bakewell

Main Area

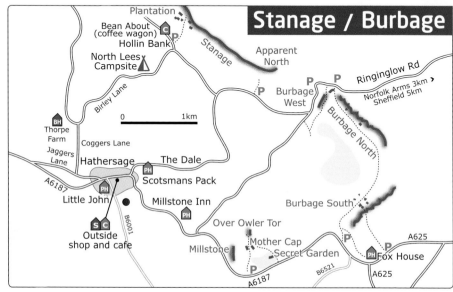

Stanage / Burbage

Plantation
Bean About (coffee wagon)
Hollin Bank
Stanage
Apparent North
North Lees Campsite
Ringinglow Rd
Norfolk Arms 3km
Sheffield 5km
Birley Lane
Burbage West
Burbage North
Thorpe Farm
Coggers Lane
Jaggers Lane
Hathersage
The Dale
Scotsmans Pack
A6187
Burbage South
Little John
Millstone Inn
Over Owler Tor
Outside shop and cafe
B6001
Mother Cap
Secret Garden
Millstone
Fox House
A625
A6187
B6521
A625

The Plantation boulders are the crown jewels of Peak grit. A scattering of golden globes gives probably the most celebrated bouldering in the country with historic classics across the grades. A must-visit venue for any boulderer. It's everything that grit should be and then some. World class.

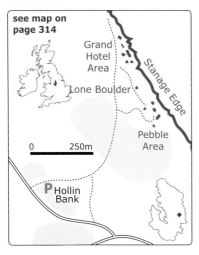

see map on page 314

Grand Hotel Area

Stanage Edge

Lone Boulder

Pebble Area

0   250m

P Hollin Bank

The bracken-covered slopes under the area's mightiest crag has been the go-to venue for generations of Sheffielders much the way Almscliffe is for the little people of Leeds. History runs deep and Joe Brown's footsteps are to be found here. In the Gritstone Renaissance of the 1970s climbers such as John Allen, Gabe Regan, Martin Veale and Mark Stokes strutted their stuff on some of the best lines that bouldering has to offer. The big man, Ron Fawcett, a Hathersage local, amazed the world with Careless Torque, the country's most prized highball (perhaps only High Fidelity, Queen Kong and Cypher come close). Ben Moon, Jason Myers, Johnny Dawes and Jerry Moffatt, have brought the boulders to maturity. Now, what about that for a roll of honour.

The problems here are all on the two groups of blocks that make up the Plantation. On the left is the Grand Hotel area called after the ramped block containing Not To Be Taken Away, acclaimed as the best highball on grit, as well as Careless Torque. A lot of the problems here, especially the better ones, are highball or have tricky landings but are well worth breaking an ankle for. Brave and well-padded highballers may well want to know about Archangel (E3), Ulysses (E6) and White Wand (E5), the three aretes on the crag up behind the Grand Hotel, and perhaps the best routes of their grade on grit.

To the right is the Pebble area with a host of famous testpieces. More popular, less highball and with more easier problems, it is a perfect compliment to the Grand Hotel. The boulder between the two areas is the Lone Boulder and there are problems all along the crag just as good as those covered here.

// Climbing: Essential gritstone climbing. Generally quite steep and powerful climbing on slopers, crimps and aretes. A few slabs, but not tons. Problems are generally non-eliminate and follow strong lines. Sit starts, stand-ups, traverses, little problems and big highballs are all common. Burly. Landings are mostly very good and most of the highballs are above flat ground. The rock is fairly fine grained and, with only a few pebble problems, is not too harsh on the skin. Good for traverses. Not brilliant for very easy stuff.

Because of the historical significance and popularity of the boulders it is great for well-known testpieces. Pebble Arete, Crescent Arete, Not To Be Taken Away, Green Traverse, Deliverance, The

Roger, Dan and Martin watch Carwen on the Green Traverse, 7A (problem 8). Photo: Niall Grimes.

Stanage Plantation

53.350705
-1.644752

Joker, Brad Pit and The Ace – if you climb at the grade then you have to do them.

// Conditions: Quite exposed, clean and very quick drying. Very sunny. Boulders face in all directions but are generally south-west facing getting the sun from late morning. A great sunset crag. Can be windy. Climbable year round. Popular. **Family friendly.**

// Approach: From Sheffield follow the A625 Ecclesall Rd to the outskirts of town then follow the Ringinglow Rd, passing the Norfolk Arms, to follow the maps to Hollin Bank (paid) parking. **From Hathersage**, take School Lane/The Dale leading off the main street from the Sheffield side of town. Follow this past The Scotsmans Pack pub, uphill, until the crag comes into view then follow the maps to Hollin Bank as above.

The Stanage Bus runs on Sundays and bank holidays from the end of March to the end of October linking Sheffield and Hathersage via the crag.

// Info: Stanage (BMC); **Peak District Bouldering** (Vertebrate); **peakbouldering.info**

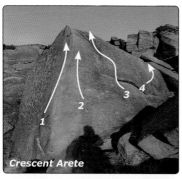

Crescent Arete

Grand Hotel

Mental Block

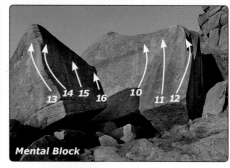

Mental Block

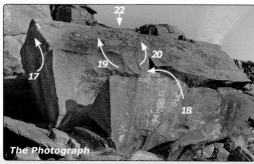

The Photograph

The Photograph

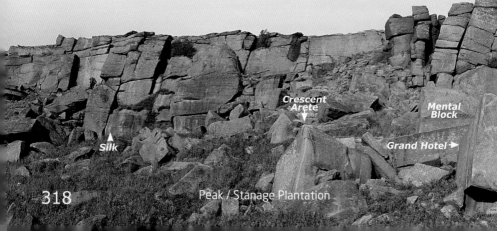

Silk

Crescent Arete

Mental Block

Grand Hotel

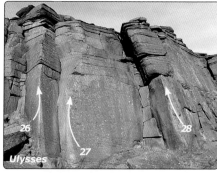

1	**Crescent Arete** 5+ *Highball: HVS.*	**9**	**Beneath the Breadline** 7B *Ground start to 8.*	**22**	**Brad Pit** 7C
2	**Crescent Arete Right-Hand** 6B+	**10**	**Scoops Groove** 4+	**23**	**Silk Start** 7A+ *Continue up left at E5.*
3	**Crescent Slab** 7A	**11**	**Scoops Slab** 5	**24**	**Fern Crack Start** 4+
4	**Crescent Groovelet** 6A	**12**	**Arete** 5	**25**	**Help the Aged** 7A
5	**Careless Torque** 8A *Highball.*	**13**	**Issue 53** 5+	**26**	**Archangel** 5 *E3.*
6	**Not to be Taken Away** 6C *Highball.*	**14**	**Back Cover** 3	**27**	**Ulysses** 6C *E6.*
		15	**Slab** 3+	**28**	**White Wand** 6A *E5.*
7	**The Storm** 7B+	**16**	**Arete** 3	**29**	**Right Spur** 6C *Sitter.*
8	**The Breadline** 6C *Climb the arete by stepping off the block opposite. E4.*	**17**	**Adults Only** 6C	**30**	**Satin** 7A *Sitter*
		18	**The Crown** 4	**31**	**Lone Arete** 5+
		19	**The Positive** 4+	**32**	**Lone Slab** 6A+
		20	**The Negative** 3	**33**	**Lone Scoop** 6A
		21	**The Aniston Slap** 6C	**34**	**Wall** 4+

Peak / Stanage Plantation

Crozzle Block

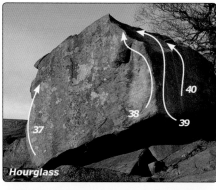

Hourglass

Steep Traverse

Green Traverse

35 **Crozzle Arete**   6B
  Arete on right. 6C on left.
36 **Crozzle Slab**   5+
37 **Glass Hour**   7A
38 **Hourglass Left**   6B
39 **Hourglass**   6A
40 **Slopey Pokey**   6A+

41 **Steep Traverse**   6C
42 **Green Traverse**   7A
43 **Green Mantel**   6C
44 **The Joker**   8A
  Lean in from the block to reach the crimps.
45 **The Ace**   8B
  Gain The Joker from the low break.

Steep
Traverse

Hourglass ▶

Crozzle
Block

Green
Traverse ▶

Joker Block

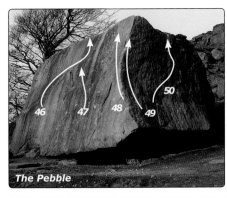

The Pebble

Business Boulder

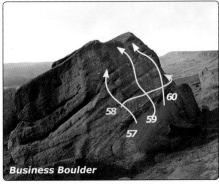

Business Boulder

46 The Ramp 3+
Hardest at the start: often used as a descent.
47 Pebble Flakes 4+
48 Pebble Arete
 Left-Hand 6A
49 Pebble Arete 6A+

50 Deliverance 7B
Dyno using layback flake.
51 Flake 3
52 Zippy's Traverse 7B
Sit start with with hands in the low slot.
53 Big Business 5
54 Jerry's Traverse 7C
55 Vague Arete 6B
56 Business Launch 6B+
57 Black Arete 4+
58 Traverse 3
59 Black Wall 4
60 Black Bulge 4+

Hamper's Hang, 7A (problem 18).

8 min | 100 probs 2 - 7C best from 3 - 7A | vertical | steep | | exposed

Apparent North

53.341226
-1.623831

The northern reaches of Stanage is the crag's other great bouldering area. A fantastic circuit with a great sense of Wuthering Heights about it.

// Climbing: Gritstone edge. Mainly vertical, fingery and technical. Perfect rock and great problems. Some highballs, great for traverses.

// Approach: See map on page 314. Park at the highpoint of the road from where the crag is easily visible.

// Conditions: Faces from south-west, to south, to south-east. Lots of sun. Exposed and very quick drying. Can be midgy. **Family friendly**.

// Info: Stanage (BMC); **Peak District Bouldering** (Vertebrate); **peakbouldering.info**

1	**Sparky Slab** 6B	12	**Lip Traverse** 7B
2	**Sparky** 2		*Sitter.*
3	**The Henge** 5	13	**Easy Walling** 5
4	**Flake** 4 *Sitter.*	14	**Trainer Failure** 4+
5	**Al's Attic** 7A	15	**Crack** 4
6	**Front Flake** 4+	16	**Canary Traverse** 5
7	**Upper Traverse** 5	17	**Minah Variation**
8	**Arete** 5		6C+ *The sidewall.*
9	**Cube Root** 5	18	**Hamper's Hang** 7A
10	**Lower Traverse** 6A	19	**Skinless Wonder**
11	**The High Road** 3+		7A+ *To the break.*
	Mantel into scoop, undercut right and climb the slabby arete.	20	**Stanage Without Oxygen** 7A+ *Highball.*
		21	**North** 5

The Henge   ◀ The Cube   Real Twenty   Apparent
                                            Foot Crack   North

The Henge

The Cube

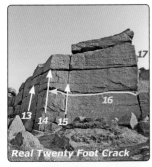

Real Twenty Foot Crack

Apparent North

Sloper Traverse

Almost a Hold

Block

Flat Wall

22 Across and Up 6B+	**27** Crimps 5+	**33** Block Arete 5+ *Sitter.*
23 Mating Toads 5+	**28** Petty Larcent 6A	**34** Wall 6A+ *Sitter*
24 Massacre Direct 5	**29** Almost a Hold 6C+	**35** Groove 5+ *Sitter.*
25 Sloper Traverse 7A+	**30** Grand Theft 5	**36** Get the Horn 5+
26 Sloper Problem 6B	**31** Zorro 4+	*Double dyno from low flake.*
	32 Block Wall 5 *Sitter.*	**37** Flat Wall Traverse 6A+

Sloper Traverse **Almost a Hold** **Block** **Flat Wall**

Burbage North

53.343378
-1.60984

While Stanage stretches itself out like a beautiful model across a sports car bonnet in a motor show, Burbage North is more coy, tucked into nooks and trees, under overhangs and up gullies. A great place, and a firm favourite with the local cognoscenti. Spot-on for some power-sapping problems and few cute solos. And oh, the view...

5 min | **130 probs** **4 - 88+** best from **5 - 7B+** | vertical | steep | roofs | | shelter

This section includes Burbage West and Burbage Bridge. The bouldering is on the bottom of buttresses and on boulders generally giving steep and fingery problems. These are often short but make up for it in fierceness and technical finesse. Ultra classic.

Go West

Famous Grouse

West Side Story

Westworld

Burbage West

Emma Flaherty on Blind Ali, 7B+ (problem 37). Photo: Niall Grimes.

Lots of historic testpieces such as Banana Finger, Remergence, Blind Date, West Side Story, as well as the hardest problem on Peak Grit, Ben Moon's Voyager Sit Start.

Burbage West is a small series of mini-buttresses, big on quality and classic lines. Conditions differ from Burbage North in that it gets only morning sun and is a great place to shelter from prevailing westerly winds.

// Climbing: Fingery and steep climbing on crimps, slopers and pebbles. Lots of burling around overlaps and small roofs. Technically interesting requiring good footwork and body positioning. Flat landings but they are sometimes a bit hard, rocky and unforgiving, so a couple of mats are useful. The First Walls have some micro-routes perfect for padded-out warm ups (but don't fall off) that will add loads to the experience. Burbage West good for vertical wall climbs.

// Conditions: Burbage North is fairly sheltered although it can still feel cold in a strong westerly wind. The problems are generally clean and quick drying although after wet periods there is often a lingering greenness. If it's not great drying weather you might be better off at Curbar. Burbage North faces south west and gets sun from late morning till sunset. Burbage West gets morning sun. A puddle sometimes forms under Remergence after wet periods so borrow a friend's bouldering mat. Climbable year round but midgy in summer. Burbage West is quick drying but a great place to find shelter from cold westerly winds. **Family friendly.**

// Approach: Roughly the same approach as Stanage (see page 314). The car park is on the left coming from Sheffield along the Ringinglow Rd. See maps for the approach from Hathersage. For Burbage West follow the track along the top of the crag and drop down. The Bridge area is directly below the parking and the three little buttresses all lie within 70m around the two bridges. The main Burbage North crag stretches off from below the parking. All the buttresses are visible from the main track. Little Slab is 20m right of Remergence. Velvet Crab is 25m right of the end of the trees near the right end of the crag and 20m below it. Nicotine Stain is near the left end of the walls behind Velvet Crab. The main track leads to the Burbage South boulders in about twenty five minutes.

// Info: Burbage, Millstone and Beyond (BMC); **Peak District Bouldering** (Vertebrate)

Stanage Apparent North

parking

Burbage Bridge

Famous Grouse

West Side Story

Go West

Westworld

Burbage Bridge

Burbage Bridge

Burbage Bridge

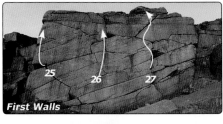

First Walls

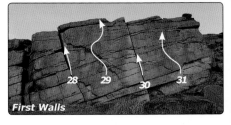

First Walls

1 **Slab** 6A	**8** **Rumblefish** 5	**15** **Westworld** 8A
2 **Breakfast** 7A *Sitter.*	**9** **Western Eyes** 7C	**16** **Not Westworld** 6B+
3 **West End Girls** 5+	**10** **Wall** 4	**17** **Arete** 6A+
4 **Famous Grouse** 7C	**11** **Wall** 5+	**18** **Wall** 4
5 **Crow Man** 5	**12** **Go West** 6A+	**19** **Rib** 6A+
6 **Groove** 3+	**13** **The Nose** 7A *Low start.*	**20** **Mermaid** 7A *Sitter.*
7 **West Side Story** 7B+	**14** **Blazing 48s** 8A	

Ringinglow Rd

First Walls

Banana Finger

◄ *parking*

Banana Finger

32 33 34

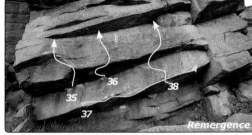

Remergence

35 36 37 38

Little Slab

39 40 41

The Terrace

42 43 44

The Sphinx

45 46 47 48 49

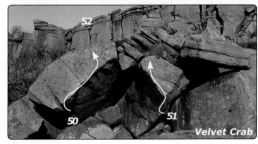

Velvet Crab

50 51 52

21	**Arete on Left**	5+
22	**Roof**	6B+

From low, no arete.

23	**Wobble Block**	6B
24	**Beached Whale Crack**	4+
25	**Route 1**	4
26	**Route 2**	3
27	**Route 3**	3
28	**Cranberry Crack**	3
29	**The Chant**	4+
30	**20 Foot Crack**	3+
31	**The Curse**	5
32	**Banana Arete**	6A
33	**Banana Finger Direct**	6C
34	**Banana Finger**	6A

35	**Hanging Rib**	6B
36	**Remergence**	6B
37	**Blind Ali**	7B+

Lip traverse, using holds on or below the lip.

38	**Blind Date**	7B+
39	**Slab**	4
40	**Slab**	4+
41	**Slab**	6A
42	**The Terrace**	7C *Sitter.*
43	**Jason's Roof**	6C+ *7C if*

started under the roof (reachy).

44 Rib 6C+ *7A+ from the low start to Jason's Roof.*

45 The Sphinx 7A+

46	**Voyager**	8B

Pinch the lip with left hand and swing on to start.

47 Voyager Sit Start 8B+

Probably more accurately a low start, not quite sitting. Start with the right hand on the fin, left on break above and left of it.

48	**Cleo's Edge**	5 +
49	**Cleo's Right-Hand**	5
50	**Velvet Crab**	7A+
51	**Zaff Skoczylas**	
	7B+	*Sitter.*
52	**Nicotine Stain**	6B

The thin seam in the wall.

Velvet Crab

◄ Little Slab

The Terrace   The Sphinx

Remergence

Burbage South

A beginner's bouldering paradise. A dozen friendly blobs of gritstone mooching around a broad field in a setting as fine as any in the land. Amongst many a gentle ruminant are a few with a bit of bite but still, for those operating in the lower grades it's a gentle pick 'n' mix of pleasure.

It's hard not to think about a blue checkered rug thrown out on the grass, some cream cheese and cherry tomatoes, chocolate milk and some spilled coleslaw. Perhaps a toddler crawling around playing with the sheep shit. Doing the odd problem as the sun shines down. People parading up and down the Green Drive, the ancient drovers' route that runs down the valley. Woof Woof, as Andy Benson would say.

// Climbing: The flanks of the boulders give generally rounded slabby or slightly overhanging climbs where your feet seldom get far above great grassy landings. The problems are still technical, often smeary, sometimes pebbly. For the harder climber the boulders will lack a bit of bite. Luckily on the crag section above there are a pack of problems with more bite than a Burnley Rottweiler. Sometimes highball, the landings here are often a bit challenging needing a few of pads.

// Conditions: The boulders are in sun all day. Clean and very quick drying. Sheltered. Midgy in summer. The crag is very shaded getting light only on summer evenings. It can be green in winter but is a great place to find shade in hot weather. **Great for families**.

// Approach: Follow the maps on page 314. There is a small layby for five cars 400m below the Fox House on the A6187. This is at the bottom of the Green Drive which leads to the boulders after 800m. Otherwise park on the verge above the Fox House (above a bus stop linking Sheffield, Hathersage and Bakewell). A rough footpath cuts across the fields from 200m above the pub and leads to the edge of the crag at a quarry after 500m. For a less rough approach walk downhill towards Hathersage to find the 5-car layby and follow the Green Drive.

// Info: Burbage, Millstone and Beyond (BMC); **Peak District Bouldering** (Vertebrate)

Me, Erin and Helen at the Pock Block.

328

Pock Block

The Sheep

The Brick

The Briquette

Useless Block

Useful Block

The Whale

The Tank

The Tank

The Armoured Car

The Armoured Car

Crag Sector

Crag Sector

1	**Mantel** 3+	**19**	**Traverse** 4	**36**	**Panzer** 6B+	**51**	**Clark's Route**
2	**Slab** 7A	**20**	**Arete** 5+	**37**	**Flake** 3+		6A *Highball arete.*
3	**Pick** 3	**21**	**Ridge** 2	**38**	**Tiger** 6A	**52**	**Sublime**
4	**Pock** 6A	**22**	**Pebble Wall** 4	**39**	4+ *Sitter.*		**Indifference** 6A
5	**Puck** 6B	**23**	**Arete** 4	**40**	**Jigsaw** 4+	**53**	**Home Cooking**
6	**The Sheep** 6C+	**24**	**Arete** 4+	**41**	**Wall** 6A+		7A *Steep highball arete.*
7	**Shearing** 5	**25**	**Crack** 2	**42**	**Wall** 6A	**54**	**Eating Out** 6C
8	**Slab Arete** 2	**26**	**Crack** 2+	**43**	**Traverse** 5		*Slab to right.*
9	**Sheep Slab** 1	**27**	**Scoop** 5	**44**	**Flakes Arete** 4	**55**	**Triangle Wall**
10	**Arete** 4	**28**	**Arete** 6A+	**45**	**Seam** 6A		6C
11	**Traverse** 4+	**29**	**Whale Ridge** 5	**46**	**Wall** 6A+	**56**	**The Alliance** 7A
12	**Vague Rib** 6A	**30**	**Whale Wall** 5	**47**	**Arete** 6A		*Twin arete.*
13	**Wall** 4	**31**	**Wall** 4+	**48**	**The Rib** 7B+	**57**	**Arete** 6A
14	**Brick Wall** 4+	**32**	**Chieftan** 5	**49**	**Layback** 6A		*Arete on right. Sitter 7A.*
15	**Brick Arete** 5+	**33**	**Jump** 6A	**50**	**Desparete** 7A+		
16	**Arete** 3	**34**	**Tank Slab** 1				
17	**Slab** 2	**35**	**Tank Edge** 1				
18	**Slab** 3						

Crag Sector

The Whale

The Tank

Useful Block

Useless Block

The Armoured Car

The Brick

The Briquette

The Sheep

Pock Block

Green Drive

Peak / Burbage South

A rattlebag of blocks, boulders and buttresses that string themselves together to give a proud wandering circuit with tons of variety on a clutch of venues. Bulging veins, shredded fingers and a great big smile on your face. A grand tour for a great day.

The circuit here only visits Millstone for a few problems and focuses mainly on a series of cool carbuncles on the moor above. However, for any climber, the central bay of Millstone, with its soaring and terrifying aretes and corners, is something that you really must see. The Taj Mahal of the Hope Valley.

// Climbing: The other tors will lead you gradually uphill and give some superb problems in a stunning location. The upper venues are very picnic-friendly. Secret Garden is quite a testpiece venue. Burly roof action on slopers and is very skin intense. Quite lowball, and loads of fun. Not so great for easy problems. Mother Cap is great for vertical climbs, sometimes highball, finger and conditions-dependant, with a summit tick. Below this Mother's Pet Rock is a very sloping sausage of gritstone, a cruel grinding beast best suited to masochists with a well-honed set of lats. Think topouts. The summit rocks of Over Owler Tor area gently contrast to the ravages below with a gaggle of easier and middling problems with a great view of the world. The Millstone problems are vertical or slabby and give very technical and fingery climbs.

// Conditions: Secret Garden is sheltered in the trees. Good for windy days but slow drying. Faces south-east and gets morning sun. The climbing on the moor above faces roughly south and gets lots of sun. Exposed, clean and quick drying. Millstone is sheltered and the problems face west and get sun from the afternoon. **Family friendly.**

1	Sitdown Groove	5+	
2	Bulge	6C+	*Sitter.*
3	Topless Crack	6A	
4	Chockstone Crack	5	
5	Beach Ball	7A	*Sitter.*
6	Secret Garden Traverse	6C+	
7	Flake	5+	
8	Bulge	6C	*Sitter.*
9	Left-Hand Man	7B+	*Sitter.*
10	Dick Williams	7B+	*Sitter.*
11	Oyster Cap	6A+	
12	David	7B	
13	Conan the Librarian	6B+	
14	Milk Cap	3	
15	Ink Cap	3+	
16	Blue Whale	6C	
17	Pet Cemetery	7A+	
18	Traverse	6C	*Finish up Ahab.*
19	Ahab	6B+	
20	Moby	6B	
21	Scrunchy Slopes	6B	
22	Li'l Arete	3	
23	Wafery Flake	6B	
24	Plop Start	2	*Highball finish is 4+.*
25	Flake Arete	3+	
26	Spider Crack	6C	
27	Jawbone	4	
28	Eye Socket	4+	*Sitter.*
29	Edge Lane	6B	*E5 solo.*
30	Green Death Start	6C	
31	Green Death Superdirect	7B	
32	Master's Edge	7A	*E7 lead.*
33	Master Chef	7B	*Spring off boulder.*
34	Technical Master Left-Hand	6C	
35	Technical Master	6B	

// Approach: See map on page 314. Park in Surprise View car park on the A6187. For Secret Garden, follow tracks along the road back towards Burbage. Near the end of the trees, and opposite a stile, cut directly into the trees on a tiny rough track. Follow this for 150m keeping your eye out for squat rocks on your left. Use the map for other venues. For Millstone find one of the descent paths from the moor top (tricky) or come all the way back to the car park and follow easier tracks to the crag.

// Info: Burbage, Millstone and Beyond (BMC); **Peak District Bouldering** (Vertebrate); **peakbouldering.info**

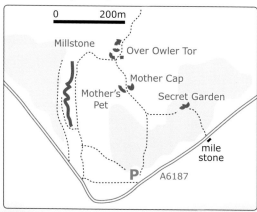

Peak / Millstone Area

Secret Garden

1　2　3　4　6　5　7　8　9　10

Mother Cap

11　12　13　14　15

Mother's Pet Rock

16　17　18　19　20

Over Owler Tor

21　22　23　24　25

Over Owler Tor

26　27　28

Millstone

29　30　31　32

Millstone

33　34　35

Over Owler Tor

Mother Cap

Secret Garden ▶

Peak / Millstone Area

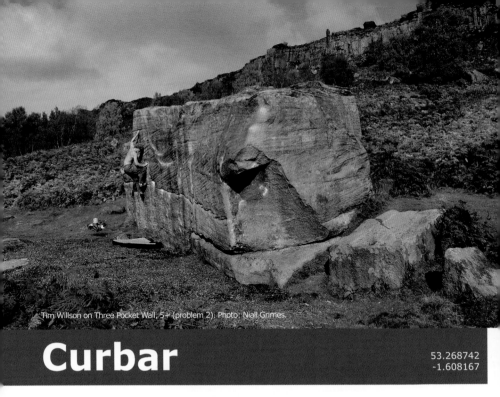

Tim Willson on Three Pocket Wall, 5+ (problem 2). Photo: Niall Grimes.

Curbar

53.268742
-1.608167

Half a dozen gritstone caravans give a popular and powerful roadside circuit. Quick drying and fairly sheltered and sandwiched between a royal crag and a heavenly view. Man alive!

Not tons here but all is good and it covers all grades apart from the very easiest. Good for sessioning something at your limit.

// Climbing: Gritstone boulders. Generally a little either side of vertical but always strenuous. Problems are short but pack it in. Landings are great and problems not high. Friendly.

// Approach: Park in Curbar Gap parking, walk downhill to Warren Lodge on the sharp bend and follow the path to Trackside. Other boulders are seen from here. For Ben's Wall contour from Bad Landing for 80m. Walk on By is in a quarried bay 40m right of the big wall above Gorilla Warfare.

// Conditions: Very reliable. Sunny, clean and quick drying. Fairly sheltered. Good year round. **Good for families.**

// Info: **Froggatt to Black Rocks** (BMC); **Peak District Bouldering** (Vertebrate); **peakbouldering.info**

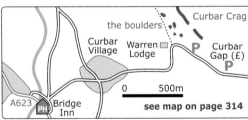

1	**Sidewall Slot** 5+
	Mantel the slot left of the arete.
2	**Three Pocket Wall** 5+
3	**Wall** 3+
4	**Strawberries** 6B+
5	**Crack** 3+
6	**Play Hard** 7C
7	**Work Hard** 8A+
	Eliminate on 6, avoiding sloper out left.
8	**6B+**
9	**Trackside** 7A
10	**Arete** 4+
11	**Slab** 5
12	**Diagonal** 3+
13	**Gorilla Warfare** 7A
14	**Hurricane** 7C *Dyno from slopers.*
15	**MP Traverse** 6C
	Start along the dark back wall.
16	**Mini Arete** 3
17	**Mini Crack** 4
18	**Mini Prow** 5
19	**BL Groove** 6B+
20	**La Musée Imaginaire** 7B
	Traverse from flatty on the lip and up 19.
21	**LMI Extension** 7C+
	Start 20 by liebacking off ramp feature.
22	**Bad Lip** 7A *Start hanging the flatty.*
23	**Ben's Wall** 7C
24	**Great White** 7C *Finish in pocket.*
25	**Walk on By** 7C+
	Climb the wall above the rock step.

Trackside

Crescent Slab

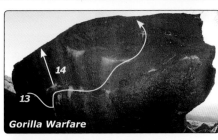

Gorilla Warfare

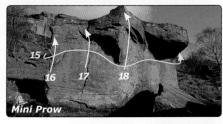

Mini Prow

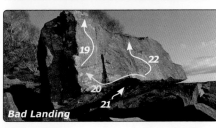

Bad Landing

Ben's Wall

Walk on By

10 min | 60 probs 3 - 8A+ best from 5 - 7B | vertical | steep | | shelter

Walk on By ▶

Gorilla Warfare ◀

Mini Prow ▼

Crescent Slab ▲

◀ Ben's Wall

Bad Landing ▲

Trackside

Peak / Curbar

Gardom's 53.262088 -1.584038

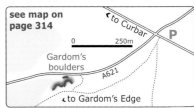

see map on
page 314

to Curbar

P

0   250m

Gardom's
boulders

A621

to Gardom's Edge

Brian Callan on Mark's Roof Original, 7A (problem 13). Photo: Niall Grimes.

1	**First Roof Left**	6A+
2	**First Roof Middle**	6C+
3	**Arete**	4
4	**Ledge Crack**	4
5	**Ledge Wall**	5
6	**West Wall**	5+
7	**Ben's Bulge**	7B
8	**The Grasper**	6C
9	**Soft on the G**	7B

The lip start is Full Power, 8A.

10   **8 Ball**   8A+

Sit start at the right end of the overhang and traverse into Soft on the G.

11	**Soft Groove**	6A+
12	**Mark's Roof Left-Hand**	6C+
13	**Mark's Roof Original**	7A

From the shelf at the back of the roof.

14   **Mark's Roof**   7B

Start as for the original and finish on slopers.

Here's a perfect little circuit for gorillas who don't like to walk very far. The scattering of boulders that loom over the fast road have a few easy problems, a load of graunchy roofs, a hard arete and a Ben Moon desperate. Good for shelter from the wind and the sun.

// Climbing: Natural gritstone outcrops. Mainly busting over roofs on sloping holds. Powerful compression moves on slopers and aretes. Better for harder stuff. Seldom very high and usually with good landings.

// Conditions: North facing and gets limited sun, mostly in the evening. The problems are quite sheltered from the wind. Good for hot days or cold, windy dry ones. Can be green after rain. Climbable year round. A nice place, good for a picnic but the road below Mark's Roof is noisy. Not busy. **Family friendly.**

// Approach: Park on the verge of the small road opposite where the road to Curbar leaves the A621. Go through a stile and follow the right-hand path to the outcrop 400m away. The path can be boggy, so if it's been wet, follow the road to below the boulders, cross a stile and scramble up the path.

// Info: Froggatt to Black Rocks (BMC); **Peak District Bouldering** (Vertebrate); **peakbouldering.info**

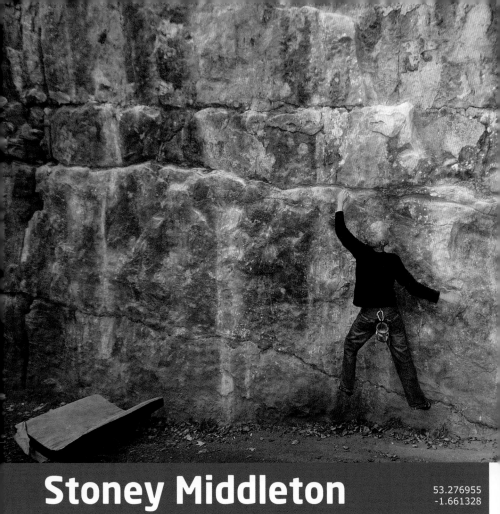

Stoney Middleton

53.276955
-1.661328

Out of vogue maybe, but quality still shines. A wall of vertical eliminates on very polished slopers and crimps and a dusty cave where everything centres around one glued hold. A must-visit venue for lovers of bouldering history. People from somewhere like Bristol will likely find it a bit of a hole.

And who says you can't polish a turd? A dusty and much maligned museum of British climbing circa 1982 and one of the early crucibles of Peak District bouldering. Stoney Middleton used to be the epicentre of Derbyshire climbing and had the country's hardest routes in 1980 at which time many 'full timers' lived at the crag. In the late 80s and 1990s, back in the days before climbing walls, dirty winter days would find the cream of the nation's climbing huddling close to the wall for shelter arguing over which footholds you were allowed on particular eliminates. When it rains Minus Ten stays dry

and while your T shirt, sandwiches and beer towel will get wet, at least the tips of your fingers will stay dry. It's not a pretty place bit it was much loved despite itself.

Trying to detail any of the problems here is beyond the scope of this guide as they rely on strict rules about where to put your hands and feet. You will need to be creative to get anything out of Stoney.

// Climbing: Quarried limestone crag. The main attraction, Minus Ten Wall, is a vertical wall of quarried limestone well peppered with finger-friendly features. Mostly crimps, flatties and slopers. Footholds are very poor so the climbing is very technical and unusually powerful given the angle. All problems are pick-the-hold-and-go style eliminates. The definition of polished. Tom's Roof (names after Tom Proctot – legend) is a grotto with a historic crimp that is used in various ways to produce more venerable eliminates. The classic

Sean Lynch traversing at Minus Ten. Photo: Niall Grimes.

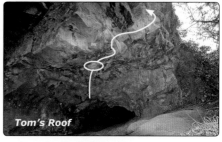

approach to Tom's Roof

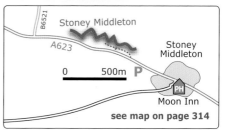

Tom's Roof

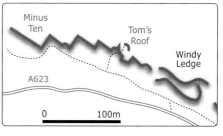

see map on page 314

original line goes from busty undercuts, out to match the polished crimp in the roof then on and out rightwards to finish at 7A. Minus Ten has a very flat landing, you'd get away with one pad although you would ill advised to fall off Tom's Roof with too much aplomb as you might take a quick ride down the cliff.

// Conditions: Minus Ten doesn't seep and stays dry in the rain. It can suffer from condensation. Some afternoon sun but generally quite shady thanks to trees. Very sheltered. Good in winter. Tom's Roof seeps after wet periods and is unreliable in winter. Not somewhere to go on the family holiday as the busy road is not far away and there is sometimes a bit of broken glass lying around.

// Approach: Park in the big lay-by just after the village of Stoney. Walk along the road then follow trails at the base of the crag to find Minus Ten. For Tom's, walk back right to the second big bay. Just past the right edge of this scramble up a gully for 25m to the cave.

// Info: Peak District Bouldering (Vertebrate)

A typical minging day at Rubicon. Dan McManus on A Bigger Tail, 7A+ (problem 4). Photo: Niall Grimes.

Rubicon

53.251016
-1.741333

Crap, like all peak limestone. However, once you accept that, Rubicon gives some of the best hard fingery test of crank-craft in town and a longtime venue of choice for strong people who want to get stronger. If you get up something here you'll think it's great. If you walk away with your trousers around your ankles you may well feel the need to slag it off. I know I do. Historical, and a beautiful place.

Rubicon is a glorified outdoor cellarboard. It specializes in tiny crimps, slimy breaks, loose rattly jugs and glassy footholds. Basically, if you're one of those people who can't handle hard climbing and deal with this by criticising the place rather than being honest about your limitations, then you will find much here to be vocal about.

It's a lovely place, beside a swan-riddled lake, with duck-style birds too. An old mill and weir, the gentle River Wye, families out a-walking, and in summer afternoons the reflection of the sun dances silver on the shaded overhang of Rubicon Roof. Just beautiful. However, you'll most likely find yourself here on a horrible wet day. Very popular with walkers, families and fishermen. Please be courteous to all.

// Climbing: Natural limestone crag. Rubicon Roof area, on the right, is good for warm ups and traversing. Many of the holds are second-joint flatties and the big traverse on the left is good for getting the blood going. The steeper bulge to the right has some harder traverses and steep eliminates (5 to 6C). The main interest is Kudos Wall, 40m to the left, a bulging wall of hardcore session problems. Holds are small and far apart. Extremely powerful. This has a dozen problems in the 7A to 8A+ range and will feel very hard if this isn't your thing. Some problems finish at 4-5m so you'll need a mat for these.

// Conditions: Very rainproof and sheltered and a good venue on a wet day. Can take some seepage in winter or in wet weather. Best in the drier months although climbing is possible year round. Can be a bit savage on a hot sunny day when the glassy crimps won't be at their best. Morning shade. **Family friendly.**

// Approach: See map on page 314. On the A623 turn off by the Three Stags Head (legendary boozer) and follow the B6465 through Wardlow towards Monsal Head. Take the first right and wind down a vale to the bottom. Turn right and park on the verge on the right after 600m, just before a fork. Follow the path right of the mill for 150m, go right over a wee bridge and there it is.

// Info: **Peak District Bouldering** (Vertebrate); **peakbouldering.info**

Kudos Wall

Rubicon Roof

1   **Dragonflight Traverse**   6B   *A long traverse
of the slabby left end of the crag.*
2   **A Miller's Tale**   6B   *Sitter 6B+.*
3   **Kudos**   7B   *Sitter 7B+.*
4   **A Bigger Tail**   7A+   *Jump to crimps to start.*
5   **A Bigger Belly**   8A+   *Sit start to ABT.*
6   **Bigger Splash Direct**   7B   *Start with right
hand on a sidepull and left hand on an undercut, slap
upwards to a jug.*
7   **Tsunami**   8A   *A sitting start to BSD. Start
sitting, with hands in thin slots. Eliminate; for 8A you
have to match the sloper. The non-eliminate way is
7C+ (Tsunamish).*
8   **The Press**   7B+   *Start with left hand as
a gaston on the BSD sidepull and right hand on poor
nubbins, then lock to small crimp and pop to jug on
BSD. 7C+ from kneeling, 8A from pockets down and
right, 8A+ from Tsunami start (aka Low Left).*
9   **A Bigger Splash**   7A+
10   **Warm-Up Traverse**   5   *Long juggy traverse
from the far left end of the bay.*
11   **Bulge**   6A
12   **Toenail Pie**   5
13   **Debris Groove**   6A
14   6B+

15   6B
16   6A+
17   **High Traverse**   5+
18   **Middle Traverse**   6A+
19   **Low Traverse**   6B+

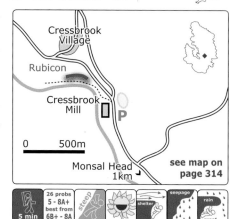

see map on
page 314

Peak / Rubicon

Phil Rose on The Press Kneeling Start, 7C+, at Rubicon (page 341, problem 8). Photo: Nic Mullin.

Tim Marsh on Pump Up The Power, 7C+, at Raven Tor (page 345, problem 16). Photo: John Coefield.

Stefan Weedkiller Traverse, 7b (problem 7). Photo: Niall Grimes

Raven Tor

53.255612
-1.775537

The epicentre of Peak District power where the ar-ea's strongest fingers have spent 30 years work-ing out fiendish problems. Best suited to weasels operating in the higher levels. Lots of famous test-piece to fail on. Rainproof and very intense. The moves are fantastic, hard and unforgiving and if you are on anything but top form then you will struggle. An essential limestone venue.

Big thanks to Rae Cowie for help on this section.

// Climbing: Limestone crag. Climbing varies from very steep to pure roof. Lots of famous named problems added by the likes of Moon, Pollitt and Moffatt in the 1980s. Always fingery. Crimps, undercuts and pockets. Sometimes a bit highball and the landings are bumpy and very hard so you'll need a few mats. Good for traverses, eliminates and link-ups. Good for training.

// Conditions: The climbing is quite conditions dependent. The holds are polished and glassy and problems will feel harder on hot or humid days. Seepage is a big problem in wet periods. Not really a winter crag. Rainproof. Sun from early afternoon but in summer evenings trees offer a lot of shade. Very sheltered. The location is beautiful but the crag is right beside a (quiet) road.

// Approach: See Main Area map on page 314. Turn off the B6049 at the Anglers Rest pub (1km west of the Youth Hostel) and follow the dead-end road to park in bays below the crag after 1km. **Make sure you don't obstruct the road.**

// Info: **Peak District Bouldering** (Vertebrate); **peakboulder-ing.info**

1   **Too Hard for Mark Leach** 6C
2   **Ben's Roof** 7C+   *Sitter. From sidepulls at the back right of the cave swing across to the left side and follow holds out to finish up 1.*
3   **Keen Roof** 8B
4   **Weedkiller Direct** 7B+   *Start from a slot. Better from a lower sitter at 7C.*
5   **Fat Lip** 8B *Link the stand-up version of problem 4 into problem 3.*
6   **Basher's Problem** 7A
     Start from undercuts at back of the roof.
7   **Weedkiller Traverse** 7B
8   **Little Extra** 7A   *From the break move up left to flat crimp then right to bigger flatty. Carry on to higher jugs at 7A+.*
9   **Undercut Problem** 7B+
     From the break, move into the undercuts then to the flatty on Little Extra via either the diagonal crimp (7B+) or sloper (7C).
10 **Ear Problem** 7C   *Move up to high crozzly ear then left to the Little Extra flatty.*
11 **Toilet Traverse** 6B+
12 **Hooligan Start** 8A+
     Pull on using left hand undercut and slap up right for crimps then flakes.
13 **Boot Boys Start** 6C
14 **Ben's Traverse** 8A *Link into 11.*
15 **Out of my Tree Start** 7B   *To jug.*
16 **Pump up the Power** 7C+
     Groove, to good flat hold out left at 5m.
17 **Rattle and Hump Start** 7A+
     To jug at 3m.

Peak / Raven Tor

Weedkiller Area

Little Extra

Powerband

18 Powerband 7C *Start on good slots on a low, right-pointing flake. and traverse left on pockets, crimps and pinches. The rules are: stay high on pinches in the middle and drop down onto the pillar using the 2 finger pocket.*

19 Power Humps 7B+ *Start as for Powerband and finish up Rattle and Hump.*

20 Staminaband 8A *Traverse into Powerband starting on a left-facing flake. Link into Pump up the Power at 8B+. F9a route grade.*

Zaff Ali on Nobody Knows, 5 (problem 18). Photo: Niall Grimes.

Robin Hood's Stride

53.158815
-1.669149

The Fontainebleau of the Peak. A magical playground of variety, quality and styles that will deliver the goods to the hardcore, the softcore and those who hardly boulder at all. Good for the soul: a treat.

The setting is rolling pastoral farmland, a bucolic paradise, and a nice change from the high moorland areas further north. It easily has enough problems for an entire day and, especially when combined with the adjacent Cratcliffe Boulders, is one of the best days out for a boulderer in the Peak District. The climbing often has a gentle, frolicking style but always demands enough huff and puff that brutes will also come away well satisfied. Hippies and hangers-on will feed off the ancient power of the place and also go home replete.

// Climbing: Natural gritstone boulders and outcrop. All sorts of variety with slabs, walls, bulges, aretes and cracks. Often technical and can be quite burly. Lots of gentle stuff too. Well weathered rock gives lots of rounded holds and features. Great strong lines. Sometimes a little high but always friendly, a mat or two is enough. Great for all grades as well as total beginners and families.

// Conditions: The problems are based around all sides of a small tor so something is always in the sun and something always sheltered from the wind. It is also at a relatively low altitude and is fairly quick drying. As such it is a good bet on days when the weather is not perfect. Good year round. The rock is a bit soft so please don't climb on any eroded rock if it is damp and generally tread very gently here. You wouldn't want to piss the spooks off. **Family friendly.**

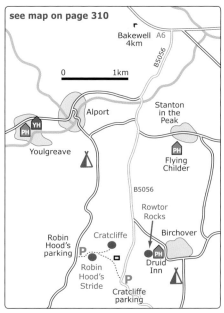

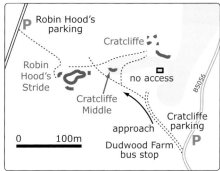

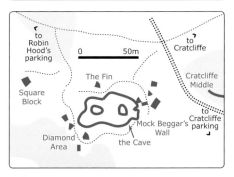

// **Approach: From Bakewell:** Follow the A6 south. After 2.6 miles turn right on the B5056 (signposted Youlgreave). Follow this taking first left, first right, then left leading to parking on the verge (park sensibly) from where the Stride can be seen. Follow the footpath to it. Alternative park as for Cratcliffe. There is a bus stop by the Cratcliffe parking (Dudwood Farm stop). **From Matlock:** Follow the A6 north for 2 miles then turn left on the B5057 (towards Winster). Follow for 4 miles to meet the B5056. Turn right towards Bakewell and park on the verge on the right after 0.6 miles (Cratcliffe parking).

// **Info: Froggatt to Black Rocks** (BMC); **Peak District Bouldering** (Vertebrate); **peakbouldering.info**

Rowtor Rocks

There's a load more smaller outcrops in the area the best of these being Rowtor Rocks, located directly behind the Druid Inn in Birchover. This has 50 problems from 4 to 7C+ (best 6A-7B) in a mad and magical setting. Tree covered so a bit slow to dry but a great venue on an extremely windy day.

The Cave

Mock Beggar's Wall

Sweet Thing

Green Block

Boomer

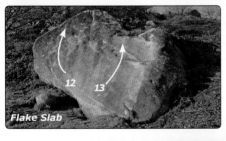

Flake Slab

The Arch

1	**Haddon Haul** 5+	
2	**Cave Problem** 7A	
	Sitter, starting on undercuts.	
3	**Hugo First** 6A *Sitter.*	
4	**The Kid** 7A *Sitter.*	
5	**Grizzly Arete**	
	7A+ *Highball.*	

6	**Dry Wit in a Wet Country** 7A+ *Highball.*	
7	**Sweet Thing** 8A+ *Sitter.*	

8	**Sweet Arete** 6A	
	Sitter 6A+.	
9	**Short Arete** 6A	
10	**Short Wall** 7A+	
11	**Boomerang-erang** 6A	
12	**Flake Slab** 6A	
13	**Slab** 3	

Boomer

Sweet
Thing

Green
Block

The Fin

The
Cave

Mock
Beggar's
Wall

Flake Slab

The Arch

Big Al

18
17
19
20

The Fin

21
22
23
24
25

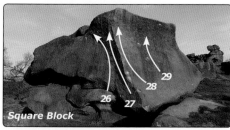

Square Block

26
27
28
29

Square Block

29
30
31
32

Diamond Area

33
34
35
36
37
38
39
40

14	**The Arch** 4+	26	**Ben's Wall** 7C	35	**Diamond Left** 6A
15	**T Slab** 4		*Avoid the arete.*	36	**Diamond Right** 6B
16	**T Slab Arete** 4+	27	**Spine Left** 6B	37	**Front On** 5+
17	**Big Al Qaeda** 7B	28	**The Spine** 5+	38	**Jerry's Arete** 7A
18	**Nobody Knows** 5	29	**Spinal Slab** 7A	39	**Boss Hogg** 5 *Swing onto*
19	**Muscle Slab** 5	30	**Angle Arete** 5		*slab using the flake then up.*
20	**Crack** 4+	31	**Slab** 4+	40	**Mantel** 6C
21	**JT** 3	32	**Corner** 1		
22	**JT Crack** 2	33	**Jams O'Mantel** 6B		
23	**Flipper Arete** 6A+	34	**Crimpy Slab** 6A+		
24	**Flipper** 6C				
25	**Vandals** 5				

The chipped wall to the right.

The Fin

Square Block

Big Al

Diamond Area

Ann Leese on Pink Arete, 4 (problem 9). Photo: Niall Grimes.

Cratcliffe

53.153835
-1.659257

Robin Hood's gentle brother gives more great quality and is the natural continuation of the circuit. Lots of gentle padding, some harder classics in a picnic-perfect setting. Great for families and beginners.

// Climbing: Lots of slabs and little bulges. Great for easy stuff. Quite rounded. T Crack and Jerry's Traverse are essential Peak ticks. Generally perfect landings.

// Approach: Follow the maps here and on page 347. T Crack, Jerry's Traverse and The Egg are all in the trees within 35m of the Top Boulders.

// Conditions: Top Boulders are sunny, sheltered and quick drying. The rest are very tree sheltered. Please avoid any damp problems as the soft rock erodes easily.

// Info: Froggatt to Black Rocks (BMC); **Peak District Bouldering** (Vertebrate)

1	**Arete** 4+	16	**Arete** 6A
2	**Slab** 4	17	**Blind Pocket**
3	**Last Arete** 6B+		**Wall** 4+
	Sitter.	18	**Arete** 5
4	**Lip Traverse** 6C	19	**T Crack** 7B
5	**Johnny's**	20	**Jerry's Traverse**
	Groove 6C		7B
6	**Slab** 4	21	**The Lark** 6C+
7	**Slab** 3+	22	**Left Egg** 5+
8	**Pink Slab** 3	23	**Eggy Scoops** 5
9	**Pink Arete** 4	24	**Egg Arete** 6A+
10	**Slab** 4+	25	**Egged On** 6A
11	**Arete** 4	26	**Slab** 4
12	**Scoop** 3	27	**Arete** 5+
13	**Arete** 6A	28	**Razor Arete** 7A
14	**Rib** 6A	29	**Razor Roof** 6C+
15	**Slab** 1	30	**Cave Wall** 5+

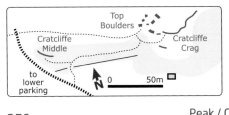

Top Boulders

Cratcliffe Middle

Cratcliffe Crag

to lower parking

N

0 — 50m

Top Boulders – Last Arete

1 2 3 4 5 6

Top Boulders – Pink Slab

7 8 9 10

Top Boulders

11 12

Top Boulders

13 14 15

Top Boulders

16 17 18

T Crack

19

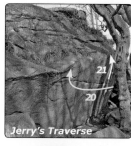

Jerry's Traverse

20 21

The Egg

22 23 24 25

70 probs
1 - 7B
best from
3 - 7B

10 min

steep · slabby · shelter

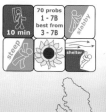

Cratcliffe Middle

26 27

Cratcliffe Middle

28 29 30

Last Arete · **Pink Slab** · **17** · **Jerry's Traverse**

11 · **13** · **Top Boulders** · **T Crack** · **The Egg**

Peak / Cratcliffe

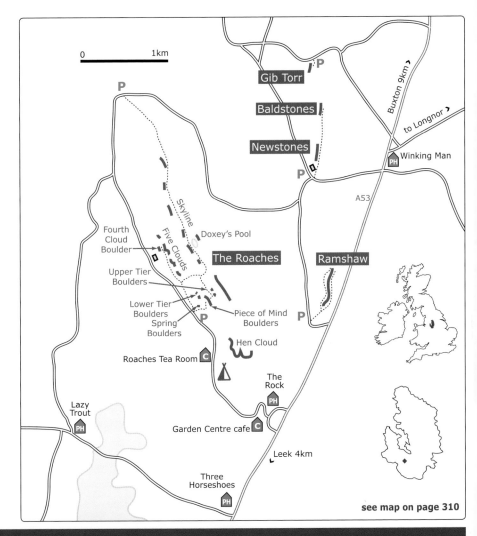

0 — 1km

P

Gib Torr

P — Buxton 9km

Baldstones

to Longnor

Newstones

P

PH — Winking Man

A53

Skyline

Five Clouds

Doxey's Pool

Fourth
Cloud
Boulder

The Roaches

Ramshaw

Upper Tier
Boulders

Lower Tier
Boulders

Piece of Mind
Boulders

P

P

Spring
Boulders

Hen Cloud

Roaches Tea Room — C

The
Rock

PH

Lazy
Trout

PH

Garden Centre cafe — C

Leek 4km

Three
Horseshoes

PH

see map on page 310

The Roaches Area

These are the fabulous crags of the Peak's Western Edges, a collection of cliffs that easily rival their more famous Eastern counterparts. The most celebrated of all are the Roaches, varied and beautiful, with a lifetime's bouldering on display. There is all styles here, quick drying crags with plenty of sun. The beautifully ugly carbuncle that is Ramshaw Rocks sits nearby, but with a different character. Steep and dark, it gets morning sun, making it a good choice for cool mornings or hot days. The rough diamonds that are the Baldstones and Newstones make for a great circuit, with loads of problems across the grades on numerous craglets. Perhaps the most fun of the three circuits described here.

The Rock is the most obvious choice of pub while the Lazy Trout finds favour with locals. The Traveller's Rest, 5km to its north, toward Buxton, is also a popular choice. In the fleshpot that is Leek, try The Wilkes' Head for an authentic local. The Roaches Tea Room does great food (01538 300345), and also has two beautiful cottages for rent. A garden centre at Upper Hulme also has a cafe.

Justin Critchlow on Fielder's Corner, 6B, Baldstones (problem 28, page 361). Photo: Niall Grimes.

David Hudson on Flake and Chips, 5 (problem 51). Photo: Mike Hutton.

The Roaches

53.156164
-1.995478

The pride of the western Peak and many people's favourite gritstone crag. A glorious west-facing bastion proudly overseeing the plains of Cheshire. The mighty crag has cast forth many perfectly-sized blocks of the best quality stone that hold brilliant problems across all grades. Lots of mini venues, each with its own fine character. It's enough to make you want to move to Leek.

// **Climbing:** Problems on gritstone boulders and crag. Great variety offering lots of forceful walls and overhangs and many technical, often slabby, walls. The rock is superb. Lots of slopers, aretes, pebbles, crimps and cracks. Not very highball and generally very friendly although the landings on the Upper Tier are hard. Probably best for easier and mid-grade stuff: super-desperate stuff is a bit thin on the ground.

// **Conditions:** Problems are mainly sunny and very quick drying. The Lower Tier Boulders are more sheltered and slower drying. Problems come into the sun from late morning and get sun from then on. Breezy. Can be exposed on cold windy days. Good year round. **Family friendly.**

// **Approach:** See map on page 352. Turn off the A53 towards Upper Hulme, 3 miles from Leek and 9 miles from Buxton. Follow the twisting road as it passes under Hen Cloud then park in laybys below the crag after 1.5 miles. Observe any parking restrictions as there are frequent ticketing sessions. Go through the main gate and follow the track towards the crag. Individual approaches given in appropriate sections.

// **Info**: The Roaches (BMC); **Peak District Bouldering** (Vertebrate); **Western Grit** (Rockfax)

to bulging 8A+. The bulging Inertia Reel Wall on the crag holds most of the hard problems at the Roaches while the boulders below are great for easy slabs and a couple of mid-grade classics. The problems are very sheltered from the wind and sun among larch trees and can be a bit slow to dry. Inertia Reel Wall can seep.

Piece of Mind Boulders (not detailed here): A scattering of smaller rounded boulders with 30 problems mostly from 3 to 6A. Not so popular but fun in a scrambly sort of way. They are at the right terminus of the Lower Tier (see photo).

The Clouds – Fourth Cloud: The Clouds are a set of little outcrops made of the most perfect grit. Each has a couple of classics but only the Fourth Cloud Boulder is detailed here. Treat yourself to an explore. **Approach:** Go through the first gate by the parking and follow a track leftwards for 400m. As it turns rightwards follow a smaller direct path that runs under the outcrops. The Third Cloud (just visible in the photo below) is the biggest. 40m left is the Fourth Cloud and the boulder sits below the left edge of this.

Upper Tier Boulders: More classics in one of the freshest settings on grit, although it can all feel a bit worn. 45 problems, mostly up to 7A, with the odd harder one. Steeper and more pully than the Lower Tier Boulders. Very exposed and quick drying. The crag behind has lots more problems. **Access:** Follow the ancient steps that cut through the Lower Tier.

Skyline – Doxey's Pool: The continuation of the Upper Tier, the Skyline, stretches off for a mile and has little eruptions of bouldering all along its length. Most classic is Doxey's Pool. 25 problems, mostly 3 – 6C with a couple harder. They truly feel on top of the world. **Access:** From the Upper Tier Boulders skirt left under the crag for 100m until a path leads to the top of the crag. Turn left and walk along the edge for 350m and the boulders are on the right, behind a muddy pool.

Spring Boulders: The first boulders on the left of the path. 40 problems from very easy up to 7A. Short, and great for slabs. However a very boggy landing means that these boulders are hard work: a small selection of the drier more accessible problems are given here.

Lower Tier Boulders: Classic. Bouldering on the crag and half a dozen boulders below. 45 problems from very easy slabs

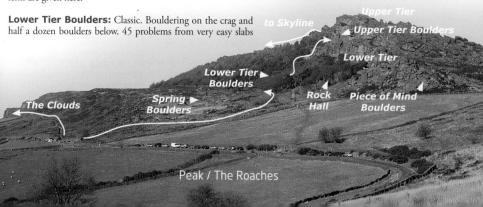

to Skyline · Upper Tier · Upper Tier Boulders · Lower Tier · Lower Tier Boulders · Spring Boulders · Rock Hall · Piece of Mind Boulders · The Clouds

Spring Boulders

Lower Tier - Crag

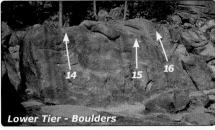

Lower Tier - Boulders

Lower Tier - Boulders

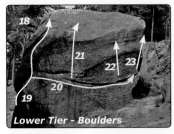

Lower Tier - Boulders

Lower Tier - Boulders

Lower Tier - Boulders

Fourth Cloud

1	**Arete on Right** 6B	
2	**Pebbly Wall** 6A	
3	**Bog Monster** 6A *Scoops.*	
4	**Bog Standard** 5 *Flake.*	
5	**Poxy** 3	
	Scooped slab on back of boulder.	
6	**Spring Slab** 7A+	
7	**C3PO** 7A	
8	**Boba Fett** 7B+	
9	**Spring Roll** 4	
10	**Inertia Reel Trav** 8A+	
11	**Ant Lives** 7A	
	Doesn't top out.	
12	**Inertia Reel** 7A+	
	Top out is harder. Sitter 7C+.	
13	**Teck Crack Direct** 6C+	
14	**Slab** 2	
15	**Blister Slab** 5	
16	**Slab** 3	
17	**Arete** 5	
18	**Three Pocket Slab** 6A	
19	**Arete** 4	
20	**Undercut Traverse** 6B+	
21	**Stretch and Mantel** 6C	
22	**Undercut Dyno** 7A	
23	**Arete** 4	
24	**Greener Traverse** 6B	
25	**Green Greenie** 5+	
	Sitter 6B+.	
26	**Pine Slab** 4	
27	**Pine Crack** 2	
28	**Chips** 3	
29	**The Arch** 4	
30	**Hard Arete** 7A+	
31	**Tetris** 7C *Sitter, into 30.*	
32	**Hanging Slab** 7A	
33	**Left Arete** 4+	
34	**The Ripple** 6B	
35	**The Boss** 6C	

36	**Wall** 4	**45**	**Staircase** 4+ *Sitter.*	**55**	**The Nose** 6C *Low start.*
37	**Arete** 4+	**46**	**Cooper's Traverse** 6B	**56**	**Staffs Flyer** 6B
38	**Mantel** 3	**47**	**Mantel** 5+	**57**	**Groovy Crack** 4
39	**Big Holes** 3+	**48**	**Mantel** 6B+ *Sitter.*	**58**	**Chipped Wall** 3
40	**Joe's Arete** 6A	**49**	**Winger** 5+	**59**	**Arete** 5+
41	**Joe's Portholes** 3+	**50**	**Wing Wong** 5+	**60**	**Wall** 6C+
42	**Nadin's Traverse** 7A+	**51**	**Flake and Chips** 5	**61**	**Arch** 6A

36 **Wall** 4
37 **Arete** 4+
38 **Mantel** 3
39 **Big Holes** 3+
40 **Joe's Arete** 6A
41 **Joe's Portholes** 3+
42 **Nadin's Traverse** 7A+
   Traverse right from low jugs to finish up 44.
43 **Reg** 6C+ *Slap the top from the long angled sloper.*
44 **Pixie** 5+ *Flake.*

45 **Staircase** 4+ *Sitter.*
46 **Cooper's Traverse** 6B
47 **Mantel** 5+
48 **Mantel** 6B+ *Sitter.*
49 **Winger** 5+
50 **Wing Wong** 5+
51 **Flake and Chips** 5
52 **Left Groove** 6B
53 **Higginson's Arm** 7B
   Sitter, with right hand on undercut below the roof.
54 **Right Groove** 6A

55 **The Nose** 6C *Low start.*
56 **Staffs Flyer** 6B
57 **Groovy Crack** 4
58 **Chipped Wall** 3
59 **Arete** 5+
60 **Wall** 6C+
61 **Arch** 6A
62 **Flake** 6A+
63 **Arete** 3
64 **Arete** 2

Mark Sharratt and Andi Turner spotting Neil Pearsons on The Lurch, 6B+ (problem 6). Photo: Niall Grimes.

Ramshaw

53.155109
-1.975307

The jutting dinosaur's spine overlooking the busy A53 is home to a burly bunch of great problems. Just as you drive under it and see endless thrusting gritstone uppercuts, your poor biceps and forearms are already starting to salivate. And rightly so. The numerous nibs, nebs and knobs give many intensely physical challenges that will thrash you and rash you. Bring it on.

// Climbing: Natural gritstone edge and boulders. Very strenuous, mainly on rounded, bulging rock. The rock is very rough gritstone and slopers abound. Mostly standard height, with a few brilliant highballs.

// Conditions: The crag faces east, getting morning sun. Exposed, but the crag areas offer good shelter. Quick drying. Crag-top boulders get lots of sun. The Lower Tier and The Press areas can stay dry in some rain. Good year round. **Family friendly.**

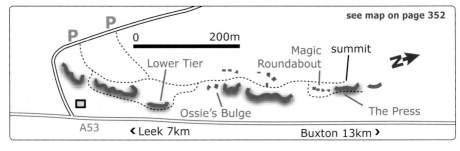

see map on page 352

P   P

0   200m

Lower Tier

Magic Roundabout   summit

Ossie's Bulge

The Press

A53   ‹ Leek 7km   Buxton 13km ›

Lower Tier

Ossie's Bulge

Magic Roundabout

The Press

1   **Roll Off**   6A   *Mantel.*
2   **Collywood**   6C+
     Sitter, starting with hands in the crack.
3   **Tierdrop**   7A   *Highball. Tops out.*
4   **Tier's End**   6A   *Groove.*
5   **The Scoop**   4+
6   **The Lurch**   6B+
     Slap left to slopers and go up or spring direct to slopers.
7   **Ossie's Bulge**   6A+   *Stand on the low flake and finish leftwards or rightwards.*
8   **Ram Air**   7B+
9   **Jamless**   5
10   **Epilogue**   7A
11   **The Rammer**   4
12   **The Pinches**   6B
13   **Dialogue**   7B+
14   **Cracked Arete**   5+
15   **Bulge**   5+   *Jump off or solo.*
16   **Press Direct**   6B   *Sitter 6C+.*
17   **Night of Lust Start**   6C+
     Sitter 7A.
18   **Foord's Folly**   6B+   *E2 crack with low crux. Jump off or solo to top.*

// Info: The Roaches (BMC); **Peak District Bouldering** (Vertebrate); **peakbouldering.info**

// Approach: The crag overlooks the A53. Turn off the A53 at the Leek end of the crag, by a gritstone farmhouse. Drive up the steep road and park on the verge after 200m. The X18 bus runs under the crag. Locations: The Lower Tier, obvious from the road, is below the crag after a couple of hundred metres. Ossie's Bulge area is about 100m past this, back on top of the crag, and very close to the main cliff-top path. Magic Roundabout Boulders are a few hundred metres further uphill along the cliff-top path, on the right, and not obvious from the path.

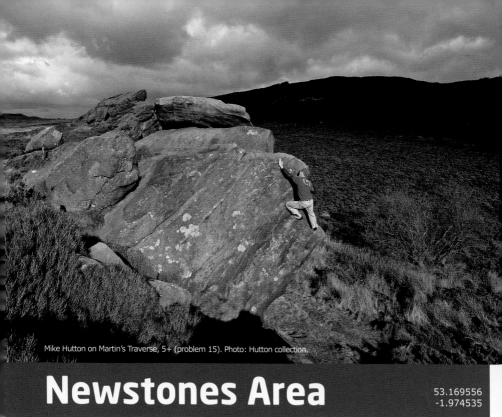
Mike Hutton on Martin's Traverse, 5+ (problem 15). Photo: Hutton collection.

Newstones Area

53.169556
-1.974535

A rocky ridgeback beloved of boulderers and picnickers alike. Lots of little rocky warts and bigger carbuncles yield gritstone fruit across the lower and middle grades but with plenty of burly action to satisfy anyone. Wild, despite a roadside setting.

// Climbing: Natural gritstone outcrops. Lots of variety. Lots of slopers, aretes, bulges and traverses. Some highballs above good landings but mostly very friendly.
// Approach: Turn off the A53 just south of the Winking Man pub and follow the road for 400m to a fork. Park in lay-bys here. Follow the path right of the house and after 100m the rocks appear on the left. This

is Newstones. Buttresses are obvious, in a straight line. For Baldstones go through the gate at the end of the crag and follow it across the moor for 300m to see the distinctive tower. The bouldering is on the next buttress.
// Conditions: Exposed. Gets morning sun and lots of shade. Can be cold on windy days. Some slow drying areas. The rock is a little delicate so please don't climb on any rock that's at all damp. Good year round. **Great for families.**
// Info: The Roaches (BMC); **Peak District Bouldering** (Vertebrate); **Western Grit** (Rockfax)

Gib Torr

A little more of the same. Conditions and rock are pretty much the same as the crags above. Please don't approach from Baldstones,: instead go round to park 100m from the crag.

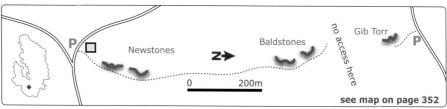

Peak / Newstones Area

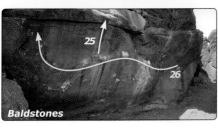

1	**Little Traverse** 6A	**11**	**Slab** 1	**23**	**Sly Superdirect** 5+
2	**S&M** 7A	**12**	**Arete** 3		*Highball.*
	Finish direct, or left at 6C.	**13**	**Arete** 3+	**24**	**Sly Direct** 6A *Highball.*
3	**Charlie's Overhang** 6B	**14**	**Ripple** 6B	**25**	**Baldstones Dyno** 6B+
	Highball.	**15**	**Martin's Traverse** 5+	**26**	**Baldstones Traverse** 7A+
4	**Arete on Left** 5+ *Sitter.*	**16**	**Hazel Traverse** 6A+	**27**	**Ganderhole Crack** 4+
5	**Bulge** 6A *Sitter.*	**17**	**Hazel Barn** 3+ *Highball.*	**28**	**Fielder's Corner** 6B
6	**Varicose** 6A+ *Sitter.*	**18**	**Hazel Groove** 6B	**29**	**Fielder's Wall** 7B
7	**Grinding Sloper** 6A *Sitter.*	**19**	**Nutmeg** 4	**30**	**Elephant's Eye** 6B+
8	**Slab** 3	**20**	**Nutmeg Groove** 5+	**31**	**Elephant's Ear** 4 *Flake.*
9	**Crack** 2	**21**	**Stallone Arete** 6C+	**32**	**Clever Skin** 7A+
10	**Traverse** 6B+ *Finish up 4.*	**22**	**Sly Stallone** 6B+ *Dyno.*		*Arete on right.*

Ian Johnson on Percy Traverse, 6B (problem 15). Photo: Niall Grimes.

Hobson Moor

53.466144
-2.018562

A popular spot for Mancunians, urban and well used, giving a bunch of fingery problems on polished walls. A dozen short trifles and a mega-pump workout traverse. Broken glass, bored youths and frantic after-workers give the ambience. You won't have an amazing time here, but you'll have a time, and it's better than being trapped in traffic at the Mottram Moor crossroads.

The crag is popular, especially on summer evenings where its quick approach and very reliable conditions mean you're guaranteed to get something out of an hour or two. Lots to warm up on, a solo or two if you're in the mood, and an arm-withering twenty-metres traverse that will get you fit for the main cliff at Gogarth.

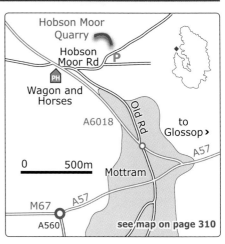

Back Wall

Sunshine Corner

Percy Area

// Climbing: Gritstone quarry. A dozen problems on the right edge of the quarry are mainly vertical and fingery on very polished rock. The main traverse on the back wall is a long drawn-out affair on flatties, pockets and cracks. Anything as hateful as that traverse has got to be doing you a lot of good. The ground is always flat but also a bit hard so a mat would be useful.

// Conditions: Mainly south-west facing. The right walls get sun from early afternoon and the back wall goes into shadow in the late afternoon. Generally very dry and not much seepage. Very sheltered. Climbable year round. Has a very urban feel.

1	**Back Wall Traverse** 6C	**9**	**Wall** 4+
2	**Crack** 4	**10**	**Slab** 5+ *Avoid the*
3	**Wall** 5		*corner on the left.*
4	**Sunshine Traverse** 6B	**11**	**Rib and Wall** 6B
5	**Parker's Traverse** 5	**12**	**Crack** 2
6	**Grain of Sand** 5	**13**	**Slab** 4
7	**Percy 97** 6B	**14**	**Arete** 3+
8	**Amphitheatre** 2	**15**	**Percy Traverse** 6B

// Approach: From Mottram crossroads follow the A6018 towards Stalybridge for 1km then take a sharp right turn opposite the Wagon and Horses pub. Fork left after 60m. After 120m take another left fork and park immediately on the verge on the right. The quarry is opposite.

// Info: Peak District Bouldering (Vertebrate)

Back Wall   **Sunshine Corner**   **Percy Area**

Wimberry

53.527784
-1.981101

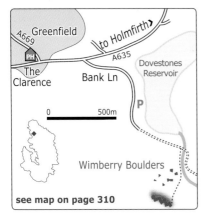

#			#		
1	**Rib** 5+		17	**Arete** 4	
2	**Local Hero** 6B+		18	**Slab** 2+	
3	**Baxter's Wall Direct** 5+		19	**South Face Direct** 5	
4	**Artificial Route** 4		20	**Hörnli Ridge** 2	
5	**Way Down** 3		21	**West's Route** 5+	
6	**Angus** 6B+		22	**Winsome** 7A	
7	**Letterbox Slot** 5		23	**Arete** 5+	
8	**Fat Slapper** 6b *Sitter 7A.*		24	**Dark Matter** 7C *Sitter.*	
9	**Slap Happy** 6C		25	**Fish Eye** 4	
10	**Crack** 3+		26	**Grouper** 6B+	
11	**Chipper** 4		27	**Fish Groove** 6B	
12	**Moby Dick** 6A		28	**Fish Arete** 6C+ *Sitter 7B+*	
13	**Elephant's Bum** 5		29	**Fish Slab** 2+	
14	**Bum Slide** 6C		30	**Slab** 4	
15	**Shell Shot** 4+				
16	**Shell Shock** 4				

A great place with great views. Never too busy.

// Climbing: Gritstone boulders giving mostly shortish powerful problems on slopers, aretes and pebbles. Some slabs too and these can get quite high. Landings are generally lovely grass but these can sometimes be a bit sloping.

// Conditions: Can be a bit green in winter. Usually less sweaty in summer than some grit. Fairly exposed hillside but it does get some shelter from the crag. A breeze will keep midges at bay in the summer. **Family friendly.**

// Info: **Peak District Bouldering** (Vertebrate); **Over The Moors** (BMC);

A coarse course in a classic setting. A fabulous hillside of dark blocks shed from one of grit's mightiest crags give one of the Peak's favourite venues. Problems across the lower and middle grades. A great summer venue and a fine place to come on a nice evening after a hard day in Manchester.

Sugar Loaf

1 2 3 4

Sugar Loaf

5 6

Sloping Top

7 8 9

The Tank

10 11 12 13 14

Shell Shot

15 16

Matterhorn

17 18 19 20

Matterhorn

20 21 22 23

The Fish

24 25 26

The Fish

27 28 29 30

// Approach: From Greenfield (good bus service) follow the A635 towards Holmfirth. 300m after the roundabout beside the Clarence Inn take a little road that dips off to the right. Follow this down to the de- lights of Dovestones Reservoir and paid parking. Follow the main track on foot for 800m. Just after the tree plantation follow a track to the boulders that lie strewn on the hillside above.

Brian Callan on Short Arete, 3 (problem 15). Photo: Niall Grimes.

Holmfirth

53.57277
-1.779501

Quarried highballing with graffiti and a charm all its own. Great for technicians, dog-walkers, and glue-sniffers. A much loved little suntrap. Nora Batty's local crag: Venus in wrinkled stockings.

This little edge, known locally as 'The Cliff', is one of those scruffy, semi-urban destinations that has always had a loyal following amongst turned-on locals. Anyone in that area will have fond memories of youthful evenings wasted at The Cliff.

// Climbing: Quarried gritstone edge. The problems are often a wee bit high but still in a very friendly way. Essentially it's bouldering in the old-school meaning of the word, being somewhere you'd never bring a rope, but you will often find yourself in an exposed situation, sometimes high above an awkward landing. Having said that it doesn't feel very threatening and while sometimes the lines are up to 6 or 7 metres high, you can often traverse off at a reasonable height. A couple of mats are nice.

// Approach: From the main junction in the centre of Holmfirth (with the zebra crossings and yellow road box) follow the A635 (Town Gate/Station Rd) towards New Mill for 600m then angle right (Town End Rd). After 500m turn right onto Cliff Rd. After 450m the cliff can be seen above a row of houses. Park before the houses at a junction with Cliff Lane. Wander down to the houses and follow a little track that cuts up between them and there is The Cliff. For the problems detailed here turn right. If coming on foot follow Dunford Rd, left up South Lane, left on New Laith Lane, left onto Cliff Rd then take the track to the cliff.

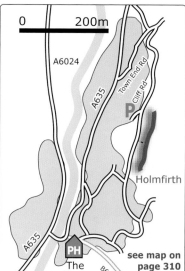

Holmfirth

The Nook

see map on page 310

1   **Devs** 4
2   **Scar Face** 4
3   **Arsenic Slab** 3
4   **Old Lace** 7A *Sidepull, sloper and up.*
5   **Upside Down Arete** 6B+
6   **Left Crack** 3
7   **Right Crack** 3
8   **Slabby Arete** 5
9   **Silent Running** 6A+
10 **Mad Mantel** 7A+
11 **First Arete Left** 5+
12 **First Arete Right** 5+
13 **Ramp** 5
14 **Traverse** 6B
15 **Short Arete** 3
16 **Short Arete Right** 5
17 **Slab** 6A+
18 **Uncle Lubin** 5+
    Sitter.

// **Conditions:** Exposed, very clean and quick drying. Gets the sun from early afternoon. Urban, but not in the bad sense of the word. Houses back onto the crag so bear this in mind. **Good for families.**

// **Info**: Google "kirklees holmfirth bouldering" for Carl Dawson's free pdf guide.

Brian Callan on First Arete Right, 5+ (problem 12).

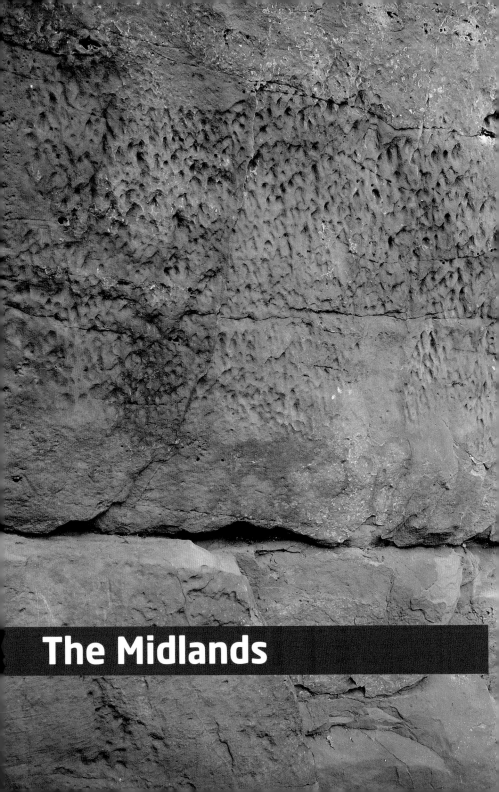

The Midlands

Sam Whittaker on Bank Job, 6B, at Nesscliffe (page 377, problem 12). Photo: David Simmonite

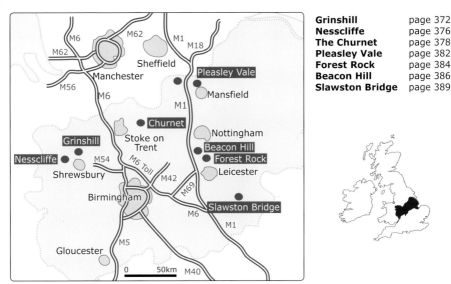

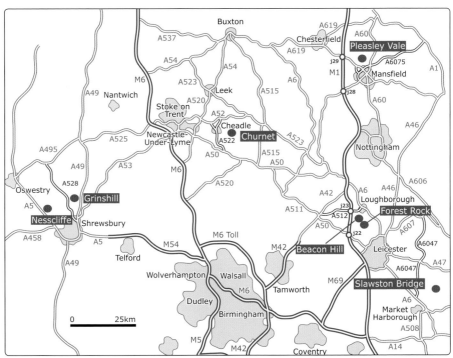

To be honest with you, I don't exactly know what people mean when they talk about the Midlands. For the purpose of this book it's anything that sits below Cheshire and the Peak and right of Wales. A little scattering of local venues, hidden gems, oddments and an abandoned bridge. Few of these are 'destinations', but Grinshill, Nesscliffe and the Churnet are definitely on the map for those in the know. The other venues are saviours for the outdoor-hankering denizens of the big cities on the hard shoulder of the M1, as well as bored travellers along this dreary highway.

Lucinda Whittaker on Berlin's Fallen, 6C, at Nesscliffe (page 377, problem 5). Photo: David Simmonite.

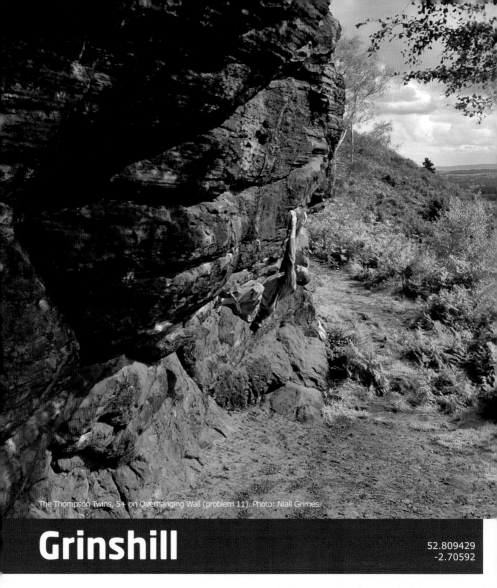
The Thompson Twins, 5+ on Overhanging Wall (problem 11). Photo: Niall Grimes.

Grinshill

52.809429
-2.70592

An esoteric gem. A full day's worth of varied quality problems spread along half a dozen buttresses that ring a Shropshire hillside. Lots of highballs, although they are generally gentle, and not gripping. A bit of climbing, a bit of a wander, some ferns, a picnic then some more climbing. You get the idea?

A nice place. A relaxing day out with some quarried, some natural outcrops of varying steepness. The area itself is popular with families and walkers, set amidst some reassuringly affluent countryside and affords some great views across the Shropshire savannah where herds of wildebeest and giraffe roam. The hillside is entwined with a network of paths and trails and finding the bouldering can sometimes be tricky. There is a large amount of climbing here. This tour will show you round and give you a bit of flavour. Check out Stuart Cathcart's quirky guidebook for the full low down.

// Climbing: Mainly natural sandstone outcrops with some quarried sections. Good and varied climbing on high quality rock. Some bulging buttresses where the climbing is either fingery or burly or both. Also vertical walls with good technical, fingery climbing. Often highball, a couple of mats will be useful, although the landings are usually very flat.

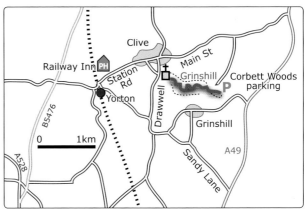

climbers parked down Drawwell, near the church, but this has caused problems for residents, so please use the Corbett Woods parking. Those approaching on public transport should approach down Drawwell. See map overleaf.

A driveway (a private road for residents) runs from the Corbett Woods parking, past Holland's Cottages, to Drawwell. The first-time visitor should follow this driveway from the parking to a clearing near the end, by the school. (This is 150m along, if you have approached from Drawwell.)

The Crinkle Wall area and The Pancake: These are just below this, gained down a small track.

Middle Rocks: From the clearing by the school a good path angles off the main track following some telegraph poles. Follow this. Middle Rocks lie below the third pole. The path to them cuts off after the second pole.

The Prow: It is easiest to return to the private driveway. Follow this for about 500m to some cottages on the left. On the right is a wide opening in the wall and a good path going into the woods. Take this, keeping right, and the Prow is at the back of the small quarry, less than 60m from the driveway.

Ass Creek: From the private driveway continue past the Prow access until, opposite the last cottage, a path leads through the wall. Enter this and turn left taking a path downhill, past a large quarry, onto a larger track at the bottom. Ass Creek is a narrow quarried channel just ahead, and across the track. The larger track leads to the parking.

// **Conditions:** The bouldering mostly faces south and gets lots of afternoon and evening sun. Lots of trees stop it being too exposed to the wind. Some buttresses dry quickly some more slowly. However the rock here is fairly delicate so please don't climb any rock that is at all damp as moisture weakens it. Good year round but a bit brackeny in summer. Best in spring and autumn. **Good for families.**

// **Approach:** Excuse the large number of maps here. I get lost easily at Grinshill so they reflect my lack of direction finding more than yours. Follow maps to the village of Clive (train station nearby and good bus service). Traditionally

// **Info**: **Shropshire Bouldering** (High Sports)

The Midlands / Grinshill

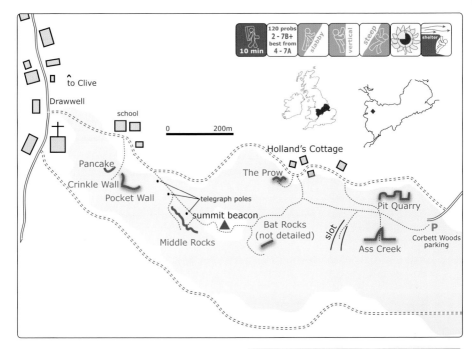

120 probs
2 - 7B+
best from
4 - 7A

to Clive

Drawwell

school

Holland's Cottage

The Prow

Pit Quarry

Pancake

Crinkle Wall

Pocket Wall

telegraph poles

summit beacon

Middle Rocks

Bat Rocks
(not detailed)

slot

Ass Creek

Corbett Woods
parking

0   200m

1	**Pancake** 6B	*Highball.*
2	**Panasea** 6A	*Highball.*
3	**The Conflict** 6A+	*Dodgy finish. Jump off.*
4	**Ali Ba Ba** 3	*Highball arete.*
5	**Black Dog** 5+	*Highball.*
6	**Shoulder Dog** 6A	*The highball wall. Other*

possible lines are around the same grade.

7	**Slapper** 4	
8	**Longest Traverse** 6B+	*Links three seperate*

traverses, finishing along the upper wall.

9	**Long Traverse** 5+	
10	**Black Bulge** 5+	
11	**Thompson Twins** 5+	
12	**Scary Landing** 6A	
13	**Cig Arete** 5	
14	**Dang Tootin** 4	
15	**Teenagers Live to Beat** 6A+	
16	**Top Traverse** 4+	
17	**Frog Leg Traverse** 6A	
18	**Up the Wall** 3+	
19	**Warts and All** 4+	
20	**Eliminator** 6C	
21	**Terminator** 7A	*Link 20 into 23.*
22	**I Was the Fourth Son of Five** 7A+	
23	**Lung La** 7A+	*Arete.*
24	**Ass Creek Traverse** 6B	
25	**Disappointment** 3	*The crack.*
26	**Worms** 4	

Pancake

Crinkle Wall

Crinkle Wall

Pocket Wall

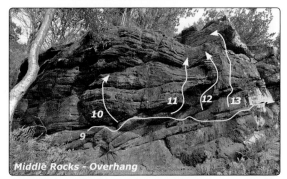

Middle Rocks - Overhang

Middle Rocks - Brutus

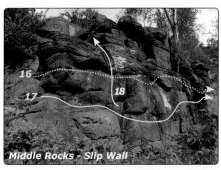

Middle Rocks - Slip Wall

Middle Rocks - Slip Wall

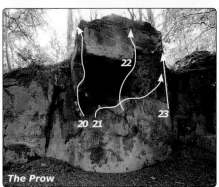

The Prow

Ass Creek

Nesscliffe

52.772032
-2.915754

Generally tough and fingery cranking on vertical walls at the base of an ancient and very impressive quarry. Huge walls of red sandstone tower over a good range of medium and hard problems that are good but it all feels a little stern. Plenty to go at but it's unlikely your fingers will last more than a couple of hours. And God, what a crag!

I found the bouldering here had a certain 'ouch' factor that you will need to be in the mood for. But lots of people love this style of climbing and coupled with very reliable conditions, Nesscliffe is justifiably popular. Climbing here will make you a better climber. However if you are looking for a more wholesome day out on a nice afternoon then Grinshill is probably a better bet.

Both the routes and the bouldering here have surged in standard, quality and quantity in the last decade thanks to the steel fingers of old-school gnarler Nick Dixon. His home-produced guide to the crag and the bouldering, Nesscliffe, which includes a DVD, is a piece of esoteric class. However the crag is served by not one, but two brilliant locally-produced guides. Long-term Shropshire devotee Stuart Cathcart's Shropshire Bouldering Guide is a unique-looking and lovingly produced volume that covers Nesscliffe as well as Grinshill and several other crags in the area. Both are very worth getting.

// Climbing: Quarried sandstone. Several different areas of vertical and beyond-vertical. Kind of like Pex Hill on its holidays. As with that crucible of Merseyside cranking, Nesscliffe demands precise footwork and clean technique. Nick's Terrace, perhaps the showpiece of the crag, is a lot steeper, more highball and has slightly bigger holds. Good for traverses. Good landings but sometimes a bit high. Your knees will thank you for a pad.

// Conditions: Thick larch woodland and a towering crag make this very sheltered. The walls take virtually no rain and the only problem is condensation. Good year round but great on a fine winter day when the sun can get through the trees. Can be humid in summer. A good breeze is useful to keep it fresh. **Family friendly.**

// Approach: Follow the maps to the village of Nesscliffe. Turn up the road opposite the Old Three Pigeons. A footpath leads directly to the crag from here but there is no parking so continue to pull-ins on the right after 300m and follow a path through the woods.

Sunset Buttress and The Alley: These two venues, not detailed here, lie above this path after 150m. They sit left and right of a broad, open Beech hillside. The Alley holds several fierce wall climbs including Cholesterol, Nick Dixon's 8A rockover, and a classic 7B+ traverse.
The Main Quarry: This lies 200m further on, beside the path (directly in front of the footpath from Nesscliffe Village). Most of the bouldering covered here is on the Kynaston's Cave area, the right section of this quarry. The Berlin Wall area is easily recognised and problems go right from here.
Nick's Terrace: This is above the huge hole of Pit Quarry. Approach up a long set of steps running up the left side of this quarry. Near the top the little bulging wall can be seen over on the right. Best to continue on and skirt safely round behind it. Don't roll off the edge.

// Info: Nesscliffe (Jasperdog Productions); **Shropshire Bouldering** (High Sports)

1   **The Highwayman's Escape**   6C+
2   **Jug U'La**   5+   *Sitter.*
3   **Dead Head**   6A   *Sitter.*
4   **Stazi**   6C+
     Use undercut for either left or right hand.
5   **Berlin's Fallen**   6C
6   **Chipper**   6A+
7   **Snail Trail**   5+
8   **ST**   6C
9   **Wing Wrapper**   4+
10   **Bonobo**   5
11   **Joys of Tom Tom**   5+
12   **Bank Job**   6B
13   **Ripple**   5+
14   **Immaculato**   6B
15   **Dreadline**   6A+
16   **Horizontal Slapping**   6A
17   **Crackle**   5
18   **Short Crack**   4+
19   **Rigpa**   7B+   *Highball.*
20   **Northumberland Wonderland**   7A
21   **Right-Hand Route**   6B   *Highball.*
22   **Little Northumberland**   7C

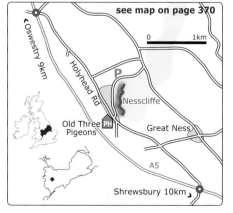

see map on page 370

0 ——— 1km

Oswestry 9km
Holyhead Rd
Nesscliffe
P
Old Three Pigeons
PH
Great Ness
A5
Shrewsbury 10km

Kynasten's Cave - Berlin Wall

1 2 3 4 5 6

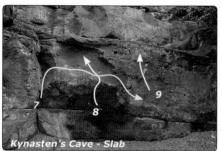

Kynasten's Cave - Slab

7 8 9

Kynasten's Cave - Ripple

10 11 12 13 14

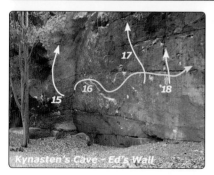

Kynasten's Cave - Ed's Wall

15 16 17 18

Nick's Terrace

19 20 21 22

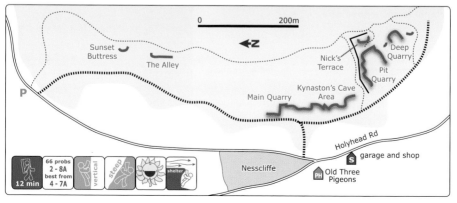

0   200m

N

Sunset Buttress
The Alley

Nick's Terrace
Deep Quarry
Pit Quarry
Kynaston's Cave Area
Main Quarry

P

Holyhead Rd

Nesscliffe

Old Three Pigeons

garage and shop

12 min | 66 probs 2 - 8A best from 4 - 7A | vertical | steep | | shelter

The Midlands / Nesscliffe

377

The Churnet

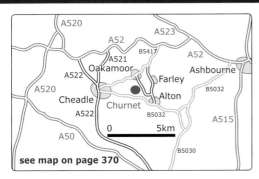

see map on page 370

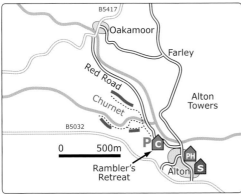

A wooded wonderland hiding arm-busting bastions of sandstone brutality. A mega-circuit of withering traverses and full-frontal up-problems all in a very reliable rain shadow. Really interesting rock. A favourite spot for familes, kids and dogs with idyllic woods and a river to mess around in and a good cafe.

The Churnet Valley is quite an extensive area. These pages deal only with the Dimmings Dale crags.

// Climbing: Steep. Sandstone outcrops giving very burly problems. Mainly sharp crimps, slopers, pockets and large pebbles. Brilliant for traverses. A few highballs, mostly on Wright's Rock, but these are far from mandatory and the landings are always perfect.

// Approach: The Red Road runs between the villages of Oakamoor and Alton. Drive along this and park by the Rambler's Retreat cafe. Crag approaches are given overleaf.

// Conditions: Generally very dry and sheltered. Lots of the crags stay dry in the rain. Generally midge-free. **Great for families.**

// Info: The Roaches (BMC); **Peak District Bouldering** (VG)

Stuart Brooks on Little Groove, 6A (problem 26) at Wright's Rock. Photo: Brooks Collection.

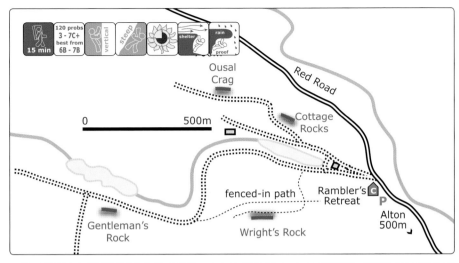

Cottage Rocks

The Midlands / Churnet

// Crag Approaches: All approaches start from the parking near the Rambler's Retreat. **Ousal Crag and Cottage Rocks:** Follow the right-hand of the two good paths which leads after a couple of hundred metres along the right side of the first big pool. After a hundred metres another track veers off uphill. Follow this. Cottage Rocks is above the apex of a right-hand bend after 200m. **Ousal Crag:** continue along the track and after 300m it can be seen in the trees on the right about 30m from the track. For Wright's Rock take the left-hand of the two good paths. Just at the start of the first big pool take a small path up the hillside on the left. Follow this to meet a fenced-in path. Cross this then go up the hillside to the crag. **Gentleman's Rock:** follow the good path along the river. After 600m there is a series of pools. Gentleman's is in the trees on the hillside to the left by the first of these pools.

Ousal Crag
1   **Ooze** 5
2   **Little Rib** 4   *Sitter.*
3   **Ousal High** 6B
4   **Ousal Low** 7A+
Cottage Rocks
5   **Crusty** 3+   *Cracks.*
6   **Sid the Sexist** 5
7   **Cottage Slab** 5
8   **Green wall** 6B
9   **Sapling Bulge** 6B+
10 **Tufa** 6A
11 **Orange Crush** 5
12 **Pocket Wall** 5
      Sitter 6B.
13 **The Wafer** 5+
14 **Strenuousity** 4
Wright's Rock
15 **Wright's**
      Traverse 7B
16 **Thorns** 4+
17 **Blazes** 6A+
18 **Quill** 7C+
19 **Simple Simon** 7B
      Crossing the low roof alone is 6B.
20 **Simple Simon**
      Indirect 7A   *Sitter, finishing at the jug. Finish up SS at 7B+.*
21 **Fingers Start** 7A
22 **Alternative Start** 6B
23 **Point Break** 7B+
      The lower section, getting established under the roof, is The Undercut, 7A.
24 **Warchild** 7C+
      The lower section, to get established on the slopers under the roof, is The Old Sloper Problem, 7A.
25 **Bhodi** 7A+
26 **Little Groove** 6A
27 **Last Wrights** 6A+
Gentleman's Rock
28 **Jill the Traverse**
      6B+
29 **Gentleman John**
      6B+
30 **High Speed**
      Imp Act 7A
31 **Low Traverse** 6B+
32 **The Nose** 6C

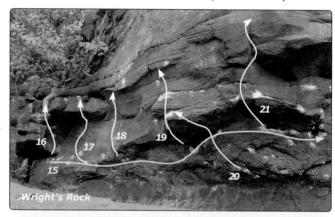

Ben Quinn on Yew Tree Corner, 6C (problem 16). Photo: Niall Grimes.

Pleasley Vale

53.180302
-1.213163

A pretty and pinchy training wall in a gentle riverside location. It would be average in a good area but in the Mansfield Watershed it's A-list. Locals and aficionados are quite sweet on it. Well caressed by the hands of the devout.

This is a great little bit of limestone bouldering often ignored for the more obvious delights of the gritstone on the other side of the M1. However, for anyone on the dark side of the tracks, this gives superb fingery training on solid rock. It is also worth travelling further for when bad weather is sitting over the Peak District. It rains less here, the crag is a great suntrap, it overhangs, and takes virtually no seepage.

// Climbing: Limestone outcrop. Steep walls with pushy climbing on crimps and pockets. Nice polished rock. Good for pumpy training traverses. Landings feel hard without a mat.

// Conditions: Very reliable. Sheltered and low lying. Hardly seeps in winter and can stay dry in the rain, as long as it's not the wrong kind of rain. Sometimes suffers from Attack of the Chavs who will soot up the walls and scatter cans. **Good for families.**

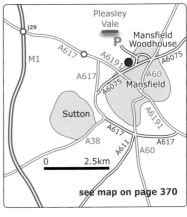

see map on page 370

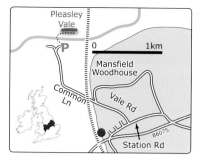

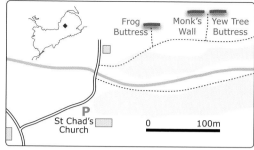

// Approach: From M1 Junction 29, follow the A617 for 4.7 miles, ignoring a Pleasley Vale sign. At a junction, go straight on (A6191) for Mansfield. After 1 mile take the A6075 signposted Mansfield Woodhouse. After 800m, go under a railway bridge (past Mansfield Woodhouse train station), and after 100m go left into Station Street. After 300m, turn left into Vale Rd. Follow this until it veers right before a bridge, and continue straight, under the bridge. Follow this until, just before a house, a small road leads right, signposted St Chad's Church. Park by the small red church. Cross the tiny bridge then follow the river rightwards. The rocks are immediately visible. If coming from Mansfield itself then get to Mansfield Woodhouse train station.

// Info: The old Rockfax Peak Bouldering Guide covered it well. Also **peakbouldering.info**

1	**Frog Traverse** 5	*9*	**Pillar Crack** 5	*17*	**Bulge Left** 6C	
2	**Grounded** 5+	*10*	**Crack** 4+	*18*	**The Pinch** 7A	*The Superdirect eliminates the slot out left and arete jug at the top at 7C.*
3	**Scrambled** 5+	*11*	**Seam** 6A			
4	**Ceiling Zero** 6A	*12*	**Yew Tree Traverse** 7A+	*19*	**Right On** 6B	
5	**Ground Zero** 5+	*13*	**Holly Tree Wall** 6A+	*20*	**Groove Move** 6A	
6	**Monk's Traveres** 6A	*14*	**Statement of Yewf** 6B+	*21*	**Bulge** 6A+	
7	**Crack** 4	*15*	**Yew Tree Wall** 7A+	*22*	**Arete** 4	
8	**Flake** 6A	*16*	**Yew Tree Corner** 6C			

Frog Buttress

Monk's Wall

Yew Tree Wall

The Midlands / Pleasley Vale

Forest Rock

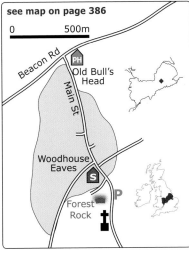

see map on page 386

A grotto of brutality nudged into the corner of a sleepy Leicestershire village. Steep as hell with very powerful climbs.

A good contrast to Beacon Hill. Instead of failing because things are too scary, here you can fail becaure they are too hard.

// Climbing: Powerful. Quarried slate-style rock. A couple of easier slabby problems and a bunch of harder, steeper ones. Often the start of routes so jump dismounts from 3 to 4 metres. Good landings. Crimps, sometimes sharp, cracks and slopers.

// Approach: See the Beacon Hill map on page 386. Forest Rock is just visible from the road, below the church.

// Conditions: Hardly any sun. Good on hot days. Fairly rainproof. Dank in winter.

// Info: **Leicestershire Rock** (BMC)

1	**Forest Wall** 2		
2	**Metal Spike Route** 6C+	*Sitter 7A.*	
3	**Sorcerer** 5+		
4	**Saucy** 6A	*Sitter 6B+*	
5	**Sorcerer Direct** 6C+		
6	**Sorcerer's Apprentice** 6C+		
7	**Sorcerer Traverse** 7B		

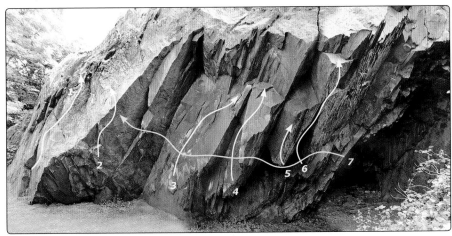

Iain McKenzie on Sorcerer Direct, 6C+ (problem 5). Photo: Amanda McKenzie.

Pillar, 3+ (problem 10).

Beacon Hill

52.72743
-1.246964

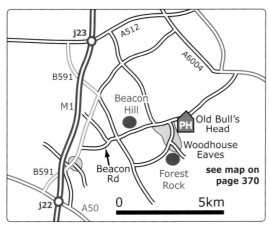

j23
A512
A6004
B591
M1
Beacon
Hill
Old Bull's
Head
PH
Woodhouse
Eaves
B591
Beacon
Rd
Forest
Rock

see map on
page 370

0   5km

B591
j22   A50

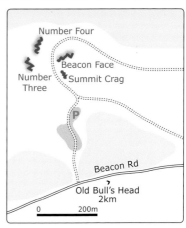

Number Four
Beacon Face
Number
Three
Summit Crag
P
Beacon Rd
Old Bull's Head
2km
0   200m

1. **Moonshot** 5+ *E1.*
2. **Moonshot Direct** 6A *E1.*
3. **V Gully** 4 *VS.*
4. **Right Arete** 4+ *HVS.*
5. **Shaft** 1 *Diff.*
6. **And You and I** 6A *E3.*
7. **Auto** 4+ *HVS.*
8. **Prop** 2 *VDiff.*
9. **Harley Street** 4
10. **Pillar** 3+ *Sitter 6A.*
11. **Jack in the Box** 3+
12. **Wall** 3+ *Direct start is 6A.*
13. **Bow** 2+
14. **Starship Trooper** 6A *E1.*
15. **Collywobble Crack** 2
16. **The Last Straw** 3+ *HS.*
17. **Relayer** 5+ *E1.*
18. **The Gully** 2 *Diff.*
19. **Starlight** 3+ *HS.*

Beacon Face

A small animal with surprisingly sharp teeth. A little mini mountain popular locally for evening bouldering / soloing sessions although it can feel scary. A superb, fresh and elevated location with a righteous view of the sunset. A cool place.

The rock is a type of hardened volcanic ash, the oldest rock in England and Wales apparently. It is formed into sharp-angled, spikey rock and these spikes sometimes gather at the bottom of routes giving one the shivers at the thought of a fall. Long falls at that as the problems can be 5 or 6 metres high. If that's not bad enough the rock has an unpredicable slipperyness about it. Bouldering at Beacon Hill gave me the sort of feelings that I associate more with Lake District E4s.

Summit Crag

That said, it is a fab little spot; quirky, unique and beautiful, and would give a great evening to bold boulderers.

// **Climbing:** Very highball microroutes with often very poor landings. Very much at the North Stack Wall end of the bouldering spectrum with some of the worst landings in the book. Crimps, cracks and slopers.

// **Approach: From south:** leave M1 at junction 22. Take A511 direction Ashby. After 0.6 miles go right at roundabout direction Copt Oak. After 2 miles (700m after Copt Oak) turn right signposted Woodhouse Eaves. Continue, crossing Shepshed Rd after 1.3 miles, then after 300m turn left into the parking. **From north:** leave M1 at junction 23. Follow A512 direction Ashby. After 800m turn left on B591 direction Woodhouse Eaves. At intersection after 2 miles cross the road and head towards Woodhouse Eaves. After 1.3 miles turn left on Beacon Rd to the parking after 300m.

// **Conditions:** Clean, exposed and quick drying. Late afternoon and evening sun. A lovely spot. **Family friendly.**

// **Info:** Leicester Climbs (BMC)

Number Four

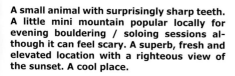

Number Three

Elspeth Yates on Bow, 2+ (problem 13, page 387), Beacon Hill. Photo: Iain McKenzie.

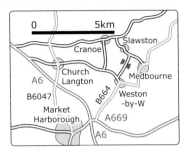

Pipe Wall

Sun Wall

Old railway bridge in a beauiful location.

I arrived here on a harassed Tuesday evening ready to hate it for being man made. As soon as I parked and got out I had my Road to Slawston experience. Little bunnies hopped, birds sang, sheep chattered, cows mumbled. This has got to be the most beautiful place in the world, I thought. The only bridge to make it into the book.

In their childhoods both Jerry Moffatt and Johnny Dawes climbed here regularly. Can you feel it?

// Climbing: Vertical crimping with traverses and routes. 5 metres high but great landing. Some belay anchors.
// Approach: From Weston-by-Welland on the B664 follow road towards Welham. After 300m turn right onto Green Lane by the Wheel and Compass. The bridge is in 1 mile.
// Conditions: Sunny, dry. **Family friendly** in a playing in the road kind of way.

1	4	*7*	5+	*13*	5+
2	5	*8*	6A+	*14*	5
3	4+	*9*	6C	*15*	4+
4	6C+	*10*	6B+	*16*	4+
5	3+	*11*	6C+	*17*	5+
6	5	*12*	5	*18*	5

50 probs
4 - 7A
best from
4 - 6B

0 min

vertical

shelter

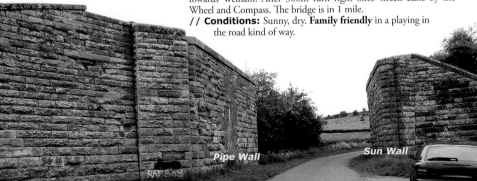

Pipe Wall

Sun Wall

Southern Sandstone

Ben Read on a 6C situated in the nooks between Odin's Wall and Honeycombe at High Rocks (page 395). Photo: James O'Neil.

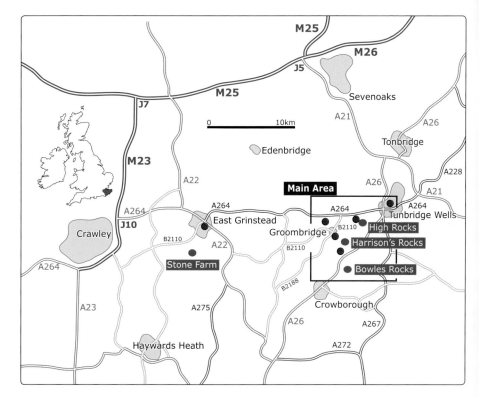

Southern Sandstone is one of those very handy, time saving places. This is because it lets most climbers decide to hate it without ever having to waste any time actually going there, passing the savings onto you, the boulderer. Bingo! I was going to write that its reputation preceeded it but when I thought about it I couldn't tell what that reputation was, in any real, specific sense. 'It's shit!' That's all I heard from the knowledgable folk who'd never been. And, I'm holding my hands up here, I too had sneered at it in the right company. As I did Helsby!

So it came as some surprise to me that I actually quite liked it in many ways. Sure, it's not Font, but neither is that little rattle of sharp mossy blocks behind Badger Rock or that squat sandstone turd up in Shaftoe.

But what it is is an area with a very strong sense of identity, insular, perhaps, aware of its cast-off reputation throughout the land. It's definitely an obscure backwater, and even many London climbers could be in the Roaches quicker than High Rocks, and northerners are unlikely to be tempted here, halfway to Fontainebleau as it is, but I really enjoyed the climbing I did here and, while I wouldn't make a special trip, I look forward to having the opportunity again.

The rock is generally a wee bit soft so can feel dusty and insecure underfoot. But if you like your challenges to be challenging then this adds an extra dimension and it demands great footwork and technical sense.

Here's what I thought: of the places I visited. Stone Farm is a harmless little spot in a pretty setting and plenty for a couple of hours; Eridge Green was ok, but didn't have anything the other crags didn't have, so no details are included here. Bowles Rocks is about as tame as a crag can be without being an indoor wall, and probably the best for training and is pretty rainproof; Harrison's, well, it's okay. Popular. High Rocks was properly impressive. I did a whole bunch of good bouldering there, although the next time I go I'm bringing my top rope.

There is one thing about the area I feel I need to mention. At every venue I went to, when I stood there and looked lost, a local would come up to me, ask what I was looking for, and then take some time showing me around. Not because I was doing a book – I usually didn't say – but because I was a fellow climber. And do you know, I didn't get that at any other area, bar the very odd exception. For that alone, Southern Sandstone gets a big thumbs up from me.

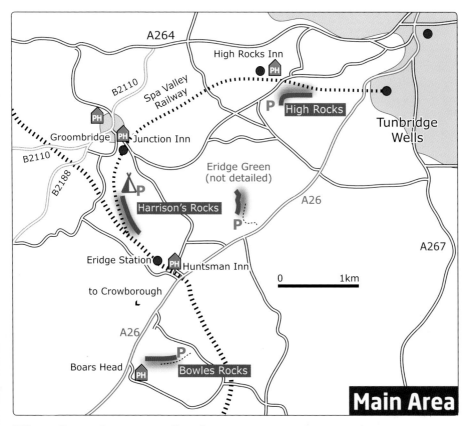

The Sandstone Code

Due to the quality and delicacy of the rock hereabouts, locals are unsurprisingly keen to protect it. Over the years a set of guidelines have been honed that seem best suited to both users and the rock. The list below is simply the set of standards that any climber would expect of themselves, and while they apply to everywhere somehow, on Southern Sandstone, they bear repeating. Included here is what to think about when you're bouldering, then specific points for when you've got the string out, and remember, no leading. Solo or top rope only.

No chipping whatsoever. On sandstone, heavy brushing/cleaning can have the same effect.

No wire or hard nylon brushing. Use a soft nylon brush or a cloth very gently if absolutely necessary.

Use as little chalk as possible, and only use tick marks when absolutely necessary.

Gently brush away any build-up of chalk and any tick marks at the end of your session.

No use of resin (pof).

No blow torching. If you come across a wet hold, dry it gently with a towel, or come back on a windy day when it will have dried out naturally.

No gardening of indigenous vegetation.

Do not leave carpet patches at the crag. Not only are they an eyesore, but they quickly become sodden, and thus useless. They also kill off the vegetation that they cover.

Use a bouldering pad to decrease the impact on the vegetation at the base of popular problems.

Do not drop litter at the crag, and take home any that you find.

Guidelines on the use of ropes

Climbs are done using a top rope, or solo. Careful positioning of the climbing rope and belay are necessary as any weighted rope moving over the rock will cause permanent damage. Use a non-stretch belay rope or sling. Make sure the karabiner hangs over the edge of the crag. Make sure moving or stretching ropes do not come into contact with the rock. Walk off when you have finished a climb, do not lower off. Do not abseil. Now go on, get!

Andrew Shilling on Craig-y-Blanco, 6B (problem 34). Photo: Niall Grimes

The proudest crag on Southern Sandstone, albeit with some drawbacks. A magical kingdom of woolly sandstone blobs, death-chasms and ariel footbridges. Well supplied with mid-grade desperates although outside the summer months your choice will be a bit limited. A great place to play and great for rich families.

Now, sit down and pour yourself a stiff belt of tequila, because I haven't mentioned the biggest drawback: it will cost you £10 to climb here! The grounds themselves are privately owned and just to visit for a walk costs £3. Climbing used to cost a fiver but the owner got fed up with people sneaking over the fence so he doubled the price to put them off. I'm not sure how that works. Local climbers are sure that if people continue to sneak in then the owner will ban climbing here. But ten pounds! You must purchase a ticket in the downstairs bar of the High Rocks Inn, where you can also buy that stiff drink to calm your nerves after paying.

High Rocks is a nook-filled ornamental wonderland that's gone a bit hairy around the edges. There is a lot of bouldering at High Rocks and what is described here is only a small sample. See the local guides.

The climbing described here has three distinct styles. As you come into the grounds the main section of crag stretches off left for 100m and is characterised by big steep or vertical walls often with undercut bases. This stretch holds 40 problems, mostly 6C to 7B+, which tend to overcome the steep lower sections of walls as far as good breaks to give powerful, dynamic moves. However the stone is a wee bit soft and much of the rock here, being north-facing and near trees, is dank for a lot of the year. And we all know that we must not climb on damp sandstone as it is weakened.

Round the corner at the right extremity of this wall the rock swings round and is a bit more open and sunny. Here is a bunch of vertical, often highball walls of harder, crimpy rock. These are much drier and should be climbable year round.

Just in front are a few boulders. The biggest, more a pinnacle, has problems around the base while beside it the Slab Boulder gives the best bouldering at the crag, mainly due to its high quality, hard rock. A good bunch of testpieces here. Quick drying. Just below this the Bowling Green boulders are a more diminuitive clutch of rounded blobby problems, with lots of easy stuff.

On the whole the bouldering is very good, but I wouldn't make a special trip for it. However if I get the chance to go back again I am definitely going to bring a top rope set-up and do some of the routes. They look fantastic. The local ethic here forbids leading. The soft rock would quickly be destroyed. See the Sandstone Code in the introduction.

// Climbing: Sandstone crag and boulders. Quite varied. Lots of harder, steep problems on slopers along the main crag. Around the boulders at the right end is crimpy stuff at all grades, sometimes on the crag, sometimes on boulders. A couple of mats is nice as a lot of the stuff on the crag will involve jumping dismounts.

// Approach: From Tunbridge Wells take the A26 south towards Crowborough. The town ends and there are fields and trees on both sides. Just over half a mile after the town ends turn right, signposted High Rocks. Follow this and after two right forks then a right turn at a junction you will find the High Rocks Inn. The car park lies to the right of the entrance to the rocks.

// Conditions: The north-facing crag section is dank outside of the summer months and will seriously curtail any climbing here. Other areas get some afternoon sun and are quicker drying. **Family friendly.**

// Info: **Southern Sandstone Bouldering; Southern Sandstone** (CC).

Tea Garden Lane

A264

Broom Lane

High Rocks Inn

P

High Rocks

Tunbridge Wells

A26

Broadwater Forest Lane

0   1km

see map on page 393

Renaissance

Vandal

Salad Days

Leglock

Kinda Lingers

Slab Boulder

1	**Pammy** 7A+ *Sitter.*	**9**	**Pet Cemetary** 7B+	**19**	**Kinda Lingers Start**
2	**Renaissance Start** 6C	**10**	**Leg Lock** 5		7A+ *Sitter 7C.*
3	**Resurrection** 7C	**11**	**The Real Slim Shady** 7A	**20**	**Lunge between**
4	**Vandal** 7B	**12**	**Rubicon Start** 6A		**Pockets** 6C+
5	**Superman** 7A	**13**	**Cut Steps** 6A	**21**	**Original Start** 6C+

5   *Jump to crimps 1m right of the crack and go.*

14   **Superfly** 7A+

6   **Punch** 6A+

15   **Dragon Start** 5+

16   **Robin's Left** 6A

7   **Telegram Sam** 6C+

17   **Robin's Route** 6B

8   **Salad Days** 6C

18   **The Rip** 6B

22   **Darth Vadar** 7A *Sitter.*

23   **Old Kent Road** 6B+

    Sitter, left and up the arete. Locally, the big sidepull at the base of the arete is avoided at 7A.

Odin's wall

Honeycomb

Bowling Green

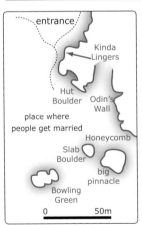

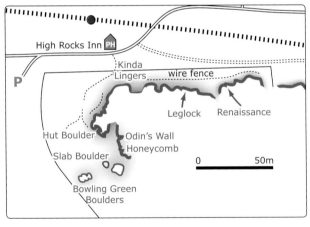

High Rocks Inn PH

Kinda Lingers

wire fence

Leglock   Renaissance

Hut Boulder   Odin's Wall
Honeycomb

Slab Boulder

Bowling Green Boulders

0   50m

entrance

Kinda Lingers

Hut Boulder   Odin's Wall

place where people get married

Honeycomb

Slab Boulder

big pinnacle

Bowling Green

0   50m

24 Z'mutt 5
Climb the pockets, traverse the ledges right and finish back left.
25 Z'mutt Direct 6B
26 Wish 7C+ *Start using left hand undercut, or using stacked pads at 7C. The sitter is Don't Pierdol, 8A+.*
27 Brenva 5 *Sitter 7A.*

28 Slab 6B+
29 Orrer Crack 5C
30 Odin's Wall 6A+
31 Something Crack 6A+
32 Degenerate 4+
33 Honeycombe 6B+
34 Craig-y-Blanco 6B
35 Dagger Crack 6A
36 Greasy Crack 4+

37 Wishful Thinking 6C
38 Émile 4+
39 Gaugin 5
40 Maze Crack 2
41 Camille 3
42 Alfred 3
43 Maze Chimney 2+
44 Elephant 6B
45 Chez's Arete 6C

Harrison's Rocks

51.106176
0.188892

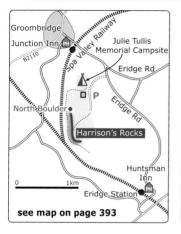

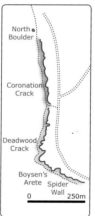

see map on page 393

North Boulder
1 **Alligator Snatch** 6B *Sitter.*
2 **Groovy Graeme** 4+
3 **Letterbox** 5
4 **Sunset Wall** 5+
5 **Torque Wrench** 6A
6 **Finger Flow** 7A
7 **West Face Route** 6A+
8 **Strong Struggle** 6C
9 **Papillion** 6B
10 **Back Breaker** 6B+
11 **The Sherriff** 6B
12 **OK Corral** 2+
The corner crack in the back of the boulder. Also the way down.
Coronation Crack - *top rope or solo*
13 **Hangover III** 6B+
14 **Long Layback** 4+
15 **Flakes Direct** 6B
16 **The Flakes** 6B+
17 **Coronation Crack** 6B+
18 **The Limpet** 7A
19 **Nut Tree** 6B+
20 **Spout Buttress** 6A
21 **Spout Crossing** 5
22 **Bow Window** 3
23 **Sashcord Crack** 3
The Vice - *highball*
24 **Wildcat Wall** 6A+
25 **Deadwood Crack** 4
26 **Tame Variant** 2
27 **The Vice** 3+
28 **Toevice** 6B
Deadwood Crack - *highball*
29 **Set Square Arete** 5+
30 **Sunshine Crack** 4
31 **The Knam** 6A+
Left-facing scoop.
32 **The Mank** 5
Rampy scoop.
33 **Dr Pepper** 6A+
34 **Piecemeal Wall** 7A
35 **Karen's Kondom** 6B
Boysen's Arete - *highball*
36 **Crowborough Corner** 6A
37 **Wailing Wall** 6A
38 **Boysen's Arete** 6B
Spider Wall - *highball*
39 **Sitter** 6A+
40 **Second Chance** 5+
41 **Last Chance** 5
42 **Spider Wall** 5+
43 **Cave Wall** 5
44 **Traverse** 6B
45 **Grant's Groove** 6B
46 **Grant's Crack** 4+

A good enough crag in many ways, but somehow lacking in bite. A few boulder problems then it's on to make the best of the crag. Relaxed, and with a holiday feel on busy days.

This might well be the most popular crag in the region and on busy weekends the crag can look like Moby Dick in it's last lashed throes of life. It has a range of challenges in a non-threatening environment. Detailed here is the worn delights of the North Boulder, the only real boulder. Due to a lack of more proper bouldering I have detailed a bunch of the routes at the crag. Problems 13 to 23 are full-bore routes while the rest are little mini-climbs that can be bouldered out by the gutsy. I have given the routes hopelessly inaccurate Font grades.

// **Climbing:** The boulder is a softish blob with a bunch of steep problems above perfect landings. Fairly physical. The crag has some fine strong lines in its mid-area then towards the right stretches out to smaller climbs that might tempt the padded boulderer. Many of these 'routes' are included here as boulder problems. Use your judgement.
// **Approach:** From the little roundabout in Groombridge follow the Corsley Road, branching left onto Station Road, past the Junction Inn and the train station. Fork right after 0.7 miles, down the right-hand of two roads, both called Eridge Road – quaint – then look for a lane cutting off on the right after 100m. Follow this to paid parking (£1 in the honesty box) beside the toilet block and campsite. The easiest approach heads in the direction of the railway line then follows paths beside the treeline to a little gate after 300m. Go through this and the North Boulder lies after 30m. Coronation Crack is 300m right of this.
// **Conditions:** Sheltered and quick drying. Afternoon and evening sun. Climbable year round. **Family friendly,**
// **Info:** Southern Sandstone Bouldering; Southern Sandstone (CC).

North Boulder

North Boulder

Coronation Crack

The Vice

Deadwood Crack

Boysen's Arete

Spider Wall

Bowles Rocks

51.07624
0.201895

A smart wall of pumpy, fingery testpieces sheltering under what must be seen as a somewhat 'ornamental' crag. Still, the problems are great fun in a basic sort of way. Very roadside and with some everdry and much quick-drying rock, it's a good choice for a quick hit. It makes me think of doilies.

If Harrison's Rocks are sliced white bread then Bowles is Sainsbury's Finest. If Harrison's is ITV, then this is BBC2. If Harrison's is a can of Foster's, then this is a glass of Harvey's Bristol Cream. The politest, best-kept crag I've ever been to.

The crag is actually on the grounds of an outdoor centre who charge £2.50 to climb there. Money well spent. It's got a very tidy, back-yardy feel and the chittering of little voices will join the birdsong as the aural motif of the experience. You better be cool with that.

// Climbing: Fandango Wall, the centrepiece of the crag, is a stoutly-overhanging gallery of crimps allowing great traverses, up-problems and link-ups. Fingery, and can be high. Best 6B – 7B. Also a bunch of varied and fun problems on high walls and slabs either side of Fandango Wall. Best 6A – 7A. Flat, hard landing; whatever mats you bring will be well appreciated.

// Approach: Follow the maps and find the entrance to the Outdoor Centre, and enter and park. Pay here and follow the crag to find the bouldering, in a bay near the end.

// Conditions: South facing, gets lots of sun. Sheltered. The problems in the middle of Fandango Wall will stay dry in some rains. **Family friendly.**

// Info: Southern Sandstone Bouldering; Southern Sandstone (CC).

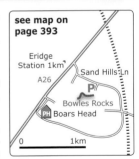

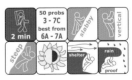

Santa Claws

Banana Groove

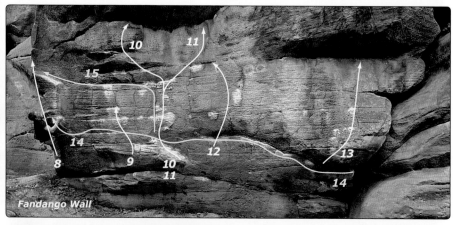

Fandango Wall

Orr's Traverse

1	**Netwall** 3 *Chopped holds.*	10	**Fandango** 6B+ *Sitter 6C.*	18	**Kemp's Delight** 4+
2	**Corner Layback** 4	11	**Fandango Right** 6C	19	**Mick's Wall**
3	**Zoom** 6C+	12	**Sonic Blue** 7B *Sitter.*		**Variation** 5
4	**Santa's Claws** 3+	13	**Pastry Direct** 7B *Sitter.*	20	**Midheight Traverse** 6B
5	**Banana Hammock** 6C	14	**Nicotine Alley** 7A		*To the flake.*
6	**Wall** 4+	15	**Tobacco Road** 6B+	21	**Wall** 6A *Sitter.*
7	**Traverse** 6C		*Start along Nicotine Alley.*	22	**Flake** 3
8	**Coathanger** 6A	16	**Orr Traverse** 5+	23	**Steep Wall** 5
9	**Fandango Direct** 6C+		*All the way to easy ground.*	24	**Short Traverse** 6B+
	Sitter.	17	**Mick's Wall Arete** 6B	25	**Nose** 6A+ *Sitter.*

Stuart Clark on SE Corner Direct, 6B (problem 30). Photo: Niall Grimes.

Stone Farm

51.095814
-0.026007

A modest little crag that might give an unassuming couple of hours of fun. A few sit starts, a bit of high-balling and a solo or two. It won't change your life but you could easily walk away happy.

This was the first crag I visited on Southern Sandstone and when I arrived at the first boulder and had a fondle and immediately thought – "God, I'd love to be in Font now." In that sense, Stone Farm reminded me of Fontainebleau.

// Climbing: Sandstone edge. Lots of slabby problems, most easy, some hard, and a few bulging boulders offering steep sitters and rounded tops. The rock is quite soft in parts. Holds are usually slopers or big rounded pockets. You'll want a mat if you want to do some highballs otherwise it's all fairly civilised.

// Approach: Follow the map from East Grinstead and through Saint Hill Green heading toward the reservoir. 400m before the water a tiny road, Admiral's Bridge Lane, cuts off on the left. Park on the verge here, which doesn't feel right, or continue for 300m to a car park on the left. From the lane's junction walk uphill for 30m and a track on the left leads to the rocks after 200m.

// Conditions: Quick drying. Some of the crag is in trees, otherwise it is very sunny. Sheltered. **Family friendly.**

// Info: SS Bouldering; Southern Sandstone (CC).

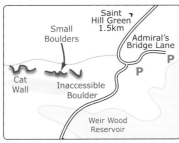

Cat Wall

Cat Wall

Small Boulders

Small Boulders

Inaccessible Boulder

Inaccessible Boulder

1	**Footsie** 6A	**13**	**Traverse** 6B
2	**Stone Farm Chimney** 2	**14**	**Wall** 5
3	**Chalk n' Cheese** 6B+	**15**	**Bulging Corner** 4
4	**Kathmandu** 6B+	**16**	**Bulging Wall** 4+
5	**Cat Wall** 6A		*5+ from a low start.*
6	**Sweet Carol** 6A	**17**	**Ashdown Wall** 5
7	**Stone Farm Crack** 3+	**18**	**Introductory Climb** 4+
8	**Pine Buttress** 6A	**19**	**Up** 4+
9	**Biometric Slab** 6B+	**20**	**Slab** 2
10	**Pine Crack** 4	**21**	**Gap 1** 3
11	**Face** 4+	**22**	**Gap 2** 2
12	**Open Chimney** 3+	**23**	**Leaning Crack Start** 5

24	**Leaning Crack Start** 4+
25	**Ducking Fesperate** 6A
	To the break.
26	**SW Corner** 4+
	Reverse and jump or traverse
right and down Primitive Groove.	
27	**Mantel** 6B
28	**Boulder Wall** 6A
29	**Primitive Groove** 3
30	**SE Corner Direct** 6B
31	**Stinging Nettle** 7A
	Sitter.

Paul Freudenthal at Reiff in the Woods (page 416). Photo: Richie Betts.

Scotland

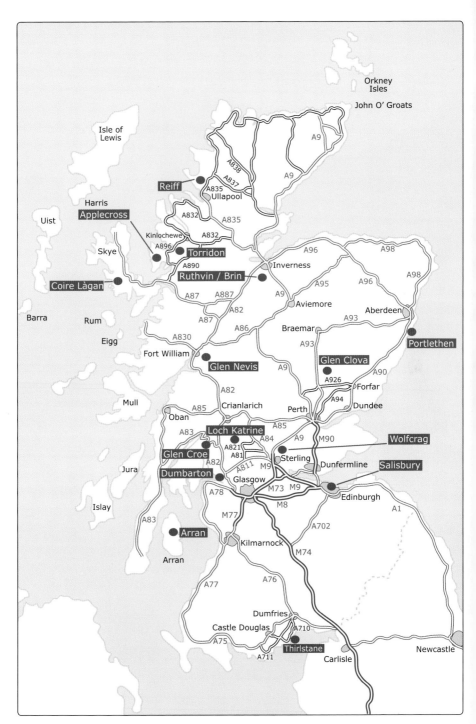

Scotland / Introduction

Amanda Lyons on The Prow, 6C, at Portlethen (page 414). Photo: Lyons collection.

Scotland / Introduction

Chris Houston on Pongo Sit Start, 8A, at Dumbarton (page 434, problem 21). Photo: Photo: Jonathan Bean.

John Watson on Sky Pilot, 6C+, High Crag, Glen Nevis (page 429). Photo: Stone Country.

It might sound obvious, but Scotland is another country. There is a map of the UK on the wall in my office. While working on this book, beavering away at Leicestershire quarries, squirreling about on Lancastrian hilltops, I always managed to ignore the massive lump that sat on top of the island, pretty much as big as all the other parts put together. I eventually started noticing it, became slightly distressed by it and in the end hung a baby-gym over the top of it so I wouldn't see it. Out of sight and all that. Then one day I peeked behind the baby gym and it was still there, and still a massive country. Something needed to be done.

So in honour of the worrying independence of that land Scotland has been treated differently in this book. In general you are only going to get information on character, conditions and approach and no problems. Mainly that's because I haven't visited the venues.

I have thought of some hollow excuses why this is okay. For a start you won't happen to 'find yourself' in Ul-lapool. You will know ahead of time giving you plenty of time to gather some info. Secondly there is simply too much climbing to make any meaningful dent on it here. Thirdly there is a perfectly good guidebook. Fourthly... not sure yet. I'll think about it.

The truth is that if I had tried to undertake Scottish research then this book would never have been finished. It would have broken the back of that weak camel that is my determination.

I have taken the easy way out. This section has been written with the help of locals beyond the border, mainly Richie Betts, John Watson, Dave MacLeod, Ian Taylor, Jonathan Bean and others.

In many ways it is the most inspiring chapter in the book, full of wild unknowns and breathtaking rock. The photographs I think are stunning. Once the dust has settled I'm going to take that baby-gym off the wall, have a look at the map and make my way north.

John Watson at Thirlstane. Photo: Stone Country.

Thirlstane

54.892504
-3.577294

A unique curio with a raft of great hard problems on steep walls inside a seaside cave. Conditions can be tricky but with the right tides and a good wind it will give a great session.

Mostly hard problems but a few easier things scattered about.

// Climbing: Steep walls either side of a cave with powerful problems. Crimps and slopers. Not too high and with a nice beach landing but a mat will keep your feet clean.

// Approach: About a mile south of Kirkbean on the A710 is a big blue sign for Southerness pointing down a road. Take this turn. Fork left after 700m then on to a sharp left-hander after 900m. 150m after the bend take a small road on the right by an Arbigland sign. Follow this to parking by the sea. Turn left and follow the shore for 150m to the cave.

// Conditions: Tidal. Cave conditions with little sun and lingering dampness if there isn't a drying breeze. Can stay dry in the rain. **Family friendly.**

// Info: **Bouldering in Scotland** (SCP)

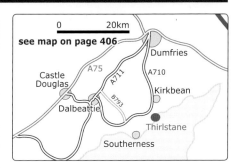

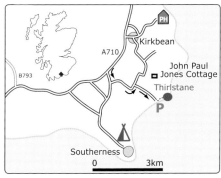

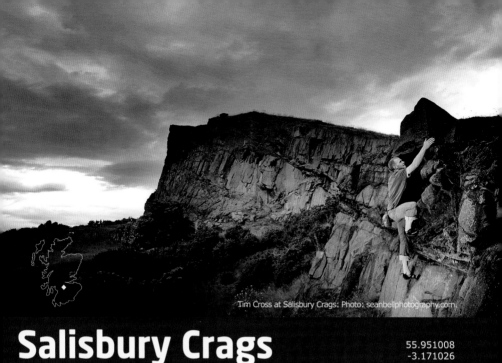

Tim Cross at Salisbury Crags: Photo: seanbellphotography.com

Salisbury Crags

55.951008
-3.171026

A century-old training ground for Edinburgh locals or highbrow tourists with a pair of boots and itchy fingers. It sits loftily above the city it gives beautiful views and a great bit of exercise for those with the right expectations. There follows an actual conversation:

Badger: "You're putting Salisbury Crags in, right?"
Me: "Don't know, is it any good?"
Badger: "Is it? I'll say. I'd say it's as good as... as good as... as good as Minus Ten Wall at Stoney Middleton."
Me: "That good?"
Badger: "No. Actually I'd say it's even *better* than Minus Ten Wall. I've probably been there over two hundred times."

// Climbing: Sandstone quarry. Fingery and technical. The main bouldering is in the South Quarry at the right end of the crags. The Black Wall is unmistakeable with a great fingery traverse (6C, a bit polished) taking the obvious line across the leaning wall in either direction. There are loads of eliminates on the same wall, and a great problem up the middle (7A, reachy and quite high). The back wall of the quarry is slabbier and has some fun smeary problems up to about 6C; these tend to be very eliminate. There's also an easyish traverse across the whole back-wall and a few scary VS-style solos, which are good for clearing the head.

// Approach: The hill with the crags is visible throughout the city. Find Arthur's Seat, or the Scottish Parliament House. From the parliament building follow the Radical Road to the crags.

// Conditions: Fresh setting, fairly exposed. Sun in the afternoon and evening. **Family friendly.**

// Info: Bouldering in Scotland (SCP)

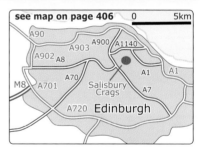

see map on page 406

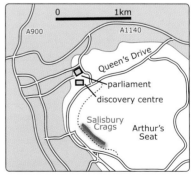

10 min | 30 probs 5 - 7B best from 6A - 7A | slabby | vertical | steep

Wolfcrag bouldering. Photo Fraser Harle.

Wolfcrag

56.15953
-3.951436

see map on page 406

j11
A9
Wolfcrag
0   2km
Bridge of
Allan
B823
M9   B998
A9
A91
j10
A84
A907
A9
Stirling

Popular quarry bouldering with easy access and reliable conditions. A great collection of easy/mid-grade problems that will be to your arms what a ten-mile cycle does to your legs. A nice place.

// Climbing: Quarried greenstone (like a fine-grained grit). Problems are mostly all vertical. Problems go part-way up the walls where you jump off or traverse to easy ground. The ground is flat and hard. Mats very useful for jumping onto. Good for training and mileage. Good for eliminates. Crimpy, sometimes chipped. The classic problem is the traverse of the entire quarry at 7A.

// Conditions: Mostly south facing. Leafy. Climbable year round although it can get very hot, humid and midgy in summer. Sometimes dank in winter. Best in spring or autumn. Very sheltered. Lots of problems can stay dry in the rain. The setting is urban and the quarry sometimes graffitied, but this has little impact on the senses of even more delicate souls.

// Approach: Bridge of Allan is easiest reached off junction 11 of the M9 and following the A9. Follow this to the bridge in the middle of town. (The train station is just on the east side of the river.) On the west side of the bridge, at the mini-roundabout, follow signs for the golf course. Carry on uphill on Blairforkie Drive then forkie right up Ferniebank Brae, still following for the golf course. At the top turn right and park: the quarry is just in the trees.

// Info: **Bouldering in Scotland** (SCP); **scottishclimbs.com**

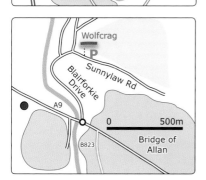

Wolfcrag
P
Sunnylaw Rd
Blairforkie
Drive
A9
0   500m
B823
Bridge of
Allan

1 min | 50 probs 4 - 7A+ best from 5 - 6C | vertical | shelter | rain proof

Glen Clova

56.866194
-3.165436

Adrian Crofton on John Peel, 6c. Photo: John Watson.

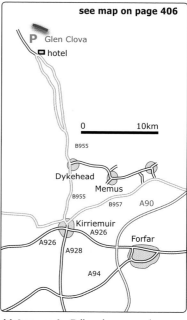

see map on page 406

Glen Clova

hotel

0   10km

B955

Dykehead

Memus

B955

B957   A90

Kirriemuir
A926

Forfar

A926   A928

A94

70 probs
4 - 7B+
best from
6A - 7A

3 min   slabby   vertical   steep   roofs   exposed

A beautiful and wild valley with a dozen blocks scattered around its base and on the scree below a crag. These provide a bunch of testpieces in the mid grades and plenty of mileage for the lower-grade climber.

The Hollow area has about 35 problems on four main boulders, mostly in the 6s. Further up the valley is the Peel Boulders area, lying under the Red Craigs crag. This is the most popular area. The Stone Country guide covers this area with 10 testpieces from 6A to 7A+, all within 150m of the road.

// Climbing: Diorite boulders. Generally steep climbing from sit starts. Plenty of slabs and walls too. Boulders are often above grass but lots too above scree. Can be sharp.

// Conditions: Plenty of sun although some are sunless in winter. Some boulders climbable year round but a few stay green. Potentially very midgy. **Family friendly.**

// Approach: Follow the maps and get onto the B955. Follow this as far as the hotel at the end of the loop. Carry on the single track road. The Hollows parking is 250m past the white house and the Peel area parking is under the crags. Each of these has space for 3 cars. If these are full do not park on the verge: carry on to the spacious quarry parking area.

// Info: Bouldering in Scotland (SCP); <u>scottishclimbs.com</u>

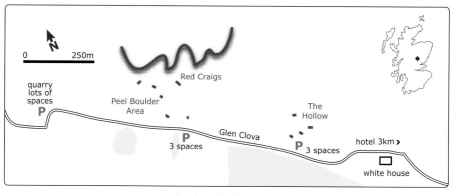

0   250m

N

quarry
lots of
spaces
P

Red Craigs

Peel Boulder
Area

The
Hollow

Glen Clova

P
3 spaces

P
3 spaces

hotel 3km ›

white house

Portlethen

57.056947
-2.116284

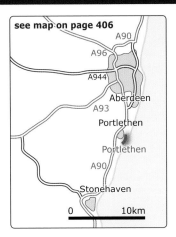

see map on page 406

A90
A96
A944
Aberdeen
A93
Portlethen
Portlethen
A90
Stonehaven

0   10km

160 probs
3 - 8A
best from
5 - 7B
10 min
steep
shelter

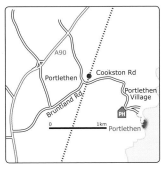

A90
Portlethen
Cookston Rd
Portlethen
Village
Bruntland Rd
PH
0   1km
Portlethen

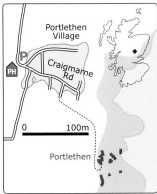

Portlethen
Village
P
PH
Craigmarne
Rd
0   100m
Portlethen

Amanda Lyons on Crack of Dawn, 6C. Photo: Lyons collection.

A great scattering of small boulders in a stunning setting will give a full session to crimpy Aberdonians. Tons of problems, mostly out of reach of the sea, and a great spread of grades, makes this the area's most popular venue.

The bolted Sports Wall, on the left of the descent path, has over a dozen overhanging highballs in the mid 6s to mid 7s. Below this the Pit Boulder holds the best problems here including Tim Rankin's 8A, Kayla.

// Climbing: Generally small boulders giving steep and crimpy sit-start problems. Physical, quite dynamic and fun. A bit sharp. Landings can be very rocky so mats are essential.

// Approach: From the A90 enter Portlethen. Head towards the railway station then take Cookston Road over the line, heading towards Portlethen Village. Upon entering the village there is a pub on a bend, The Neuk. Park around here, being careful not to obstruct the parking of any locals. Just after this take a right fork down Craigmarne Road. Several roads come off this, mostly unnamed. First on the right is the Old Coast Road. Continue past another road on the right then turn up the next (not the last one). At its end is a gap and a footpath. Follow this then go along the field to the coast. Turn right along the clifftop and after 70m follow a path down to the boulders.

// Conditions: Quick drying with very reliable conditions. Not really tidal. **Family friendly.**

// Info: **Bouldering in Scotland** (SCP)

John Cooke on Pain, 7A. Photo: Amanda Lyons.

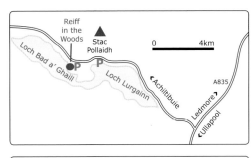

Reiff in the Woods

Stac Pollaidh

Loch Bad a' Ghaill

Loch Lurgainn

Achiltibuie

Ledmore

Ullapool

A835

0   4km

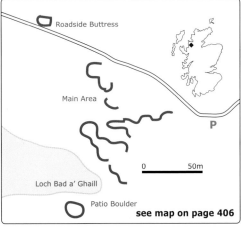

Roadside Buttress

Main Area

Loch Bad a' Ghaill

Patio Boulder

0   50m

see map on page 406

Richie Betts on Red Handed, 7A. Photo: Ian Taylor

A collection of beautiful sandstone boulders and walls located on the stunning Coigach Peninsula north of Ullapool. The position amongst the trees and outlook to the west over Loch Bad a' Ghaill are superb. A wonderfully atmospheric venue that manages somehow to be roadside and yet still feel remote and hidden away. A proper destination. Developed by Ian Taylor. Thanks to Richie Betts for the information here.

// Climbing: Sandstone boulders and outcrop. A varied circuit of easy and mid-grade problems with a few classic harder testpieces thrown in. A good mixture of slabs, vertical walls, aretes and crack problems on compact featured sandstone. Most of the boulders are close together, so it is possible to get plenty done in a short session. The Patio Boulder, obvious across the Loch below the main area, has three superb problems well worth the extra effort to get to.

// Approach: Leave the A835 at a junction 11 miles north of Ullapool and 8 miles south of Ledmore. Follow the minor road westwards in the direction of Achiltibuie. About 4 miles from the A835 there is a small parking on the left, for Stac Pollaidh. Another two miles past this, and as Loch Bad a' Ghaill comes into view, there is a small parking area by some trees. Park carefully here just before the bend. Most of the bouldering is in the trees on the left (south) side of the road. For other areas see instructions.

// Conditions: Very sheltered. Avoid during the midge season unless it's very windy. Can be damp and humid in still conditions but the more exposed boulders will dry quickly in a westerly wind. Catches the afternoon sun, even for a short time in winter. Evenings here can be superb in the right conditions and the sunsets magical. **Family friendly.**

// Info: Ullapool Bouldering by Ian Taylor available from North West Outdoors in Ullapool; **Bouldering in Scotland** (SCP); **scottishclimbs. com**

Main Area: This has 50 problems 4 to 7B. The Scooped Wall is the quickest area to dry and the usual warm up spot, while the sheltered square cut boulders nearest the road are the Cubes and have

Reiff in the Woods

58.033099
-5.233698

a number of fine wall problems. The Leaning Wall has some excellent steeper problems including the obvious dyno challenge of The Main Issue, 7B.

The large boulder in front of the Cubes is the Cave boulder. Its steep front face contains one of the best problems in the North West. TP and QC, 7A, starts in the break under the roof, heel-toe locks out to the lip and then moves right and up the slabby arete. All on perfect rock.

Roadside Buttress: On the north side of the road about 50m futher along is a small steep alcove hidden in trees. The Crack, 7A+, follows the obvious left-slanting steep crack and is particularly worthwhile.

The Patio Boulder: This is the large heather-topped boulder seen below and across the loch from the main area. Approach by dropping into the small valley south of the parking area (10 minutes from the road). It contains 3 superb highball problems to date; The Breathalyser (5) is the obvious hand rail traversing the west wall, Teewhuppo (6B) moves left from the start of the hand rail and climbs straight up the wall and Red Handed (7A) climbs the arete to the left.

Brin / Ruthven

Brin 57.336992,-4.2133
Ruthven 57.322721,-4.26321

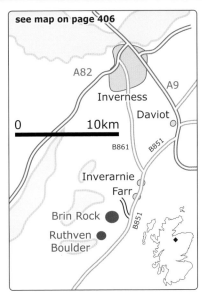

see map on page 406

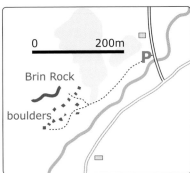

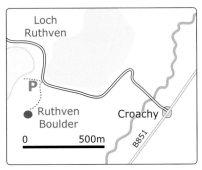

Two close together venues combine to give a superb and varied day out. Brin Rock is a densely wooded and mossy hillside with two dozen blocks giving four score of steep problems. The Ruthven Boulder is a mega-block in a fine open location overlooking a loch with two dozen steep problems in the mid-grades. And when they met, it was moider!

Brin Rock

An interesting woody venue with lots of problems. Sheltered and good on a cold windy day outside of summer. Atmospheric.

// Climbing: Gneiss boulders, some small, some middling and some big. The rock is quite sharp and angular giving powerful, aggressive climbing on crimps and slopers. Generally fairly steep. Landings can be awkward so a few mats and a spotter are very useful. Originally developed by Dave Wheeler.

// Approach: On the A9 between Inverness and Aviemore take the A851 towards Fort Augustus. After 6.5 miles take a turning toward Dunlichity and Brin House. Park after 100m just after the bridge. Brin Rock, the crag, can be seen on the hillside. The boulders are on the slope below. Walk across the field and cross the fence by the third gate. The bouldering begins on the slope just above.

// Conditions: Very tree-shrouded in an old mossy woods. Savage midges in summer. Generally clean and quick drying.

// Info: Bouldering in Scotland (SCP); scottishclimbs.com

The Ruthven Boulder

Said to be among the best boulders in Scotland set in a fresh family friendly location. A short walk to a destination that's guaranteed to tire the fingers and arms. Little legs. Big biceps. It's a boulderer's dream come true.

// Climbing: Gneiss boulders with lots of starred problems. Some great 7As. Always steep, with crimps and slopers. Powerful. Flat grass landings.

// Approach: Follow the Brin approach. A mile south of the Brin parking turn right in Croachy towards Loch Ruthven. Park before the loch after about a mile. The boulder is visible on the skyline along a muddy path.

// Conditions: Clean and quick drying. Exposed and a better bet than Brin in summer in terms of midges. **Family friendly.**

// Info: Bouldering in Scotland (SCP)

Ben Litster on The Dude, 7A, at the Ruthven Boulder. Photo: John Watson.

Mike Shorter on Squelch, 6C. Photo: John Watson.

Torridon

57.542687
-5.500631

One of the best blocks in Scotland in one of the best locations in Britain. The collections of boulders at the head of Loch Torridon, known specifically as the Celtic Jumble, has been a long-time favourite. The centrepiece of the Jumble, the mighty Ship Boulder, is a truly stunning block, a national destination. As well as that there's tons more quality to sniff out. And oh! the mountains.

The climbing is concentrated several blocks to the left, behind and right of the Ship Boulder. The Stone Country guide details 21 problems well spread from 4 to 7B. Loads more on the outcrops behind recently developed by Richie Betts with help from others.

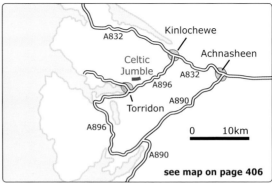

see map on page 406

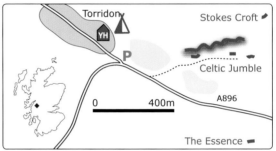

// **Conditions:** Reasonably sheltered boulders, almost at sea level. The problems face in all directions but most are generally south facing. Climbing possible year round but on a still summer day midges will make existance impossible. The best boulder, the Ship Boulder, suffers from a boggy landing so some civil engineering / a tarpaulin is needed to keep you feet dry and your mat from getting sodden. However this landing is nowhere near as boggy as it used to be. Generally quite clean although they don't get tons of traffic so the surface can be a wee bit sandy. There's a good cafe and shop in Torridon village.

// **Info**: Bouldering in Scotland (SCP); **scottishclimbs.com**

// **Climbing:** Sandstone boulders and outcrop. Mostly steep and physical. Be prepared for a tough time on Malcolm's Arete. The Ship Boulder is 4 – 5m high and other boulders are smaller. Mostly good landings but sometimes rocky so a couple of pads are useful. It's fair to say that the landing below the Ship Boulder is soft. Climbing mostly on crimps and slopers.

1	**Malcolm's Arete** 7A+
2	**The Mission** 7B
3	**Dandy Don's** 6B
4	**Bogmen** 6A+
5	**Descent**
6	**North Face Direct** 5+
7	**Swamp Monster** 6C
8	**Indentation** 5
9	**Squelch** 6C

// **Approach:** Follow the maps and park in the information centre car park in Torridon. Walk back along the road and follow a path across a bog to the obvious boulders.

10 **Stokes Croft** 8A *On the outcrops higher up and right of the lower areas. Arete from a sitter.*
11 **The Essence** 7B+ *Ship's prow feature from a sitter. This lies on the south side of the road.*

Scotland / Torridon

Murdoch Jamieson on The Essence, 7B+, Torridon (problem 11). Photo: Richie Betts.

Dan Varian on Stokes Croft, 8A, Torridon (problem 10). Photo: Richie Betts.

Celtic Boulder

Spaceship

The Ship

Dinosaur Area

Applecross

57.409831
-5.644484

Remote and tranquil, the Applecross peninsula has some excellent bouldering in magnificent surroundings. The Kishorn Boulders have a well established circuit and more recent discoveries in Coire nan Arr and on the Bealach na Bà give the area a more varied appeal. Well worth combining with a trip to Torridon, half an hour drive away to the North. Big thanks to local developer Richie Betts for this section.

There are loads more areas and problems beyond the three covered here but the venues below will give the visitor a proper taste of Applecross quality.

// Climbing: Sandstone boulders. A mix of slabs and walls with the odd roof problem thrown in. A good circuit of easy and mid grade problems at the Kishorn Boulders on featured pink sandstone with superb friction. Generally good landings and clean rock. Some excellent harder roof and wall problems in Coire nan Arr and up on the Bealach itself.

// Approach: Leave the A896 a few miles north of Lochcarron, following the single track Bealach na Bà road towards Applecross for 2 miles until the road crosses the Russell Burn, just before a tight bend. Park carefully here for Coire nan Arr and Kishorn Boulders. Carry on up to park at the top of Bealach na Bà for the Sanctuary Cave.

// Conditions: Plenty of sun at the Kishorn boulders, even in winter. Coire nan Arr has more shade, afternoon sun on Bealach na Bà. Wellies recommended for moving between boulders in all but the driest conditions. Climbing is possible year round but hope for a breeze in summer and for some sun during the short days of winter. Most of the rock is superbly clean although some of the north facing problems may need a quick brush. Wild, but **family friendly.**

// Info: **Bouldering in Scotland** (SCP)

Kishorn Boulders

The original classic circuit. There are 30 problems from 4 to 7C+. Best for its circuit of easier problems from 6A to 6C. Park at the parking as mentioned in the main approach. The boulders are all close.

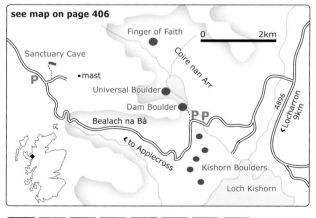

see map on page 406

Coire nan Arr

This is really made up of 3 separate areas. From the parking mentioned in the main approach head up the valley. Best for exploring the harder problems on the Dam and Universal Boulders. However the furthest, an hour's walk, is:

Finger of Faith Area

Remote and hardly ever visited. Special. At the head of the coire is a cluster of boulders including the Finger of Faith. About 20 problems from easy to 7A+ so far. To quote Richie Betts, the developer: "It's an hour to walk in to here and I've only been twice. I not aware of anyone else having been. I don't have names for the problems and I've already forgotten exactly what did or didn't get done. It's that kind of place."

Universal Boulder

A block sitting on the left side of the lake. 15 minute walk. It has three problems, 6B, 6C and 7B. The Universal, 7B, is one of the best problems in the North West. It takes the centre of the wall facing away from the car park.

Dam Boulder

This is at the bottom of the lake. 5 minute's walk. 4 problems, two 6Bs, a 6C and a 7A (the left arete of the roof).

The Sanctuary Cave

Three powerful roof problems from 7A to 7B+ plus the highball wall climb Don't Mess with the Shek, 7A+. Park at the large car park at the top of Bealach na Bà (GPS:57.418926,-5.708438). The cave is on a north-facing terrace about 300m inland from the car park. Walk up the mast track for 200m and cut off left down a shallow valley following one or two rock steps. The cave marks the south western end of the terrace. Don't Mess with the Shek is 150 metres further along the same terrace. Developed by Nic Ward.

65 probs
3 - 7C+
best from
6A - 7A

5-60 min

slabby · vertical · steep · roofs · exposed

Richie Betts on Finger of Faith, 6A. Photo: Betts Collection.

A numberless sprawl of gabbro blocks nestled under Britain's finest mountainscape. Boulders everywhere, some of them bouldered on. Three surrounding venues covered too.

The blocks lie all around the coire at the head of the Allt Coire Làgan burn. Included too are three other smaller areas.

// Climbing: Lots of big blocks with steep problems and slabs. Lots of sitters, some highballs. Hellish rough rock. Landings are awkward without a mat.

// Approach: Get onto Skye at Kyle of Lochalsh. Follow A87 for 23 miles to Sligachan. Take the A863 for 5 miles and then the B8009 towards Carbost. Before the town turn left and follow the road to Glenbrittle. Follow maps from here.

// Conditions: High and very clean. Quick drying.

// Info: Bouldering in Scotland (SCP); **Gabbrofest** (betaguides.com)

Picnic Boulder: And why not! 500m before the main boulders and beside the path. Some great 6s and 7s.

Culnamean Boulders: A civilised 10-minute walk along the land rover track leads to the first stream. A few boulders lie around here with a few nice problems in the 6s.

Sron na Ciche Boulders: A 40-minute walk (see map) leads to half a dozen blocks holding 30 problems, mostly 5s and 6s, as well as an 8A and 8B. However these *may* be fantasies.

Chieftan Arete, 6C. Photo: John Watson.

see map on page 406

A87
A863
Skye
A87

Coire
Làgan

0   40km

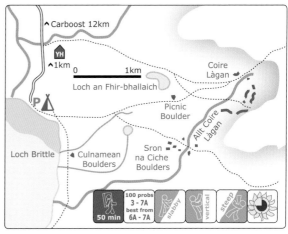

⌃Carboost 12km

YH
⌃1km

0   1km

Loch an Fhir-bhallaich

P

Coire
Làgan

Picnic
Boulder

Allt Coire
Làgan

Loch Brittle   Culnamean
Boulders

Sron
na Ciche
Boulders

100 probs
3 - 7A
best from
6A - 7A

50 min

slabby   vertical   steep

Howff Boulder Slab, 4+, on the Cir Mhor boulders, at the head of Glen Rosa. Photo: John Watson.

Arran

A few places to visit when on this lovely island. Varied quality.

Glen Rosa: The premier mountain circuit on the island with a great number of granite boulders strewn along a couple of miles of stunning upland. Most folk can switch off now as it's a solid two hours or more to get there and as if that isn't bad enough, the quality improves with altitude.

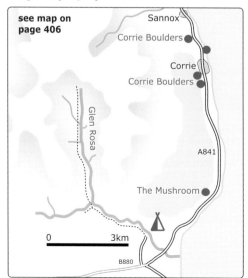

see map on page 406

Sannox
Corrie Boulders
Corrie
Corrie Boulders
Glen Rosa
A841
The Mushroom
0   3km
B880

The Mushroom: A funny sandstone outcrop in a wooded, secretive setting with a few steep mid-grade problems. Slow drying and somewhat delicate – do not climb if it is at all damp. It has a little friend just opposite. Head north out of Brodick on the A841. A mile after a sharp right-hand bend and Rosa Bridge is the entrance to Brodick Castle. 300m later is a track on the left signed Merkland Woods. 800m later, still on the A841, is a gravel parking on the right. Walk north for 100m from here, cross the wall and start looking. It's close.

Corrie Boulders: Roadside blocks. Tidy boulders giving a dozen problems. The Cat Stone is a mile south of Sannox: roadside. Clach an Fhion is near the hotel in Corrie on the seaward side of the road. Other boulders are either side of a path into the woods just south of the last house in the village of Corrie. 25 problems, 3 - 7A.

// Info: **Bouldering in Scotland** (SCP); **Arran Bouldering** by Claire Youdale and John Watson (SCP)

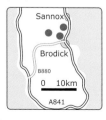

Sannox
Brodick
B880
0   10km
A841

Dave MacLeod on Waterfall Arete, 5+, Skeleton Boulders. Photo: Claire MacLeod.

Glen Nevis

56.770753
-5.036845

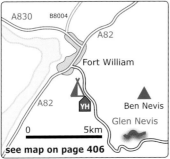

see map on page 406

A breathtaking mountain valley, as grand as they come, with good blocks dotted along its flanks. Some roadside, some a wee bit of a trek. Classic stuff, especially if you like midges.

The bouldering in the glen has mainly been developed by those two A-listers of Scotting power, Dave Cuthbertson and Dave MacLeod. Indeed Dave Mac's 2011 addition to Sky Pilot crag, 7 of 9, is one of the hardest problems in the land at 8B+, and very highball to boot.

The Stone Country guide details ten individual boulders and outcrops with 35 problems mainly in the middle and upper grades. Lots of steep stuff. Covered here are four of the areas towards the west end of the glen.

// **Climbing:** Steep and burly climbing on crimps and slopers. Landings are generally flat (and sometimes boggy) and the problems not too high. However Sky Pilot can get pretty highball.

// **Approach:** From Fort William take the road down Glen Nevis. 5 miles from Fort William, and 2.7 miles after the youth hostel, the road swings left over a bridge. Park just before or after the bridge. There is more parking down the valley but don't park in any passing places. See map for individual boulders.

// **Conditions:** Sunny and open but quite high and prone to bad weather. The boulders dry quickly. Landings can be boggy. Can be extremely midgy although Sky Pilot catches a helpful breeze. **Family friendly.**

// **Info**: Bouldering in Scotland (SCP)

The Cameron Stone: This is visible from the road about 100m before the more obvious Heather Hat boulder. It has ten steep problems from 4 to 7C+.

Heather Hat: It's got a heather hat! Six classics from 6B to 7B+. Maizie Gunn's, 6B, is the leftmost line, a low start to the hanging arete. The roof to the right is Pagan Uileann, 7A+. The leftwards lip traverse is Midnight in a Perfect World, 6C+.

Sky Pilot: AKA High Crag, is visible from the road and is a half-hour bash round the left of the larger crag at lower level. This has ten problems, 6A to 8B+. Gaining the niche near the left side is Sky Pilot, very highball 6C+. 7 of 9, 8B+, is an up-line two metres left of Sky Pilot. The easy groove right of centre is Auto Roof, 6A. Beetle Back, 7C is a rightwards traverse, finishing up Auto Roof.

Skeleton Boulder: Probably the nicest spot to boulder in the UK, according to Dave MacLeod. 600m further up the road from the other areas, and 150m after a right-hand bend, is a small car park on the right above a wooden footbridge. (This is 150m before two big pines straddle the road.) Cross the bridge and walk up the hill for 20 mins to a shoulder covered in big old Scot's pines near a steep waterfall. It is 100m uphill from Whale Rock, a classic trad crag, and clearly visible. Amongst these are two great boulders. A handful of superb problems from 6B to 8A+ in a great setting including Waterfall Arete 5+.

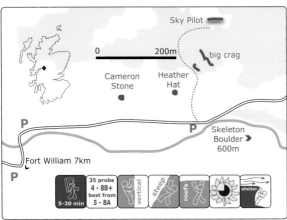

Scotland / Glen Nevis

Alan Cassidy on Precious, 7C. Photo: John Watson

Glen Croe

56.199984
-4.8195

A glen of high-quality, if a little spread out, problems. Generally steep, powerful and fingery with lots of hard session-style testpieces. Developed by Dave MacLeod and Michael Tweedley.

Just use the map to locate the boulders. Be prepared for the odd hunt around. The one boulder worth a special mention is the Kennedy Boulder, a heart-stopping 40-minute yomp up the hillside (visible from the road). This has 10 Bowderstone-style power problems up its steep front face, mostly quality offerings across the 7s.

// **Climbing:** Steep and powerful on crimps and flatties. Some awkward or boggy landings.
// **Approach:** See maps. The middle parking is called Honneymoon Bridge.
// **Conditions:** Best in spring and summer. Often boggy. Not much winter sun.
// **Info:** **Bouldering in Scotland** (SCP); **scottishclimbs.com**

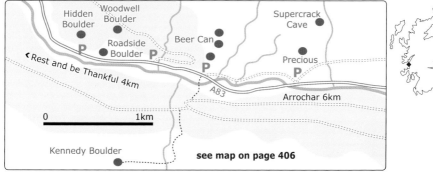

Anne, Nigel and Dave at Mind Trick, 6A. Photo: John Watson

Loch Katrine

56.229934
-4.42027

A picturesque wonderland with a clutch of blocks of highest quality schist. A heavenly setting, great friendly lines and endless fresh air could give you a truly heartwarming day out. Magic.

// Climbing: Schist boulders. Great landings, but sometimes a little boggy. Steep walls and bulges. Most problems are sitters.

// Approach: From the A821 turn towards Loch Katrine. Park in a layby at a forestry track after 700m. Follow the track for 800m then cross the river on a footbridge. Turn right and follow along the river, past the dam then straight on. The boulders all lie near the rough track. 20 – 35 minute walk.

// Conditions: Ferns and midges ruin summer visits. Best in spring and autumn after a dry spell. Neither massively exposed nor sheltered. **Family friendly.**

// Info: Bouldering in Scotland (SCP)

Fight Club: A squat boulder with a gravel patio near the burn. The classic, Fight Club, 6C+, is on the uphill face, from a sit on the left, traversing right to finish up the nose.

Art School Boulder: This is in the next stream, 50m before twin 'sentinel' boulders. Follow the stream, over the fence, to find the hidden block. The downstream arete is Art School, 6B. Watercolour Challenge, 6A+, is the upstream face.

Jawa Boulder: The left of the two 'sentinels'. Jawa, 6C, is the centre of the wall facing away from the loch. Mind Trick, 6A, is the short groove just left.

Tourist Boulder: The right-hand sentinel. Tourist Trap, 6C+, is the left arete of the block as seen on the approach from below.

Hydroponicum: On the opposite side of the path from the sentinels, and perhaps a bit before. Hydroponicum, 5+, the groove and slab on the right side of the loch-facing face.

Bealach Boulder: A low flat boulder near the bottom of a scattering of boulders. The Knob, 6C, is the middle of the lower wall.

Sebastopol: A barrel-shaped boulder down the burn. Lock, Stock and Barrel, 7C, is the lowest overhanging arete.

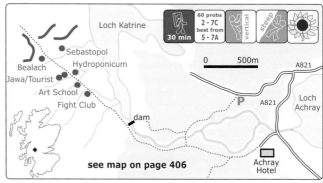

see map on page 406

Dumbarton

The steelworks of Scottish bouldering. A hard-edged proving ground for the greats of Caledonian cranking. A messy back yard for Glasgwegian climbers and little local delinquents. Always a place of intensity and wild times, and very much somewhere with its own special ambience. It's having a resurgence these days.

One of the most urban bouldering spots in the book. The outlook is across the remnants of the Clyde's industrial past. The rocks are a gallery for generations of graffiti. Broken glass is common. Neds, local youths with little to do other than drink cans of cheap lager, throw stones and break glass, permanently scamper around the rocks. This all makes it sound bad. It's not. It's just the place's special character, but you'd better be prepared for it.

It's the sort of crag where you will try an unattractive little sitter in a damp crevice and for some reason be unable to move on until you do it and you get it with the skin of your teeth as the sun disappears over the Clyde. You know the kind of place.

Most of the harder problems in Scotland are here. Powerful eliminates, link-ups and strong natural lines. Wads include Bryan Sheilds, Dave Cuthbertson, Andy Gallagher, Malcolm Smith, Dave MacLeod and Will Atkinson. The king lines on the crag behind include Chemin de Fer, E5, the left-hand crackline, and Cubby's Requiem, E7, the right-hand one. This was once the hardest route in Britain. Rhapsody, Dave MacLeod's E11, is a direct finish to this.

// Climbing: Basalt boulders. Burly, almost Germanically so. Really forceful moves on miserly slopers and staunch crimps. Generally steep. There's the odd slab too. Landings are okay but a bit slopy and the more mats and spotters the better.

// Approach: Best located from Dumbarton East train station on the A814 Glasgow Road in Dumbarton. This is gained from the Glasgow side by following the A82 north from Glasgow and following the signs or if coming from the north, take the B830 till you meet the B814 and turn left at the roundabout. From the train station follow the A814 west, away from Glasgow for 100m then turn seaward on Victoria Street. Follow this for 250m to meet the football stadium and park. Walk between the stadium and the outcrop to reach the boulders. Good bus and train service to Dumbarton.

// Conditions: Very quick drying. Sheltered. Quite sunny and it can get hot but there is always plenty of shade to escape to. Good all year. Very urban and scruffy but not threatening.

// Info: The crag has a website all its own with loads of videos and great topos: **dumby.info**. It also has its own guidebook from Stone Country: **Dumbarton Rock**. Also covered by **Bouldering in Scotland** (SCP): **scottishclimbs.com**

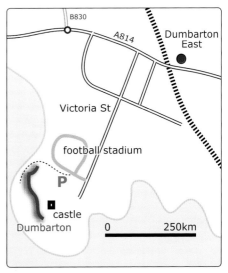

Toto by night. Photo: Jonathan Bean.

Eagle Boulder

1   **Zig Zag**   5   *Meander up the undercut slab.*
2   **Blue Meanie**   5+   *Line of good holds climbing the bulge at the top corner of the Eagle boulder.*
3   **Supinator**   6B   *The high crack in the centre of the face.*
4   **Gorilla**   6C   *Start on left hand crimp and sloper and gain layaway. Finish left on the jug at the lip.*
5   **Silverback**   7C   *Start on the right hand crimp and climb the hanging arete.*
6   **Pressure**   8B   *Sit start at a low pillar and trend left to a flat jug then up the hanging ramp.*

Home Rule Boulder

7   **The Beast**   3+   *The juggy arete.*
8   **Mugsy**   7A   *Start on the rail and jump to the right hand sloper then move up and left to a finger jug. Finish left or up the groove.*
9   **Mestizo**   6A+   *Hanging arete from jump start. 7A+ from a sitter down right.*
10   **Physical Graffiti**   6C   *Bold, crimpy, highball line up the centre of the face.*
11   **Home Rule**   6A   *Use a high foot and undercut pinch to gain the rail. Finish up and right.*

Suckers Boulder

12   **Toto**   6B   *Awkward and technical leftward-slanting crack. Finish on triangular jug.*
13   **The Shield**   7B+   *Pull on the shield feature and throw for the top. Sitter 7C.*

BNI Boulder

14   **Imposter Arete**   4   *The hanging highball arete. Start on top of Pongo boulder.*
15   **Good Nicks**   6A+   *Climb the rising crack then lunge left to the lip. Finish up the slab.*
16   **Sabotage**   8A   *Climb the hanging 45-degree arete to the lip then mantle onto the slab.*

Pongo Boulder

17   **Hard Cheddar**   5+   *Traverse right along the lip to gain the arete.*
18   **Slap Happy**   7A   *Start on jug and gain sloping right hand crimp. From here pull to the top rail.*
19   **In Bloom**   7C   *Traverse the face left-to-right on a slopy, crimpy rail. Finish up Pongo.*
20   **The Tickle**   8A   *Dyno from the centre of the rail to the top of the Pongo crack.*
21   **Pongo**   6C+   *Jump start from the handrail to gain the crack. Finish up this and top out below the big block. Sitter 8A using original beta, or 7B+ with newly found finger lock method.*

Sea Boulder

22   **Steptoe**   4   *Arete.*
23   **Erewhon**   5   *Arete.*
24   **Commercial Route**   4   *Wall.*

Warm Up Wall

25   **Friar's Mantle**   5   *The ramp feature up the centre of the wall.*

Dumbarton Rock. Photo: Photo: Jonathan Bean.

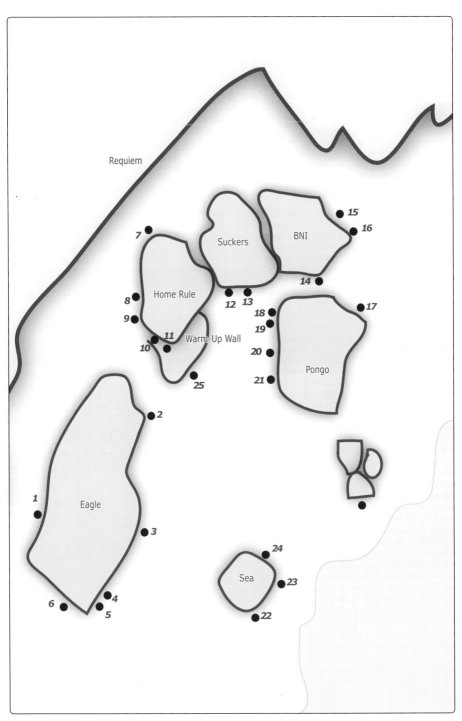

Requiem

7

Suckers

BNI

15

16

Home Rule

8

9

12 13

14

18

17

11

Warm-Up Wall

10

19

20

Pongo

25

21

2

1

Eagle

3

24

Sea

23

4

6

5

22

Problems index

This index covers only problems with proper, accepted names. Problems called things like Pocket Wall are not included.

Index

Index

// U

// V

Index

// W

// X

// Y

// Z

Barnaby Carver on The Groove, 7B+, Clodgy (page 47, problem 11). Photo: Carver collection.

Chris Plant on Groove from Sitter, 7A, Honister Boulders, (page 199, problem 4). Photo Jon Bassindale.

Niall Grimes on the Pocket, 6C+, Langdale Boulders, (page 207, problem 5).